THE JEWISH RESPONSE TO
MISSIONARY CHRISTIANTY

ALSO BY GERALD SIGAL

THE JEWISH RESPONSE TO MISSIONARY CHRISTIANTY

Why Jews don't believe in Jesus

Gerald Sigal

ISBN-13: 978-1508807773
ISBN-10: 1508807779

Printed by Createspace

CONTENTS

PART I
THE JEWISH SCRIPTURES

PART II
THE NEW TESTAMENT

ACKNOWLEDGMENTS

This volume is the product of many years of research. In that period of time I have been privileged to discuss its contents with outstanding scholars and laymen. In particular, I want to give special mention to Rabbi Tsvi Kilstein. He is not only a scholar in countering the fraudulent Christian missionary arguments but in many other fields as well. He is a dear friend who has been a motivating force urging this project on. Mention must be made of my grandson, Shalom Noach Jaffe, the cover designer and my technical support in setting up the manuscript. Last, but never least, is my wonderful wife, Frances, who read parts of the manuscript and made many helpful comments and suggestions.

INTRODUCTION

For Jews adhering to traditional Judaism the Torah is God's words revealed directly to Moses. Subsequent additions to the Jewish canon are God inspired works often recording God's interaction with the prophets of Israel. The Jewish Bible in its original language is the clearest expression of God's written word to His people. This despite copyist errors and lost knowledge of certain word meanings and the like that have interfered with a clear transmission of the biblical text.

Christians maintain that the Christian Greek Scriptures (New Testament) are a continuation and clarifying fulfillment of the Jewish Bible, what they call the "Old Testament." In connection with this assertion, it should be noted that through incorrect translations, misinterpretations and reliance on the Greek Septuagint for certain renderings the Christian "Old Testament" is not the same Bible as used by Jews. On investigation, we find that the New Testament and the subsequent theological developments derived from interpretations of its contents are greatly at odds with biblical teachings. For example, the author of Mark's parenthetical expression (7:19) that by Jesus' teaching, all foods were declared clean, that is, biblical dietary laws were abrogated in their entirety.

In the Gospel of John the Christian community replaces Judaism. This theme of replacement is expressed most especially in its attitude toward the Temple and the biblical feasts. The Temple has been replaced by the body of Jesus (John 2:19-21). The Sabbath and feasts are reinterpreted or replaced by Jesus (chapter 5, the Sabbath; chapter 6, the Passover; chapter 7, the Feast of Tabernacles; chapter 10, the feast of the dedication of Temple). In effect, according to the Gospel of John, Christianity has become a new religion separate from Judaism. In the Gospel of Matthew, Jesus (and by extension Christianity) has become the fulfillment of Judaism (Matthew 5:17). The first part of the Letter to the Hebrews (1:1-4:13) claims that God's definitive word has been spoken in the *Son* and that his word has a priority over any communication made through angels or through Moses. The second part of the letter (4:14-10:31) teaches that Jesus is the eternal high priest whose supposed sacrifice on the cross has atoned for sin once and for all, establishing a so-called new covenant between God and humanity. Accordingly, the first (Mosaic) dispensation has been abolished, the author announces, and the second one has been established (10:9): there is only one tabernacle and that is in heaven (8:1-2, 9:24); the law and the priesthood have been changed (7:12); and the new covenant has made the old one obsolete (8:13). Though in its first decades the church could profess its faith in Jesus as messiah and still remain within Judaism, the author of Hebrews no longer sees that as a possibility. In this, he adopts a position similar to that found in the Gospel of John.

By the second century C.E. Jewish Christians who adhered to the Torah and resisted the introduction of pagan influenced doctrines (e.g., virgin birth, divine/dual nature) were marginalized and declared heretical by the Gentile dominated church and eventually disappeared. All expressions of Christianity today descend from Gentile Christianity including those who call themselves Hebrew Christians or Messianic. They are followers of Gentile Christianity no matter how much of Jewish ritual they try to incorporate into their belief system.

The proper genre for the Gospels is historic fiction. The setting is often historical: topography, cities and towns, mention of the high priest, the Sadducees and the Pharisees, the Sabbath and Jewish holy days, and so on. But the story line itself is froth with fiction, in many cases culled from biblical verses now applied to Jesus as if he was their fulfillment. Matthew, in particular, is infamous in his use of Scripture to enhance his fictional rendition of the life of Jesus. For example, his newly born Jesus is taken to Egypt to avoid the wrath of Herod (Matthew 2:15 cf., Hosea 11:1), while Luke's Jesus is tranquilly taken back to Nazareth. Needless to say, Matthew's use of Isaiah 7:14 (cf. Matthew 1:23) has to appeal to a Greek rendering to support his proclaiming of a virgin conception. The list is long of Christian scriptural abuse through taking passages out of context and mistranslations of the Jewish Scriptures: Isaiah 9:6, Isaiah 53, Daniel 9, Psalms 22 and 110, and so on. Christians have a right to their opinions, but they do not have a right to manufacture fallacious facts.

Christian missionaries have been known to taunt their Jewish opposition saying: "If Christians want Jews to believe in Jesus, why is the Jewish community so afraid? Is the Christian faith so powerful and that of the Jews so frail that the mere mention of belief in Jesus is seen as a danger to the Jewish community?" But, you see, many Jews do not know the essential truth of the fallacious nature of Christianity. And they do not know that what the missionary offers is like a drink of water that looks pure but contains cholera; like the pig that stretches forth its cloven hoof to show it is kosher while keeping its mouth closed to hide that it does not chew the cud. They do not know that missionaries follow the dictum of Paul who boasted that he would "become all things to all men" (1 Corinthians 9:22) in order to convert them — "whether in pretense or in truth" (Philippians 1:18). Against such enemies of Jews and Judaism, against such distorters of the Jewish Bible, against the false teachings of the New Testament and subsequent Christian doctrines one must be prepared not only to personally respond but to teach others why this misinformation must be rejected. The missionary seeks out those who are vulnerable in one way or another. Jews must be prepared to show why the missionary and would would-be missionary should be rebuffed.

Part 1
THE JEWISH SCRIPTURES

Chapter 1

THE MEANING OF *'ELOHIM*
(Genesis 1:1)

Genesis 1:1, states: "In the beginning God created the heavens and the earth." Here the word for God is *'Elohim*, having a plural form as though it meant "gods." Trinitarians maintain that this is proof that God is a plurality. A careful investigation of the actual use of this word in the Jewish Scriptures unequivocally shows that *'Elohim*, while plural in form, is singular in concept. In biblical Hebrew, many singular abstractions are expressed in the plural form, e.g., *rachamim*, "compassion" (Genesis 43:14, Deuteronomy 13:18); *zekunim*, "old age" (Genesis 21:2, 37:3, 44:20); *n'urim*, "youth" (Isaiah 54:6, Psalms 127:4).

The commentator Rashi offers a significant insight into the meaning of the word *'Elohim*. In commenting on the phrase *yesh l'eil yadi*, "there is power in my hands" (Genesis 31:29), he writes: "And anywhere *'eil* denotes holiness [as in a Name of God], [it is] because [it connotes] 'strength' [see Proverbs 8:28] and 'great power' [Isaiah 40:26]." That is, *'El* generally means "God," and, in particular the God of Israel, because He is the sum of all power, but it can also refer to other "powers," real or imaginary, as well (e.g., human authorities, angels, idols).

The Jewish Scriptures teach us that *'Elohim* is an honorific title, which expresses the plural of majesty. The underlying reason for the grammatically plural form *'Elohim* is to indicate the all-inclusiveness of God's authority as possessing every conceivable attribute of power. The use of the plural for such a purpose is not limited merely to *'Elohim*, but also applies to other words of profound significance. For instance, Isaiah 19:4 uses *'adonim* ("lords") instead of *'adon* ("lord"): "Into the hand of a cruel lord" (literally "lords," even though referring to one person),[1] and Exodus 21:29 reads: "Its owner [literally *be'alav*, "its owners"] also shall be put to death." Thus, we see that the plural of a noun is sometimes used to signify one person, as a mark of

2

honor and distinction or for emphasis.

'*Elohim*, in the first verse of Genesis, does not show the existence of a plurality of persons in the God of Israel. Concerning human authority, it may indicate a plurality of persons. We read in Exodus 22:8: "Both parties shall come before the *'elohim* ["judges"], and whom the *'elohim* ["judges"] shall condemn, he shall pay double to his neighbor." However, Jacob wrestles with *one* being, yet that being is referred to as *'elohim* (Genesis 32:31); and the angel that appears to Manoah, the father of Samson, is also referred to as *'elohim* (Judges 13:22). Note the words used by the woman in speaking to Saul when, upon seeing Samuel, she exclaims: "I see *'elohim* coming up out of the earth" (1 Samuel 28:13). Here, *'elohim* is followed by the verb in the plural. Yet only a single individual is referred to, as is seen from verse 14: "And he said to her: 'What is his appearance?' And she said: 'An old man is coming up; and he is wrapped in a robe.'" Thus, even joined to a plural verb the noun may still refer to a single individual.

'*Elohim* means "gods" only when the Bible applies this plural word to pagan deities. The pagan Philistines apply the title *'elohim* to their god Dagon (Judges 16:23-24, 1 Samuel 5:7). The Moabites, likewise, used the word *'elohim* to describe their god Chemosh (Judges 11:24). If trinitarian Christians are correct in their argument that the use of *'Elohim* with a singular verb means there are three coeternal, coequal persons in one god, then the same thing *must* be true for the Philistine god Dagon and the Moabite god Chemosh. They must be respectively a plurality of persons in one god. How else could trinitarians explain the Philistines saying of Dagon: "Our god [*'eloheinu*] has delivered" (Judges 16:24)? Here, the verb is singular, yet the subject is, literally, "our gods" in the plural. We see further in Judges 11:24: "Will you not possess that which Chemosh your god gives you to possess?" Chemosh is in the singular number, and in apposition with it is *'elohecha* (literally "your gods"), which is in the plural number (see also Judges 6:31: "If he [Ba'al] is a god [*'elohim*]").

The episode of Elijah's confrontation with the priests of Baal gives the reader further insight into the essential oneness of God as taught by the Jewish Scriptures. Elijah demonstrates God's power and primacy on Mount Carmel. He challenges the 450 priests of Baal.

Each side is to sacrifice a bullock before the assembled Israelites. Now they will see whose prayers calling down fire to consume the respective offerings would be answered. The prophets of Baal cry out, slashing themselves with knives and swords until their blood flows, but to no avail. Elijah prays: "Answer me, *Y-H-V-H*, answer me," and a divine fire descends from heaven to consume Elijah's offering. All the assembled Israelites cry out: "*Y-H-V-H* — He is God [*'Elohim*]" (1 Kings 18:39).

Throughout this passage, Baal is referred to as "he," in the third-person singular, in conjunction with the plural *'elohim*. *Y-H-V-H* is also addressed in the same language. Yet, where is the plurality of Baal if one wants to insist on trinitarian grammatical guidelines? There is simply no justification for the notion that *'Elohim* denotes a plurality in the essence of God.

Some trinitarians justify the use of the plural with Dagon, Chemosh, and Baal on the basis of the assumption that they were not the name of one idol only, but were the names of innumerable idols throughout the respective kingdoms where they were worshiped. Hence, Dagon, Chemosh, and Baal though in the singular form, are collective nouns, which embraced every idol of the realm. But, this interpretation is unattested and forced. It is nothing but a theory invented to support a theological need. That the plural form of *'elohim* does not imply the plurality of the divine essence is a fact that was already known in ancient times. This is reflected in the Septuagint version of the Scriptures, which renders *'Elohim* with the singular title *ho Theos* ("The God").

One also needs to consider the frequent use of the singular *'Eloha*. For example we find: "Then he forsook God [*'Eloha*] who made him" (Deuteronomy 32:15); "You that forgot God [*'Eloha*]" (Psalms 50:22); "At the presence of the God [*'Eloha*] of Jacob" (Psalms 114:7). If *'Elohim* refers to a triune deity, how can one account for the alternate deployment of *'Elohim* and *'Eloha*? Isaiah declares: "Thus says the Lord, the King of Israel, and his Redeemer the Lord of hosts: I am the first, and I am the last, and besides Me there is no God [*'Elohim*]" (Isaiah 44:6). This is followed in verse 8 by: "Is there a God [*'Eloha*] besides Me?" If the truth of the doctrine of the Trinity depends in any measure on the plurality in form of the noun *'Elohim*, the use of *'Eloha*, the singular of the noun, most decidedly disproves it.

[1] For *'adonim* used in this way, see also: Genesis 24:9, 10, 51; 39:2-20; 40:1; 42:30, 33; Exodus 21:4, 6, 8; Judges 19:11, 12; Malachi 1:6.

Chapter 2

US AND *OUR*
(Genesis 1:26, 11:7)

God said: "Let us make man in our image, in our likeness" (Genesis 1:26) and "Come, let us go down, and there confound their language" (Genesis 11:7). Trinitarians maintain that these verses are prooftexts of an alleged triune deity, but this claim is erroneous.[1] The inference that "Let us make man in our image, in our likeness" refers to a plurality in God's essence is refuted by the subsequent verse, which relates the creation of man to a singular God, "And God created man in His image" (Genesis 1:27). In this verse, the Hebrew verb "created" appears in the singular form. If "let us make man" indicates a numerical plurality, it would be followed in the next verse by, "And *they* created man in *their* image."[2] Although God often acts without assistance, He makes His intentions known to His servants. Thus, we find, "Shall I conceal from Abraham that which I am doing" (Genesis 18:17); "He made known His ways to Moses, His doings to the children of Israel" (Psalms 103:7); "For the Lord God will do nothing without revealing His counsel to His servants the prophets" (Amos 3:7). Obviously, the plural form is used in the same way as in the divine appellation *'Elohim*, to indicate the all-inclusiveness of God's attributes of authority and power, the plurality of majesty. As Isaiah relates: "I heard the voice of the Lord, saying, 'Whom shall I send, and who will go for us?'" (Isaiah 6:8). It is customary for one in authority to speak of himself as if he were a plurality. Hence, Absalom said to Ahithophel, "Give your counsel what we shall do" (2 Samuel 16:20). The context shows that he was seeking advice for himself' yet he refers to himself as "we." In the Book of Ezra we find that "Rehum the commander and Shimshai the scribe wrote a letter against Jerusalem *to Artaxerxes the king*" (Ezra 4:8). In the king's answer, he says, "Peace, and now the letter which you sent to *us* has been plainly read before me" (Ezra 4:18). There we see that although the letter is sent specifically to the king, the king's reply speaks of "the letter which you sent to us."[3]

A misconception similar to that concerning Genesis 1:27 is held by trinitarian Christians with reference to the verse, "Come, let us go down, and there confound their language" (Genesis 11:7). Here, too, the confounding of the language is related in verse 9 to God alone, "because the Lord did there confound the language of all the earth." In this verse, the Hebrew verb *balal*, "he confounded," appears in the singular form. Also, the descent is credited in verse 5 to the Lord, alone, "And the Lord came down to see the city and the tower." In this verse, the Hebrew verb, *va-yeired*, "and He came down," appears in the singular form. If a doctrine of plurality of persons is to be based on the grammatical form of words, the frequent interchanging of the singular and the plural would vitiate such an attempt as being without merit. We may safely conclude that the Jewish Scriptures most emphatically refute every opinion, which deviates from the concept of an indivisible unity of God.

Chapter 45 of Isaiah, using, Y-H-V-H, unequivocally asserts that He alone is the creator and ruler of all things in the universe. The six uses of *'Elohim* in this chapter (verses 3, 5, 14, 15, 18, 21) show that the term *'Elohim* is used synonymously with Y-H-V-H, and that both epithets refer to the absolutely indivisible one-and-only God. The singularity of God, expressed in the first-person singular in verse 12, clearly shows who is meant by the phrase, "Let us create man in our image, in our likeness": "I, even I, have made the earth, and created man upon it; I, even My hands, have stretched out the heavens, and all their host have I commanded." The prophet states further: "Y-H-V-H, your Maker, that spread out the heavens, and laid the foundations of the earth" (Isaiah 51:13).

[1] When the sages originally made the translation of the Torah for King Ptolemy II Philadelphus (283-245 B.C.E.) they made ten emendations to the text. Instead of "Let us make man in our image, in our likeness" they emended the text to read, "I will make man in the image and the likeness" (Midrash *Tanchuma*, *Shemot* 1:22).

[2] Genesis 1:26-27. "And God said: 'Let us make Adam [here *Adam* does not refer to a specific male being, but to humankind generally] in our image, after our likeness; and let them have dominion … [the human collectivity throughout history is to have ascendancy over creation].' And God created Adam in His own image, in the image of God created He him [the first human]; male and female created He them [this refers to God's original statement—humankind is to consist of male and female made in the image and likeness of God]."

Genesis 5:1-2. "This is the book of the generations of Adam [his descendants]. In the day that God created Adam, in the likeness of God made He him [the first human]; male and female created He them [humankind is to consist of male and female made in the image and likeness of God], and blessed them, and called their name Adam [here *Adam* does not refer to a specific male being, but to humankind generally], in the day when they were created [male and female were created on the same day]."

[3] A *midrash* finds a lesson in interpersonal relations in "Let us make man in our image." It says: "Now if a great man comes to obtain permission [for a proposed action] from one that is less than he, he may say, 'Why should I ask permission from my inferior!' Then they will say to him, 'Learn from Creator, who created all that is above and below, yet when He came to create man He took counsel with the ministering angels'" (*Bereshit Rabbah* 8:8). According to this *midrash*, God addresses Himself to the angels and says to them, "Let us make man in our image." It is not that He invites their help, but that it is the conventional manner of speech to express oneself in this way and not necessarily that God sought angelic help in the creation of man.

Chapter 3

THE SEED OF THE WOMAN
(Genesis 3:15)

Some Christians explain the genealogical discord between Matthew and Luke by claiming that the determination of the Messiah's genealogy is to be different because biblically he is biologically supposed to be different. God declares to the *serpent*: "And I will put enmity between you and the woman, and between your seed and her seed; he will strike your head, and you will strike at his heel" (Genesis 3:15). Christians take the verse to mean that a miraculous birth took place. Their assumption is that this "seed" of the woman is not only the Messiah but that conception took place without a human father. None of this is stated explicitly or implicitly in the text of this verse. The Christian claim that the Messiah will not have a human father and will receive his familial identity through adoption is totally unfounded. There is absolutely no reason to assume that Genesis 3:15 is messianic or that the Messiah is to be born in a supernatural way.

The phrase "her seed" has nothing to do with the determination of messianic lineage. The woman mentioned is Eve. "Her seed" is representative of all her future descendants and the direct reference here is to the hostility between mankind and *serpents*, representing the *nachash*. The *nachash* (Heb. "serpent"), the "beast of the field" that caused Eve to transgress God's directive, having been instrumental in causing the expulsion from the Garden of Eden would be an object of antagonism.

Christians assume this verse to be descriptive of an enmity between Jesus ("her seed") and Satan ("your seed"). They support this position by reference to three New Testament passages: 1 John 3:8-9, Hebrews 2:14, and Romans 16:20.

1 John 3:8-9 states: "The Son of God appeared for this purpose, that he might destroy the works of the Devil. No one who is born of God practices sin, because His seed remains in him; and he cannot sin, because he is born of God" (see also 1 John 5:18). Hebrews 2:14

contends that the reason Jesus became flesh and blood was so "that through death he might render powerless him who had the power of death, that is, the Devil." Despite all these claims the works of Satan have not been destroyed and Satan has not been rendered powerless. Indeed, if Jesus accomplished all this by his death there would be no sinners among those who accept him and reject Satan, for the claim is that those who practice sin are not of God but of the Devil (1 John 3:8). However, there has never been a lack of sinful behavior among Christians. The author of 1 John wrote: "If we say that we have no sin, we are deceiving ourselves, and the truth is not in us" (1 John 1:8). What is more, even when they supposedly receive forgiveness for their sins (1John 1:8) there is no guarantee that they will not repeat the sin (cf. 1 John 3:8-9). Jesus simply did not bring about deliverance from the power of Satan for his followers. Paul admits as much when he says: "For we wanted to come to you, even I, Paul, once and a second time, but Satan hindered us" (1 Thessalonians 2:18). Most revealing is Paul's statement of a hope now deferred some two thousand years: "And the God of peace will crush Satan under your feet shortly [*tacheos*]" (Romans 16:20). Well, Satan is still around and Paul's "shortly," the imminent first century sudden appearance of Jesus, has become an empty promise. It is obvious that Jesus' death did not render Satan powerless as promised.

Jesus' death did not render Satan powerless, Satan was not crushed in the "shortly" timeframe promised by Paul, and sin was not abolished. The christological interpretation leaves believers in Jesus with a series of unfulfilled promises and prophecies.

Since God was not addressing a man, but the *serpent* in the presence of the woman, it was not necessary nor would it have been grammatically correct for Him to have said: "I will put enmity between you and the woman, and between your seed and *his* seed." It must read, in order to make sense, as found in Genesis: "I will put enmity between you and the woman, and between your seed and her seed." Thus, the grammatical consistency of the sentence is upheld in reference to those addressed. In Genesis 16:10, God's message to Hagar states: "I will greatly multiply your seed" not "I will greatly multiply his [Abraham's] seed." Since God's message concerning Hagar's descendants is addressed directly to a woman, an occurrence not commonly found in the Bible, it is grammatically necessary to refer to these descendants as *her seed*. This was also the case concerning Eve. "Her seed" simply refers to her descendants, just as when addressed to a man, "his seed" means his descendants. As with Isaiah 7:14, no indication of virgin conception, messianic or otherwise, is found in Genesis 3:15. It is left to New Testament exegetical acrobatics to make the fallacious and distorted claim of a virgin conception.

Chapter 4

THE FIRST HUMAN BIRTH
(Genesis 4:1)

Christians seek prooftexts of their claim that Jesus was born in a supernatural way. As a result, they interpret, "I have acquired a male with [the help of] the Lord" (Genesis 4:1) to mean that Eve thought she had conceived supernaturally, with God as the father of her child, and had given birth to the Messiah. Christians claim this to be a forerunner of what happened to Mary. They claim prophetic power for Eve because, in accordance with Christian belief, she knew that the Messiah was to be born of the union of God with a female. However, they deny the mother of humanity the fundamental knowledge of the biological process of birth. Thus, according to them, Eve was not aware of the part played by Adam in the birth of her child. This is evidently not the case since the verse, as it reads in full, states: "And the man knew Eve his wife; and she conceived and bore Cain, and said: 'I have acquired a man with [the help of] the Lord.'" Adam is clearly acknowledged as the father of her child. This fact is not given simply to enlighten the reader but most of all this knowledge is principally attributed to Adam and Eve, themselves.

What Christians choose to ignore, is that Eve is grateful to the Almighty for His help in the process of birth. She feels the personal closeness of the Divine Presence to herself. Eve felt this way since divine aid is most essential in facilitating birth. We see this in Jacob's words to Rachel: "Am I in God's stead, who has withheld from you the fruit of the womb?" (Genesis 30:2). This is explicitly stated in Ruth 4:13: "And he [Boaz] went in to her [Ruth], and the Lord gave her conception, and she bore a son." This interaction of God, man, and woman in the birth process can be expressed as: God + Man + Woman = Child. The Rabbis have aptly phrased it by stating that: "There are three partners in man: The Holy One, blessed be He, his father, and his mother."[1] There is simply no messianic significance to be found in this verse.

[1] B.T. *Kiddushin* 30b, B.T. *Niddah* 31a.

Chapter 5

THE SEED OF PROMISE
(Genesis 3:15, 17:8)

God made two significant promises to Abraham concerning the everlasting possession of *'Eretz Yisrael*, the Land of Israel, by his descendants:

> [F]or all the land which you see, to you will I give it, and to your seed forever. (Genesis 13:15)

> And I will give to you, and to your seed after you, the land of your sojournings, all the land of Canaan, for an everlasting possession; and I will be their God. (Genesis 17:8)

These verses are used by Paul to promote his claim that Jesus is the Messiah. In actuality they debunk his arguments. Focusing in on the word *zer'a* ("seed") he comments: "Now the promises were spoken to Abraham and to his seed. It does not say, 'And to seeds,' referring to many; but, referring to one, 'And to your seed,' who is Christ" (Galatians 3:16). Did Paul exploit this word for its homiletic possibilities, rather than adhering to grammatical convention? Homiletically, the preacher has wider latitude to hyperbolize in getting his point across, but if Paul meant that his comments are to be taken literally there is a problem. Whatever Paul's intention, the fact is that there is no place in the Jewish Scriptures where the *plural* of "seed" (*zer'aim*) is used so as to refer to human offspring. In every instance, the singular word "seed" is used in a plural sense (e.g., Genesis 13:16, 17:10, 22:17-18). Hence, Genesis 17:8 reads: "and I will be their God." In this verse the third-person plural pronoun, "their," refers to "your seed [singular]." Obviously, there is no valid theological statement that can be made by emphasizing that *zer'a* is singular and, therefore, points to one individual. Grammatical convention negates any claim that these verses refer to Jesus, because of the appearance of the noun *zer'a* in the singular.

Chapter 6

ABRAHAM'S THREE VISITORS
(Genesis 18-19)

Christians take Genesis 18 and 19 as proof for their trinitarian views. In their search for evidence in support of the doctrine of the Trinity, they claim that the three angels who appeared to Abraham as he sat in his tent door under the oaks of Mamre were actually the first, second and third persons of the Trinity. Although the complexity of the context may lend itself to several interpretations, the Christian understanding of these chapters as referring to a triune god is totally unacceptable on scriptural grounds alone.

Genesis 18:1 may be interpreted as Y-H-V-H speaking to Abraham prior to the arrival of the three men mentioned in verse 2. Most probably, however, verse 1 acts as an introductory remark informing the reader that Y-H-V-H spoke to Abraham, with the following verses being the details of how that encounter was accomplished. The text of Genesis 18 and 19 is not clear as to whether Y-H-V-H spoke at any time, directly to Abraham or solely through an angel, in the guise of a man, who acted as an intermediary. But these are minor problems compared to the problems involved in the Christian interpretation. The latter are of a nature that reveals the shallowness of the theological assertions of Christians concerning these two chapters.

As mentioned, Christians believe that the three men who visited Abraham are the three personalities of the so-called Trinity. But, then, which part of God would they say is Y-H-V-H who speaks to Abraham after two of the men depart (Genesis 18:22)? If the three angels are the three persons of the Trinity, then how could Y-H-V-H say: "You cannot see my face, for man shall not see Me and live" (Exodus 33:20)? Abraham and Sarah would have died had they gazed upon the supposed Father, Son and Holy Spirit, unless what they saw was not God but three angelic beings manifested in human form for the several purposes assigned to them. Even John exposes the error when he declares that "no man has seen God at any time" (John 1:18, 1 John 4:12). Since a number of people saw the faces of the three angels and still lived, we must presume that they were not God.

Of the three visitors, one is specifically sent as a messenger from *Y-H-V-H* to Abraham. Through him, *Y-H-V-H* speaks, in Genesis 18, to Abraham. He is the one who delivers God's message concerning the birth of Isaac, and it is through him that *Y-H-V-H* speaks to Abraham concerning the possibility of saving the two cities. Thus, for example, in verse 22: "And the men turned from there, and went toward Sodom; but Abraham stood yet before *Y-H-V-H*," and in verse 33 it says: "And *Y-H-V-H* went His way, as soon as He had left off speaking to Abraham." As *Y-H-V-H's* agent the messenger speaks as *Y-H-V-H* and is referred to accordingly. The authority which he expresses is not his own but God's. It is God who oversees all events, and that is why, even though the Scriptures describe the angels as going to Sodom, *Y-H-V-H* states, in verse 21: "I will go down now, and see whether they have done altogether according to the cry of it, which has come to Me, and if not, I will know."

In Genesis 19:1, two of the men are now referred to as angels, literally, "messengers," while the third, having accomplished his mission of speaking to Abraham, is no longer involved in the narrative. That is why only two of the visitors are mentioned as arriving at their destination. The text indicates that the function of these two men is to bring about the destruction of Sodom by exposing through their mere presence, all the evil that resides in the hearts of the inhabitants. The two angels are never referred to as God, as should be expected if the Christian position is correct. They are portrayed as God's agents carrying out His commands. Simply stated, they cannot be God if they are sent by Him to do His bidding. At no time do the two angels take the initiative in making critical decisions concerning Sodom. Hence they exclaim: "[W]e will destroy this place, because their cry has become great before *Y-H-V-H*; and *Y-H-V-H* has sent us to destroy it" (Genesis 19:13).

It is obvious that it is not the angels who decide to destroy Sodom and Gomorrah; they only act as agents for *Y-H-V-H*. He made the decision and sends them to carry it out. At no time do the Scriptures say that the two angels declare "we heard their cry" or "we have come on our own initiative." The angels only speak in terms of what they are commanded to do. In contrast, *Y-H-V-H*, apparently through the medium of the third man, speaks with authority throughout the narrative. However, this *man* is not God in human form, as Christians argue, but an angel in the guise of a human being. In the end, it is God, and not the angels, who causes the destruction of the wicked cities, as is clearly stated in Genesis 19:24: "Then *Y-H-V-H* caused to rain upon Sodom and Gomorrah brimstone and fire from *Y-H-V-H* out of heaven."

From verse 24, Christians infer that there were two divine personalities, one on earth, conversing with Abraham, and the other in heaven. The one on earth rained down fire upon the two cities from the one in heaven. There is, however, no grammatical basis for such an inference. Actually, in accordance with the construction of the Hebrew language, we find that in the first half of the verse, the reader is informed who caused the brimstone and fire to fall upon the two cities, and in the second half of the verse he is told for emphasis, not only from whom it came but also from where. The verse emphasizes that it is "from *Y-H-V-H*," in order to leave no doubt as to who is in command of events. Furthermore, the technique of speaking in the third person about Himself is used by God in other scriptural contexts (e.g., Exodus 3:12, 24:1; Numbers 19:1-2; Zechariah 1:12-17). It is a common feature of the Scriptures to repeat the noun rather than make use of a pronoun. In addition, an individual will frequently speak of himself in the third person instead of using the first person. Examples of this may be seen in the following: Lamech said, "Hear my voice you wives of Lamech" (Genesis 4:23), not "my wives"; similarly David said, "Take with you the servants of your lord" (1 Kings 1:33), not "my servants"; and Ahasuerus said, "in the name of the king" (Esther 8:8), not "in my name." In the same way, the use of "from the Lord" rather than "from Him," in the verse under discussion, conforms to the biblical usage.

These very verses, by which Christians attempt to prove their claims, demolish, in effect, the theory of a coequal triune partnership.

If the destruction of Sodom and Gomorrah is the act of a triune god, in which all three personalities take part, it would show them to be unequal partners. It is stated in Genesis 19:13: "[W]e will destroy this place, because their cry has become great before *Y-H-V-H*, and *Y-H-V-H has sent us* to destroy it," implying that two of the divine personalities are inferior in status since they do the bidding of the third. The claim that any, or all, of these three angels was God is a contradiction of the biblical text of Genesis 18 and 19.

Chapter 7

THE MEANING OF *'ADO-NAI*
(Genesis 18:30)

The word, *'adon*, "lord" (plural, *'adonai*), may be used in the singular or the plural to refer to a divine or human lord. But, how are we to understand the meaning of the related word form *'adonoi* (with the long vowel *qametz*), used over four hundred times in the Bible in reference to *Y-H-V-H*? To this end, we need to establish the meaning of the *-ai* (alt. *-oi*) ending in *'adonoi*. It may be that this is an honorific title in the first-person singular suffixed form of the plural noun *'adonim*. This understanding fits well in passages in which *Y-H-V-H* is addressed reverently as "my Lord" (e.g., Genesis 18:30). Additional support for this understanding of the expression is seen in the fact that both the singular and plural first-person suffixed forms, (*'adoni, 'adonai*), are used exclusively for addressing people (cf. Genesis 23:6, 19:2). On the other hand, it may be that the *-ai* (-oi) is an emphatic suffix which strengthens the meaning of the root word so that the term denotes "Lord without equal," "Lord of all." This understanding finds support in that *'adonoi* occurs in passages where God speaks of Himself and where accordingly the meaning "my Lord" is improbable (e.g., Ezekiel 13:9, 23:49; Job 28:28). It also occurs in passages in which more than one human speaker is represented, making a singular suffix seem incongruous (Psalms 44:24).

The intensity of meaning expressed in the term *'adonoi* ("Lord of all") fits every citation of this word found in the biblical text. Interestingly, the Septuagint does not render the term with a pronoun; it translates as *Kyrios*, "Lord," not *Kyrios mou*, "my Lord." *'Adonoi* apparently is a divine epithet when used in conjunction with *Y-H-V-H* or as a parallel to it. Hence, it is written: "*Y-H-V-H*, you made a place for your dwelling, a sanctuary, *'Ado-nai*, your hands established" (Exodus 15:17). One may conclude therefore that although *'adonoi* may be a plural of majesty meaning "my Lord" in some passages where God is being addressed (e.g., Genesis 15:2), it means "Lord of

18

all" everywhere that it is used (e.g., Isaiah 48:16 — *'Ado-nai Y-H-V-H*).

A *midrash* states:

> The Holy One blessed be He said to Moses, "You wish to know My
> name? I am called according to My deeds. Sometimes, I am called
> by [the name] *'El Shaddai*, by [the name of Lord of] Hosts [*Tzeva'ot*],
> by [the name] God [*'Elohim*], by [the name] Lord [*Y-H-V-H*]. When
> I judge humankind, I am called 'God.' And when I make war against
> the wicked, I am called ['Lord of] Hosts.' And when I suspend
> [judgment for] a person's sins, I am called *'El Shaddai*. And when
> I have mercy on My world, I am called 'Lord' [*Y-H-V-H*].'" For
> God is none other than the quality of mercy, as it says, "Lord, Lord,
> merciful and gracious God . . ." (Exodus 34:6). That is [what it
> means when it says,] "I will be that which I will be": "I am called
> according to My deeds." (Midrash *Shemot Rabbah* 3:6) See also:

> The Almighty said to him [Moses], "You want to know My name? I
> am called by name according to My deeds. When I sit in judgment
> of the world, I am called *'Elohim*. When I take revenge against the
> wicked, I am called *Tzeva'ot*. When I suspend [punishment] of sins,
> I am called *'El Shaddai*. When I dispense mercy, I am called *Rachum*.
> Thus, My name depends on My deeds." (Midrash *Tanchuma, Shemot*
> 1:20)

According to these *midrashim*, God can be known only through
His deeds, and the various names of God are merely labels reflecting
God's actions. God cannot be fully known through His names. He is
only known through how He reveals Himself, that is, "I Will Be What
I Will Be" (*'eheye 'asher 'eheye*).

Chapter 8

JACOB WRESTLES WITH AN ANGEL
(Genesis 32:25-31)

Christians use the biblical story of Jacob's wrestling with an angel as proof of their belief in a triune deity. As with Genesis 18 and 19, they claim that this narrative proves God manifested Himself in human form.

> And Jacob was left alone; and a man wrestled with him until the breaking of the day. And when he saw that he did not prevail against him, he touched the hollow of his thigh; and the hollow of Jacob's thigh was strained, as he wrestled with him. Then he said: "Let me go, for the day is breaking." But he said: "I will not let you go unless you bless me." And he said to him: "What is your name?" And he said: "Jacob." Then he said: "Your name shall no more be called Jacob, but Israel; for you have striven with a divine being ['*elohim*] and with men, and have prevailed." And Jacob asked him, and said: "Tell me, I pray, your name." But he said: "Why is it that you ask my name?" And he blessed him there. And Jacob called the name of the place *Peni'el*: "For I have seen a divine being ['*elohim*] face to face, and my life is preserved." (Genesis 32:25-31)

The word '*elohim* may mean an angel ("divine being," or "divine power") and this, indeed, is its meaning in our verse: "I have seen an angel [or "a divine being"] face to face." Further confirmation for this rendering is found in Hosea 12:4-5. In speaking of Jacob, the passage, written in parallel style, says: "And by his strength he strove with a divine being ['*elohim*]; so he strove with an angel [*malach*], and prevailed."

Jacob calls the place *Peni'el*—"The face of God" or "The face of a divine power." The name *Peni'el* is the most natural and proper commemoration of the incident that Jacob could give, since it honors God, who sent the angel. The importance of only honoring God is highlighted by the angel's refusal to divulge his name to Jacob when the latter requests it. The angel is aware that the knowledge of his name would not be of any benefit to Jacob, for all the power he possesses is directly from God. Therefore, in striving with the angel, Jacob is, in effect, striving with God.

Only God must be honored, not his messenger. The messenger only represents the one who sends him and in whose name he repeats the message exactly as given to him. To see the messenger is equivalent to seeing the sender. As a result, *Peni'el* ("The face of God" or "The face of a divine power") is the only appropriate name Jacob could give to honor the sender rather than the messenger.

Any interpretation which would have Jacob seeing God is in direct contradiction to the teaching of the Jewish Bible, in which God says: "You cannot see My face, for man shall not see Me and live" (Exodus 33:40). The fact that Jacob sees "*'elohim* face to face" only goes to prove that the divine being that Jacob wrestles with is not God. But, since the angel represents God, Jacob views the messenger as if it is God Himself. It is quite clear that this angel is not God manifested on earth as a human being. At no time does the Jewish Bible teach this belief.

Even the author of the Gospel of John agrees that God does not manifest Himself in a human form. He emphatically declares the impossibility of seeing God at any time (John 1:18, see also 1 John 4:12). Of Jesus, who trinitarians assert is God incarnate, that is, God in the flesh, John says he is "the only begotten god [alternately "son"]" whose function is to explain God (John 1:18). He does not consider Jesus to be the Lord God of Israel, only an angelic being who bridges the gulf between God and man. There is no legitimate reason to believe that Jacob's encounter with an angel testifies in any way to a claim that God has ever appeared in human form or to a belief in a triune deity.

Chapter 9

THE SCEPTER AND THE STAFF
(Genesis 49:10)

Christians attempt to demonstrate that the Messiah had to come prior to the end of Jewish sovereignty in 70 C.E. by citing Genesis 49:10: "The scepter shall not depart from Judah, nor the ruler's staff from between his feet, until Shiloh comes; and to him shall be the obedience of peoples." Shiloh is identified with the Messiah according to the traditional commentaries of both Judaism and Christianity. Some Christians understand the text to mean that Judean sovereign authority will end, following the coming of the Messiah. Since the termination of what little Jewish self-government remained took place approximately forty years after the death of Jesus, the verse is taken to imply that Jesus was the Messiah.

But if this text is taken to mean that the scepter shall not depart from Judah until the Messiah comes, as Christians assert, then there is an historical discrepancy that needs to be dealt with. Moses, who ruled over Israel, was a Levite. Joshua of the tribe of Ephraim followed him as ruler. The judges who held office prior to the establishment of the monarchy were not necessarily of Judean origin. But, did this prophecy only apply to the period following the establishment of the monarchy? The last Judean king, Zedekiah, was taken into captivity around 586 B.C.E. The returnees from the Babylonian exile and subsequent generations were under foreign domination (Persian, Greek, Roman) except for a relatively short period of independence during the reign of the Hasmoneans (165 B.C.E. to 63 B.C.E.), who were a priestly family of the tribe of Levi. At the time of Jesus' death, the highest sovereign Israelite authority was that of the high priest, a descendant of Levi. As such, for approximately six hundred years, before the birth of Jesus, the scepter of leadership was wielded by rulers outside the tribe of Judah. The Christian interpretation of this verse simply does not bear out according to the historic facts. What is called for is an interpretation that takes historical reality into consideration.

22

The phrase "the scepter shall not depart" is a prophetic pronouncement declaring that the right to the scepter of leadership is permanently assigned to the tribe of Judah, regardless of who is actually exercising authority over Israel at any given time. The phrase "until Shiloh comes" does not mean that at this time the scepter of leadership will depart from Judah. On the contrary, it indicates that from then on, the scepter—the kingship—will forever remain in actuality within the tribe of Judah.

Sometimes the word *'ad*, "until," is understood as *'ad v'lo 'ad bichlal*, "until [a given point], but not including that point." For example, Rashi explains, "Until the morrow of the seventh week you shall count" (Leviticus 23:16): "But [the limit denoted by] 'until,' [i.e., the morrow itself] is not included [in the counting]. They [i.e., the days to be counted] are forty-nine days." The context of verse 16 indicates that *'ad* should be understood as not including the fiftieth day, for if the fiftieth day were included the term "seven weeks" in verse 15, "You shall count for yourselves ... seven weeks, they shall be complete," would be inexact. At other times, it is understood as *'ad ve'ad bichlal*, "until [a given point], and including that point." Rashi explains, "I gave from Gilead even until the brook Arnon, within the brook and the border; even until the brook Jabbok" (Deuteronomy 3:16): "The entire brook and also beyond its border, that is, 'until' [i.e., the brook] is included and more than that."

There are talmudic discussions on the meaning of the word "until" as used in different contexts. For example, "Our *mishnah* [*Berachot* 4:1] said: R. Judah says: The Morning Prayer may be recited until four hours" (B.T *Berachot* 26b). The rabbis in the *Gemara* then analyze R. Judah's ruling. Does the word "until" in the *mishnah* mean it includes the fourth hour itself or does it mean that the fourth hour is not included? They conclude that the word "until" used by R. Judah means "until and including" the fourth hour" (B.T. *Berachot* 27b). In B.T. *Niddah* 58b we find the following statement, "'Up to' ['*ad*] may sometimes include the terminus and sometimes exclude it." In sum, sometimes "until" means *inclusive of* and sometimes *exclusive of* and the exact meaning must be derived from the context in which it is used.

Those Christians under discussion are in error in their

understanding of the Hebrew word *'ad*, "until" as used in Genesis 49:10. They suppose that "until" means "before," "up to a certain time, but not including anything following that time." They arrive at this incorrect conclusion through a misreading of the biblical text. The Hebrew word *'ad*, "until," does not mean exclusively, "before," or "up to a certain point but not beyond." It also has a meaning parallel to "until" as found in the verse, "[H]e [Jonathan] and his sons were priests to the tribe of the Danites until the day of the captivity of the land" (Judges 18:30b). Were Jonathan and his sons priests only up to the day before what is called "the day of the captivity of the land"? Or, were they priests even on that eventful day? A plain reading of the text would show that "until" here includes at least part of "the day of the captivity of the land." How the adverb *'ad* ("until") is used is dependent on context. For example, "For I will not leave you until I have done that which I have spoken to you" (Genesis 28:15), and "No man shall be able to stand before you until you have destroyed them" (Deuteronomy 7:24). Did God leave Jacob after doing all that He promised him? Were the enemies of Israel who were killed able to stand after they were destroyed? In light of Jewish history, "until" in Genesis 49:10 means *inclusive of* the following period.

Even after the Messiah comes, the scepter will still belong to Judah. The right to the scepter will never depart from Judah until the Messiah comes, at which time his scepter will be wielded over all nations (Isaiah 11); up to that time it was wielded over Israel alone. As for Genesis 49:10, there is nothing in it to suggest that it applies to Jesus. The majority of the world's population has never been followers of Jesus.

Chapter 10

THE ANGEL OF THE LORD
(Exodus 3:2-8, 10-16, 18)

The Angel of the Lord

Some trinitarians claim that whenever the Scriptures mention *malach 'Adon-ai* (*Y-H-V-H*), "an angel of the Lord," the angel is Jesus. They translate all passages mentioning such an angel as "*the* Angel of the Lord," although the Hebrew may just as well mean "*an* angel of the Lord" (literally "a messenger of the Lord"; cf. Judges 2:1, 6:11-22). True, in the construct state, when the second noun has the definite article, the first noun is automatically definite without the need for the article, however, with proper nouns, which are automatically definite, only context determines whether the first noun attached to it is to be taken as definite or indefinite. The context, in all the verses where *malach 'Adon-ai* occurs, strongly indicates that it is not to be taken as definite.

Even when the noun "angel" (*malach*) appears with a definite article in a scriptural passage, it is not used in the sense of a definite personality, but only as a reference to the particular angel mentioned previously in the text. The angel is always an impersonal being whose name is not necessary, since he is simply a messenger (the Hebrew word *malach* means "messenger" as does the Greek *anggelos*) to whom God, in whom all power resides, has entrusted a specific mission (1 Chronicles 21:16, 27; Zechariah 1:12-17). It is for this reason that the prophet Haggai, who conveyed God's message to Israel, is also called "a messenger of the Lord" (Haggai 1:13). The Hebrew term applied to Haggai, *malach 'Ado-nai*, is the same that is translated as "an angel of the Lord" and points to his prophetic role as an intermediary. Similarly, the priest is designated as "a messenger of the Lord of hosts" (Malachi 2:7). The angel who appears to Abraham does not swear by his own name but merely conveys God's message: "'By Myself I have sworn,' says the Lord" (Genesis 22:16). God sends angels to act in

His name, not in their own names. Therefore, to Jacob an angel says: "Why is it that you ask my name?" (Genesis 32:30), and to Manoah an angel says: "Why is it that you ask my name, seeing it is hidden?" (Judges 13:18).[1] There is no indication that these verses all refer to one specific angel. The angels that appeared to various biblical personalities were acting only as messengers bearing God's word. That the words of a messenger of God may be attributed directly to God is evident from Isaiah 7:10, which reads: "And the Lord spoke again to Ahaz." Ahaz received this message through Isaiah, but it is nevertheless reported as if God Himself spoke directly to him because a messenger represents the one who sends him. Therefore, an action of an angel may be credited directly to God, who gave him the message (Zechariah 3:1-8).

In describing the beginning of Moses' career as a prophet the Torah states:

> And an angel of the Lord appeared to him [Moses] in a flame of fire out of the midst of a bush; and he looked, and, behold, the bush burned with fire, and the brush was not consumed. And Moses said: "I will turn aside now, and see this great sight, why the bush is not burnt." And when the Lord saw that he turned aside to see, God called to him out of the midst of the bush, and said: "Moses, Moses." And he said: "Here am I." Then He said: "Do not come near; put off your shoes from your feet, for the place on which you are standing is holy ground." And He said: "I am the God of your father, the God of Abraham, the God of Isaac, and the God of Jacob." And Moses hid his face; for he was afraid to look at God. Then the Lord said: "I have surely seen the affliction of My people who are in Egypt and have heard their cry because of their taskmasters; for I know their pains; and I have come down to deliver them out of the hands of the Egyptians.... Come now, and I will send you to Pharaoh, that you may bring forth My people the children of Israel out of Egypt." But Moses said to God: "Who am I, that I should go to Pharaoh, and that I should bring forth the children of Israel out of Egypt?" And He said: "Certainly I will be with you; and this shall be the sign to you, that I have sent you: when you have brought forth the people out of Egypt, you shall serve God upon this mountain." Then Moses said to God: "Behold,

when I come to the children of Israel, and shall say to them: The God of your fathers has sent me to you; and they shall say to me: 'What is His name?' what shall I say to them?" And God said to Moses: "I WILL Be WHAT I WILL BE"; and He said: "Thus you shall say to the children of Israel: I WILL BE has sent me to you." And God also said to Moses: "Thus shall you say to the children of Israel: The Lord, the God of your fathers, the God of Abraham, the God of Isaac, and the God of Jacob, has sent me to you; this is My name forever, and this is My memorial to all generations. Go, and gather the elders of Israel together, and say to them: The Lord, the God of your fathers, the God of Abraham, of Isaac, and of Jacob, has appeared to me.... And they shall hearken to your voice. And you shall come, you and the elders of Israel, to the king of Egypt, and you shall say to him: The Lord, the God of the Hebrews, has met with us. And now let us go, we pray you, three days' journey into the wilderness, that we may sacrifice to the Lord our God." (Exodus 3:2-8, 10-16, 18)

Trinitarians cite this passage as further evidence of their allegation that the term "angel of the Lord" refers to part of a triune deity. To them, the text seems to indicate that the angel who appears as a fiery manifestation to Moses is the same being as the God who afterwards speaks to him. However, on further examination, the textual evidence leans in favor of the view that this angel of the Lord functions here solely as a fiery manifestation which attracts Moses' attention, while it is the God of Israel who actually "appeared," that is, made Himself known and spoke to Moses. Yet, the issue of whether God Himself speaks at some point or an angel speaks in God's name to Moses cannot be conclusively decided one way or the other. In any case, the angel is not one-third of God.

For our discussion, a final decision as to whether God speaks directly to Moses or through the medium of an angel is not crucial. Even if one believes that the angel, rather than God, speaks to Moses, it should be remembered that when, as God's representative, an angel (messenger) appears before a person, it is considered as if God Himself has appeared. As stated above, an angel repeats the exact message given to him by God. If, in verse 14, it is actually an angel that speaks directly to Moses, then he is merely conveying the

Lord's message concerning His name. That the message in this verse, even if delivered through an intermediary, is actually from the Lord is indicated by the fact that whenever an angel of the Lord is asked in the Scriptures for his name, he always refuses to give it. This is understandable, since he is only a messenger, with his own personal identity being of no importance. Therefore, he is identified with the sender of the message. Yet, in verse 14, the God of Abraham, Isaac, and Jacob does give His name. In so doing, He indicates that He is not synonymous with what the Bible calls "an angel of the Lord." All in all, "an angel of the Lord" can in no way be identified as part of the divine essence.

The Septuagint renders *malach 'Ado-nai* (*Y-H-V-H*) as *anggelos Kyriou* with the meaning "an angel of the Lord" (e.g., Judges 6:11) and "the angel of the Lord" is rendered by *ho anggelos Kyriou* (e.g., Judges 6:12). The author of the Gospel of Matthew writes: "But when he [Joseph] had considered this, behold, an angel of the Lord [*anggelos Kyriou*] appeared to him in a dream, saying, 'Joseph, son of David, do not be afraid to take Mary as your wife; for that which has been conceived in her is of holy spirit.' …And Joseph arose from his sleep, and did as the angel of the Lord [*ho anggelos Kyriou*] commanded him, and took [her] as his wife" (Matthew 1:20-24). The wording, "an angel of the Lord," reappears in Matthew 2:13, 19; 28:2. The author of the Gospel of Luke writes: "An angel of the Lord [*anggelos Kyriou*] appeared to him [Zacharias], standing to the right of the altar of incense" (Luke 1:11). Luke 1:19a identifies the angel of the Lord as Gabriel: "And the angel … said to him [Zecharias], 'I am Gabriel, who stands in the presence of God." It is further stated: "Now in the sixth month the angel Gabriel was sent from God to a city in Galilee, called Nazareth, to a virgin … and the virgin's name was Mary" (Luke 1:26-27).[2] Elizabeth later exclaims: "And blessed is she [Mary] who believed that there would be a fulfillment of what had been spoken to her by [the] Lord [*Kyriou*]" (Luke 1:45). Although the things spoken were supposedly said to Mary by Gabriel, an angel of the Lord (Luke 1:26-27), Luke's Elizabeth refers to them as spoken by the "Lord." In Luke 2:9-10 it is stated, "And an angel of the Lord [*anggelos Kyriou*] suddenly stood before them [the shepherds] … And the angel said to them…." The author of Luke understands the angel's message as having come from the Lord rather than from the angel, hence in Luke 1:15 the angel's message is said to come from the Lord.

As mentioned above, some Christians maintain that "angel of the Lord" refers to Jesus in the Jewish Scriptures. In considering the New Testament usage of "angel of the Lord" with and without the definite article one must ask how if this angel is Jesus, he can be in the womb of Mary while speaking to her (Luke 1:30) and Joseph (Matthew 1:20) respectively in the third person, he can speak to the shepherds in the fields when he was in the manger (Luke 2:9), or is able to roll away the stone from the tomb when he was supposedly inside the tomb (Matthew 28:2). Moreover, is Jesus to be identified as the angel Gabriel who the author of Luke identifies as the *angel of the Lord*? One might say that the biblical "angel of the Lord" is not the same angel identified as such by the New Testament. But, if "angel of the Lord" is consistently a title of Jesus in the Jewish Scriptures why is that name inexplicably handed over to another angel in the New Testament? It would be, indeed, strange if the New Testament angel (Gabriel) is now called after this name if it was a special title belonging to Jesus.

[1] Some Christian Bibles translate this verse as: "Why is it that you ask my name, seeing it is wonderful?" "Wonderful is a secondary meaning which is used in the sense of "incomprehensible," "marvelous." It is not to be understood as a proper name identifying the angel. The Hebrew word *peli* ("hidden," "wonderful") indicates that the name is beyond the realm of human knowledge.

[2] "Gabriel," means "Man of God," or "Strength of God." In his only biblical appearance (Daniel 8:15-16, 9:21) he is described as a man. Enoch 40:2 describes him as one of the four presences who look down from heaven (9:1), a holy angel (20:7), set over all powers (40:9). He is also the angel set over Paradise, over the serpents and the cherubim (20:7), and has the power to destroy the wicked (54:6). (See *The Apocrypha and Pseudepigrapha of the Old Testament in English*, Ed. R.H. Charles, Oxford: Clarendon Press, Vol. 2, 1913.)

Chapter 11

THE ATONEMENT PROCESS
(Leviticus 17:11)

Fulfilling the Torah's requirements

Christians argue that the multiplicity of biblical laws makes it impossible for one to have a proper relationship with God based on those laws because no one person could possibly fulfill all of the Torah's requirements. But, this conclusion involves a misunderstanding as to the goal of the Torah. In its entirety, it is addressed not to the individual but to the community. The individual is expected to carry out such laws, which come within the scope of his or her life. The Torah is a source of directives available to guide a Jew's life, to the extent that situations arise to which such directives may apply. There was never any intention on the part of God, however, that any one person attempt to carry out all enactments of the Torah. For example, some laws apply to only certain individuals. But, even more significant, the Torah, itself, shows what is to be done when one is not able to fulfill an obligation specified by the commandments—the atonement system.

The nature of biblical sacrifice

Christians mistakenly believe that without a blood sacrifice the Jewish people can have no assurance that their sins are forgiven. Their reasoning is based on Leviticus 17:11: "It is the blood that makes an atonement for the soul." The Christian presumption is that where there is no blood there is no atonement. They assume that the fasting and repentance of *Yom Kippur*, the Day of Atonement, cannot give any assurance of sins forgiven. They insist that God will only accept an offering of a blood sacrifice to atone for one's sins. Finally, the Christian misunderstanding of the text is compounded by the claim that there can be no salvation without the supposedly atoning blood of Jesus. Jesus, by his death and supposed sacrifice for humanity's sins, is said to have made atonement for all who believe in him, and so there is no longer any need for a Temple or a sacrifice or a priesthood. Following the death of Jesus, it is alleged, the Temple was destroyed, and the priesthood abolished, since they were no longer needed. Jesus was now to be the unblemished lamb that would bear away the sins of the world.

Read in context, Leviticus 17:11 is part of a passage whose major emphasis is not on how to secure general atonement from sin, but is concerned mainly with the specific prohibition against consuming blood. "And whatever man of the house of Israel, or of the strangers who sojourn among you, who consumes any blood, I will set My face against that person who consumes blood, and will cut him off from among his people. For the life of the flesh is in the blood, and I have given it to you upon the altar to make atonement for your souls; for it is the blood that makes an atonement for the soul. Therefore, I say to the children of Israel, 'No one among you shall consume blood, nor shall any stranger who sojourns among you consume blood.'" However, in presenting the prohibition against consuming blood the biblical text provides significant information concerning sacrificial animal offerings. In the case of animal offerings, the blood of the sacrifice serves as the atoning agent, not another part of the body. Blood symbolizes the life of the animal and, as such, it is given as a means by which to atone for sins.

To fully understand how Christians have misinterpreted Leviticus 17:11, let us first investigate the nature of the physical and spiritual contents of the Temple atonement system. The physical sacrifice portion is an unblemished clean animal, while the spiritual sacrifice portion is a repentant mental attitude expressed through sincere prayer.

The ceremonial service of the biblical sacrificial system serves as a reminder that the consequences of unrepentant sin leads to suffering and even death. It serves as an external symbol of an inner understanding expressed through the act of prayer, the service of the heart. A prerequisite of prayer is that one who prays does so with "clean hands." That is, it must be done with sincerity and repentance and with the intention of seeking inner change. To those who offer insincere prayer God declares, "And when you spread forth your hands, I will hide My eyes from you; also when you make many prayers, I will not hear; your hands are full of blood. Wash yourselves, make yourselves clean, put away the evil doings from before My eyes, cease to do evil" (Isaiah 1:15-16). God knows when a person is sincere in his/her supplications and answers accordingly.

Offering sacrifice is only part of the Temple process of atonement. Sins were not automatically removed when an animal was slaughtered on the altar, as if something took place that made the individual's own moral actions irrelevant. Rather sacrifice symbolically connected the worshiper to God, thereby providing the external basis for effective repentance. Nevertheless, sacrifice is not an alternative to contrite repentance. Sincere confessionary repentant prayer must always accompany atonement even with a blood sacrifice offering. Atonement is not granted to the sinner by virtue of the sacrifice alone, without the accompanying act of confessionary repentance. The confession of sin (*vidui*) is an essential part of repentance (Leviticus 5:5, Numbers 5:7). Even where the Torah mandates a specific offering there cannot be atonement without an oral confession. As long as a person refuses to acknowledge his wrongdoing, he cannot repent sincerely.

Sin cannot be erased by the mere observance of the technical rite of blood sacrifice. The penitent sinner must perceive the sacrifice as though he were offering himself as the victim on the altar. True atonement lies in the "broken spirit" and "contrite heart" of the penitent (Psalms 51:18-19; 16-17 in some versions). The sinner must face the gravity of his guilt and act to relieve its burden. He does this by putting his two hands between the horns of the sacrifice and pressing down with all his strength on the animal. This *leaning* was performed on all personal sacrifices by the individual bringing it and was accompanied by a confession (B.T. *Yoma* 36a). By actually laying his hands on the animal prior to slaughter and expressing his feelings in words of confession the sinner obliterates and consumes his sinful pride, just as the sacrificial offering burns and is to be consumed on the altar. The awareness of guilt is the first step. Remorse over past actions must be followed by a resolution for change in the future; only then is the way open to full repentance. In any event, atonement comes directly from God and is, in fact, an act of divine grace.

The efficacy of contrite prayer

Many passages in Scripture declare that sincere repentant prayer, without an accompanying blood sacrifice, can and does provide a means for full atonement and forgiveness of sin. For example, Solomon's prayer at the very dedication of the First Temple (1 Kings 8:22-53) does not mention sacrifice, but prayer is emphasized as a means for obtaining remission of sin:

> If Your people go out to battle against their enemy, by whatever way You shall send them, and they pray to the Lord toward the city which you have chosen, and toward the house which I have built for Your name; then hear in heaven their prayer and their supplication, and maintain their cause. If they sin against You — for there is no man that does not sin — and You are angry with them, and deliver them to the enemy, so that they carry them away captive to the land of the enemy, far off or near; yet if they take thought in the land to which they are carried captive, and repent, and make supplication to You in the land of their captors, saying: "We have sinned, and have done iniquitously, we have dealt wickedly"; if they return to You with all their heart and with all their soul in the land of their enemies, who carried them captive, and pray to You toward their land, which You gave to their fathers, the city which You have chosen, and the house which I have built for Your name; then hear their prayer and their supplication in heaven Your dwelling place, and maintain their cause and forgive Your people who have sinned against You, and all their transgressions which they have transgressed against You, and give them compassion before those who carried them captive, that they may have compassion on them; for they are Your people, and Your inheritance, which You did bring out of Egypt, from the midst of the furnace of iron. Let Your eyes be opened to the supplication of Your servant, and to the supplication of Your people Israel, to hear them whenever they cry to You. (1 Kings 8:44-52)[1]

Indeed, Daniel, living in exile centuries later, did exactly as Solomon proposed:

> He went into his house — now his windows were open in his upper chamber toward Jerusalem — and he kneeled upon his knees three times a day, and gave thanks before his God, as he had done

33

previously. Then these men came joined together, and found Daniel making petition and supplication before his God. (Daniel 6:11-12)

In a contrite supplication before God, Daniel confesses his sins and the sins of the people of Israel:

And I set my face toward the Lord God, to seek by prayer and supplication, with fasting, and sackcloth, and ashes. And I prayed to the Lord my God, and made confession, and I said: "I beg of You my Lord, the great and awesome God, who safeguards the covenant and the loving-kindness to those who love Him and keep His commandments. We have sinned, and have dealt wickedly, and have done evil, and have rebelled, and have deviated from Your commandments and from Your ordinances. Nor have we listened to Your servants the prophets who spoke in Your name to our kings, our princes, and our fathers, and to all the people of the land. To You, O Lord, belongs righteousness, but to us shamefacedness, as of this day: to the men of Judah, and to the inhabitants of Jerusalem, and to all Israel, that are near, and that are far off, through all the countries where You have driven them, because of the betrayal with which they betrayed You. O Lord, to us belongs shamefacedness, to our kings, to our princes, and to our fathers, because we have sinned against You. To my Lord our God is the compassion and forgiveness, for we have rebelled against Him; neither have we listened to the voice of the Lord our God, to follow in His teachings, which He placed before us by His servants the prophets. All Israel have transgressed Your law, and have deviated, so as not to listen to Your voice, and so there has been poured out upon us the curse and the oath that is written in the Law of Moses the servant of God; for we have sinned against Him. And He has confirmed His word, which He spoke about us, and about our judges who judged us, to bring upon us a great calamity; so that under the entire heaven has not been done as has been done upon Jerusalem. As it is written in the Law of Moses, all this calamity has come upon us; yet have we not entreated the countenance of the Lord our God, that we might turn from our iniquities, and comprehend Your truth. And so the Lord has hastened the calamity, and brought it upon us; for the Lord our God is righteous in all His works which He has done, and we have not listened to His voice. And now, my Lord our God, that has brought Your people out of the land of Egypt with a mighty hand, and You have made for Yourself a name as of this day; we have sinned, we have done wickedly. My Lord, according to all Your righteousness, let Your anger and Your fury, I pray, be turned away from Your city Jerusalem, Your holy mountain; because for our sins, and for the iniquities of our fathers, Jerusalem and Your people have become a reproach to all that are round about us. Now therefore, O our God, listen to the prayer of Your servant, and to his supplications, and cause Your face to shine upon Your sanctuary that is desolate, for my Lord's sake. O my God, incline Your ear, and hear; open Your eyes, and see our desolations and of the city upon which Your name is proclaimed; for we do not present our supplications before You because of our righteousness, but because of Your great compassions. O my Lord, hear, O my Lord, forgive, O my Lord, be attentive and do, do not delay, for Your own sake, O my God, because Your name is proclaimed upon Your city and Your people." And while I was speaking, and praying, and confessing my sin and the sin of my people Israel, and presenting my supplication before the Lord, my God, for the holy mountain of my God; and while I was speaking in prayer, the man Gabriel, whom I saw in the vision at first, approached me in swift flight about the time of the evening offering. And he enabled me to understand, and he spoke with me, and he said, "Daniel, now I have come forth to make you skillful in understanding. In the beginning of your supplications, a word came forth, and I have come to tell it, for you are beloved; now contemplate the word and understand the vision. (Daniel 9:3-23)

Daniel asks in the name of all Israel for forgiveness and restoration to the land of their forefathers. His prayer for restoration and rebuilding of Jerusalem and the Temple is answered although the sacrificial system was still not reinstituted and Jerusalem lay in ruins. There was no "mixing" of prayers of repentance with sacrifices being offered in the Temple. It was the time of day for the evening offering but no sacrifices were being presented in the destroyed Temple at that time. Only the prayers of repentant sinners could bring about national restoration and the rebuilding of the Temple. Solomon's request was that heart-felt prayers offered from exile toward the Temple, not specifically toward the ruins of the Temple, should be received by God. Nevertheless, it is obvious from the description of Daniel's supplication that God received prayers offered even toward the ruins of the Temple.

Nehemiah, himself still in exile, saddened by the news that the Jews in Judah were in great distress confessed the sins of the "sons of Israel" wherever they may be:

And it happened when I heard these words that I sat and wept, and I mourned for days, and I fasted and prayed before the God of heaven. And I said, "I beseech You, O Lord God of heaven, the great and awesome God, who keeps the covenant and loving-kindness to those who love Him and to those who keep His commandments. Let Your ear now be attentive and Your eyes open to listen to the prayer of Your servant, which I pray before You today, day and night, concerning the children of Israel, Your servants, and I confess the sins of the children of Israel, which we sinned against You; and I and my father's house have sinned. We have dealt corruptly against You, and we have not kept the commandments, the statutes, and the ordinances that You commanded Moses, Your servant. Remember now the word that You commanded Moses, Your servant, saying, 'If you deal treacherously, I shall scatter you among the nations. And if you return to Me and keep My commandments and perform them — if your exile is at the end of the heaven, from there I shall gather them, and I shall bring them to the place that I chose to cause My name to rest there.' Now they are Your servants and Your people, whom You redeemed with Your great strength and with Your strong hand. I beseech You, O Lord, may Your ear now be attentive to the prayer of Your servant and to the prayer of Your servants, who wish to fear Your name, and cause Your servant to succeed today, and grant him mercy before this man." And I was the king's butler. (Nehemiah 1:4-11)

God responded to Solomon's prayer saying, "I have heard your prayer, and have chosen this place for Myself as a house of sacrifice. . . .[I]f My people, who are called by My name, shall humble themselves, and pray, and seek My face, and turn from their wicked ways; then I will hear from heaven, and I will forgive their sin, and I will heal their land. Now My eyes shall be open and My ears attentive to the prayer of this place" (2 Chronicles 7:12-15). This did not preclude

God's answering sincere prayer made elsewhere. God did not answer Solomon's prayer point by point but the unfolding of events in Jewish history shows that He did grant all that Solomon requested. The fact that Nehemiah's prayer request, as Daniel's before him, was granted without his providing a sacrificial offering shows that sincere repentance without the shedding of blood can bring forgiveness even for one living in exile. But, God did warn Solomon that if the people of Israel went too far in their sin, He would uproot them from their land and destroy the Temple (2 Chronicles 7:17-22). What would be left for them to do, but to reach out to God for forgiveness? In Leviticus 26:40-45, God declares that once the Israelites have repented their sins and those of their forefathers, He would show mercy to them and end their exile. With the Temple destroyed, only sincere repentant prayer could be offered as a means of achieving atonement. This Daniel did at a time when the sacrifices were suspended; this Nehemiah did when sacrifices were again reinstituted, but he was still in exile.

The absence of the Temple service has not prevented the Jews from seeking God in humility and establishing a relationship with Him at the personal level, which is the goal of the sacrificial offering made with a contrite spirit. This does not mean that the exile or the absence of Temple sacrifice is what God ultimately intends for the Jewish people, but restoration of the full atonement procedure as provided by the Torah will come according to His timetable.

Meanwhile, as we learn from the prayers of Daniel and Nehemiah, "All Israel are responsible for one another."[2] They do not speak only of their own sins or dwell on the sins of others, but include themselves within the national commonality. They do not request personal reward for their own merits, but would have all Israel benefit from the divine recognition of their merits. Their prayers reflect national responsibility and national repentance leading to national atonement and forgiveness. As such, there is not only an individual atonement taking place but a national atonement as well.

That which is acceptable to God

The sacrificial atonement system of the Torah was given exclusively to the Jewish people: "I have given it [the blood] to you ... to make atonement for your souls" (Leviticus 17:11). A blood sacrifice, in itself, was never enough; it always had to be accompanied by sincere confessionary repentant prayer: "And it shall be, when he shall be guilty in one of these things, that he shall confess that he has sinned in that thing: and he shall bring his guilt offering to the Lord for his sin which he has sinned ... and the priest shall make atonement for him concerning his sin" (Leviticus 5:5-6). Thus, the Jewish Scriptures confirm that beside blood, confession was also needed in order to receive forgiveness. But, it is clear from a careful perusal of the Scriptures that sin can be removed through genuine remorse and sincere repentance even without the shedding of blood. Non-Jews can also find remission of sin through sincere confessionary repentant prayer (Jonah 3:5-10, Daniel 4:27). Jonah tells the idol worshipers of Nineveh to turn from their evil ways; he does not say that unless they begin offering sacrifices to Y-H-V-H or become Jews they are doomed. Their response to his warning is to repent: they fast, pray and turn from their evil. What is God's response? "And God saw their deeds, that they had repented of their evil way, and the Lord relented concerning the evil that He had spoken to do to them, and He did not do it" (Jonah 3:10). Spiritually, the contrite heart has always been the constant immutable human portion in the atonement process. A transgressor, whether Jew or Gentile, fulfilling this requirement may expect the Almighty to forgive his sins and allow him to enter fellowship with God. For what does God require "but to do justly, and to love mercy, and to walk humbly with your God" (Micah 6:8). God asks of the sinner: "Return to Me ... and 1 will return to you" (Zechariah 1:3). Acknowledge responsibility for sins committed and sincerely attempt to do better in the future.

God's mercy

It should be noted that God is often merciful and forgiving even when there is an absence of sincere repentance. The psalmist writes, "But He, being full of compassion, forgives iniquity, and does not destroy; many a time He turns His anger away and does not stir up all His wrath. For He remembered that they were but flesh, a wind that passes away, and comes not again" (Psalms 78:30). The prophet Micah declares: "Who is a God like You, that pardons iniquity, and passes by the transgression of the remnant of His heritage? He retains not His anger forever, because He delights in mercy" (Micah 7:18). Isaiah records that redemption may be forthcoming even when undeserved, for God's own reasons. "I, even I, am He that blots out your transgressions for My own sake, and will not remember your sins" (Isaiah 43:25). The prophet informs us that in some cases God's "redemption" precedes Israel's "return." "Remember these things, 0 Jacob, and Israel, for you are My servant; l have formed you, you are My servant: 0 Israel, you should not forget Me. I have blotted out[3] as a thick cloud, your transgressions, and as a cloud, your sins. Return to Me, for I have redeemed you.... The Lord has redeemed Jacob, and does glorify Himself in Israel" (Isaiah 44:21-23). Individually, there is no atonement without repentance, but nationally it is possible that sin reaches a degree where after permitting suffering of the nation God forgives for His own sake lest the nations mock Him (Isaiah 43:25). Thus, God's redemption is not always dependent on repentance preceding forgiveness.

No matter what occurs, Israel is always God's chosen servant people expressed as a singular entity: Isaiah 41:8, 44:1-2, 45:4, 48:20, 49:3. "They are the offspring whom the Lord has blessed" (Isaiah 69:1).

Sacrificial blood loss

Biblically, sacrificial death must be directly attributable to the loss of blood and this shed blood is essential for achieving atonement. When the sinner sees what happens to the animal he is moved to consider that were it not for God's mercy he, himself, would suffer the punishment. The sin-offering is a dramatic enactment of the severest punishment and has the effect of making the sinner aware of how great his sin is. With this awareness, the sinner will experience remorse. As the blood escapes the slaughtered animal's body, the sinner reflects upon the ebbing of life. The graphic sight of the blood serves as a visual aid to evoke awareness of the punishment for sin.

Emphasis is placed on the shedding of blood not the

mere death of the sacrifice. Fulfillment of the so-called "old covenant," under which Jesus was put to death, meant that an actual blood shedding as demanded by God's Law had to take place. The manner in which the animal offering dies is apparently crucial because "the life is in the blood" (Leviticus 17:11). This may refer to the fact that the life sustaining elements (nutrients and oxygen) are in the blood. Blood, the principal carrier of life, is considered the life-force of the animal. Physiological malfunctions of body organs due to blood loss notwithstanding, implicit in the biblical text is the conviction that when slaughtering an animal sacrifice death is caused by blood loss. Indeed, no other cause of death is acceptable.

The biblically mandated method of slaughtering an animal causes the maximum loss of blood and a quick death. Animals offered on the altar were sacrificed by the traditional method that was given orally to Moses on Mount Sinai. This method, shechitah ("slaughtering"), is extended to the slaughter of animals for food, "...then you shall kill ... as I have commanded you [orally, on Mount Sinai]" - Deuteronomy 12:21. Death, by the shedding of blood, is an inevitable result of using shechitah. A portion of the sacrificial animal's shed blood is used for the remission of sin process (which also includes an accompanying sincere confessionary repentant prayer).

Leviticus 17:11 states that "...the blood ... I have given it to you upon the altar to make atonement for your souls...." This verse is extremely important for an understanding of the biblical atonement system. In this verse God provides for the expiation of sin: "... the blood ... I have given it ... to make atonement...." It specifies to whom the sacrificial atonement system of the Torah was given. This system was given exclusively to the Jewish people: "I have given it [the blood] to you ... to make atonement for your souls." Non-Jews could find remission of sin solely through sincere confessionary repentant prayer (Jonah 3:5-10, Daniel 4:27). Verse 11 also sets the spatial limitations on where the blood shed for atonement may be offered: "I have given it [the blood] ... upon the altar." Biblically, the sacrificial animal's blood is acceptable to God only if offered "upon the altar," first, that of the Tabernacle, and later of the Temple. Once the Temple was built, no altar might properly be built or sacrifice offered outside the Temple in Jerusalem (Deuteronomy 16:2, 5-6). The Temple is the sole designated area in which animal sacrifice is permissible (Deuteronomy 12:5-6, 11; 1 Kings 5:5, 8:19, 1 Chronicles 22:10).

The sacrifices of our lips — Hosea 14:3

The understanding that under certain circumstances prayer alone is sufficient in the atonement process is expressed in Hosea 14:3: "Take with you words, and return to the Lord; say to Him: 'Forgive all iniquity, and accept that which is good; thus we will pay bullocks — our lips.'" The stich at Hosea 14:3c is best rendered in English as": Thus, we will pay [our sacrificial obligations of] bullocks [with] our lips." The Septuagint has a variant rendering that differs from that of the Hebrew Masoretic text. The Greek reads: "that we offer the fruit of [our] lips [as sacrifices to you]." This shows either that its translators emended the text, loosely interpreted the text, or that they used a variant Hebrew text that left off the final *mem* in *parim*, "bullocks," resulting in the vocalization of the word as *peri*, "fruit." (Hebrews 13:15 reads: "the fruit of lips" and reflects the Septuagint phrase.) This conjectured variant text renders the stich: "we will pay [to You] the fruit of our lips," that is, we will fulfill our spoken vows to God. This has led to a modern scholarly debate about which version represents the original text. Some modern scholars have adopted the Septuagint's version, usually with further emendations, as the correct text. They believe it gives a clearer sense of the meaning than the Masoretic text. Other scholars suggest emending the text by moving the final *mem* to the beginning of the next word to produce *peri misfateinu*, "fruit from our lips," that is, the prayers coming from our lips.

A close examination of the Masoretic text makes both the ancient and modern emendations of the text at Hosea 14:3c unnecessary. The Masoretic text makes sense as it stands.

To understand the stich at Hosea 14:3c a number of points need to be considered:

- First, the Masoretic biblical text consists of not only the words and their vocalization, but also of the trope, that is, the cantilization/

41

punctuation. In this stich, the trope under the words are *mercha*, *tipcha* and *sof-pasuk* respectively. The tropes *mercha* and *tipcha* place emphasis on *unshallema parim* ("Thus, we will pay bullocks"), creating a clause that effectively separates these two words from the word *sefateinu* ("our lips"). This can be indicated in translation by a dash. The Hebrew understands the presence of "with" between the two parts of the stich.

- Second, the text is not written in prose, but is poetry. Therefore, understanding it must take account of the nature and form that characterizes the poetic style used to express the divine message. The noun *parim* functions as an adverbial accusative of state. Semantically, "bullocks" is the debt or obligation being discharged, "our lips" being the means of payment. *Unshallema* (*shilleim*, "to pay") is in the pi'el form of the verb. The pi'el is used in the causative sense. The thought expressed by the use of the pi'el in this stich is that we will "make restitution" for our absent sacrificial obligations through the sincere prayers coming from our lips. In the poetic diction of the prophet we will "replace," "restore," "repay" the sacrificial offerings owed God with something of equal value (cf. Exodus 21:36, 2 Samuel 12:6, 2 Kings 4:7). Consequently, sincere repentant prayer, in effect, is equal to sacrificial offerings *brought with a contrite heart*. As a result of the aforementioned, the literal rendering of the stich: "Thus, we will pay bullocks — our lips," is for greater clarity expressed as: "Thus, we will pay [our sacrificial obligations of] bullocks [with] our lips."

- Third, time and place of composition must be considered. The prophetic message is timeless for the Jewish people of all generations, but in the immediate historical context, Hosea prophesied in the Northern kingdom of Israel. His message was for all Israelites of both kingdoms and, in part, addressed the worthlessness of sacrifices when not accompanied by repentance and obedience to God (Hosea 5:6, 6:6). In the context of this stich, the prophet is addressing a procedural problem confronting the repentant sinner living in the Northern kingdom, but its implications are far reaching. In urging his fellow Israelites to repent their iniquities, he is aware that the religio-political difficulties prevented free access to the Jerusalem Temple. Therefore, Hosea stresses the universal principle of the biblical sacrificial system — inward devotion and repentance expressed through contrite prayer brings God's forgiveness.

In the immediate context, if the Israelites of the Northern kingdom will heed the prophet's message and repent, God "will heal their backsliding" and turn His anger away from them (Hosea 14:5), There is no dependency or inclusion in someone else's sacrifice; one's own prayerful repentance can bring God's forgiveness. The context of the full verse calls for turning to God with repentant prayer wherein the sinner asks for forgiveness. The prophetic message is that in the absence of the full atonement system God's forgiveness of sins is still possible through contrite prayers of our lips.

Availability of God's forgiveness

As we have seen, the sacrificial system is a part of one method the Almighty provides for attaining forgiveness of sin. Biblically, a Jew could generally obtain forgiveness through sacrifice accompanied by repentant prayer, repentant prayer alone, or out of the pure mercy of God. A blood sacrifice in itself was never the sole means of atonement, but a portion of a larger process. The prophet Hosea states: "For I desire loving-kindness, and not sacrifices, and knowledge of God more than burnt offerings" (Hosea 6:6). Loving-kindness and showing knowledge of God are greater than any blood sacrifice. Without knowledge of God, there is no belief in Him. It is belief in God and putting one's faith in Him, and not the offering of a blood sacrifice that biblically establishes a relationship with God. Today, Jewish people without Temple, active priesthood, or animal offering, by faith in God, by coming to Him with contrite repentant prayer, maintain their biblically based relationship with Him. Simply put, a Jewish relationship with God is based on belief and trust in the Almighty. The role of Torah is crucial in having this relationship. The purpose of Torah is not simply to save individuals from sin. Its primary purpose is to bring into existence God's promise that through the Torah the Jewish people become "a holy people before God" (Deuteronomy 26:19). When the individual Jew acknowledges

God's preeminence and accepts upon himself God's commandments he identifies himself with God and establishes a relationship with the Almighty. Atonement is then open to the person of faith.

How can a Jew today receive forgiveness of sins? Repentance and not bloodshed is the quintessential biblical form of atonement valid in all generations. When a Jew sins, he/she may come before God in sincere repentance to receive forgiveness through contrite prayer. "Yet even now, says the Lord, turn back to Me with all your hearts, and with fasting, and with weeping, and with lamentation" (Joel 2:12; cf. Esther 4:3). Although the Temple stood when these words were enunciated, there is no mention of a blood offering. Instead, there is a call to: "Blow the *shofar* in Zion, sanctify a fast, call a solemn assembly" (verse 15) and to, "Let the priests, the ministers of the Lord, weep between the porch and the altar" (verse 17).

Indeed, the offer to humble oneself before God and be reconciled to Him is made to all humankind. Some moral precepts of Torah, the Noahide Commandments, are incumbent on Gentiles. These are the natural laws which any just person can be expected to follow by observation and reason. Minimally, non-Jews are to live by moral and civil rules and establish the proper institutions necessary to uphold the basic structure of society. For example, a tone of righteousness and mercy is to be set in relationships of human to human and human to animal life in the command to abstain from eating flesh from a living animal (Genesis 9:4), have responsibility to maintain the sanctity of life, whether one's own or someone else's (Genesis 9:5), and to have respect for human life, which entails prescribing capital punishment for murder (Genesis 9:6).[5] On a deeper spiritual level, non-Jews may also establish a personal relationship with God (2 Kings 5:15-18) and find remission of sin through sincere repentance (Jonah 3:5-10, Daniel 4:27).[6] But, it was not necessary for a person to become a Jew to be righteous and have a place in the world to come.

God's relationship with the Jewish people is unique, but does not preclude God's concern about all humanity. Thus, God declares through the prophet, "And there is no God else beside Me; a just God and a Savior; there is none beside Me. Look to Me, and be saved, all the ends of the earth; for I am God, and there is none else" (Isaiah

45:21-22).

Not by blood alone

There is historical precedent from Jewish history to guide us as to the biblically prescribed manner by which to obtain atonement today. Jewish history, prior to the Common Era, shows that the absence of a blood sacrifice does not prevent one from gaining atonement for his/her sins. If this were not so, Manasseh would not have been able to repent while in Assyrian imprisonment and receive the forgiveness necessary for his subsequent restoration to the throne (2 Chronicles 33:11-13). Jews were first exiled to Babylonia in the seventh century B.C.E., that is, even prior to 586 B.C.E., and had no means of offering a blood sacrifice to obtain atonement through the sacrificial system (especially after 586). Did God write them off as generations lost in sin with no means of atonement and forgiveness? Where was their blood atonement? Yet, in accordance with Jeremiah 29:12-13, forgiveness was forthcoming; the Jews were permitted to return to their homeland. Also, traditional Jews, loyal to the God of Israel, could not offer sacrifices in the Temple during the three-year period of its desecration by the Hellenized Jewish collaborators of the Seleucid king Antiochus IV Epiphanes. Following his command, they caused an altar to Zeus Olympios to be erected within the Temple precincts. According to 1 Maccabees (cf. 1:54, 4:52) the sacrifices in the Temple were discontinued for three years (168-165 B.C.E.). During this period unclean animals were offered in the Temple. No Jew adhering to the Lord God of Israel could offer sacrifices at this time. It must be assumed that during that period of Temple desecration God did not leave those loyal to Him without any means of atonement. In this period, there could have been no other means for obtaining atonement other than through repentance devoid of a blood sacrifice. Furthermore, by the first century C.E., the Jewish population spread into other regions making it impossible for most of them to travel to the Temple. This meant they could not offer personal atonement sacrifices in the Temple that required their presence. Did God leave them with no means of atonement for sins committed?

The period prior to Jesus' crucifixion saw the Jewish people endure exile and persecution in which they had no means of bringing blood atonement. Yet, it appears they were under the Mosaic Law's requirement to do so. Since no Temple sacrifice was possible, and Jesus had not yet died to provide the supposed everlasting means of atonement, that is, his atoning blood, a grave problem would seem to have arisen: Did God leave these Jews in their sins, with no means whatsoever for atonement? In adhering to the position that only blood can obtain forgiveness of sin, Christians are claiming that God condemned these Jews to die in their sins, without any means of atonement available. Why? For not doing the impossible!

Did God mock His people throughout the ages by placing them in situations where no blood sacrifice system was available to them, yet no other means of atonement was possible? Did He demand either those blood sacrifices or eternal damnation? The claim that Jesus' blood was shed as an atoning sacrifice, once and for all times, for those who accept him, does not provide an answer for those Jews preceding Jesus' generation, especially under conditions where no blood sacrifices could be made. God Himself gave the Jewish exiles in Babylonia the answer to this dilemma, and its message echoes across the centuries:

> And you shall call upon Me, and go, and pray to Me, and I will hearken to you. And you shall seek Me, and find Me, when you shall search for Me with all your heart. (Jeremiah 29:13)

Jeremiah unequivocally told the exiles that God did not discard them, as even in the lands of their exile they did not lack the means for achieving the atonement of their sins. Not by the blood of bullocks slain, but by the offering of their lips, that is, prayer, were they able to effect atonement. And so it is with Jews throughout the ages — by prayers and repentance they make atonement for their sins and God in His mercy forgives.

Prayer without a blood sacrifice was biblically recognized as a means of atonement: "And the people came to Moses and they said: 'We have sinned, because we have spoken against the Lord, and against you; pray to the Lord, that He take away from us the serpent.' And Moses prayed for the people" (Numbers 21:7). There were even times when non-blood material offerings provided a physical atonement: Incense (Number 17:12-13), jewelry (Numbers 31:50), a red hot coal (Isaiah 6:6-7), fine-flour (Leviticus 5:1-13). The holy incense, without the use of a blood sacrifice, could effect atonement: "And Aaron took as Moses spoke, and he ran into the midst of the assembly; and behold, the plague had already begun among the people; and he put on the incense, and he made atonement [*va-yechapper*] for the people. And he stood between the dead and the living; and the plague was stopped" (Numbers 17:12-13). Stopping the spread of this plague — not atoning for sins — is the main subject of this passage. Nevertheless, in this singular case, we are informed that incense made atonement for the people, providing a protective barrier between the "dead and the living." On returning from battle, the Israelites brought jewelry as an atonement offer for their sins: "And we have brought the Lord's offering, what every man has found, articles of gold, armlets, and bracelets, signet rings, earrings, and girdles, to make atonement [*le-chapper*] for our souls before the Lord" (Numbers 31:50). This demonstrates that atonement could be attained without animal sacrifices. In each instance, no shedding of blood was required for forgiveness of sin to take place.

Isaiah provides a graphic example showing that it is incorrect to say that there must be shedding of blood in order to obtain forgiveness of sin. He states, "Then flew one of the seraphim to me, having a live coal in his mouth, which he had taken with the tongs off the altar; and he touched my mouth with it, and said: Behold, this has touched your lips; and your iniquity is taken away, and your sin forgiven" (Isaiah 6:6-7). Christians emphasize that the burning coal was taken from the altar and therefore had some connection with the blood atonement of the sacrificial system. But, the biblical point made is simply that atonement could be achieved through an object other than blood. Despite the Christian contention that there is no substitute for the shedding of blood, we find that Isaiah is forgiven his past misdeeds by means of a live coal that touched his lips. This unique method of atonement may never be used again, but it shows that means other than blood sacrifices can effect atonement for our sins. However, while the Bible records these unique one-time atonement episodes the theme of contrite repentance alone as a means of attaining atonement is in contrast commonplace. In the atonement process brought about by repentant prayer no shedding of blood is required, only the contrite heart and the will of God.

David sinned by transgressing three of the Ten Commandments (the tenth, seventh, and the sixth), in his affair with Bathsheba. He admitted to Nathan that he had sinned against the Lord, and Nathan answered him: "The Lord has put away your sin, you shall not die" (2 Samuel 12:13). David did not offer a blood sacrifice to attain forgiveness? This is attested in Psalm 51, in which David confesses his sin before God. This psalm shows that the contrite heart may achieve forgiveness from sin:

> Deliver me from bloodguiltiness,
> O God, God of my salvation;
> So shall my tongue sing aloud of Your righteousness.
> O Lord, open my lips;
> And my mouth shall declare Your praise.
> For You have no delight in sacrifice, else I would give it;
> You have no pleasure in burnt-offering.
> The sacrifices of God are a broken spirit;
> A broken and contrite heart,
> O God, You will not despise.
>
> (Psalms 51:16-19)

The next two verses result from the return to David of the prophetic ability (apparently removed on account of his sin) for which he prayed in verses 13-14: "Cast me not away from Your presence; Your holy spirit take not from me. Restore to me the joy of Your salvation; and let a willing spirit uphold me." David poured out his heart in contrite repentance before God. In return, God shows that David is forgiven by restoring to him his prophetic ability. In a pouring out of the prophetic spirit David exclaims: "Do good in Your favor unto Zion, build the walls of Jerusalem. Then You will desire the sacrifices of righteousness, burnt-offering and whole-offering; then will they offer bullocks upon Your altar" (verses 20-21). With his renewed prophetic abilities, David foresaw a time when the nation of Israel would come before God as he did without sacrificial offering but with a contrite repentant spirit. He then prayed for the rebuilding of Jerusalem and its Temple for a repentant nation, who will then offer their sacrifices before God.

The poor man's offering

What does the Torah say concerning a poor man who cannot afford the price of a blood sacrifice?

> But if he cannot afford two turtledoves, or two young pigeons, then he shall bring his offering for that which he has sinned, the tenth part of an *ephah* of fine flour for a sin-offering; he shall put no oil upon it, neither shall he put any frankincense on it, for it is a sin-offering. And he shall bring it to the priest, and the priest shall take his handful of it as the memorial portion and make it smoke on the altar, upon the offerings of the Lord made by fire; it is a sin-offering. And the priest shall make atonement for him for his sin that he has sinned in any of these things, and he shall be forgiven; and the remainder shall be the priest's, as the meal offering. (Leviticus 5:11-13)

The poor man's meal offering is accepted by God as the equivalent of a blood sacrifice. Significantly, although this meal offering is used on the altar it is not a shedding of blood. As is always the case, "the priest shall make atonement [*ve-chipper*] for him," but his particular sin-offering "for that which he has sinned" was not "blood" but "flour." In this case, it is the offering of flour as a sin-offering upon the altar that makes atonement. The text states clearly, "it [the flour] is a sin-offering." Once again, we see that blood sacrifice is not essential for attaining atonement. The poor man's atonement is not conditioned by any other physical factor. The flour is placed on the portion being burnt on the altar, but the blood of an atonement sacrifice is dashed on the side of the altar (Leviticus 1:5; see also Exodus 29:12, Leviticus 9:9). It is this dashing of blood on the side of the alter that brings atonement not the burnt offering on the altar. Thus, a different set of rules is applied for the poor man's offering.

As we see, God provides the means for bloodless atonement even in situations that are not the norm. Certainly, the absence of the Temple and the sacrificial system is the most unusual of circumstances. The above citations highlight the lesson that God has never left Israel without the means for atonement.

Deliberately committed sins

Interestingly, animal sacrifices are mentioned only for unwitting sin, that is, sins committed unintentionally (Leviticus 4:2, 13, 22, 27; 5:5, 15). With one exception, there is no blood offering provided for sins that are deliberately committed. The one exception is for swearing falsely to acquit oneself of the accusation of having committed theft (Leviticus 5:24-26). One who wittingly sins has no means of atonement (Numbers 15:30) other than to come directly to God with prayer and a contrite heart.

[1] Solomon's prayer differs from other prayers found in the Bible in that it does not necessarily address the immediate and actual needs of a particular individual, but the possible situations in which any person in the corporate entity of Israel may find himself/herself.

[2] B.T. *Shavu'ot* 39a.

[3] *Machiti,* "I blotted out." *Machah* is used here in the sense of "covered over" as with a cloud and not in the sense of "erased."

[4] The phrase "as I have commanded you" cannot refer to verse 15, for in that case the verb would not be in the past tense, but the participle would be used (cf. Deuteronomy 11:8, 13, 22, 27, 28; 12:11). "As I have commanded you" refers to the method, previously taught, by which "you shall kill" animals for food. But, no such method is taught in the Scriptures. This shows that God had previously instructed Moses in a method of slaughtering animals that had not been written down. The Talmud relates, "It is written, 'Then you may kill of your herds; and of your flocks which the Lord has given you as I have commanded you.' Rabbi says, 'This teaches that Moses was commanded [orally] concerning the gullet and concerning the windpipe and concerning [the fact that] most of one of them, in a fowl, and most of both of them in a bovine animal [should be severed at the time of slaughtering]'" (*Chullin* 28a). The Laws of *shechitah*, the Jewish method of slaughter, were communicated orally from God to Moses and were then passed on, as part of the body of Oral Law, from one generation to another.

[5] The Noahide Commandments relating to the just and humane responsibilities of all humanity are derived from a midrash on the flood narrative in which God makes a covenant with all humanity never again to destroy the world. The rainbow, a sign of safety visible to all humanity, symbolizes this covenant.

The rabbinic sources enumerate from six to ten Noahide Commandments. They include monotheism, avoidance of murder and theft, organizing courts and promulgating justice (civil law), and avoiding incest and other sexual transgressions, as well as abstaining from eating the flesh of living creatures. This list can be derived from the story of Noah in Genesis read in conjunction with the rules governing resident aliens, especially as found in Leviticus 17-26 (see also

B.T. *Sanhedrin* 56a; Rambam, *Hilchot Melachim* 9:1). The earliest version of the Noahide Commandments known is probably that of Jubilees 7:20-21.

[6] Offerings to invoke God's protection for the Gentile nations were made in a limited sense in the Temple. "R. Eleazar stated. To what do those seventy bullocks [that were offered during the seven days of the Festival of Sukkot] correspond? To the seventy nations.... R. Yochanan observed. Woe to the idolaters, for they had a loss and do not know what they have lost. When the Temple was in existence the altar atoned for them, but now who shall atone for them" (B.T. *Sukkah* 55b). Rashi states, in his commentary on Numbers 29:13-32, "The bullocks of the festival are seventy, in allusion to the seventy nations.... And during the days of the Temple they [the bullocks] protected them from afflictions [*yissurin*]. In his commentary on *Sukkah* 55b, he implies that what is meant by "afflictions" are those problems related to the absence of rain. Rashi states that the sacrifice of the seventy bullocks over the course of the festival "make atonement for them [the seventy nations] that rain should fall throughout the world." Many of the observances and prayers of Sukkot are associated with water and rain. It is a time to thank God for His past kindness and to beseech His continued benevolence in the form of plentiful rain for crops. The seventy bullocks represent that Israel, a nation of priests (Exodus 19:6), beseeches God to extend His benevolence throughout the world.

There is recognition in rabbinic literature that the burnt offering of the seventy bullocks in the Temple was considered to be for the benefit of humankind. Therefore, Rabbi Yochanan declares that the altar "atoned" for them. Rabbi Yochanan's statement means that the sacrifice of the seventy bullocks effectuates a protection specifically concerning offenses of the nations of the world that might cause God to withhold rain? The nations receive God's benevolence in the form of rain despite their grievous sins based on Israel's sacrificial offerings made on their behalf in the Temple. These were not sin-offerings or guilt-offerings, brought to atone for transgressions, but sacrifices acknowledging in advance God's kindness to the nations. By, in effect, advocating God's benevolence to the nations, it was said that the offerings upon the altar effectuated a protection that can be considered as if they atoned for the nations. In this scenario, the Temple service provides a protection that is referred to as "atonement" in that it results in God not punishing the nations through withholding of rain. What occurs is not actually atonement and therefore requires no pre-condition of repentance.

This is not the same as what occurs in the Book of Jonah. Jonah calls upon the people of Nineveh to repent their evil ways and use of violence (Jonah 3:8) or their city will be "overthrown." "Overthrown," is the same Hebrew verb, expressing complete destruction, used to describe the overthrow of Sodom (Genesis 19:25). If the offering of the seventy bullocks atoned for all the sins of the people of Nineveh there would be no need for Jonah to be sent to warn the city's inhabitants. In addition, if Gentile repentance was needed to accompany the sacrifices the nations were unaware of this obligation. The Sukkot offering on behalf of the nations had to do with the issue of rain and not with the general problem of their sins. Nineveh's sins were outside the narrow scope of atonement (or better yet *protection*) obtained through the offering of the seventy bullocks and therefore needed repentance by the people of Nineveh in order to attain atonement.

Jeremiah expressed the concept that Israel's prayers and sacrifices protect the nations of the world from adversities when he advised the exiles to "seek the peace of the city where I have caused you to be carried away captive, and pray to the Lord for it; for in its peace you shall have peace" (Jeremiah 29:7). In 1 Maccabees 7:33, we are told that a burnt offering was made in the Temple on behalf of the Syrian king. For the sake of Israel, God protects the nations. In the Messianic Era, "It shall come to pass, that every one that is left of all the nations that came up against Jerusalem shall go up from year to year to worship the King, the Lord of hosts, and to keep the feast of Sukkot. And it shall be, that whoever of the families of the earth that does not go up to Jerusalem to worship the King, the Lord of hosts, upon them there shall be no rain" (Zechariah 14:16-17). Considering that the reason for the offering of the seventy bullocks during Sukkot is established in Jewish tradition as having to do with rain, the withholding of rain as punishment for not going to Jerusalem to worship God is the appropriate punishment.

Chapter 12

Y-H-V-H IS INDIVISIBLE
(Deuteronomy 6:4)

The Nicene Creed

It is a fundamental belief of most Christians that God consists of three beings in one: God the Father, God the Son and God the Holy Spirit. This belief, called the Trinity, is diametrically opposed to the Jewish belief in the absolute oneness of God. It is also the antithesis of the teaching of the Torah, the Prophets and the Writings concerning the oneness of God.

The Christian interpretation of the nature of God as a triune being found its official expression in the Nicene Creed, which became the foundation for both Catholic and Orthodox Christian and later Protestant beliefs on the subject of the Trinity. In the year 325, the Council of Nicaea was convened at the insistence of the still pagan emperor Constantine, who sought to secure through this body an authoritative declaration of Christian belief that would meet with his approval. His goal was to end the violent dissension in the Christian church concerning the nature of God. The Council condemned some of the theories discussing God's nature then current, including that of Arius, which asserted that the Son was created by the Father. By his political power, Constantine, a treacherous and unbaptized pagan, gave Christianity its doctrine concerning the nature of the deity it worshipped. This is the man who declared as indisputable law the Nicene Creed.

The Nicene Creed asserts, in essence, that God is one, but within that *One* are three, equally sharing in His being and substance. The three sharing this godhead are designated a triune unity. The overall Christian church, after many lengthy, often violent, disputes, included the doctrine in its fundamental teachings with variations among the many church divisions. But this teaching, the result of theological and doctrinal speculation, is not even a pale reflection of what is taught in the Jewish Bible. In their effort to shore up this teaching, trinitarian Christians distort the meaning of the Hebrew word *'echad* ("one") as applied to the absolute unity of God.

Y-H-V-H is One (Deuteronomy 6:4)

The word *'echad*, "one," is used in the Jewish Scriptures in either a compound or absolute sense. In this study of the word we want to know in what sense is it used in the *Shem'a*, "Hear, O Israel, the Lord our God, the Lord is One" (Deuteronomy 6:4). It is true that in such verses as Genesis 1:5: "And there was evening and there was morning, one day," and Genesis 2:24: "Therefore shall a man leave his father and his mother and shall cleave to his wife, and they shall be one flesh," the term *'echad*, "one," refers to a compound united one. That is, day and night constitute one day of twenty-four hours and a man and woman can constitute one couple. However, *'echad* often also means an absolute one. This is illustrated by such verses as 2 Samuel 13:30: "Absalom has slain all the king's sons, and there is not one of them left"; 2 Samuel 17:12: "And of all the men that are with him we will not leave so much as one"; Exodus 9:7: "There did not die of the cattle of Israel even one"; 2 Samuel 17:22: "There lacked not one of them that was not gone over the Jordan"; Ecclesiastes 4:8: There is one [that is alone], and he has not a second; yea, he has neither son nor brother." Context determines if "one" is compound or absolute. Clearly, the word "one" used in these verses means an absolute one and is synonymous with the word *yachid*, "the only one," "alone." Ecclesiastes 4:8 makes this abundantly clear. Two parallel modifying clauses are added to emphasize that "one" is used to speak of a human who is singularly alone within the family structure. In speaking of God, no such modifying clauses are necessary, since the biblical record recognizes no divisions or persons in the ontological being of God. The Bible, with even greater refinement implicitly teaches that *'echad* in Deuteronomy 6:4: "Hear, O Israel, the Lord our God, the Lord is One," is used as a single, absolute, unqualified one.

The preponderance of implicit scriptural evidence is that "the Lord is one" is not a mere numerical designation, but an ontological statement as well. Thus, there will come a day when "the Lord [*Y-H-V-H*] shall be King over all the earth; in that day shall the Lord [*Y-H-V-H*] be one, and His name one" (Zechariah 14:9). What does it mean that "the Lord" will someday be "one," isn't "the Lord" one now? Sometime in the future, the whole world will recognize this fact, but those indoctrinated with trinitarianism, in particular, will come to realize the ontological oneness of Y-H-V-H. Presently, they admit to Y-H-V-H being God but say that that "one" is in the form of a triune being. However, "in that day" they will come to realize that "Y-H-V-H is one" not just in that He is the only true and unique God, which they already admit, but that He is one in His very essence of being. They will discard the trinitarian doctrine and no longer think of Y-H-V-H as one part of or a combination of "God the Father, God the Son and God the Holy Spirit." Furthermore, "in that day shall His name be one" in that He will not be called "Krishna," "Allah," or the "Great Spirit," but the whole world will come to realize that just as He is ontologically one and there is no other god beside Him so is His Name one - Y-H-V-H. They will declare as did Naaman, a non-Israelite, "Behold, now I know that there is no God in the whole world, except in Israel.… Your servant will never again offer a burnt-offering or a peace-offering to other gods, only to Y-H-V-H" (2 Kings 5:15-17).

As applied to God, the word 'echad has three connotations. First, there is no God other than Y-H-V-H (read as HaShem ["the Name"] or 'Ado-nai ["my Lord," "Lord of all"] in Hebrew and rendered as "the Lord" or "Jehovah" in many English translations). Second, though we perceive God in many roles — kind, angry, merciful, wise, judging, etc. — these different manifestations are neither contradictory nor an indication of division of His ontological essence. Any action or state of being that we might ascribe to God refers to something that God created in order to interact with his creation — not to God Himself. Third, when we speak of the oneness of God, it is not like the oneness of anything in His creation. While matter can be broken down into sub-atomic particles God's unique oneness cannot be subdivided. God declares: "I am the first, and I am the last, and beside me there is no God. And who is like me?" (Isaiah 44:6-7). There is no mention here of a triune god unless one wants to claim that "I am the first" is God the Father, "I am the last" is the third person of the Trinity, the Holy Spirit and "besides Me is no God" designates the Son, Jesus, as "no God" (cf. the claim of Hebrews

8:1 that Jesus sits at the right hand of Majesty, i.e., God.). God says in no uncertain terms that "I am the Lord that makes all things, that stretches the heavens, alone; that spreads abroad the earth by Myself" (Isaiah 44:24). "By Myself," following the *qere* (the marginal reading), *mei'iti*, "from Me," "from Myself," "without help." Following the *ketiv* (the written consonantal text), *mi iti*, "who [was] with Me?" There is no being beside God equal to Him, outside of Him or as part of His essence. God Himself, not part of the wholeness of God, brought about the creation. Only through trinitarian gymnastics do Christians reconcile this verse with Paul's exaggeration, "For in him [Jesus] all things were created … all things have been created through him and for him" (Colossians 1:16).

Chapter 13

OF MIRACLE WORKERS AND PROPHETS
(Deuteronomy 13:2-4)

The New Testament claim that Jesus performed miracles is one more exaggeration on the part of early Christians seeking to impress would-be converts. But the assertion that Jesus performed miracles is irrelevant as far as proving anything concerning his being the Messiah. Deuteronomy 13:2-4 declares:

> If there arise in the midst of you a prophet or a dreamer of dreams and he gives you a sign or a wonder, and the sign or the wonder come to pass, whereof he spoke to you saying: "Let us go after other gods, which you have not known, and let us serve them"; you shall not listen to the words of that prophet, or that dreamer of dreams; for the Lord your God puts you to proof, to know whether you do love the Lord your God with all your heart and with all your soul."

Jesus did not fulfill any biblical messianic expectations during his lifetime. So-called "fulfillments" are the result of inserting stories into the Jesus myth that would appear to be fulfillments of biblical passages. But, the fraudulent nature of this usage is readily seen. He was neither the singular ruler promised nor did he exercise any real authority. Ezekiel declares: "And David My servant shall be king over them; and they all shall have one shepherd ... and My servant David shall be their prince forever" (Ezekiel 37:24-25). Jesus also did not fulfill the prophecies which speak of the benefits the people of Israel were to enjoy under the Messiah's rule and leadership (e.g., Ezekiel 34:25-31, 37:21-28; Isaiah 11; Jeremiah 23:6, 30:10-11). The prophecies concerning the Messiah and the benefits of his rule over Israel each form an integral unit. One cannot fragment them in order to proclaim limited fulfillment of prophecy during Jesus' lifetime and to rationalize that the remaining fragments will be fulfilled during a second appearance. There was a total lack of fulfillment by Jesus of these messianic prophecies. Christians wait in vain for an expected fulfillment of messianic prophecies during a so-called "second coming" of Jesus. According to New Testament calculations, their count is off. Their hope would have to refer to a *third coming*. The *first coming* would cover the period prior to Jesus' death and the *second coming* would span the period from his alleged resurrection to his alleged ascension said to be forty days later. A *third coming* was to occur *speedily* within the lifetime of his contemporaries, but it never happened.

What the historical Jesus actually believed or did is an unknown. All that we know of "Jesus" is what the authors of the New Testament wrote about him. Even if it were true that the New Testament's Jesus performed miracles Deuteronomy 13:2-4 warns against following him. He is depicted (especially by Paul, the author of Hebrews, the Gospel of John and Revelation) as a sinless angelic being, a demi-god. In the New Testament the character of Jesus is transformed into a god-like being—the very thing Deuteronomy 13:2-4 warns us against. A careful study of the Gospels reveals that this New Testament Jesus is a fictional character, a false prophet and a dreamer of false dreams. But, on further reflection we realize that the Gospel's Jesus did fulfill one prophecy found in the Jewish Scriptures: That fictional Jesus was a false prophet and all that went with it.

Chapter 14

A SECOND MOSES
(Deuteronomy 18:15, 18)

The Torah declares that "The Lord your God will raise up for you a prophet like me [Moses] from among you, from your brethren, to him you shall listen…. I [the Lord] will raise up for them a prophet like you from among their brethren; and I will put My words in his mouth, and he shall speak to them all that I shall command him" (Deuteronomy 18:15, 18). Christians allege that these verses are a prophecy that refers to Jesus. This tendentious interpretation has no basis in fact. It is simply Christian wishful thinking that has them apply these verses to Jesus.

The singular noun *navi'*, is most likely used in a plural sense generically and does not refer to a particular prophet. The people of Israel are promised that God will raise up prophets to guide Israel just as Moses himself did. This does not mean that these prophets will be like Moses in their level of prophetic stature. The uniqueness of Moses is unsurpassed. What is promised is that following the death of Moses, God will still send prophets to Israel who will possess the true prophetic spirit associated with Moses. The Torah's message to Israel is that they should beware of false prophets as described in verses 20-22: "But the prophet who will presume to speak a word in My name that I have not commanded him to speak, or that shall speak in the name of other gods, that prophet shall die. And if you say in your heart, 'How shall we know the words which the Lord has not spoken?' Know that when a prophet speaks in the name of the Lord, if the things do not follow, nor come to pass, that is the thing which the Lord has not spoken, but the prophet has spoken it out of presumption; you shall not be afraid of him." The people of Israel are to be ever watchful against false teachers who would attempt to undermine the Torah given by God at Mount Sinai. The true prophet, the true teacher of Torah, will continue in the path and tradition of Moses. Among the teachings of the New Testament's Jesus were those that undermined God's Torah (e.g., Mark 7:14-15, 18-19; Mark 10:11-12, Luke 16:18). Moreover, as we shall see, he never fulfilled the major promise to return to his contemporaries. As a result, this so-called "second coming" has been constantly put off to a future date by those professing to be his followers.

Chapter 15

THE LAW: A CURSE OR A BLESSING?
(Deuteronomy 27:26)

Deuteronomy 27:26 states: "Cursed be he who does not establish the words of this law to do them." Paul, seeking to deprecate the Torah in an effort to enhance his new belief system alleges that any person who violates a biblical commandment is eternally cursed. He concludes that since it is inevitable that one will break a commandment one is actually cursed by the Torah, the Law of God. He writes: "For as many as depend upon works of law are under a curse; for it is written: 'Cursed is everyone who does not abide by all the things written in the book of the Law, to do them'" (Galatians 3:10). What Paul is trying to do is substantiate his claim that man is under "the curse of the Law" and condemned by the Law, because he is unable to obey it (Galatians 3:13). But, if he is speaking to Gentiles, they never were under the law in the first place! If he is speaking to Jews his allegation is totally without merit.

Let us look at verse 26 carefully to ascertain what it is really saying. A better understanding of this verse is given by the rabbinic sages of the Talmud. They explain that the phrase "he who does not establish," does not apply to an ordinary person breaking a commandment. It applies to the authorities in power who fail to enforce the Torah in the Land of Israel (J.T. *Sotah* 7:4). It is the responsibility of the nation's leadership, under the pain of a curse, to set an example for the nation and make the Torah the guiding principle in the life of the people.

Paul's distortion of Deuteronomy 27:26 is even more evident if verse 26 refers to an individual's obedience to the Torah. Paul's conclusion is fallacious and downright dishonest. The Torah's commandments include those which instruct on how to achieve atonement from sin, because God knows mankind does sin. Obviously, all is not lost if one violates a precept of the Torah. This verse declares as cursed those who reject the offer to atone as stipulated by the Torah. This would include those who insincerely pay lip service to the atonement process, and who thereby fail to take the opportunity to rectify their relationship with God. Such a person brings a curse upon himself. The person who rejects God's offer to repent and return to Him with a contrite heart and instead decides to lead a sinful life is cursed. Simply put, Paul twists the meaning of the verse to advance his agenda — "whether in pretense or in truth" (Philippians 1:18). One is not punished simply for not abiding by every commandment for which he or she is responsible, but is punished if that person does not sincerely avail himself/herself of the atonement process.

Chapter 16

'EL, 'ELOHIM AND Y-H-V-H
(Joshua 22:22, Psalms 50:1)

Trinitarian Christians make use of *'El*, *'Elohim* and *Y-H-V-H*, employed in Joshua 22:22: "*'El, 'Elohim, Y-H-V-H, 'El, 'Elohim, Y-H-V-H*" ["God, God, the Lord, God, God, the Lord"] and Psalms 50:1: "*'El, 'Elohim, Y-H-V-H*", as proof of their doctrine. In actuality, these three distinct appellations are juxtaposed for the express purpose of heightening the effect, and they do not at all imply that God is a triune personality. Using the names in ascending order heightens the effect. The first of these, *'El*, is the most general, the second, *'Elohim*, is the ordinary name, and the third, *Y-H-V-H*, is the most specific name for God used in the Scriptures. As a rule, these names are used with the following connotations: *'El*, the Mighty One; *'Elohim*, the Judge; *Y-H-V-H*, the Merciful One. Their use certainly does not imply any division in the absolute unity of God's essence. In 2 Samuel 22:32, David uses these three words: "For who is God [*'El*] but the Lord [*Y-H-V-H*]? And who is the rock except our God [*'Eloheinu*]?" Obviously, no division in the absolute unity of God is intended in this verse, since its entire thrust is to impress us with the ontological oneness of God

Chapter 17

PROVING THE EXISTENCE OF A QUATERNARY
(1 Samuel 16:15)

Proving the existence of a Quaternary

Trinitarians manipulate the Scriptures to establish the triune doctrine. If they had a Quaternary to prove, this would be demonstrated just as easily from the biblical text. That this observation is not an exaggeration can be seen from the words *ruach 'Elohim* ("the spirit of God"), found in Genesis 1:2. According to trinitarianism, the phrase "the spirit of God" represents one distinct entity of the triune deity. Following this exegetical approach to its logical conclusion, we will obtain not a trinity but a quaternary. If the divine spirit is to be treated as an entity in itself, then the evil spirit should be granted similar status, for just as the "holy spirit" is referred to as a spirit of God, so is the "evil spirit." This is clearly found in the words of Saul's servants to him: "Behold now, an evil spirit of God is terrifying you" (1 Samuel 16:15), and the subsequent use of this term in verse 16: "when the evil spirit of God comes upon you." Are we to surmise, then, that there really exists a divine quaternary—Father, Son, Spirit of God and Evil Spirit of God (see also Judges 9:23, 1 Kings 22:21f.)? Evidently, the terms "spirit of God" and "evil spirit of God" express certain aspects of God's will and action rather than His essence.

Or perhaps proof of a Quaternary can be found in Stephen's alleged vision just prior to his death. "But being full of holy spirit, he gazed intently into heaven and saw the Glory of God and Jesus standing at the right hand of God" (Acts 7:55). One could argue that we have here the "Holy Spirit" indwelling Stephen, the Glory of God standing at the right hand of God, Jesus also at the right hand of God, and God. In this case, the doctrine of the Quaternary would be: the Father, the Son, the Glory of God and the Holy Spirit.

A further indication of the futility of the viewpoint expressed by

64

Christians is found in Proverbs 3:19: "The Lord by wisdom founded the earth; by understanding He established the heavens." According to many Christians, "wisdom" is to be considered a real being, the second member of the Trinity, and the agent by which God created the world. But to follow this reasoning one may very well say that "understanding" also represents a real being and the agent by which God created the heavens. No doubt, if Christians needed to prove God a quaternary, they would claim that not only "wisdom" but also "understanding" is a distinct personality within the nature of God.

Chapter 18

THE VIRGIN MISCONCEPTION MYTH
(Isaiah 7:14-16)

Isaiah 7:14-16:   Therefore the Lord Himself shall give you a sign: behold, the young woman shall conceive, and bear a son, and shall call his name Immanuel.   Curd and honey shall he eat, when he knows to refuse the evil, and choose the good.   Yes, before the child shall know to refuse the evil, and choose the good, the land whose two kings you have a terror of shall be forsaken.

Conceiving the myth

The sign of Isaiah 7:14 occupies a prominent place in Christian theology.   Christians claim this verse found fulfillment in the manner of conception and birth of Jesus.   However, verse 14 shows that the prophet does not emphasize the circumstances of the child's conception but, rather, the state of political affairs a few years later when he has reached the age of moral development.   The birth of Jesus took place some seven hundred and fifty years after Isaiah enunciated these words.

We learn from chapter seven that an attack was aimed at Jerusalem (Isaiah 7:2-6).   In Isaiah 7:3, the prophet's son Shear-yeshuv, on God's command, accompanies his father in his encounter with King Ahaz. Isaiah now offers to provide a sign from God to show He is always with His people, but Ahaz refuses.   Nevertheless, Isaiah delivers God's message that the enemies' plan would fail.   God gives Ahaz a divine sign that all would surely come to pass as Isaiah prophesied (Isaiah 7:3-16).   This sign revolves around the formative years of a child named Immanuel.   The name given to the child to be born, *Immanu'el*, literally means, "With us is God."[1] The words *'immanu'el* also appear in Isaiah 8:10, but do not refer to the child so named.

In verse 14 the prophet speaks of a sign being given. Isaiah's words, in general, and the word *'ot*, "sign," specifically indicate his prophecy had relevance for his contemporaries. The *'ot*, the "sign," of Isaiah 7:14 could not refer to an event in the distant future. The sign was not the manner of conception, but the imminent birth of a child, naturally conceived, whose very name would illustrate God's concern for His people and that God is still "with us." The child to be born was not the Messiah and Isaiah 7:14 was never considered a messianic reference by the Jewish people. Christianity incorrectly claims that the Jewish Scriptures foretell a virgin conception of an individual who was to be both a god and a man.

Isaiah's words, in general, and the word *'ot*, "sign," specifically indicate his prophecy had relevance for his contemporaries. The word *'ot* is used in the Bible in reference to an event that is to take place in the near future. This understanding is reinforced by the manner in which the word *hinnei* ("behold") is used by the prophet to introduce the passage. In the seventy-eight times it is used in Isaiah it is used of future events. Its use in combination with *'ot* provides a compelling argument that the passage is announcing an imminent birth. There had to be a fulfillment in Isaiah's time or his words, which were directed toward his contemporaries, would have had absolutely no meaning for his generation. On word usage alone, the *'ot*, the "sign," of Isaiah 7:14 could not refer to an event in the distant future. All indications are that the sign was not the manner of conception, but the imminent birth of a child, naturally conceived, whose very name would illustrate God's concern for His people and that God is still "with us." The birth of Immanuel was a sign of the continuity of the people of Judah in this period of crisis and was foremost a sign of God's concern for His people.

Several suggestions have been proposed to identify the mother and child. Frequently, she has been identified with a present wife of Ahaz or a young woman about to be married to him and pointed out in person by the prophet. The child has been identified with one of his children, notably Hezekiah.[2] Another proposal is that *ha-'almah*, "the young woman," is Isaiah's own wife, specifically the prophetess of Isaiah 8:3, or one of several wives. A third proposal is that the young woman was betrothed to Isaiah and soon to be married to the prophet. A fourth proposal identifies the child Maher-shalal-hash-baz, born to Isaiah's wife (Isaiah 8:3), with the child Immanuel, giving the child a double identity.[3] Without any definite clue, it must be concluded that the identity of *ha-'almah* remains a matter of speculation.

Christians contend that the "Holy Spirit,"[4] one-third of the Godhead, entered into union with a virgin so that she could conceive and bear Jesus, another one-third of the Godhead. They imagine that God not only performed the miracle of a virgin conception[5] but also in the process, part of Him, became the human being so conceived. The idea of divinity incarnate was widespread in the ancient pagan world. As a result, it is not surprising that deification of Jesus took place in the pagan environment in which the New Testament was written. It should be noted, however, that the authors of the New Testament considered Jesus to be the incarnation of an angelic being, but not God Himself. He was thought to be *a* god, but not *the* God. The trinitarian conception, which saw Jesus as the second person of the Godhead, was a later innovation. In any case, both perspectives of Jesus presently espouse the doctrine of a virgin conception.

Could God bring about such a miracle as is proclaimed in the doctrine of the virgin conception? The Jewish Scriptures teach that God is omnipotent: "Behold, I am the Lord, the God of all flesh; is there anything too hard for Me?" (Jeremiah 32:27). Technically, God, being Almighty, can do whatever He wants, without being limited or determined by the laws of nature that effect that which He created. Omnipotence implies that God can do anything He desires, which would include a virgin conception and even His taking on of a human form. It may even be assumed that He can commit suicide or even create a God that is greater than He is. He may even be said to have the ability to create something that can be existent and non-existent at the same moment in time. We are taught, however, by the Jewish Scriptures that God is consistent and unchanging in His ways: "For I the Lord do not change" (Malachi 3:6). God performs the miraculous, but He is not irrational and does not do that which is self-contradictory or absurd. In fact, it is irrelevant whether God can actually do that which is self-contradictory and absurd. Ability, whether in God or man, does not automatically mean that an action must follow. In His relationship with man, God sets limitations upon Himself as to what He will or will not do (Genesis 9:14-17; Exodus 32:13; Deuteronomy 7:8; Psalms 89:4, 132:11). As a result, we are not concerned here with what God *can* do but with what God *does* do.

Now to the all-important question: Did God perform a miraculous virgin conception and birth and become flesh, a god-man? In truth, nowhere in the Jewish Scriptures is the notion of virgin conception to be found.

Matthew and Luke claim a virgin conception for Jesus whom they regard as a divine being, but not God Himself.[6] Both Matthew and Luke state that Jesus was conceived by a holy spirit (not "God, the Father," who thus, is not logically "the Father" of Jesus in the trinitarian concept of the Godhead)[7] without the aid of a human father. How did the respective authors of Matthew and Luke substantiate their claim? They claim that Jesus' mother was a virgin, and God, not Joseph was his father, so that he was really God's son from his very conception. Based, in part, on the Septuagint's rendering of Isaiah 7:14 (or some related recession) Matthew's text reads: "Behold, the virgin shall be with child and shall bear a son, and they shall call his name Emmanuel" (Matthew 1:23). It should be noted that the virginity of Mary in the Gospel of Matthew does not depend on the Hebrew of Isaiah 7:14. Matthew's citation is taken from a Greek rendering and is used to give spiritual support to a previously conceived notion.

Matthew cites this Greek version of Isaiah 7:14, not the Hebrew original, as an intrinsic prooftext to substantiate his claim that the Messiah is to be conceived by a virgin in accordance with God's prophetic plan. His belief in the virgin conception leads on to the prophecy rather than *vice versa*. It is useful to him that the Septuagint's translator of Isaiah renders *'almah*, "young woman," as *parthenos* "virgin." Luke also thinks in terms of a virgin conception, but no scriptural basis is given for it as in Matthew's citing Isaiah 7:14. The Jewish Scriptures, even in their Greek rendition, do not support the claim of a virgin conception.

Parthenos (virgin)

The etymology of the Greek word *parthenos* is uncertain. A

complicating factor is that there are several instances of the word being used in Greek literature of women who were not virgins. From the general meaning of "girl," "young woman," with no reference to sexual experience, the evidence shows that the word evolved in Greek literary use to where it specifically indicated a "virgin" in the technical sense of the word, that is, a woman with no sexual experience.

None of the authors of the Gospels was writing history. Matthew, in particular, wrote by remodeling stories from the Jewish Scriptures. He seems to think the Bible is a source of information about Jesus. Since he had no actual details of Jesus' birth to work with, he created his birth narrative by utilizing his imagination, pagan birth myths, and the Jewish Scriptures. As a result, Matthew claims that the virgin conception of Jesus was to fulfill the sign of Isaiah. But, actually, Isaiah does not say this. The Hebrew word Isaiah uses, *'almah*, means a "young woman," with no reference to her sexual experience. It is evident that *'almah* may be used of a young woman who is a virgin. The evidence shows that *'almah* simply means "young woman." There is a Hebrew word for "virgin," *betulah*, but Isaiah did not use it. It is the Septuagint which renders the Hebrew *'almah*, "young woman," with the Greek word *parthenos*, "virgin."

A Hebrew/Aramaic Gospel of Matthew

If we presume an original Hebrew/Aramaic Gospel of Matthew, certain questions arise. Was it the same as the later Greek text of the Gospel of Matthew? Did the author of the Hebrew Gospel of Matthew, in addressing his born-Jewish Christian audience, depend on the Septuagint's use of *parthenos* to biblically justify the virgin conception doctrine that developed among some Christians? If the author of Matthew addressed a Hebrew/Aramaic speaking audience without a dependency on the Septuagint what would the word *'almah* originally have meant? There was no tradition of biblical interpretation which rendered *'almah* as "virgin." Despite the claim that Matthew wrote in Hebrew/Aramaic[8] appears that his use of Isaiah 7:14 to support a virgin conception derives from the Septuagint's mistranslation of the Hebrew text. It is doubtful that an original Hebrew Gospel of Matthew, if it ever existed, would contain Isaiah 7:14 as a prooftext in support of a virgin conception.

If verse 14 was used in an original Hebrew/Aramaic text, it may have appeared simply as a birth of a child prooftext without the intention of promoting a virgin conception.

In the Hebrew text of Isaiah there is nothing mentioned concerning a virgin conception of the Messiah. In fact, nowhere do the Jewish Scriptures predict a virgin conception of the Messiah. It suggests that *parthenos* was used initially by Matthew, not because a virgin conception had occurred but simply to have his text conform to the wording found in Septuagint Isaiah 7:14.

As we have observed, Matthew's supposed prooftext of a virgin conception is not scripturally based on a Hebrew manuscript, but on the Septuagint's version of Isaiah 7:14 whose translator used the Greek word *parthenos* "virgin," to translate the Hebrew *'almah*, "young woman."

'Almah

The Christian understanding of the scriptural uses of *'almah* is usually governed by the attempt to prove that the word means virgin in Isaiah 7:14. Christians attempt to translate this verse in the Hebrew text to conform to the way Matthew used the Greek Isaiah 7:14 as a reference to a virgin conception. Of the relevant scriptural verses where *'almah* is used, Genesis 24:43, Exodus 2:8, Isaiah 7:14, Psalms 68:26, Proverbs 30:19, Song of Songs 1:3, 6:8, only the Septuagint's Genesis 24:43 and Isaiah 7:14 translates *'almah* as *parthenos*.

It is understandable that the Septuagint translates *'almah* in Genesis 24:43 in this way since Genesis 24:16 already says that Rebekah is a *betulah*, "virgin." In Genesis 24:16 it renders both *na'arah*, "damsel," and *betulah*, "virgin," as *parthenos*: "And the *parthenos* [*na'arah*] was very beautiful in appearance, she was a *parthenos* [*betulah*], neither had any man known her." Clearly, *'almah* is to be equated with *na'arah*, the two terms being interchangeable; *betulah* is used to refer to the fact that this "young woman" was a virgin.

In Genesis 24:43, "it shall come to pass, that the *'almah* who comes out to draw water," the word *parthenos* in the Septuagint translates *'almah* who, in this case is Rebekah. Although correct in that Rebekah was a virgin, the Septuagint translation does not precisely render the

Hebrew in context. In verse 16 of the chapter, it is said of Rebekah: "the *na'arah* was very fair to look upon, a *betulah*, whom no man had known," which is precise and accurate in the use of the two words. The Septuagint, however, has, "the *parthenos* was very fair in appearance, a *parthenos*, whom no man had known," which is tautological and an inexact translation of the Hebrew. It cannot be maintained, on the basis of this inaccurate translation that the Hebrew word *na'arah* means "virgin." The Septuagint inaccurately rendered *na'arah* as *parthenos* in verse 16 and in a similar fashion inaccurately rendered *'almah* as *parthenos* in verse 43.

The Septuagint, as noted, has *parthenos* for all three terms: *na'arah* (verses 14, 16a, 55); *'almah* (verse 43) and *betulah* (verse 16), and uses *pais* (maiden, child) twice for *na'arah* (verses 28, 57). Although factually correct (for Rebekah was, in fact, a virgin), the Septuagint does not exactly convey the differences between the three terms in its rendering of the passages. Consequently, the rendering of *'almah* by *parthenos* in verse 43 may in no way be adduced as proof that *'almah* means "virgin."

The Septuagint renders *na'arah* twice in Genesis 34:3, "he loved the *na'arah*, and spoke kindly to the *na'arah*," as *parthenos*. This is inexplicable since the passage is concerned with the sexual assault of Dinah who consequently was no longer a virgin. This brings further into question how *parthenos* is used for translating purposes. Unqualified support cannot be found for the rendering of *'almah* as "virgin" by referral to Septuagint usage. The quote from Isaiah 7:14 found in Matthew 1:24 follows the Septuagint (or a related rendering), but does not do so exactly. The Greek translation gave Matthew an opportunity to exercise his inclination to find some sort of biblical basis for his claims. This is significant in that it was not *the* biblical text, but *a* Bible translation that was used to support his theological assertions.

The remaining passages in which *'almah* is found are consistent in showing that the word simply means "young woman" (Genesis 24:43; Exodus 2:8; Psalms 68:26; Proverbs 30:19; Song of Songs 1:3, 6:8). In the occurrences of *'almah* in the Jewish Scriptures there is never any reference to sexual experience *as such*. The word simply indicates a young woman sexually mature, whether a maiden living in her father's house (Exodus 2:8), a young woman soon to become a bride (Genesis 24:43), young women living or working in the king's palace (Song of Songs 1:3, 6:8), a young woman in a relationship (perhaps sexual) with a man (Proverbs 30:19), or the young women in a religious procession (Psalms 68:26).

As we can see, the basic controversy revolves around the meaning of the word *'almah* in Isaiah 7:14. The use of the word in the Jewish Scriptures leads to the conclusion that the word refers to a sexually mature young woman, capable of having sexual intercourse, without specifying whether she has had it or not. A study of the masculine form of the word *'almah* supports this conclusion. In 1 Samuel 17:56, Saul, referring to young David, tells Abner: "Inquire whose son the young man [*ha-'elem*] is." In 1 Samuel 20:22 the word *'elem* is used of Jonathan's young servant: "But if I say to the young man [*ha-'elem*]." In verse 21 (twice), verses 35-36 (three times), and verses 37-41 (seven times) the word *na'ar* is used of the same "lad." It is thus apparent from the two occurrences of the word, and the contexts, that *'elem*, "young man," "lad," is used synonymously with *na'ar*, "boy," just as *'almah* is used as a synonym for *na'arah*. There is no reference to sexual experience, but simply to age.

The *'almah* is a young woman of marriageable age and within this word virginity is neither included nor excluded. If one renders this word as "virgin," it introduces an implication that does not convey the contextual meaning of the word. In short, without Matthew's interpretation of the Greek rendering of Isaiah 7:14, one would never suppose that *'almah* was the specific word for a virgin.

Betulah

It is a fact of biblical usage that *betulah* is the Hebrew word for "virgin," consistently used in passages which leave no room for speculation or uncertainty as to its meaning (e.g., Leviticus 21:14; Deuteronomy 22:15-19, 23, 28). The word *betulah* is derived from the root *btl*, "to sever," "to separate." It stands for the "woman separated (from man)," that is, a virgin, a woman who has had no sexual experience. The word *betulah* is found some fifty times in the Jewish Scriptures, in all of which the meaning may be presumed to be "virgin." There is no question as to the meaning of *betulah* despite attempts to interject Genesis 24:16 or Joel 1:8 in order to prove the contrary.

According to some Christians, proof that *betulah* does not always mean "virgin" can be derived from the fact that Genesis 24:16 uses the qualifying words "neither had any man known her" in its description of Rebekah: "And the maiden [*na'arah*] was very fair to look upon, a virgin [*betulah*] neither had any man known her." This verse actually presents no problem; the Bible quite often adds an interpretive phrase to a word in order to emphasize the meaning. For example, Numbers 19:2: "Speak to the children of Israel, that they bring you a red heifer, faultless, in which there is no blemish." One could assume that anything that is faultless has no blemish in it. In 2 Samuel 14:5 it says: "Alas, I am an *'almanah* [widow], my husband being dead." Will the Christians question the meaning of *'almanah*? Surely we could assume that if she is a widow her husband is dead. Therefore, it should come as no surprise that the verse should say, "a virgin, neither had any man known her."

Some Christians argue that the verse: "Lament like a *betulah* girded with sackcloth for the husband of her youth" (Joel 1:8) provides clear proof that *betulah* does not necessarily mean "virgin." But the argument is faulty since this verse may refer to a young woman who is bereaved of the man to whom she had recently been betrothed and with whom she did not consummate her marriage before his death. In biblical times a betrothal was considered as binding as a marriage and there were formal ceremonies to celebrate it. (cf. Deuteronomy 22:23-24, where such a woman is punished as an adulteress if she cohabits with another man.) This loss is truly a deep tragedy, hence its use as a simile for extraordinary lamentation. The idea of extreme sorrow and anguish is here portrayed by the figure of a betrothed maiden who laments the death of her future husband. According to the Torah, during the period in which a couple is betrothed, before the actual marriage, they were legally bound to each other and could separate only through a formal act of divorce. Deuteronomy 22:23f. makes it clear (cf. also Genesis 29:21) that a betrothed virgin was known as a "wife." Consequently, her betrothed would be termed "husband." This also seems to be the understanding of the verse as found in the Septuagint. There it is rendered, "Mourn for me, for a bride [*numphe*] girded with sackcloth [who mourns] over the husband of her virginity [*ton andra autes to parthenikon*]." There is no doubt that the word as used in Joel 1:8 as always elsewhere in the Jewish Scriptures has the meaning of "virgin."

The word *betulah* is often used in passages where the absence of sexual experience is not a significant factor; in such passages it means simply "girls," "maidens" (cf. 2 Chronicles 36:17; Psalms 148:12; Isaiah 23:4; Jeremiah 31:13, 51:22; Lamentations 1:4, 18; 2:10, 21; Ezekiel 9:6; Amos 8:13; Zechariah 9:17; Job 31:1). It is also used metaphorically: "virgin daughter of Zion" (1 Kings 19:21; Jeremiah 14:17, 18:13, 31:4, 21; Lamentations 1:15, 2:13; Amos 5:2); "virgin daughter of Sidon" (Isaiah 23:12); "virgin daughter of Egypt" (Jeremiah 46:11); "virgin daughter of Babylon" (Isaiah 47:1). Nevertheless, when used in passages where *betulah* is used to define a legal status it refers to *virgo intacto*. In all instances where *betulah* is translated in the Septuagint text it is rendered *parthenos* or its equivalent. It is evident that *betulah* is the precise word to be used where it is necessary to refer to the complete absence of sexual experience on the part of a woman

'Almah, despite a two-millennium misunderstanding by Christians of Isaiah 7:14, 'Behold a young woman [LXX: "virgin"] shall conceive and bear a son,' indicates nothing concerning the chastity of the woman in question. That being the case, does anyone seriously doubt that the respective authors of the Gospels of Matthew and Luke considered Mary, prior to her pregnancy, as anything but *virgo intacta* in the strictest sense as found in legal documents (e.g., Matthew 1:18; Luke 1:27, 34)? Therefore, Matthew's use of Isaiah 7:14 is based strictly on the Greek rendering using *parthenos*. The Greek text is not based on the literal Hebrew word *'almah* found in verse 14, which says nothing concerning the virginity of the woman in question. If God wanted to make the point that the child to be born was born of a virgin he would have inspired the prophet to use the word *betulah* which in legal texts has the meaning of *virgo intacta*.

Specifically, there is no reason to assume from the context that virginity is a critical factor in Isaiah 7:14. Nothing is known of the young woman's state of virginity at the time Isaiah spoke, nor is that knowledge critical for exegetical purposes. Even if in all occurrences of the word in the Jewish Scriptures it were proven that the *'almah* in each case was, in fact, a virgin, that would not prove that *'almah* in Isaiah 7:14 means "virgin." The original meaning of the word and its use in the Jewish Scriptures have demonstrated that the word designates a young woman, without regard to her sexual experience; whether she is a virgin or not must be determined, if possible, from the context in which the word appears. Even if it were granted that by saying "the young woman of marriageable age" Isaiah could have been, in fact, referring to a virgin, the question still remains. If it was the prophetic intention to declare parthenogenesis, the word *betulah* was available in the Hebrew language to make Isaiah's meaning unmistakable?

Why was *parthenos* used in the Greek rendering of Isaiah 7:14? The Greek, *parthenos*, like the Latin, *virgo*, was used generally for "girl" or "young woman" (cf. Genesis 24:14, 43). The Septuagint understood by *parthenos* a virgin in its strict sense. Thus, the mother of Immanuel was at the time of Isaiah's pronouncement a virgin, but not at the time of his conception. How *parthenos* is used in the Septuagint and specifically in its rendering of Isaiah 7:14 may be summed up as follows: By *parthenos* the Septuagint translator meant that the prophet was referring to a "young woman," then unmarried, who would be married and in a normal way become pregnant and bear a son.

The 'ot

What was the purpose of the *'ot*, the corroborating sign, the divine attestation, of the message the prophet delivered? The timing of the event proclaimed in Isaiah 7:14 can be fixed to some degree from the general context, from which it is indicated when the entire sequence of events would culminate (verse 16). The prophet is addressing himself to a contemporary situation and his message is delivered to a king who faces dangerous enemies. The word *'ot*, "sign," is used in the Bible only for events happening in the near future, or in some cases, as the weekly Sabbath, occurring at fixed intervals. This confirms that the time period is within a few years of Isaiah's announcement. Thus, there is no doubt in the prophet's message that the *'ot* will be fulfilled and that, before this promised child, Immanuel, should be old enough to exercise moral discrimination, "the land whose two kings you have a horror of shall be forsaken" (verse 16). That is, Israel and Syria will have been left desolate. There is no mistaking the immediate and historical purpose of Isaiah's message.

Did the promised *'ot* pertain to the supernatural conception and virgin birth of the child? To entertain the thought of this possibility is mere conjecture without probability, for the following reasons:

- There was absolutely no notion of parthenogenesis among the Israelites, nor was there anything in biblical tradition to make the notion credible.

- If the prophet had meant to say that a virgin would give birth to a son, he would have had to use the word *betulah*, which is the word for virgin (it should be noticed that *betulah* occurs elsewhere in Isaiah: cf. 23:4, 12; 37:22; 47:1; 62:5), and even then, the statement, "a *betulah* will conceive and bear a son," would have been understood as meaning that a young woman, who was *at that time* a virgin, would, in the normal way, conceive and bear a son.

- Virginal conception is *no* sign to anyone but the woman herself.

- To make explicit and unmistakable the prediction that a boy would be born of a virgin, the prophet would have had to describe the event with considerable detail and precision.

Even if the more technical word *betulah*, had been employed, the term might have described the *young* woman merely at the moment when the prophet spoke. Consequently, it is without merit to maintain that the promised *'ot* had to do with a supposedly extraordinary conception and birth of the child. Isaiah's message was relevant to the situation facing Judah, at the time the *'ot* was promised to Ahaz. The sign was not just the birth of the child, but the naming and early childhood of the boy who was to be born. It involved the whole and sudden sequence of events that would take place before he reached the age of moral discrimination and which are prophesied in 7:14-17, and expanded in 7:18-25.

Could a virgin conception/birth of a child serve as a *sign*? In the Scriptures a sign does not have to be supernatural, but it does have to be visible, something that can be seen. For example:

- Genesis 1:14: Where the celestial sources of light serve as signs to determine seasons, days and years.
- Genesis 4:15: Where God gives Cain a sign so that anyone who finds him will not kill him.
- Genesis 9:12-17: Where God places the rainbow in the sky as a sign.
- Genesis 17:11. Male circumcision is a sign of God's covenant.
- Exodus 3:12: When the Israelites come to worship God at Mount Sinai, this will be the sign to Moses that he has been sent by God.
- Exodus 12:13: The blood on the doorpost is a sign.
- Exodus 13:16: The *tefillin* (phylacteries) on our arm and head are a sign that God redeemed us from Egypt.
- Exodus 31:13: The observance of the Sabbath is a sign that God sanctifies Israel (see also Ezekiel 20:12, 20).
- Joshua 4:5-24: The stones set up in the Jordan River are a sign that God dried up the water so that the children of Israel could cross.
- Judges 6:17-22: The angel incinerates Gideon's meal as a sign.
- 1 Samuel 2:34: The death of his sons on the same day is a sign to Eli.
- 2 Kings 19:29: A sign is what will be eaten from the harvest.
- 2 Kings 20:8-11: The shade of the sundial moves backwards ten degrees as a sign to Hezekiah.
- Isaiah 8:18: Children are signs for Israel.
- Isaiah 19:20: The altar and pillar in Egypt are a sign.
- Isaiah 20:3: Isaiah going unclothed and barefoot is a sign for Egypt and Cush.
- Isaiah 37:30: The sign based upon what will be eaten from the harvest.
- Isaiah 38:7-8. The shade of the sundial moves backwards as a sign to Hezekiah.
- Jeremiah 44:29: The deliverance of the king of Egypt into the

hands of his enemies will be a sign for Israel.

- Ezekiel 4:3: Placing an iron pan as a wall between himself (Ezekiel) and Jerusalem is a sign to the house of Israel.
- Psalms 86:17: David asks for a sign "so that my enemies may see it and be ashamed."

Who could see if Mary was a pregnant virgin? According to Matthew, Joseph, Mary's betroth, initially thought that she had been unfaithful (Matthew 1:19-20). Since a sign had to be visual, something that could be seen, a virgin conception/birth would hardly qualify. Certainly, a sign concerning an impending invasion that is meant to reassure that God is with His people and that all will be fine is not to be found in a conception/birth supposedly taking place 750 years later.

In both the Hebrew text and the Septuagint translation the sign was not the manner in which the child would be conceived, but in the precise timing whereby the child, Immanuel, would serve as a sign of God's presence and protection. Neither the Hebrew nor the Greek of Isaiah 7:14 referred to a virgin conception. Furthermore, there was nothing in the biblical understanding of Isaiah 7:14 on which to base the belief in the virgin conception of Jesus. It is a claim stated in the Gospels of Matthew and Luke,[9] but not at all in Isaiah 7:14. At most, Isaiah 7:14 was used to give biblical expression to an already existing Christian belief in the virgin conception of Jesus.

Why does the Septuagint use parthenos?

The Hebrew phrase *ha-'almah harah ve-yoledet ben* literally rendered is "the *'almah* pregnant and shall bear a son." Wanting to indicate that the *'almah*, "young woman," was still a *betulah*, "virgin," at the time of the annunciation of the prophecy, the translator into Greek must have decided to render the term *'almah* as *parthenos*. The complete verse rendered from the Masoretic text reads: "Therefore the Lord Himself shall give you a sign: behold, the young woman shall conceive [literally "she is pregnant"], and shall bear a son, and she shall call his name Immanuel."[10] The Septuagint's use of *parthenos* is legitimate exegesis when properly applied to indicate that the young woman was a virgin at the time of prophecy but not at conception. Virgin conception is not indicated by the text. For Matthew the Septuagint's translation of *ha-'almah*, "the young woman," as *parthenos*, "virgin," proved fortunate. *Parthenos* in Matthew 1:23 refers to a virgin, and is used to indicate a virgin conceiving and remaining in that state after conception: "and [Joseph] kept her a virgin until she gave birth to a son," but no mention is made of being a virgin following the birth. This is inconsistent not only with the Hebrew *'almah*, but with the Septuagint's use of *parthenos* in Isaiah 7:14. Matthew uses *parthenos* in a manner that conforms to the pagan divine birth-myth motif and shows a disregard for the Septuagint's reasoning in rendering *'almah* as *parthenos*.

It is clear:

- That Isaiah's words, in Hebrew, say nothing of a virgin-birth.
- That the notion of partenogenesis did not exist in Israelite thought.
- That the sign was relevant to the situation of which the prophet spoke and was meant to vindicate the prophet's message.
- That Isaiah was definitely speaking of a child soon to be born.

The untenable Christian claim

The virgin conception story cannot gain any substantiation through reference to the Jewish Scriptures or by appealing to their Greek translation. Isaiah 7:14 appears to be Matthew's biblical justification for claiming a virgin conception, but it was not the source of the belief (even the author of Luke presents the virgin conception without reference to this verse). The belief originated in the pagan notion that divine conception occurs by the union of virgins and gods and that this was a common way in which heroes and famous persons were conceived. In reality, both parents' contributions are necessary for human DNA. The human mother provides the X and a human father provides the Y chromosome to create a *fully* human being.

Apparently, the virgin conception notion developed independently of Paul's teachings. He wrote: "But when the fullness of time came, God sent forth His son, born of a woman, born under the Law" (Galatians 4:4). If Paul thought Jesus was born of a supernatural virgin conception we should expect him to be more explicit and write "virgin" rather than "woman." Paul thought Jesus was an angelic being, but not God or part of God.

There is no reason to accept the Christian contention that Septuagint Isaiah 7:14 referred to a virgin conception and was so interpreted by the Jewish people during the pre-Christian era. The idea of a virgin conception is simply not biblical. In the attempt to express the belief that Jesus was the son of God the idea was promulgated that Jesus did not become God's son during his lifetime or at his alleged resurrection, but was God's son from the first moment of his existence in Mary's womb. Impregnation of virgins by a god was a well-known pagan religious symbol for divine origin. This subtle blending of pagan legend and the interpretive Greek rendering of verse 14 with the Jewish scriptural motif of certain individuals being referred to as sons of God transformed Jesus into the virgin conceived Son of God of Christianity.

Isaiah is speaking of a specific young woman whose identity is known to him and King Ahaz, for the word 'almah has a definite article prefixed to it—"the young women," ha-'almah. Did the promised 'ot pertain to the supernatural conception and virgin birth of the promised child? Even if the more technical word betulah, had been employed, the term might have described the young woman merely at the moment when the prophet spoke.

While many Christians maintain that Matthew's description of a virgin conception for Jesus is a literal or direct fulfillment of Isaiah 7:14 others realize how untenable this notion is. They maintain that in time, the prophecy was fulfilled exactly as God said it would. The prophecy of Isaiah 7:14, therefore, was literally fulfilled during the days of Isaiah. According to this Christian explanation, Isaiah's 'almah was a virgin up until the night of her wedding; Mary, in a much greater manner, was a virgo intacta until after the birth of Jesus (Matthew 1:24-25). Those who maintain this notion explain that Matthew knew that Isaiah 7:14 did not literally predict the virgin conception of Jesus, but he understood it to be a historical parallel and type.

The typology argument is bogus. It is a vain imaginative attempt to explain a fallacious Christian doctrine that has no biblical support. They cannot honestly have it both ways. If 'almah means "virgin" in Isaiah 7:14, then the Christian's must believe that there were two

81

virgin births in history, one in the days of Isaiah and the second one being that of Jesus. Christians must rely on the Septuagint's rendering of 'almah as parthenos, virgin" to justify their understanding of the verse. As we have seen, even the Septuagint does not understand the verse as referring to a virgin conception. In addition, if we transpose Isaiah 7:10-16 to be contemporaneously with Jesus, how did his alleged manner of conception and early life fulfill the promises made in the complete sign given by Isaiah? For example, when did his mother give Jesus the name Immanuel? The virgin conception motif was a non-biblical teaching. Typology remains another vain attempt to explain Matthew's misuse of Isaiah 7:14.

At no time was Isaiah 7:14 ever considered by Jewish sources to mean the Messiah would be born of a virgin. In the second century debate between Justin Martyr and Trypho over the meaning and interpretation of Isaiah 7:14, Trypho, the Jew, takes the position that 'almah means a young woman and that the promised child was Hezekiah. In the New Testament, only Matthew and Luke contain virgin conception stories *and* genealogies. An 'almah conceiving and giving birth is not unusual. If, on the other hand, virgin conception were the sign given by Isaiah, then the child's mother would be the one person who could be positive that it really was a virgin conception. Who could say with certainty that she was a virgin following her child's conception or at his birth?[11] A virgin being with child would not be an outstanding sign? The sign is a message imparted by the name of the male child, that is, Immanuel — "God with us," born to the young woman, and the events that subsequently followed his birth. In the New Testament, everyone assumed Joseph was the father of Jesus (Luke 3:23) and Jesus is never called Immanuel. The birth of the child, Jesus, did not give hope to his contemporaries, as did the birth of Immanuel to Isaiah's contemporaries. Matthew and Luke in their respective versions of the birth annunciation relate a direct command that Mary's child be called Jesus, not Immanuel (Matthew 1:21 to Joseph; Luke 1:31 to Mary). It is not the alleged events surrounding Jesus conception or birth that gives hope and comfort to Christians but the alleged events surrounding his death.

Isaiah 7:14 states that on divine command the young woman

"shall call his name Immanuel"; 1 Chronicles 22:9 records the Lord's declaration to David, regarding his son "for his name shall be Solomon." Matthew merely gives his own rendering of Isaiah's words. It is he alone who connects Isaiah 7:14 to the newborn Jesus. The divine naming of the child Immanuel in Isaiah's time was part of a unique revelatory sign. Matthew's connection of the name Immanuel with Mary's child is based on imitation not divine decree.

Such names as Immanuel, "God is with us" (Isaiah 7:14), and "A wonderful counselor is the mighty God, the everlasting Father, the ruler of peace" (Isaiah 9:5) do not refer to God incarnate any more than the name Elihu, "My God is He" (Job 32:1; 1 Samuel 1:1; 1 Chronicles 12:21, 26:7, 27:18), refers to anyone but an ordinary human being.

It is a common fallacy among Christians to explain the name Immanuel (Isaiah 7:14, see also Isaiah 8:8) as if it predicted that God would dwell on earth in a thoroughly human body. This claim is derived from Matthew's misuse of the statement in Isaiah 8:10 that *'immanu 'el*, "God [is] with us." It is erroneously assumed that verse 14 foretells of a miraculous conception followed by a virgin birth of a person who is to be a god in a tangible human form. God's dwelling among His people is signalized in the name *Shechaniah*, "God dwells [among us]" (see Ezra 8:3; 1 Chronicles 3:21, 22). Who more than Mary and Joseph should have remembered the "miraculous" events surrounding the birth of Jesus? According to Luke, Mary finds Jesus in the Temple teaching the teachers (Luke 2:42-50). She scolds him for causing so much trouble, whereupon he replies with the enigmatic questions: "Why is it that you were looking for me? Did you not know that I must be concerned with the affairs of my Father?" Luke's Gospel adds: "And they did not understand the saying which he spoke to them." Mary does not understand; Joseph does not understand. If Mary and Joseph were both visited by angels before their son's birth, how is it that they are so completely surprised only twelve years later? Does not Mary remember that Jesus was supernaturally conceived in a way never experienced by any other creature?[12] If a virgin conception took place would it not carry for Mary some implications as to who Jesus was?

The virgin conception of Jesus myth was unknown to the earliest Christian communities. The use by Matthew of Isaiah 7:14, but not by Luke, shows the use of the biblical text is an afterthought, an attempt to give biblical credence to the virgin conception and subsequent birth narrative. Isaiah 7:14 is simply not the impetus for a supposed virgin birth story explaining God's incarnate intervention in human affairs. As described in Matthew, the alleged virgin conception is a miraculous fulfillment of a non-existent prophecy. Isaiah's words have nothing to do with the conception of Jesus whatsoever. Matthew wanted to give biblical fortification to his virgin conception process contention. He did it by referring to the Septuagint's rendering, not the Hebrew text. Matthew 1:24 shows either a lack of understanding of the Greek translator's motivation for rendering *'almah* as *parthenos*, or a deliberate misuse of the Septuagint. In any case, the evangelist may claim a virgin conception for Jesus, but the origin of his contention lies somewhere else than in either the Hebrew biblical text or the Greek Septuagint text. All said, in addition to not referring to a "virgin," Isaiah's sign occurs in a historically specific context (Isaiah 7:1). Isaiah is simply not talking about what Matthew says Isaiah is talking about, but rather, about an event in Isaiah's own time. The misapplication in Matthew 1:23 of the Septuagint's interpretative rendering of Isaiah 7:14 does not give anyone the right to force upon the Hebrew text of Isaiah 7:14 the meaning found in Matthew's text. Simply stated the crucial word in Hebrew, *'almah*, means one thing while *parthenos* in the Septuagint means another. Matthew's claim of a virgin conception constitutes a miraculous misconception.

[1] The technical term for a compound name with a divine element is a "theophoris" or "theophorous" name. It is derived from a Greek word meaning "bearing [derived from] a god." Theophoric names are common in the Bible (For example, *Samuel*, "His name is El," *Ishmael*, "God hears [requests]," *Daniel*, "God is my judge").

[2] Later Jewish commentators identified the "young woman" as the mother of Hezekiah (that is, the wife of Ahaz); a similar understanding may be found in the Septuagint rendering of this passage. Whereas the Hebrew text reads "and she [the mother] shall call (*kar'at*, 3rd sg. fem.) his name Immanuel," the Septuagint translators read the verb as a 2nd sg. masc. (pointed *kar'ata*), "you [Ahaz] shall call his name Immanuel," thereby implying that the boy would be the son of Ahaz. This translation (*kaleseis*) is found not only in the Septuagint but also in the Greek versions of Aquila, Symmachus, Theodotion, and in the Old Latin (Syriac Peshitto

and Vulgate have the passive, "shall be called").

[3] The first mention of Maher-shalal-hash-baz, in the phrase, "concerning Maher-shalal-hash-baz" (Isaiah 8:1), introduces not Isaiah's son but rather a prophecy concerning the forthcoming Assyrian attack. The child's birth occurs in Isaiah 8:3. Some commentators then assume that according to their respective commands, the mother names the child, "God is with us" (Isaiah 7:14), and the father, "Speedily to the spoil, hurrying to the plunder" (Isaiah 8:3). According to their explanation, the child's ability to differentiate between good and evil (Isaiah 7:15-16) and ability to say "my mother" or "my father" (Isaiah 8:4) occurs simultaneously. The name Maher-shalal-hash-baz refers to God's promise to defeat Samaria and Damascus and to send Assyria to carry off the wealth of these two nations, before turning to devastate Judah. Throughout all these vicissitudes and adversities, the name Immanuel stands as a sign to the people of Judah that "God is with us." Thus, according to this understanding of the text, the child, Immanuel/Mahar-shalal-hash-baz, is God's assurance to Judah that He oversees history. Though plundered, pillaged, and despoiled to the point of near certain destruction they shall not be destroyed.

[4] The lack of the definite article before "holy spirit" in the Greek of Matthew 1:20 (also missing in the parallel description in Luke 1:25) may simply mean "a holy spirit." This phrase is anarthrous in the Greek of both Matthew 1:18 and Luke 1:35, that is, literally "a holy spirit" not "the holy spirit." The phrase, "of a holy spirit," in Greek is genitive and has no definite article. Most Christian renderings supply the definite article before "Holy Spirit," in conformity with trinitarian belief. This should not lead the reader to assume that the respective authors of Matthew or Luke were expounding the notion of "the Spirit" as a person, much less the third person of the Trinity. The trinitarian concept of the divinity was a later Christian development.

[5] "Virgin conception" should not be confused with "immaculate conception." In 1854 Pope Pius IX proclaimed the Roman Catholic Church dogma of the "Immaculate Conception," whereby Mary's own conception was considered stainless so that she remained immune to what Christians refer to as original sin.

[6] The Gospel of Mark, considered the earliest of the Synoptic Gospels, and the Gospel of John, the last of the Gospels to be written, include neither the mode of Jesus' conception nor details of his infancy.

[7] If "a holy spirit" or the "Holy Spirit" is a separate person within the triune god one might say that God, the Father, is the father of the Son, the second person of the triune god, and that the Holy Spirit is no less part of the triune god than is the Father and the Son. But, if the Son is no less part of the triune god than the Father and the Holy Spirit then, in essence, the Son fathered himself. In addition, if the second member of this triune god is "begotten" in Mary (in a fleshly form) by the "Holy Spirit," the third member of this group (Matthew 1:20) or, in its alternate form, the "Holy Spirit will come upon . . . [Mary], and the power of the Most High will overshadow . . . [her] (Luke 1:35) then there is a time period when the three "gods"

85

are neither co-equal or united (cf. Philippians 2:7-8).

[8] Eusebius (260?-340?) quoted Papias, Bishop of Hierapolis (c. 140 C.E.) as writing, "So then Matthew, indeed, in the Hebrew language put together the Logia in writing" (*Ecclesiastical History* 3. 39. 16). Eusebius also quoted Origen (185?-254?) as writing concerning the Gospels, "The first is written according to Matthew, the same that was once a publican, but afterwards an apostle of Jesus Christ, who having published it for Jewish converts, wrote it in Hebrew" (*Ecclesiastical History* 6. 25. 4). Jerome (fourth- fifth centuries C.E.) wrote that Matthew "composed a Gospel of Christ in Judea in the Hebrew language and characters, for the benefit of those of the circumcision who had believed" (*Epistulae* 20.5). Some scholars have argued that when the church fathers said "Hebrew" they really meant "Aramaic." We should also note the use of the Greek word *hebraisti*, "in Hebrew," (John 19:13) to indicate the linguistic origin of *Gabbatha* ("the Pavement"); *Gabbatha* is Aramaic. If the author of Matthew originally wrote in "Hebrew" (Aramaic), then what the church has is a Greek rendering of his "inspired" text.

[9] Isaiah 7:14 does not appear to have entered the formulation of Luke's version of the virgin conception.

[10] The Masoretic text of Isaiah 7:14 contains the word *ve-qar'at*, rendered "and she shall call." This word has the consonants *qr't* which would normally represent a second person singular form of the verb "to call." On this basis, the Septuagint derives the reading "you [second person feminine singular] shall call." Actually, the Masoretic Hebrew text preserves here an old third person feminine form "she shall call." The *Book of Isaiah*, published by the Hebrew University, contains notes on the textual evidence concerning tense variations of this verb found among certain Septuagint and Dead Sea Scroll manuscripts. On page 26 of this work the first apparatus shows that the manuscripts of the Septuagint are not always in agreement, using here the second or third person. The running commentary on the bottom of the page (the left side in English, the right side in Hebrew) shows that some manuscripts of the Septuagint have here the second person singular future indicative active; others have the second person plural future indicative active; yet others have here the third person singular future indicative passive; still others have here the third person plural future indicative active. The same running commentary gives the information that the readings of the Septuagint almost equal the readings of the Vulgate, Targum, and Peshitta.

The second apparatus shows that the complete Isaiah scroll from the Dead Sea Scroll collection has here *ve-qar'a*, which is "and he shall call," "and one shall call" (*The Book of Isaiah*, ed. Moshe H. Goshen-Gottstein, Jerusalem: Magnes Press, 1975, p. 26. See also Millar Burrows, *The Dead Sea Scrolls of St. Mark's Monastery*, vol. I, "The Isaiah Manuscript and the Habakkuk Commentary," New Haven: The American Schools of Oriental Research, 1950, Plate VI.).

[11] Verification of Mary's post-natal virginity is claimed in the Christian Apocrypha. Dating from about 150-200, the Proto-Gospel (Protevangelium) of James is perhaps the earliest of the apocryphal infancy gospels. In the Proto-Gospel of James, Joseph

calls for a midwife to assist in Jesus' delivery, telling her, "Mary is betroth to me; but she conceived of the Holy Spirit." As the midwife approaches Mary, she exclaims: "My soul is magnified today, for my eyes have seen wonderful things; for salvation is born to Israel." But when the first midwife informs a second midwife, Salome, that "a virgin has brought forth," Salome is not convinced: "As the Lord my God lives unless I put (forward) my finger and test her condition, I will not believe that a virgin has brought forth." Salome refuses to believe that a virgin has given birth unless she can test Mary's condition with her finger and find her still a virgin. It is only after performing this gynecological examination of Mary that Salome believes. Salome's role is that of a witness of the virgin birth. This story underscores a basic problem in the Christian claim that a virgin conception and birth took place. Apparently, first century of the Common Era Jews did not know that 'almah is supposed to be understood to mean a virgin. (See Proto-Gospel of James 19:1-20; 3 in J.K. Elliott, trans., *The Apocryphal New Testament*, Oxford: Clarendon Press, 1993.)

Apparently, the story of Salome (reminiscent of Thomas' skepticism recorded in John 20:25) was known to the philosopher and theologian Clement of Alexandria (active c. 190-215). He wrote that "[Mary], after she had delivered Jesus was examined and found to be a virgin." (Clement of Alexandria, *Stromateis* VII, c.16)

[12] See Baas Van Iersel, "The Finding of Jesus in the Temple: Some Observations on the Original Form of Luke ii 41-51a," *Novum Testamentum* 4 (1960), pp. 161-173.

Chapter 19

WHO IS THE CHILD?
(Isaiah 9:5-6)

Who is the child?

Isaiah presents many of his messages through the use of prophetic names (Isaiah 7:3, 14; 8:3). In one such passage he declares:

> For a child has been born to us, a son has been given to us; and the government is upon his shoulder; and his name is called A wonderful counselor is the mighty God, the everlasting Father, the ruler of peace; that the government may be increased, and of peace there be no end, upon the throne of David, and upon his kingdom, to establish it, and to uphold it through justice and through righteousness from henceforth even forever. The zeal of the Lord of hosts does perform this. (Isaiah 9:5-6)

In this passage, the prophet presents his message by devising a prophetic name for Hezekiah. The name is in the form of a sentence which although given to Hezekiah declares the power and benevolence of God. Christians allege that this passage predicts the birth of Jesus and that the name lists his attributes. A perusal of Isaiah's prophecy shows it to be a carefully crafted testimony to God's great love for His people.

Hezekiah is called, "a wonderful counselor" because this portion of the name is predictive of what God will do for the king and the people of the kingdom of Judah.

> The Lord of hosts has sworn, saying: "As I have thought, so shall it be, and as I have purposed, so shall it stand, that I will break Assyria in My land, and upon My mountains trample him under foot; then shall his yoke depart from off them, and his burden depart from off their shoulder." This is the purpose that is purposed upon the whole earth; and this is the hand that is stretched out upon all the nations. For the Lord of hosts has purposed, and who will annul it? And His

hand is stretched out, and who shall turn it back? (Isaiah 14:24-27)

Be not afraid of the words that you have heard, with which the servants of the king of Asshur have blasphemed Me. Behold, I will put a spirit in him, and he shall hear a rumor, and shall return to his own land; and I will cause him to fall by the sword in his own land. (Isaiah 37:6-7)

Hezekiah is called "the mighty God" because this portion of the name is predictive of God's protecting of Jerusalem through the wondrous elimination of the threat posed by Sennacherib's army.

Therefore thus says the Lord concerning the king of Assyria: He shall not come to this city, nor shoot an arrow there, neither shall he come before it with shield, nor cast a mound against it. By the way that he came, by the same shall he return, and he shall not come to this city, says the Lord. For I will defend this city to save it, for My own sake, and for My servant David's sake. (Isaiah 37:33-35)

Hezekiah is called "the everlasting Father" because this name is predictive of God's adding years to his life. "Go, and say to Hezekiah: 'Thus says the Lord, the God of David your father: I have heard your prayer, I have seen your tears; behold, I will add to your days fifteen years'" (Isaiah 38:5).

Hezekiah is called "the ruler of peace" because this name is predictive of God's fatherly kindness toward him. Punishment for lack of faith in the Almighty will be postponed and peace will prevail during the last years of his rule. "Then said Hezekiah to Isaiah: 'Good is the word of the Lord which you have spoken.' He said moreover: 'If but there shall be peace and security in my days'" (Isaiah 39:8).

Fulfillment is found in Isaiah 9:6, when, following the Assyrian defeat, Hezekiah's prominence increased and peace reigned for the rest of his life (2 Chronicles 32:23). Archaeological evidence shows that there was a sudden population increase in Judah following the fall of the northern kingdom. Apparently, many refugees fled south, thus bringing to fulfillment the statement "that the government may be increased." This is followed by "and of peace there be no end" ('ein ketz), a hyperbolic description of indefinite amount concerning the rest of Hezekiah's reign (cf. Isaiah 2:7, Ecclesiastes 4:8, 16; 12:12).

'Olam, rendered as "forever," (can have the meaning of *an indefinite length of time*) may refer to the long term effects of Hezekiah's reforms. In this passage it may also refer to the reaffirmation of God's promises to David. On account of Hezekiah's zeal in eradicating idolatry from the Temple, the house of David was once more confirmed as the only legitimate dynastic line that God would accept over his people "from henceforth and forever." The notability of Hezekiah lies in his buttressing Israel's spiritual future. He resanctified religious worship and reestablished the pure monotheistic faith of Israel. He eliminated idolatrous practices through the cleansing of the palace and the Temple of images and pagan altars, and centralized the worship of God in Jerusalem. Despite the apostasy that occurred during the reign of Hezekiah's son Manasseh his accomplishments would outlive him, leaving an everlasting, indelible impact on the history of his people. Thus, God, through Isaiah, bestows upon Hezekiah this name which honors the king by enunciating the wondrous acts God will do for him, and, through him, for the people of Israel.

Christians allege that the name "A wonderful counselor is the mighty God, the everlasting Father, the ruler of peace" refers to an incarnate divine Jesus. They contend that such a name can only be applied to God Himself. To make their claim about Jesus more plausible to the reader of this verse, Christian Bibles generally translate the verbs in verse 5 in the future tense, instead of the past, as in the Hebrew text. This gives the deceptive reading: "For a child *will* be born to us, a son *will* be given to us; and the government *will* rest on his shoulders; and his name will be called Wonderful Counselor, Mighty God, Eternal Father, Prince of Peace." Thus, rather than the prophecy referring to someone already born at the time the prophecy is enunciated it is made to refer to someone yet to be born.

Some Christians admit that "wonderful counselor" and "ruler of peace" can be applied to a man, but allege that the phrases "mighty God" and "everlasting Father" cannot constitute part of a man's name. Assuming this passage is messianic they also maintain this prophetic name illustrates that the Messiah has to be both God and man. Their reasoning is warped. Who says this passage is messianic? And what of names such as Elihu, "My God is He," which refer to an ordinary human being (Job 32:1; 1 Samuel 1:1; 1 Chronicles 12:21, 26:7, 27:18)? They make the same error regarding the name Immanuel, "God is with us." There are many biblical examples of humans being given names that have the purpose of declaring or reflecting a particular attribute of God (for example, Eliab, Eliada, Elzaphan, Eliakim, Elisha, Eleazar, Tavel, Gedaliah).

Despite all claims to the contrary made by Christians, Jesus did not in any way fulfill the prophecy of Isaiah 9:5-6. A wonderful counselor does not instruct his followers that if they have faith and believe they can be agents of destruction (Matthew 21:19-21; Mark 11:14, 20-23). A mighty God is not subservient to anyone (Luke 2:51, Hebrews 5:8), for no one is greater than he is (Matthew 12:31-32; John 5:30, 14:28). Moreover, he does not ask or need to be saved by anyone (Matthew 26:39, Luke 22:42), for he cannot die by any means (Matthew 27:50, Mark 15:37, Luke 23:46, John 19:30). He who is called the Son of God the Father (John 1:18, 3:16) cannot himself be called everlasting Father. One cannot be simultaneously the son and the Father; it is an obvious self-contradiction. He who advocates family strife (Matthew 10:34-35, Luke 12:49-53) and killing enemies (Luke 19:27) cannot be called a ruler of peace. There is nothing in this passage that can be associated with the life of Jesus. Jesus is simply not the "child born to us."

Chapter 20

OUT OF THE STOCK OF JESSE
(Isaiah 11)

Isaiah 11 is generally accepted as a passage which speaks of the Messiah and the messianic age. In verse 1 the prophet states: "And there shall come forth a shoot out of the stock of Jesse, and a branch out of his roots shall bear fruit." The phrase, "out of the stock of Jesse" is a reference to the Davidic dynasty, from which will come an invigorated leader of Israel ("the shoot") who will be the Messiah.

Christians, recognizing that this chapter speaks of the Messiah and the messianic age attempt to apply it to Jesus. But, for this passage to have any connection to the life of Jesus it would need to be referring to his so-called first coming, and that is not the case. This prophecy concerns the "shoot" coming "out of the stock of David," which would refer to the Messiah's ancestry at the time of his birth not at a supposed second coming. And it should be noted that Davidic ancestry in general and lineal descent from the regal line in particular is not firmly established for Jesus by the pertinent New Testament narratives.

This presents a serious problem for the Christian interpretation of Isaiah 11. This chapter, which Christians identify with Jesus, gives a very positive and widely accepted leadership portrait of the individual described. It stands in stark contrast to the portrayal of the suffering servant of Isaiah 53:1-2, who Christians also identify with Jesus. The servant is portrayed in difficult circumstances, from his very beginning. Now, if Isaiah's two prophecies (11:1 and 53:1-2) are both applied to Jesus, they would have to refer to his so-called first coming and this leads to an irreconcilable contradiction. The respective passages simply could not both be referring to one person and are mutually exclusive of each other.

Some Christians divide this passage into two separate periods, one during Jesus' lifetime and the other after his supposed future return following his death. Nonetheless, it is apparent that there is but one "coming" indicated in the passage. This is confirmed by verse 10 where all the events listed in verses 2-9 occur. There the individual spoken of is called, "a shoot of the stock of Jesse," and typical of biblical poetic style parallel to this he is called "a branch out of his [Jesse's] roots shall bear fruit." This can only refer to one's earthly existence and not to a supposedly resurrected divine being coming back at some future date. Christians claim that Jesus appeared first to offer a means of salvation for mankind. They then claim that he will return a second time, at which time he is supposed to judge and rule the world. This Christian explanation, however, has nothing in common with the text of Isaiah 11. The subject of this passage is not portrayed as a resurrected divine being returning to earth as its judge and king.

Some Christians claim that verse 2, "The spirit of the Lord shall rest upon him" was fulfilled at Jesus' baptism (Matthew 3:16, Mark 1:10, Luke 3:22). This explanation also has no textual support. It is said that "God anointed him [Jesus] with the Holy Spirit and with power" (Acts 10:38; see also John 3:34). Are we to assume that Jesus, one-third of a triune deity, needed the "Spirit of God," another one-third of the deity, to descend upon him by permission of still another one-third of this deity? The author of Acts claims that Jesus had the ability to do wonders because God anointed him and that "God was with him." But, now, think about this! If Jesus was a coequal part of a triune God, he would not need to be anointed by another part of this God and have this other God "with him" in order to perform miracles. Even more so, if Jesus was God in any way, whatsoever, he could not stand in a relationship with God that is outside of God. If the New Testament Jesus, at any time, gave up any of his supposed pre-incarnation godly powers he could not be God in any ontological subdivision. God cannot be diminished or subdivided.

Christians choose those verses that they think have been fulfilled in a first coming by Jesus and leave the remainder to be fulfilled during a second coming. A perusal of the entire chapter 11 shows that there is no evidence to suggest a two part division within the prophecy. Needless to say, this passage has nothing to do with Jesus.

Chapter 21

GOD'S SPIRIT
(Isaiah 48:16)

Trinitarians maintain that the terms *ruach hak-kodesh*, "holy spirit"; *ruach tov*, "good spirit"; and *rucho*, "His spirit," are not abstract manifestations of God's power but, on the contrary, refer to a separate entity within God's essence that has a personality and consciousness of its own. Thus, they say, it can feel emotion as when the children of Israel "embittered His spirit" (Psalms 106:33), it can feel sorrow as when they "rebelled and grieved his holy spirit" (Isaiah 63:10), and the "spirit" can give instruction (Nehemiah 9:20; Psalms 104:30, 143:10; Zechariah 7:12). They also ask why Micah raises the question as to whether "the spirit of the Lord" can become impatient (Micah 2:7).

The fact is that these terms are figures of speech referring to manifestations of God that are intimately felt. Certainly, God's presence is without bound but the use of these terminologies is descriptive of a perception of the divine that is felt although not tangible to the touch. This divine manifestation is called in later Jewish literary sources the *Shechinah*, "the Divine Presence," from the verb *shachan*, "dwell," "abide" and indicates intimate contact between God and the children of Israel as He dwells among His people. That is why it is the term used to show divine displeasure at Israel's rebellion when that rebelliousness takes place at times when that intimate relationship is manifest. God's holy spirit is not a person but is a manifestation of God's imperceptible power by which He accomplishes His divine purpose and will. Essentially, it is a synonym for an aspect of God's power, not a personification of part of His very essence.

The terms, *ruach hak-kodesh*, *ruach tov*, *rucho*, and *Shechinah*, expressing the intimate relationship of God dwelling among His people make them excellent midrashic vehicles for expressing homiletical teachings. Thus, there are *midrashim*, which have dialogues between God and His *ruach ha-kodesh* or His *Shechinah*, but they were never meant to be interpreted literally. Such dialogues are pedagogical tools used by the rabbis for teaching Torah.

We see that it is God who put His holy spirit in the midst of the children of Israel: "Then His people remembered the days of old, the days of Moses: 'Where is He that brought them up out of the sea with the shepherds of His flock? Where is He that put His holy spirit in the midst of them?'" (Isaiah 63:11). The holy spirit is thus a manifestation of an aspect of His power which is, so to speak, subordinate to God's will since God may dispense it to His chosen ones. If the holy spirit is one part of a coequal triune deity, how can David make a request of one part of this triune deity: "Cast me not away from Your presence" about matters controlled by another part of this triune deity: "And do not take Your holy spirit from me" (Psalms 51:13)? The fact is that often in the Jewish Scriptures something may be personified that is not actually a person. For example, Moses calls upon heaven and earth to witness his exhortation, "Give ear, heavens, and I will speak; and let the earth hear the words of my mouth" (Deuteronomy 32:1); the universe praises the Creator, "The heavens declare the glory of God; and the firmament proclaims His handiwork" (Psalms 19:2); Zion speaks of her estrangement from God, "But Zion said: 'The Lord has forsaken me, and the Lord has forgotten me'" (Isaiah 49:14); Zion gives birth, "For as soon as Zion travailed, she brought forth her children" (Isaiah 66:8); Zion hears and shows emotion, "Zion heard and was glad" (Psalms 97:8); "wisdom" and "understanding" are personified as females who can speak with emotion: "Wisdom cries aloud in the streets; she utters her voice in the squares" (Proverbs 1:20-23); " Does not wisdom call? and understanding put forth her voice?" (Proverbs 8:1 ff., see also Proverbs 9:1-6).

There are some trinitarians who maintain that the personification of *chochmah*, "wisdom," found in Proverbs 8:22-23 refers to an actual person, namely, Jesus: "The Lord created me as the beginning of His way, the first of His acts of old. I was set up ages ago, from the beginning, from the origin of the earth." The verb *qanah* means, "to create" (cf. Genesis 14:19, 22; Deuteronomy 32:6; Psalms 139:13). Since it is clearly stated that God created "wisdom," it becomes self-evident that whoever or whatever is personified by "wisdom" cannot be God, for that which is created cannot be God. Although "wisdom" is figuratively given a personality of its own, it is a subservient creation of God. In fact, "wisdom" has neither a personal life of its own nor any ontological existence whatsoever.

A further indication of the futility of the viewpoint expressed by trinitarians concerning wisdom is found in Proverbs 3:19: "The Lord by wisdom founded the earth; by understanding He established the heavens." As we have seen, many of these Christians consider "wisdom" to be a real being, the second member of the Trinity, and the agent by which God created the world. But to follow this reasoning one may very well say that "understanding" also represents a real being and the agent by which God created the heavens. No doubt, if trinitarian Christians needed to prove that God is a Quaternary, they would claim that not only "wisdom" but also "understanding" is a distinct personality within the essence of God.

Paul personified the concept of sin, "But sin, taking opportunity through the commandment, produced in me coveting of every kind; for apart from the Law sin is dead. And I was once alive apart from the Law; but when the commandment came, sin became alive, and I died; and this commandment, which was to result in life, proved to result in death for me; for sin, taking opportunity through the commandment, deceived me, and through it killed me" (Romans 7:8-11). Following the trinitarian thought process is it to be presumed that Paul meant that sin was actually an entity with its own personality and conscious?

Christians who are looking for trinitarian allusions in the Jewish Scriptures translate part of Isaiah 48:16 as, "The Lord God and His Spirit have sent me." However, a proper rendering reads: And now the Lord God ['Ado-nai Y-H-V-H] has sent me, and His spirit." The last two Hebrew words in this verse are *shelachani ve-rucho*, "He has sent me, and His spirit", with "me, and His spirit" being the direct objects of "sent." Although a definite direct object is usually preceded by the participle *'et*, this grammatical rule is frequently not observed in the Bible (e.g., Exodus 15:9; Judges 5:12; Psalms 9:5, 20:3-4, 45:4). In fact, *'et* rarely occurs in the poetic parts of the Bible. Thus, the meaning of the verse is that God has sent Isaiah accompanied by His prophetic spirit. There is no mention of the third member of the Trinity doctrine. Instead, Isaiah affirms that God, who has placed within him the power of prophecy, sent him.

The spirit is always at the disposal of God to bestow upon whomever He chooses, as stated in Numbers 11:17, 25, 29; Isaiah 42:1, 44:3; Joel 3:1. If this spirit referred to the third member of a coequal triune deity, how could it be ordered about at the discretion of the other members of this group? Such a condition makes it obviously impossible to consider the spirit as being an associate of God, let alone coequal with Him.[1] Thus, we see that the Jewish Scriptures do not teach that "spirit" refers to the third person of a triune deity. God says to Moses:

> And I will take of the spirit which is upon you, and I will put it upon them.... And He took of the spirit, which was upon him, and He put it upon the seventy men, the elders, and it came to pass, when the spirit rested upon them, that they prophesied.... And Moses said ..."would that all the Lord's people were prophets, that the Lord would put His spirit upon them." (Numbers 11:17, 25, 29)

[1] In the Talmud and midrashic literature, the angel Metatron is regarded notably as the defender of the rights of Israel (cf. *Chagigah* 15a). In the Babylonian Talmud, Metatron is mentioned in three places (*Chagigah* 15a, *Sanhedrin* 38b, and *Avodah Zarah* 3b). The first two references are significant because they are used in connection with polemical refutations of heretical beliefs in "two Powers." The tractate *Chagigah* relates that Acher (Elisha ben Avuyah) saw Metatron seated (next to the Divine Throne) and said, "perhaps there are two powers," that is, Metatron himself being a second deity. The citation explains that Metatron was given permission to be seated only because he was the heavenly scribe recording the good deeds of Israel. It was shown to Elisha that Metatron could not be a second deity by the fact that Metatron was carried out and received sixty fiery lashes to emphasize that Metatron was not a god, but an angel, and could be punished.

In tractate *Sanhedrin* 38b, a min ("heretic") challenges the Amora, R. Idit, on why it is written in Exodus 24:1, "And to Moses He said: 'Come up to the Lord,'" instead of "Come up to Me." The heretic claims that the verse shows that there are two deities: the one who commanded Moses to ascend, and the one to whom Moses was commanded to ascend. R. Idit answered that the verse refers to Metatron "whose name is like that of his Master, for it is written, 'For My name is in him [Exodus 23:21]'" (that is, Metatron acts as God's emissary). When the heretic argued that, if that were so, Metatron should be worshiped as a deity. R. Idit pointed out that Exodus 23:21 also says, "be not rebellious against [*tmr*] him." This, R. Idit, explained, should be understood to mean "do not exchange Me for him." Metatron is not to be worshiped; to God alone belongs that honor. To worship Metatron, thereby "exchanging him for God," is rebellion against him in that that is not within the God-given authority with which he is to deal with Israel. The verse continues, "he [the angel] will not pardon your transgression, for My name is in him." Metatron cannot on his own pardon transgression, a power which God has not placed within his authority. The limits of his authority are set by God, in whose name he comes and who alone is the ultimate guide of Israel.

There is not a single instance in Jewish sources of Metatron being represented as *synthronos*, the co-occupant of the Divine Throne, a second power or deity. He always remains the servant of his Master, no matter what functions and powers he may exercise.

Chapter 22

WHY JESUS IS NOT THE SUFFERING SERVANT

(Isaiah 52:13-53:12)

THE TEXT: ISAIAH 52:13-53:12

13. Behold, My servant shall prosper, he shall be exalted and lifted up, and shall be very high.

14. According as many were appalled at you –– so marred was his appearance unlike that of a man, and his form unlike that of the sons of men.

15. So shall he startle many nations, kings shall shut their mouths because of him; for that which had not been told them shall they see, and that which they had not heard shall they perceive.

1. Who would have believed our report? And to whom has the arm of the Lord been revealed?

2. For he grew up before Him as a tender plant, and as a root out of a dry land; he had no form nor comeliness that we should look upon him, nor appearance that we should delight in him.

3. He was despised, and rejected of men [e-shim: "men of high status"], a man of pains, and acquainted with disease, and as one from whom men hide their face: he was despised, and we esteemed him not.

4. Surely our diseases he did bear, and our pains he carried; but we considered him stricken, smitten of God, and afflicted.

5. But he was wounded as a result of our transgressions, he was crushed as a result of our iniquities. The chastisement of our welfare was upon him, and with his wounds we were healed.

6. All we like sheep did go astray, we turned every one to his own way; and the Lord has visited upon him the iniquity of us all.

7. He was oppressed, though he humbled himself and opened not his mouth; as a lamb that is led to the slaughter, and as a sheep that before her shearers is dumb; and opened not his mouth.

8. From dominion and judgment he was taken away, and his life's history who is able to relate? For he was cut off out of the land

of the living; as a result of the transgression of my people he has been afflicted.

9. And his grave was set with the wicked, and with the rich in his deaths; although he had done no violence, neither was there any deceit in his mouth.

10. And it pleased the Lord to crush him — He made [him] sick. If he would offer himself as a guilt-offering, he shall see seed, he shall prolong days. And the purpose of the Lord will prosper by his hand.

11. From the labor of his soul he shall see; he shall be satisfied. With his knowledge, the righteous one, my servant, shall cause many to be just. And their iniquities he shall bear.

12. Therefore will I divide him a portion with the great, and he shall divide the spoil with the mighty; because he had poured out his soul to death: and he was numbered with the transgressors; and he bore the sin of many, and made intercession for the transgressors.

Herein we concentrate on showing why Isaiah 52:13-53:12 does *not* refer to Jesus. In countering Christian claims concerning the Suffering Servant passage it is really sidestepping the issue to discuss if it refers to the coming Messiah or national Israel.

Some Christians claim that it was only with the commentary of Rashi (1040-1105), seeking to refute the Christian interpretation that the Jews began to refer Isaiah 52:13-53:12 to the entire nation of Israel. The allegation that interpreting the passage as referring to Israel began with Rashi is refuted even by an early third century Christian source. In *Contra Celsum*, written in 248 C.E. (Some 800 years before Rashi), no less than the Church Father Origen records that the Jews contemporary with him interpreted this passage as referring to the entire nation of Israel. He wrote:

I remember that once in a discussion with someone whom the Jews regard as learned I used these prophecies [Isaiah 52:13-53:8]. At this the Jew said that these prophecies referred to the whole people as though of a single individual, since they were scattered in the dispersion and smitten, that as a result of the scattering of the Jews among the other nations many might become proselytes. In this way he explained the text: "Thy form shall be inglorious among men"; and "those to whom he was not proclaimed shall see him"; "being a man in calamity."[1]

Significant though it is to establish this identification the conversation with Christians is really about their claim that the passage refers to the Messiah and then their jumping to the conclusion that it therefore refers to Jesus.

In developing the Jesus myth several traditions developed among distinct groups of followers of what was eventually called *Christianity*. Various strains of tradition were brought together in forming the New Testament. They were not uniform in their message as each told the Jesus story from the perspective of its own community needs. Isaiah's suffering servant played a decisive role in forming the Jesus myth among certain Christian groups. It provided an outline to guide them in describing what they imagined Jesus' ministry to have been. There is no doubt that the New Testament authors had the suffering servant in mind in developing their respective works. But this does not prove Jesus is the servant. In the traditions coming down to them concerning Jesus they did not fully eliminate the contradictions between the description of the servant and the description of Jesus. As a result, we are still able to get a glimpse of why Jesus is not the servant from their very own writings.

For a full discussion of how and why the passage refers to Israel see Gerald Sigal, *Isaiah 53: Who is the Servant?* Bloomington, IN: Xlibris: 2007

Isaiah 52:13: "Behold My Servant"

My servant

There are a number of reasons why Jesus cannot be considered the servant. The phrase, "My servant," presents a problem for the trinitarian doctrine: servant and master are two separate entities. A servant by definition is always in an inferior position to his master. John's Jesus acknowledges: "A slave is not greater than his master, neither one who is sent greater than the one who sent him" (John 13:16). The sending of Jesus would have taken place while the trinity trio supposedly were all equal. If Jesus is an incarnate member of a coequal triune deity he could not become less than equal to the other two parts and still be coequal and of one essence with them (cf. Philippians 2:5-11). Moreover, when is Jesus ever called directly "My servant"? In Matthew 12:18 the phrase appears as part of a prooftext, not as an appellative

The supposed "two natures of Christ"

Jesus is the god that never was. Some Christians differentiate between what is called "the two natures of Christ." It is claimed that Jesus was fully God and fully man at the same time, but mysteriously interwoven yet separate. Thus, it is said, Jesus could be knowledgeable about some things and ignorant about others. Jesus' statement that "A slave is not greater than his master, neither one who is sent greater than the one who sent him" refutes consideration of this two nature doctrine. This statement says that a slave is of lower status than his master. Anyone sent on a mission by another person is of inferior status. In the case of Jesus, this would make his supposed supernatural nature inferior to that of God the Father even before becoming incarnate and even if done voluntarily. It would mean that there was a period of time when the coequality of the triune deity was reduced to a dyad. This state of inequality continues presently in that Jesus supposedly mediates between God the Father and mankind (1 Timothy 2:5, Hebrew 9:24), but it is God the Father who makes the final judgment not the "mediator." This is not coequality.

Learning obedience

Did the author of Hebrews have Isaiah 53 in mind when he said that Jesus "learned obedience from the things which he suffered" (Hebrews 5:8)? Why did Jesus have to learn to be obedient if he is God? Whom did he have to obey? Can equals in any triune deity exercise dominance, one over the other? How can God's servant be none other than one-third of Himself. Those who claim a preexistent supernatural being was incarnate in the form of Jesus cannot escape the question: Why did this incarnate being have to learn to be obedient through suffering if in both his humanity and divinity he was sinless to begin with and therefore was already obedient to God?

52:13: "He shall be exalted and lifted up, and shall be very high"

Exalted, lifted up, very high

Rewarding the servant: The servant is to be raised to a higher position in the estimation of those who were previously appalled at the sight of him. Does "He shall be exalted and lifted up, and shall be very high" refer to Jesus' alleged rewards after death in heaven and on earth? Some Christians believe that the meaning of these words is to be found in Philippians 2:5-11, which speaks of Jesus' supposed exaltation in heaven and on earth following his death. But why should such a divine creature receive a reward for doing what he was programmed to do from the very start? If he was one-third of God or some sort of a supernatural being makes no difference.

Jesus is portrayed unlike a mere human who has free will and is capable of making the wrong choices and sinning. The Gospels' Jesus had no choice but to do as he was programmed to do. In fact, no matter what the temptation placed before the New Testament's Jesus he could not sin, he had no free will. The New Testament's Jesus could not deviate from the alleged preordained divine program. Unlike a martyr who has no firsthand knowledge of what to expect for his sacrifice, Jesus, it is said, did have that firsthand knowledge. If Jesus knew where he came from and he knew where he was going, and if he knew exactly what his rewards would be for his obedience to the will of God he sacrificed nothing.

The rest of the story

The fact is that Jesus' death through crucifixion was no remedy for sin. He did not die in man's place; his death was not a ransom price paid for all eternity. His death was no sacrifice. Jesus' death was the means by which the New Testament says he obtained great rewards for himself of which he was fully aware they would be his if he allowed himself to be executed (Philippians 2:7-11). Jesus sacrificed absolutely *nothing* if he was a supernatural being. He knew what his mission on earth was, he knew that his was a temporary death (John 10:17), he knew he would be restored to life with an in tacked body, and he knew he was to be well rewarded for allowing himself to be executed. As an equal member of the supposedly triune god he rewarded himself for his troubles.

Did the Jesus of Christian theology have free will and could he sin? Jesus is described as lacking a basic human characteristic — free will. Where there is no free will being sinless is no problem. Free will is an innate quality of the human species not a consequence of a sin nature. The presence of free will allows for one to make decisions — right or wrong. Adam and Eve possessed free will prior to eating from the Tree of Knowledge. Their choice to partake of its fruit was a free will decision. Their sin was disobedience to God's instruction. Their ability to choose between obedience and disobedience indicates the presence of free will.

Whether the Jesus of the Gospels was tempted at various points in his life is not the issue. It is said that Jesus "has been tempted in every way, just as we are — yet without sin" (Hebrews 4:15). John said about Jesus: "In him there is no sin" (1 John 3:5). Hebrews states that in his alleged post-resurrection state Jesus is "a high priest, holy, innocent, undefiled, separated from sinners, and exalted above the heavens" (Hebrews 7:26), but we are here concerned with him while alive. There are two specific issues involved.

- If Jesus did not sin, why did he not sin?
- If Jesus did not sin, was he truly human?

The New Testament envisions Jesus as a supernatural being who could not sin. Then again it is said that because Jesus was a man, he could be tempted — but because he was God he could not sin. A temptation might be genuine, in that it has an enticement factor. But one man's temptation leaves another indifferent. It is not simply ability to be tempted that is of concern, but what one's response to that temptation is. According to the New Testament, Jesus was tempted (Satan's temptation — Matthew 4:1-11, Mark 1:12-13) but without free will being part of his nature he had no choice but to reject Satan's offer.

Jesus could experience genuine temptations being offered to him, but he would not be tempted to give into them. Jesus allegedly had no ability to even consider the temptation because as a supposed divine entity he could not sin. That being the case, his physical body might appear to be human but his humanity was deficient in his ability to make free will decisions. Without free will Jesus was *not* in a significant sense a true human being.

52:14: "So marred was his appearance unlike that of a man, and his form unlike that of the sons of men"

Let the truth be told

Although many post-New Testament descriptions of Jesus on the cross paint a gruesome agonizing picture of his suffering the Gospels do not describe his appearance as being in a form unrecognizable as a human being. Isaiah's description is best understood when one views pictures of horrific Jewish suffering during the Holocaust and the contempt of their oppressors toward them. That is literal fulfillment of the verse not one that comes from the imagination of Christians contemplating on the agony of crucifixion,

52:15: "So shall he startle many nations"

The Hebrew text

What is the meaning of the word *nazah*? Some Christians maintain that *nazah*, which has the meaning of "sprinkle" carries with it the thought of expiation in verse 15. It is thought the verse portrays the servant as a priest who "sprinkles" (that is, spiritually cleanses) the nations. They then claim that this verse refers to the supposed power of Jesus to make "many nations" the beneficiaries of his blood. That is, Jesus was expected "to make propitiation for the sins of the people" (Hebrews 2:17) and have their "hearts sprinkled from an evil conscience" (Hebrew 10:22). However, this interpretation is problematic.

Both grammatically and in terms of the sacrificial system the correct meaning of verse 15 has *no* relationship to the priestly sprinkling of atonement blood at all. In every other instance where the object or person sprinkled is indicated, the verb is used in conjunction with a preposition (such as "onto," "upon," or "before"). This combination does not occur in verse 15. The proper rendering of the verb, *nazah*, in this verse is not "sprinkle," but "scatter" in the sense of being startled and confused. It indicates the astonishment of the nations as they scurry about in shock over the turn of events. In sprinkling, one scatters a liquid into innumerable droplets. Similarly, the inhabitants of the nations will be scattered as well. There is no reference here to Jesus spiritually cleansing the nations.

52:15: "[K]ings shall shut their mouths because of him; for that which had not been told them shall they see, and that which they had not heard shall they perceive."

What did the kings hear about Jesus and when did they hear it?

Attempting to apply verses 52:13-15 to Jesus is an exercise in futility. Some Christians say verse 15 refers to a situation when Jesus returns a second time. Why do they say after a second coming? Because the person of Jesus has already been exalted, lifted up and made very high by the great homage paid by national rulers, but not to the satisfaction of many Christians. The behavior of the majority of these rulers has never been anything to be proud of and these Christians hope for a more ethical and moral fulfillment.

Although rulers of nations with populations professing to be followers of Jesus have paid homage to Jesus does this fulfill verse 15? What is it that these rulers were not told that they now saw, what is it that they did not hear before that they now understand? Look at the behavior of the rulers of Christian Europe and other continents: the kings, queens, nobleman and other rulers elected and unelected, to whom this supposedly refers. There are an estimated 2.6 billion people in the world (and eighty-one countries with Christian majorities) who call themselves Christian, although many deny that those outside their denomination, sect or group are Christians. From a Christian perspective, is it simply reverential acknowledgement of Jesus as a superior being to themselves that is called for in verse 15? Or was there to be an elevated sense of morality, temperance of blood lust and pecuniary appetite as well? For, in truth, the rulers of these Christianized nations continued and still continue to support perverse behavior.

53:1: "Who would have believed our report [literally, "what we have heard"]?"

As we enter chapter 53, a change of speakers occurs. In Isaiah 52:13-15 God is the speaker, now in verses 1-8 it is as if it were the representative spokesman for the Gentile nations who is speaking.

The spokesman declares: "Who would have believed our report?" The Gentile nations, as expressed through their spokesman, can scarcely believe what they have to say let alone expect others to believe what they are about to tell them. These nations, recovering from their speechlessness, are still in a state of amazement at the turn of events they are witnessing. "Then," as the psalmist writes: "they will say among the nations: 'God has done great things for these [Israel]'" (Psalms 126:2b).

53:1: "And to whom has the arm of the Lord been revealed?"

What nation, the spokesman declares, has had God's "protective arm," revealed to it as is now obvious for the servant nation, Israel? With greatness and glory, God now manifests His judgment upon the faithful servant, Israel, and upon those Gentiles who reviled His people, Israel.

Verse 1 uses metaphors to describe the historical development of the Jewish people.

The "arm of the Lord" signifies God's power and is a biblical metaphor descriptive of God's physical redemption of Israel from the oppression of other nations. To whom has the "arm of the Lord" been revealed? It is explicitly stated: "Israel saw the great work that God inflicted upon the Egyptians, and the people feared the Lord, and they believed in the Lord, and in His servant Moses" (Exodus 14:31). We read further that the "arm of the Lord" is displayed for the protection of the people of Israel: "Your right hand, O Lord is glorious in power; Your right hand, O Lord dashes in pieces the enemy" (Exodus 15:6); "The great trials which your eyes saw, and the signs, and the wonders, and the mighty hand, and the outstretched arm with which the Lord your God brought you out; so shall the Lord your God do to all the peoples of whom you are afraid" (Deuteronomy 7:19); and "The Lord has made bare His holy arm in the eyes of all the nations; and all the ends of the earth shall see the salvation of our God" (Isaiah 52:10). Thus, on the one hand, the "arm of the Lord" is displayed to Israel for it to have faith in the saving power of the Almighty and on the other hand it is revealed to the nations so that they will have an appreciation of what God will do for the nation of Israel.

There are Christians who identify "arm of the Lord" with Jesus but this claim is nothing but wishful thinking.

Who is not the servant and who is?

Matthew misuses the Jewish Scriptures. Matthew 12:18-21 literally applies to Jesus the announcement of Isaiah 42:1-4, which speaks in lofty terms of the servant. But what of the verses in this same chapter which speak of the servant as being figuratively blind and deaf: "Who is blind, but My servant? (verse 19)? This passage shows the servant disobedient and rebellious at times yet still considered as God's servant. When does the New Testament portray Jesus as figuratively blind and deaf, a disobedient and rebellious sinner? It does not and cannot, and still call Jesus sinless (1 Peter 2:22). But then, he *cannot* be the servant mentioned in Isaiah 42:1. A perusal of this chapter shows that Isaiah is speaking of neither the Messiah nor Jesus, but of a people/nation (verse 22) and that the prophet identifies that people/nation as Jacob/Israel (verse 24). In, *Ve-hu 'am bazuz ve-shasu*, "But he/it is a people/nation robbed and spoiled" (verse 22), the "he/it" refers to the people of Israel as identified in verse 24: "Who gave Jacob for a spoil, and Israel to the robbers?" It is clear that when Isaiah speaks of *My servant* it is God's servant Israel as a nation not any individual Israelite; it is the combined national experience that is spoken of.

53:2: "[H]e grew up ... a tender plant, and as a root out of a dry land ... no form nor comeliness ... nor appearance that we should delight in him."

The futile search for Jesus in Isaiah 53:2

The early years:

- Was Jesus' apparently humble and inauspicious origin proof that he was the servant?

- His situation was no different than myriads of others living in Judea or Galilee.

- Does the description of the downtrodden rejected servant of verse 2 fit the one of Jesus depicted in the Gospels?

Luke states: "And Jesus kept increasing in wisdom and in physical growth [*helikia*, cf. Luke 12:25, 19:3], and in favor with God and men" (Luke 2:52). As Jesus was growing up was he a frail, unsightly child? Was he repulsive? In the Gospel, it is asserted that Jesus was tall, wise and enjoyed popularity even in the years prior to his active ministry. It suggests that his reported handsome appearance, charismatic personality and wisdom attracted a positive interest from others.

As the Gospels' story unfolds, throughout Jesus' entire lifetime, he is greatly desired by an ever growing multitude of people who come to hear his spiritual message. Even if some only superficially admired Jesus and later found him disappointing it would still not match the intensity of the servant's rejection from a tender age. The Gospels' description of Jesus simply does not fit the physical description of the servant or the reaction to his presence that is found in verse 2.

The ministry years:

- The Gospels report that there are those who opposed Jesus, but compare this opposition to the alleged popularity he enjoined even while going to his death.

- A number of Gospel stories tell of enthusiastic crowds following him from the very beginning of his preaching and even when he was taken to be executed.

- These stories contradict the description of the servant found in verse 2.

Christians in search of answers

Some Christians suggest that "no form nor comeliness ... nor appearance that we should delight in him" refers not to physical being but to humility. To the contrary, the Gospels describe a different Jesus who was neither a humble person nor was he a loving person. It is easy to love those who agree with you; much more difficult is the ability to love those who disagree.

- The heralded loving, meek and mild Jesus of the supposed new dispensation of God's salvation exhibited rabid intolerance of those who disagreed with him (Matthew 23:13-29, John 8:44).

- He was haughty and cruel in both word and deed (Matthew 15:1-20; Matthew 21:12, Mark 11:15-16, Luke 19:45, John 2:15; Matthew 21:18-21, Mark 11:13-14; Matthew 8:32, Mark 5:13, Luke 8:33; Matthew 10:34-35, Luke 12:49-53; Matthew 23:34-36, Luke 11:49-51; Luke 19:27).

Was it permissible for Jesus to act as he did because he was allegedly God and therefore could do as he pleased? This is begging the question. The specific issue here is not whether Jesus was a supernatural being but whether he *literally fulfilled* the passage in Isaiah.

Paul claims the pre-incarnate Jesus "humbled himself" (Philippians 2:8) but apparently this humility did not extend to relations with ordinary people who disagreed with him, while he was in his supposed incarnate state. Did Jesus carry out faithfully the role of the servant as specifically enunciated by the prophet? By what authority it is claimed he spoke acrimoniously is not at issue. What is at issue is that once having spoken and acted in a haughty and cruel manner the Gospels' Jesus disqualified himself from being a literal fulfillment of verse 2. This is because in all instances where the New Testament uses Isaiah 53 it alleges *literal* fulfillment by Jesus not a metaphorical fulfillment (Matthew 8:17; Mark 15:28; Luke 22:37; John 12:38; Acts 8:32, 33; Romans 10:16, 15:21; 1 Peter 2:22, 24-25).

Another unjustified Christian contention presented is that this verse refers to the Jewish rejection of Jesus' message at the time of his death. If the Gospel reports are accurate, we can assume that not only did he have followers from among the Jewish leaders of the nation (e.g., Joseph of Arimathea, Nicodemus) but that outside of Jerusalem his still loyal following was unaware of events in the capital and that even there, besides his secret followers (John 12:42) great multitudes were still loyal. On the way to being executed Luke claims that "there were following him a great multitude of the people, and of women who were mourning and lamenting him" (Luke 23:27). Overall, the great majority of Jesus' Jewish contemporaries in the Land of Israel and the Diaspora never heard of him. Therefore, the question of large-scale contemporary Jewish rejection of Jesus does not enter the picture. Other Christians wrongly see this verse as a reaction to Jesus' physical state at his crucifixion. Luke's narrative shows that those who followed Jesus to his execution were not turned away by his supposed haggard appearance (Luke 23:27).

The rejection of Jesus in the light of verse 2

Overall, those contemporaries who reject Jesus are vocal, but appear to be in the minority compared to the multitudes bewailing his fate. The type of rejection the Gospels say Jesus experienced in his last hours of life is by no means that expressed in the wording of verse 2. According to all the Synoptic Gospel accounts, those relatively few individuals who allegedly ridiculed Jesus, prior to his execution and at the crucifixion site itself, did not deride his physical condition but, rather, his messianic pretensions (Matthew 27:41-43; Mark 15:29-32; Luke 22:63-64, 23:35-37).

Considering the Gospels' description of the physical attributes ascribed to Jesus, his lack of humility and the enthusiastic reaction to his message by individuals and crowds he could not be regarded as the fulfillment of Isaiah 53:2.

53:3: "He was despised, and rejected of men ... and as one from whom men hide their face: he was despised, and we esteemed him not."

Comparing the description of the servant with that of Jesus.

Rejection of the servant contrasts greatly with the Gospel accounts of the extent of Jesus' popularity *throughout* his life generally (Luke 2:52) and during his public ministry in particular. The servant is said to be "despised," "rejected," one "from whom men hide their face" and not "esteemed. In the case of the servant, disappointment at a lack of true loyalty is not the issue. In verse 3, nothing is said about the servant's adversaries at one time being his followers, let alone that they had unworthy motives in initially following him. They never were the servant's followers to begin with. What do the Gospels say about Jesus?

The Synoptic Gospels in particular insist that Jesus was greatly admired by large segments from every level of society. It is further claimed that wherever Jesus went crowds flocked about him. The Gospels claim that it was not only the poor masses that followed him, but even people of means were attracted to him. What is more, they maintain, many were his loyal followers. Even though the Gospels claim that the Jewish rulers condemned Jesus they nevertheless assert that Jesus had many followers even from among the ruling class. They speak of Jesus as one who, while losing, at times, many of his followers, always had, even at the end of his life, a great many faithful adherents from every strata of society. Nevertheless, John says that

Jesus felt many followed him for unworthy motives and so he said to them: "You seek me, not because you saw signs, but because you did eat of the loaves, and were filled" (John 6:26). John also claims that "He came to his own, and his own received him not" (John 1:11). However, overall the Gospels allege that Jesus was enthusiastically received and esteemed and that this feeling did not end with his death.

Quotable quotes
- The Gospels' Jesus is described by average folk with superlatives titles (e.g., *the Prophet* [like Moses] *who is to come into the world*—John 6:14, *Messiah* [*Christ*]—Luke 23:39, *Son of David*—Matthew 20:30). These words of praise are the exact opposite of those used to describe one who is despised and rejected.
- The Gospels claim that when Jesus' notoriety spread throughout all the districts surrounding Galilee he taught in the synagogues and was "glorified by all" (Luke 4:14-15).
- "And the news about him went out into all Syria" (Matthew 4:24).
- As his fame grew, it is maintained: "a great crowd came together with those who went to him from the various cities" (Luke 8:4).
- "And great crowds followed him from Galilee and Decapolis and Jerusalem and Judea and from the other side of the Jordan" (Matthew 4:25).
- It is reported the press of the crowds was tremendous (Luke 7:11; 8:19, 45).
- In the city of Nain, a large part of the populace calls Jesus a great prophet and says that God has visited His people (Luke 7:12, 16).

Who do the Gospels say followed Jesus?
The Women:

Many of those who followed him were women who contributed to the needs of Jesus and his disciples (Luke 8:3). While Jesus and his male disciples traveled through the cities and villages of Galilee "proclaiming and preaching the kingdom of God" they were accompanied by women: "who had been healed of evil spirits and sickness," including "Mary, called Magdalene ... Joanna, the wife of Chuza, Herod's steward, and Suzanna, and many others, who were contributing to their support out of their private means" (Luke 8:1-3). At Jesus' execution "many women were there looking on from a distance, who had followed Jesus from Galilee, ministering to him" (Matthew 27:55). Luke also mentions that after his execution "the women who had come with him out of Galilee followed after, and saw the tomb and how his body was laid" (Luke 23:55). Mark maintains that there were "women looking from afar, among whom were Mary Magdalene, Mary mother of James the younger and of Joses, and Salome," adding that they had followed him in Galilee and "ministered to him." He adds that there were also: "many other women who had come up with him to Jerusalem" (Mark 15:40-41)

Other followers, wise and otherwise:

John states that many of the Jews believed in Jesus (John 12:11). Many of the rulers secretly believed in him (John 12:42). Luke mentions that even some of the Pharisees warned Jesus that Herod was planning to kill him and urged him to escape (Luke 13:31). Mark relates how Jairus, ruler of the synagogue, became a believer (Mark 5:36). When Jesus entered Jerusalem, it was to the accompanying shouts of "Hosanna" coming from the crowds (Matthew 21:9) that declared: "This is the prophet Jesus from Nazareth of Galilee" (Matthew 21:11). Matthew and Mark respectively inform us that Jesus taught the crowds in the Temple and that his enemies were afraid to arrest him because they feared the multitudes who listened to him enthusiastically (Matthew 21:46; Mark 12:12, 37). When his enemies made their final plans to arrest him, they decided: "Not during the festival, lest there be an uproar among the people" (Matthew 26:5, Mark 14:1-2; see also Luke 22:2).

Was Jesus abandoned by everyone in his last hours?

The Synoptic Gospels maintain that at the crucifixion "many women were there looking on from a distance" who were supporters of Jesus (Matthew 27:55; see also Mark 15:40, Luke 23:49). Luke adds that besides the women "all those acquainted with him were standing at a distance" (Luke 23:49). In addition, "all the multitude who came together for this spectacle, when they observed what had happened, began to return, beating their breasts" (Luke 23:48). John mentions a number of women supporters of Jesus being present at the crucifixion as well as "the disciple whom he loved" (John 19:26). John alleges that after Jesus' death, Nicodemus, a Pharisee and "a ruler of the Jews" (John 3:1), joined Joseph of Arimathea, a rich man, in preparing the body for burial (John 19:39). Joseph was not only a disciple of Jesus (Matthew 27:57, John 19:38), but a counselor (member of the Sanhedrin) who "had not consented to their plan and action" (Luke 23:50-51). Joseph took the bold but dangerous step of asking Pilate for the body. We should not forget Mary Magdalene and the "other women" who it is said came to the tomb (Matthew 28:1, Mark 16:1, Luke 24:10, John 20:1 [Mary alone]), and the alleged multitude who, throughout it all, continued their loyalty to Jesus despite his sentence and crucifixion. As he went to be crucified, "there were following him a great multitude of the people, and of women who were beating themselves and bewailing him" (Luke 23:27). The overall Gospel accounts claim that besides this "multitude" Jesus had a large and loyal following throughout Judea, Galilee and the surrounding territories. This group, it is alleged, consisted of people from among every level of society. These were individuals who did not know of events in Jerusalem and who still looked to Jesus as the Messiah.

Jesus' popularity in review:

Do the Gospel's describe Jesus as a person who "was despised and rejected," or from whom people fled? The words: "He was despised and rejected of men ... and as one from whom men hide their faces ... and we esteemed him not" cannot be applied to Jesus if one is to believe the Gospel narratives.

The Gospels claim that Jesus enjoyed widespread popularity during his lifetime among all classes of society. The evangelists report that the chief priests and the scribes sought to take Jesus "by craft" but, as we have seen, *not during the festival* because they feared a popular demonstration against them if the people learned of Jesus' arrest (Mark 14:1-2). Mark has these plans for the arrest of Jesus take place two days before Passover: "After two days was the Passover and Unleavened Bread" (Mark 14:1). Hence, very shortly before his death, we are told, Jesus' enemies expressed fear of the wrath of the people if they should arrest him. As we have seen, the Gospels claim that even just before the end of his life, Jesus had a significant following among all social classes. According to the Gospel narratives, the Jewish leaders had been cautiously avoiding involvement of the Jewish masses in the scheme to execute Jesus (Matthew 21:46, Mark 14:1-2, Luke 22:2). It is claimed that the Jewish masses were favorably impressed with the "prophet" Jesus (Matthew 21:11, 46; Mark 6:15; Luke 7:16; John 6:14).

According to the Gospels, did the masses turn against Jesus?

The Gospels claim that the Jewish leaders feared that the one prisoner whom the crowd would want Pilate to release during his annual amnesty would be Jesus (Matthew 27:15, Mark 15:6, Luke 23:17, John 18:39). The Gospels maintain that Pilate discounted the seriousness of the charges brought against Jesus because he knew that the Jewish leaders sought his death out of *envy* (Matthew 27:18, Mark 15:10). Therefore, he sought a way to release the *innocent* Jesus rather than the guilty Barabbas (Luke 23:20, John 19:12). Desperate, because of Pilate's maneuver to release Jesus (Matthew 27:22-23; Mark 15:9, 14; Luke 23:20, 22; John 19:4, 12) the Jewish leaders supposedly felt compelled to sway the Jewish crowd against the extremely popular Jesus. The "chief priests and elders" allegedly attempted to persuade not only Pilate (Matthew 27:12-13; Mark 15:1-3; Luke 23:2, 5, 14; John 18:30-31, 19:6-7, 12) but a crowd of their own people that Jesus should be executed (Matthew 27:20, Mark 15:11).

But, now we come to a question that has ramifications throughout the centuries as it was and is used to justify blaming *all* Jews for the death of Jesus. How large a crowd could possibly have gathered outside the judgment hall? Even if we accept that a crowd actually stood there demanding that Pilate execute Jesus (Matthew 27:22; Mark 15:13; Luke 23:21, 23; John 18:39-40), it must have constituted only an extremely small fraction of the people then in Jerusalem. In this alleged incident, the evangelists have distorted developments in order to condemn the entire Jewish people for their rejection of the messianic pretensions of Jesus. Matthew 27:25 neatly packages the slander to incorporate Jews of every generation: "Then answered all the people, and said: 'His blood be on us, and on or children.'"

Contrary to this report of rejection, the major thrust of the Gospels argues for popular support, not only in the country as a whole, but even in those last hours in Jerusalem itself (Luke 23:27). Primarily we see how the Gospel narratives insist on a strong unwavering following for Jesus even as he was being crucified. Yet, they feel compelled to condemn the Jews. If the people who were Jesus' contemporaries saw him in action and yet rejected his assertions why should those who were not there accept him? Thus there is a tension in the Gospels between claiming on the one hand that he was greatly admired and followed and on the other that he was rejected.

Christian theological needs

The argument that Jesus died without any significant following is an argument necessitated by the theological need to have Jesus' life conform to the Christian concept of the suffering servant. But the Gospels argue that Jesus had a significant following among the well-born as well as among the common people even at the time of his crucifixion. This faithful following, we are told, was not composed of ignorant masses following a mere miracle-working prophet. The Gospels allege that the masses adhered to a messianic belief that Jesus, who was believed to be the son of David (Matthew 9:27), was not only the prophet promised in Deuteronomy 18:15 (John 7:40), but was in fact, the very Messiah himself (John 7:41). Even though there was a division among the crowd over who Jesus was (John 7:43), and many of his disciples left him (John 6:66), the assumption to be drawn from the Gospels' silence is that thousands of people throughout the country still believed in him as the Messiah at the time of the crucifixion.

It should be noted that according to the Gospel narratives, the general Jewish populace did *not* have occasion to directly reject Jesus' messianic assertions since he had *not* openly claimed to be the Messiah (Matthew 16:20, Mark 8:29-30, Luke 9:20-21). To whatever reason one may attribute the description of Jesus' large following, the fact still remains that the Gospels insist the members of the various classes of society did not generally reject him. On all accounts, there is little resemblance between the life of Jesus as portrayed in the Gospels and the life of the servant as depicted by Isaiah 53. There is only one logical conclusion to be drawn and that is that Jesus is not the servant portrayed by Isaiah.

5:4: "Surely our diseases he did bear, and our pains he carried; but we considered him stricken, smitten of God, and afflicted."

The servant as a vehicle for bearing "our" diseases and pains.

Did Jesus heal the sick and infirm? Matthew makes use of Isaiah 53:4. He writes: "This was to fulfill what was spoken by the prophet Isaiah, 'He took our sicknesses and carried our diseases'" (Matthew 8:17).

The context shows that Matthew understands this verse literally to mean "he took away sickness," and thus he sees Jesus' supposed miracles as fulfilling prophecy concerning healing the infirm rather than as a reference to his allegedly removing sin by dying on the cross. However, whether literally or figuratively Jesus never bore the "diseases" or "pains," that is, the humiliation and adversity of Israel or, for that matter, of any other people.

Faith healing and miraculous cures are not impossible. However, they are attributed to Jesus not because they happened but rather because pre-Gospel Christian tradition expected them to happen. Certain illnesses may be relieved or even disappear because of the deep trust the infirm place on the "faith healer," but that does not necessarily mean the "healer" is working under a divine mandate. In the case of Jesus, it may be that he brought about some faith-healing "cures" but these were magnified and replicated more in story than in reality.

Nagua'

The servant is considered as one "stricken," (*nagua'*). *Nagua'* is used in the Jewish Scriptures in connection with being stricken with what is called "leprosy" (*nega' tzara'at*, "the plague of leprosy" Leviticus 13:9).

Jesus was not stricken physically with leprosy or anything resembling it, so Christians cannot claim that he literally fulfilled this verse. Even metaphorically, nagua' cannot be applied to Jesus who was not shunned as a loathsome pariah. The application to Jesus of nagua', that is, stricken metaphorically in the manner of one who has leprosy and treated as a leper by fellow human beings, is unwarranted. The respectively supportive, indifferent, or hostile audiences Jesus confronts in the Gospels show a variety of responses to his message, but none can be compared to nagua'; not even in the description of his last few hours of life.

53:5: "But he [Israel] was wounded as a result of our [the nations of the world] transgressions, he was crushed as a result of our iniquities."

Christian renderings of the Hebrew text attempt to convey the message that the servant vicariously took upon himself the sins of the people, and this caused him, and not them, to suffer the consequences. This conclusion is arrived at by a distortion of the text. That is, they claim the servant took on the iniquities of others and thereby, allowed their sins to be expiated through his suffering. This is a distortion of the meaning of the text that attempts to evade the real reason Jesus was executed. A correct rendering of the text reveals that the nations of the world come to the realization that the servant's suffering stemmed from *their* actions and sinfulness toward him. (The singular used here for a plural collective community.) The realization here is that the servant's pain is not because of his own sins. He (Israel) bears the pain inflicted on him by others. This verse reflects the nations' realization that the servant (Israel as a corporate entity) suffered the consequences of their (the nations') own persecution imposed in order to hide their own iniquities.

Why was Jesus arrested and executed?

Jesus was an apocalyptic revolutionary. His insurrectionist activities brought upon him Roman condemnation and execution. Jesus probably expected divine intervention with God sending His angels to annihilate the Roman's. His execution by a method reserved for rebels is evidence that the Romans considered him a seditionist. Certainly, a movement with a messianic intimation and inherent kingship connotations raised concern among Roman officials entrusted with the maintenance of the *Pax Roma* (Roman Peace). John's Jesus acknowledging that he considered himself a king (John 18:37) was an admission of guilt of a serious offense under Roman law. Under Roman law only the emperor could appoint a king.

The Gospels' Jesus did not suffer because of the iniquity of others, but because he challenged Roman sovereignty over Judea. Pressing his messianic pretensions was, to the Roman administration of the country, a challenge to Roman rule. It was common knowledge, of which Pontius Pilate was certainly well aware, that anyone who claimed to be the Messiah must also claim to be king of the Jews. The Gospels' Jesus challenged Roman rule by the way he is said to have entered into Jerusalem (Matthew 21:7-11, Mark 11:7-11, Luke 19:35-39, John 12:12-13). Jesus' manner of entry into Jerusalem and the accompanying acclaim the Gospels say he received from the people was seen as the commission of an act of treason against the emperor. This assured his arrest and crucifixion. From the moment Jesus was hailed as the son of David he was a marked man. The seizure of the Temple courtyard was also by its nature a subversive act against Rome (Matthew 21:12, Mark 11:15-16, Luke 19:45, John 2:14-15). The Romans could not see Jesus' offense as solely against the Jewish priesthood. They would understand it as directed against their control over the symbol of Jewish nationhood, the Temple. Pilate had no alternative but to treat Jesus as a political threat. Despite the evangelical attempt to exonerate Pilate (Matthew 27:24; Mark 15:14; Luke 23:4; John 18:38, 19:4) by blaming the Jews (John 19:11) and thereby Rome from responsibility for the crucifixion, it must be remembered that this method of execution was reserved for political crimes *against* Rome. Blaming the Jewish people and their leaders for Jesus' death was the early church's response to widespread Jewish refusal to accept the false claims made on behalf of Jesus. Jesus was executed for his own challenge to the Roman Empire. He imagined himself to be the Messiah, the king of the Jews, and died for that mistake. Jesus' death was *not* a vicarious sacrifice for the benefit of mankind in general or for the Jewish people in particular. Jesus' death was the result of his *own* failure to recognize his limitations. One of the limitations Jesus had was that he did not qualify to be the servant.

53:5: **"The chastisement of our [the nations] welfare was upon him [Israel], and with his wounds we were healed."**

The scourging mystery

"[W]ith his wounds we were healed." Christians claim this refers to Jesus receiving "stripes," that is, being scourged prior to his crucifixion. But, was Jesus scourged prior to his crucifixion? And, if he were scourged, how did this "heal" anyone?

It is commonly assumed that Jesus underwent great suffering and blood loss as a result of being scourged by the Romans prior to his crucifixion. This sentiment is based on an erroneous understanding of the Gospels. According to Matthew, Mark and John, Jesus was scourged prior to his crucifixion. Matthew and Mark relate that at the end of the trial Pontius Pilate, the Roman governor, "scourged and delivered him [Jesus] to be crucified" (Mark 15:15, Matthew 27:26). That is, Pilate scourged him after sentencing. John writes that Pilate scourged Jesus in the course of the trial (John 19:1), before he brought him out to face "the Jews" once more (John 19:4-5).

Some Christians have tried to harmonize the different Gospel versions by claiming there was a double scourging. But Luke has a completely different development of the scourging narrative. The scourging in Luke's version of Passion events presents a problem in that Jesus does not undergo scourging at any time prior to or after his arrival at the execution site. Luke alludes to scourging but there it is offered as an alternative punishment to crucifixion. It would be a beating that would be the full penalty; that is, more like a warning than a sentence. According to Luke, Pilate said: "I will punish him and release him" (Luke 23:16) and "I have found nothing deserving of death in him; I will therefore punish him and release him" (Luke 23:22). In the end, Luke's Jesus never undergoes scourging, although he allegedly predicts his own scourging: "For he will be delivered up to the Gentiles, and will be mocked and mistreated and spit upon, and after *they have scourged him*, they will kill him; and the third day he will rise again" (Luke 18:32-33). Scourging appears to have been a customary preliminary administered to those about to be crucified. The condemned, usually stripped naked, was beaten and mocked all the way to the execution site. In addition, he was bound or nailed to the crossbeam (*patibulum*) either before starting on his way or on arrival at the place of execution. He was required to carry or drag the crossbeam all the way to the execution site. Such procedures were apparently not followed when the Gospels' Jesus was led to his death. After the Roman soldiers abused and mocked him (Matthew 27:30, Mark 15:19) they "put his own clothes on him" (Mark 15:20, see also Matthew 27:31) and the Synoptic Gospels maintain that he did not carry the crossbeam for most of the distance (Matthew 27:32, Mark 15:21, Luke 23:26).

The crossbeam mystery

According to the Synoptic Gospels, Jesus was unable to carry the crossbeam the entire distance to the execution site and the Roman soldiers pressed one Simon of Cyrene into service to carry it the rest of the way (Matthew 27:32, Mark 15:21, Luke 23:26). Why was Jesus unable to carry the crossbeam the full distance? It has been suggested that Jesus had become so physically weak from the scourging that he simply could not continue under the weight of the crossbeam. The soldiers, it is presumed, pressed Simon into service to prevent Jesus from collapsing of exhaustion before they could execute him. The theory seems to gain support from the short time that it took for Jesus to die once he was crucified (Mark 15:44, John 19:33). How weak could Luke's Jesus have been when, relieved of the burden of the crossbeam, he is said to have turned to the "daughters of Jerusalem" and to have spoken to them at some length (Luke 23:28-31). But, of course, this is in the Gospel of Luke where Jesus never undergoes scourging!

The Johannine mystery

According to John's version of the story, Jesus carried his own crossbeam the entire distance. Some Christians maintain that Simon is not mentioned in John because in Johannine christology there is no room for Jesus needing or accepting help from human beings. This is tantamount to saying Johannine christology is derived by rejecting any fact that would deny the making of the Johannine christological myth.

The rest of the story

John's claim that Jesus was "scourged" during the trial before Pilate (John 19:1) leaves open the extent of injury incurred by Jesus at the hands of the Romans. Generally, the normal Roman thoroughness,

121

when it came to torture, would have left no doubts of torture being inflicted. Jesus would have bled profusely and would have had great difficulty standing on his feet. Yet, Jesus is portrayed as confronting Pilate without any kind of impairment due to pain or discomfort being hinted at in the text (John 19:11). It must be assumed that if Jesus was scourged before sentencing, as reported (Matthew 27:26, Mark 15:15, John 19:1) he was not tortured as severely as was the normal Roman practice. Furthermore, the Gospels make no mention of any scourging taking place at the site of the crucifixion. According to the Gospels, Jesus did not undergo the scourging and suffering that is normally associated with crucifixion and may not have been scourged at all.

Christian attempts to explain away the absence of any mention of the effects of scourging on Jesus are in the nature of afterthoughts to clarify an inexplicable omission. Knowing the New Testament propensity to describe a persecuted Jesus, it stands to reason that the evangelists would be anxious to describe a scourged Jesus. Surely, the evangelists would not leave it up to their readers to take for granted that horrible physical torture had been inflicted upon Jesus. If Jesus was bloodied or injured as a result of scourging, the Gospels would surely have recorded it. That this was not done leads us to the assumption that his alleged trial and sentencing left him unscathed with his outward appearance unchanged—even his clothing remained unbloodied by the encounter. One would have to assume that, at worst his was a superficial symbolic scourging that left no outward marks. There are simply no accounts of a scourged-ravaged Jesus.

The Gospels themselves furnish proof that this was the case. Normally, the condemned would be bound or nailed to the crossbeam of the cross. In some cases, he dragged it. As the condemned made his way to the execution site he was continuously whipped. But not Jesus!

Moreover, Jesus was *not* led naked through the streets. The usual Roman procedure was to have the condemned led naked to the place of execution and being scourged as he went. Matthew (his information derived from Mark) and Mark claim Jesus was scourged; nevertheless, they have Jesus dressed again before he is taken to the crucifixion site.

Jesus is finally deprived of his clothing only at the place of execution (Matthew 27:35, Mark 15:24, Luke 23:34, John 19:24). Perhaps, on account of Jewish sensibilities concerning public display of nudity, the Romans made a concession on this point, in Judea. The Gospel narratives maintain that Jesus was given his own clothing to wear when he was led to the place of execution. They claim the Roman soldiers "put his own outer garments on him" before he was led to the place of execution (Matthew 27:31, Mark 15:20). This unequivocally shows that Jesus was *not* naked as he walked to the execution site, but was dressed in his own clothes. Confirmation that Jesus' scourging was superficial (if it happened at all) is found in this claim that he was given his own clothes to wear to the execution. Apparently there was no adhesion of his garments to bleeding wounds. On arrival at the execution site the clothes he wore, both his outer garments and his inner garment, were not bloodstained and torn by the whiplash of the blows struck as the condemned marched to his execution. If his clothes were blood-soaked and torn they would have been of no substantial value to the soldiers. The author of John writes:

> The soldiers therefore, when they had crucified Jesus, took his outer garments [*himatia*] and made four parts, a part to every soldier and also the inner garment [*khitona*]; now the inner garment was seamless, woven in one piece. They said therefore to one another, "Let us not tear it, but cast lots for it, to decide whose it shall be;" that the Scripture might be fulfilled, "They divided my outer garments among them, and for my clothing they cast lots." (John 19:23-24; see also Matthew 27:35, Mark 15:24, Luke 23:34)

If Jesus wore clothing on a scourged ripped-raw body, the clothing removed from him would be shredded and soaked in blood. For what purpose, except to *fulfill* Psalms 22:19, would the soldiers divide up such bloodied and totally torn clothing? The presumption must be that the clothing he wore to the execution site was in good, usable condition. It follows that Jesus' physical condition was not greatly altered by what the evangelists call a "scourging." Conversely, the tale of the *parting of the garments* could be a fabrication. It could be that there was neither a *scourging* nor a *parting of the garments*.

Victims of crucifixion were attached to the crossbeam by being

123

tied or nailed, and then the crossbeam was raised, with the body affixed to it. The crossbeam was then inserted into a slot cut into the vertical beam (*starous*) permanently set in the ground. There are *no* Gospel descriptions of the crucifixion that mention whether Jesus was tied or nailed to the cross. Information that Jesus was nailed to the cross is culled by some from alleged post-resurrection episodes. But, the claim that Jesus was nailed to the cross is *never* explicitly stated in the Synoptic Gospels. In Luke 24:39 the allegedly risen Jesus is made to say, "See my hands and my feet," which can imply the imprint of nails or of rope burns. This verse is the only New Testament passage concerning the crucifixion to mention Jesus' feet. John 20:25, 27 explicitly mention imprints of nails being present in Jesus' hands. The presence of "the risen Jesus" in this scene illustrates the fictive mythological aspects of this episode. The question is, on the one hand, to what extent does it reflect an historic description of the means by which Jesus was attached to the cross and, on the other hand, to what extent does it reflect the early church's mythmaking use of the Septuagint's version of Psalms 22:17, which says: "They have dug [into] my hands and my feet"?

As mentioned above, the Synoptic Gospels say that Jesus did not carry the crossbeam for most of the way to the execution site. They maintain that following Jesus' sentencing: "[A]s they came out [of the governor's palace], they found a man of Cyrene, Simon by name: him they compelled to bear his cross" (Matthew 27:32; see also Mark 15:21 and Luke 23:26). This would show that Jesus' hands were neither bound nor nailed to the crossbeam since it was easily transferred to Simon of Cyrene. Only John insists that Jesus bore his cross by himself (John 19:17).

Not by blood loss

Presuming Jesus was nailed to the cross, did blood oozing from the nail wounds cause his death? The Roman method of execution by crucifixion was designed as a punishment to be prolonged in order to serve as a lesson to both the victim and all onlookers. Since no vital organ would be pierced crucifixion usually caused a slow death. If the victim expired within a short time he would deprive his executioners of satisfactorily meting out the sentence in accordance with their concept of justice. Moreover, with a quick execution the purpose of the terror induced by the threat of crucifixion would be somewhat lost on society. Having the victim languish in agony for a number of days was a part of the crucifixion process. Any means of heightening the tortured victims pain, which would cause undo shortening of the period spent on the cross would be self-defeating and, as such, avoided. Therefore, while nailing the victim to the cross, as opposed to the option of tying, was part of the punishment thought to have been used on Jesus, it did not, in itself, necessarily cause a shortening of the time spent on the cross before death occurred. In crucifying a victim, the Romans would simply not use methods of torture which shortened the time of suffering. Nailing was used because it added suffering, but it was still possible for a person to live for days nailed to the cross. Indeed, if nailing the victim to the cross made for a quick death through loss of blood Pilate would not have expressed surprise that Jesus had already died and would not have sought verification of this from the centurion (Mark 15:44). The amount of blood oozing from such wounds did not cause the victim to bleed to death. Oozing blood would be minimal prior to death because the arms were in an elevated position the blood pressure was very low and the large nails would have sealed the wounds. Surely, if there had been any significant blood loss the early Christians would have noted it and the evangelists would have enthusiastically introduced it into their narratives. Jesus' blood was not shed during the process of death by crucifixion to the extent that it was the cause of death. It should be noted that none of the possible physical points of blood loss described in the Gospels conforms to that required in the actual shedding of blood sacrificial process found in the Jewish Scriptures.

Did a Roman soldier shed Jesus' blood?

John claims that "one of the soldiers pierced his [Jesus'] side with a spear, and immediately there came out blood and water" (John 19:34). According to this Gospel, the Roman soldiers did not break Jesus' legs because he was *already* dead. Chronologically, John 19:33 establishes the time of the inflicting of the wound in Jesus' side (John 19:34) as subsequent to his death. John's sequence of events is contradicted in some manuscript versions of Matthew 27:49, which state: "And another man took a spear and pierced his side, and blood and water came out." This addition to the verse places the time of the inflicting of the wound as prior to Jesus' death. However, verse 49 is an interpolation unsupported by many ancient New Testament manuscripts. While this verse addition appears in the Codex Sinaiticus, in the Vatican Manuscript 1209 and in the Codex Ephraemi rescriptus it is omitted in Codex Alexandrinus and Bezae Codices, as well as in some other important manuscripts. Its insertion into the text of Matthew reflects an awareness of John 19:32-34.

While John writes that Jesus was already dead when the soldier pierced his side with a spear and blood and water began to come out of the wound, the interpolated account in Matthew has him speared prior to death. This contradicts John's sequence. Since all the manuscripts contain John 19:32-34, as presently constituted, but are not unanimous on the presence of Matthew's addition, this addition is generally thought to be a later interpolation and is discounted. Therefore, the interpolation in Matthew is not acceptable evidence that Jesus was alive while being pierced with the spear and that he died from the subsequent loss of blood resulting from that stab wound.

An incident of a soldier piercing the side of an already deceased victim does not constitute biblical blood atonement sacrifice. Blood oozing from a wound inflicted after death does *not* qualify as the shedding of blood required of an atonement offering. Biblically, in a blood atonement offering the animal *must* actually die as a result of blood loss by a properly inflicted wound. But, the piercing of Jesus' body by a spear did *not* cause his death, nor was it the proper means of slaughter. Jesus did *not* die as a result of blood loss (Matthew 27:46-50, Mark 15:34-37, Luke 23:46, John 19:28-30). Jesus' blood was *not* sacrificially shed by a Roman soldier's spear thrust into his side.

Did Jesus fulfill the Torah's requirements for blood sacrifice (Matthew 5:17-18)?

Under no circumstances can one say that Jesus shed his blood as a sin-offering as would be necessary under the conditions set by New Testament doctrine itself. It is not true that "Christ died for sins, once for all ... so that he might bring you to God" (1 Peter 3:18). Jesus did not die as a result of blood loss from any wounds. There was *no* shedding of blood, hence, *no sacrifice!* Some Christians maintain that

Jesus died of a broken heart for the sins of mankind. This position is an error unsupported by medical research or Christian theology.

Where is the Christian's blood atonement for sin?

Hebrews 9:22 states that without the shedding of blood there is no forgiveness of sins. It does not say: "Without a broken heart, there is no forgiveness of sins." If Jesus died in any way other than by the shedding of blood, he could not be the savior that is preached in Christian doctrine (Acts 13:38-39, 2 Corinthians 5:21). Accordingly, the sins of those who believe in Jesus as their atonement for sin remain unforgiven. What the New Testament claims is that it is not just any pre-crucifixion suffering by Jesus that brings "healing," (atonement). His "wounds" did not bring atonement; it was his death that supposedly achieved this end. What is alleged to bring atonement is not the spilling of blood through blood sweating or scourging but rather the shedding of Jesus' blood in death as an atonement sacrifice for sin. Therefore, "with his wounds we were healed" cannot be a reference to Jesus healing anyone (that is, bringing atonement) at any point in his life.

What does "with his wounds we were healed" have to do with Jesus? Did he take upon himself the punishment that was due "us"? The author of 1 Peter gets it all wrong when he writes: "and he himself bore our sins in his body on the cross, that we might die to sins and live to righteousness; for by his wounds you were healed" (1 Peter 2:24).

What event supposedly "healed"? Was it the scourging of Jesus or blood loss bringing on death? It is said that Jesus underwent a scourging as part of the preparation for crucifixion, but was anyone "healed" by his "wounds"? Isn't it the Christian claim that Jesus' death was a blood atonement sacrifice for mankind's sins? Paul assures Christians: "In him [Jesus] we have redemption through his blood, the forgiveness of sins" (Ephesians 1:7). Any suffering Jesus underwent prior to that moment of death does not come into consideration as a New Testament blood atonement sacrifice. Not only is scourging not in the category of a blood sacrifice but, in the case of Jesus, it would have been administered prior to the actual crucifixion and the death that ensued. According to Paul, it is "redemption through his blood"

127

that Jesus brought atonement. Then, for a Christian there is nothing else that brings or effects atonement, only Jesus' blood. There is no reliance in Christianity on Jesus' alleged miracles, teachings or suffering prior to death for obtaining atonement, only his blood. According to this christology, if nothing effects atonement but Jesus' blood shed in death (which clearly never happened), then, as stated above, that means that *not* even the suffering allegedly undergone by Jesus prior to the crucifixion counts toward anything. Therefore, linking "with his wounds we are healed" to Jesus wearing a crown of thorns, or being scourged, or nailed to a cross, has no relevance in an attempt to link Jesus to the description of the ordeal undergone by the servant. For Christians, "wounds" *do not* heal sins only the blood of Jesus. The trouble with this belief, however, is that Jesus' blood was *never* shed.

Christians translate the meaning of "stripes" in order to allude to Jesus allegedly being whipped prior to his execution. The translation of "stripes" actually encompasses a wide range of physical abuse. "His wounds," "his bruises," rendered as "his stripes," reflects the wide ranging cumulative results of centuries of beatings with fists, clubs, and whips suffered by the servant at the hands of his tormentors. Thus, it represents the very condition of exile itself and the suffering Israel must endure to achieve the spiritual and national regeneration needed to fulfill its role in God's plan. Israel is often spoken of as "bruised" and "wounded" due to suffering at the hands of the nations, both those ordained by God and those representing the free will excesses of the nations (Jeremiah 30:12-17).

53:6: "the Lord has visited upon him the iniquity of us all"

The pre-Gospel church and its developing christology

The pre-Gospel church developed its christology by utilizing biblical passages. The phrase "the Lord has visited upon him the iniquity of us all" found in Isaiah 53:6 was a significant source for the christological belief that Jesus died for the sins of the world. This unverifiable contention is belied by Jesus' non-fulfillment of the sum total of Isaiah 53's prophecy. The New Testament teaches that an innocent sinless Jesus literally took upon himself someone else's guilt!

The Jewish Scriptures teach something entirely different.

Only the blood of the sinner will suffice, where blood of the innocent has been shed: "[T]he land cannot be cleansed of the blood that is shed therein, but by the blood of him that shed it" (Numbers 35:33). Only the blood of the actual murderer (i.e., the sinner) can expiate the crime. The scriptural teaching has far wider application for "No man can by any means redeem his brother, or give to God a ransom for him" (Psalms 49:8). Each individual must personally atone for his sins; his sins cannot be literally transferred to another human being. The biblical doctrine is that God does not want innocent human blood to be shed. One person cannot transfer his guilt to another.

The New Testament doctrine that Jesus' blood was shed as atonement for sinners is totally inconsistent with the teachings of the Torah. The New Testament idea of a sinless human sacrifice totally contradicts the biblical concept against the shedding of the innocent blood of a human being. Those who claim Jesus was also part of the Godhead have to explain how any part (in any form) of the everlasting eternal God of Israel could die even for a moment. The blood of Jesus, it is said, had to do with the principles typified by those sacrifices. But who says so? This notion is not found in the Jewish Scriptures; it is the author of Hebrews who makes this non-biblical claim. But, even he attempts to show as much literal fulfillment as his imagination can cull from the commandments governing sacrifices. Consequently, he says: "For the bodies of those animals whose blood is brought into the holy place by the high priest [as an offering] for sin, are burned outside the camp. Therefore Jesus also, that he might sanctify the people through his own blood, suffered outside the gate" (Hebrews 13:11-12). Notice that in the biblical system the blood of the animal sacrificed was offered *within* the Sanctuary and the body burned outside the camp (Exodus 29:14; Leviticus 4:12, 21, 16:27). Where is the coherent actual or typological comparison with Jesus who is said to have suffered and sanctified the people with his blood "outside the gate" and whose body was not burned?

Throughout the New Testament, whatever its authors think they can claim as literal fulfillment of prophecy is seized upon (e.g., John 19:24, 33-37). The rest is relegated to the category of Jesus

129

figuratively fulfilling the image and purpose of the biblical system. They speak of the Torah's commandments as being a "shadow of what is to come" (Colossians 2:17) and emphasize Jesus receiving a "more excellent ministry ... a better covenant ... enacted on better promises" (Hebrews 8:6). The only way the early Christians could keep their group alive after Jesus' failure was to hide behind the unverifiable claim that he figuratively fulfilled with his blood the "image and purpose" of blood sacrifices and that this act pointed to something greater than animal sacrifice? The Christian claim has no basis in the word of God and their use of verse 6 does not bring Jesus any closer to being the servant spoken of.

Isaiah 53:7: "as a sheep that before her shearers is dumb; and opened not his mouth"

The silence that was a bit too loud

Was Jesus humble and silent when he stood before the Jewish officials and then Pilate? In these encounters, Jesus did not show the humility and silence with which Isaiah describes the servant in verse 7.

Before the Jewish officials:

The alleged encounter between the high priest, the elders, and Jesus is one of vigorous verbal exchange. The Synoptic Gospels claim, Jesus acknowledged before the Sanhedrin his claim that he was the Messiah. When the high priest asks him whether he is the Messiah he answers in the affirmative. Jesus declares: "I am, and you will see the Son of Man sitting on the right hand of power, and coming in the clouds of heaven" (Mark 14:62; see also Matthew 26:63-64, Luke 22:69-70). Matthew and Luke have Jesus answer the high priest in the affirmative, with a statement similar to that which John uses for Jesus' answer to Pilate: "you say that I am" (Mark 15:2, Luke 23:3). This is not silence!

Jesus was not silent before Pilate:

Jesus did not show humility and silence during his trial before Pilate. John claims that Jesus even taunted Pilate. When Pilate said: "Do you not know that I have authority to release you, and I have authority to crucify you?" Jesus defiantly answered: "You would have no authority over me, unless it had been given you from above" (John 19:10-11). John's Jesus is depicted as skillfully defending himself. He pleads shrewdly that his messianic teaching was a nonviolent, "not of this world" movement, one which the Romans need not fear. At no time does he humble himself, but, on the contrary, presents a clever verbal defense before Pilate (the one man who could condemn him to death). Jesus claimed that his kingdom was not of this world, giving the impression that it would not be in conflict with the Empire. He wanted to convince Pilate that he was not the leader of a seditious movement and that his intentions were peaceful. Contrary to what many Christians would have us believe, the Gospels say that Jesus presented a strong defense before the Jewish officials and Pilate. He was *not* "dumb" before his accusers, Jewish or Gentile, and it cannot be said of him that "he humbled himself and did not open his mouth." Jesus declared himself to be a king. John's Jesus with no sense of humility opens his mouth and declares to Pilate: "You say that I am a king. For this I have been born, and for this I have come into the world, to bear witness to the truth. Everyone who is of the truth hears my voice" (John 18:37).

It is farfetched to believe that after Jesus declares he is a king that Pilate went out to the Jews and said: "Behold, I am bringing him out to you, that you may know that I find no guilt in him" (John 19:4). Jesus' alleged regal reception upon his arrival in Jerusalem by an enthusiastic crowd could not have gone unnoticed by Pilate (Matthew 21:8-11). Declaring oneself to be a king without being appointed or recognized as such by the emperor could only be interpreted by Pilate as a seditious act and a capital offense the punishment of which was within his exclusive jurisdiction.

The futility of identifying Jesus with the sheep metaphor

There is no literal or typological parallelism between Jesus and "as a sheep that before her shearers is dumb; and opened not his mouth." A sheep led to its slaughter is oblivious to its fate. Ignorance is why the animal is silent. Jesus was *not* silent. He was supposedly *not* ignorant of his role or fate and he was *not* led unresisting and oblivious to his death. Jesus complained of his innocence during his alleged interrogation by the high priests who are said to have ordered his arrest (John 18:19-20) — and, in so doing, he made false statements denying he taught in secrecy. Jesus argued with Pilate during their encounter and protested his innocence (John 18:33-38, 19:10-11). He is also said to have complained to God concerning his impending fate. Although Jesus supposedly ultimately agreed to comply with the will of God, in the Garden of Gethsemane he first asked that God not have him die (Matthew 26:39, Luke 22:42). It is also said that Jesus cried out in sorrowful disappointment when he was hanging on the cross, asking why God abandoned him (Matthew 27:46). This raises *a crucial question*: Did Jesus not know his death was essential for mankind's salvation?

• *The crucial answer*: Jesus' actions show he never heard of that later Christian claim. He did not expect to die and all supposed self-predictions to the contrary are later additions to the narrative.

• *The crucial conclusion*: On examination of the claims made on behalf of Jesus, when they are compared to what the passage says of the servant they are found to be seriously lacking any sort of fulfillment. Jesus is simply not the servant.

53:8: "As a result of the transgression of my people [the nations] he [Israel] has been afflicted."

The literal rendering of this verse is: "From the transgression of my people the stroke [*nega*] to them." That is, because of the transgressions of the Gentiles the servant (Israel) suffered. The speaker is the Gentile spokesman.

As regards the word *lamo*, "to them," grammarians recognize that it is also in a sense singular, "to him" (as it is in *non-poetic usage*), because it agrees with certain singular nouns. As in this verse, *lamo*, *the poetic form* of *lahem* ("to them"), is used often in referring to a collective noun. Examples are, Genesis 9:26 (where it refers to Shem, that is, the descendants of Shem); Psalms 28:8 where it refers to the people of verse 9; Psalms 73:10 (also in reference to "people"); Isaiah 44:15 (in reference to *'el* [a god] and *pesel* [a carved image], which are also to be understood respectively as referring collectively to all false gods); and finally Isaiah 53:8.

The translator of the Hebrew, into the Greek Septuagint,

understood the proper use of *lamo* when rendering Isaiah 44:15: "That it might be for men to burn: and having taken part of it he warms himself; and they burn part of it; and bake loaves thereon; and the rest they make for themselves gods, and they worship them."

Lamo is generally rendered "to him" as it refers to the collective noun, *servant*, that is, the Jewish people, not a single individual. In such an instance, *lamo* can be translated in the singular. Although it must always be understood to be in the plural in relation to what numerically constitutes the entity that is given the appellative *servant*. The plural nature of the poetic form *lamo* is supported by the manner in which it is used in the Jewish Scriptures. Isaiah uses *lamo* eleven times: 16:4, 23:1, 26:14, 26:16, 30:5, 35:8, 43:8, 44:7, 44:15, 48:21 and 53:8. This poetic usage especially works well in verse 8. Although the subject of chapter 53 is given throughout in the singular, the change to the plural form in verse 8 is fully accounted for when the servant of God is considered to stand collectively for the people of Israel. That the plural *lamo* in verse 8 refers to the servant as a collective noun *excludes* any possibility that it pertains to an individual. Therefore, it cannot refer to Jesus.

53:9: "his grave was set with the wicked"

The burial of Jesus

How was Jesus' grave "set with the wicked"?

Some Christians connect "wicked" with the two *lestai* ("thieves," "brigands") executed alongside Jesus (Matthew 27:38, Mark 15:27; "others," in John 19:18). Other Christians connect the *lestai* with, "a company of evil-doers have enclosed me" (Psalms 22:17 [verse 16 in some versions]). But, crucifixion was not the punishment for common criminals. *Lestai* was a derogatory Roman term for insurrectionists, who, by armed action opposed Roman rule. These two men were more likely put to death for opposing Roman rule of the land of Israel and not for being "wicked." In any case, the Gospels say, Jesus was *not* buried with them. The point is made by Christians that he was buried in a new empty tomb. As such, he was buried *alone* and there is nothing in the New Testament narrative to illustrate how "his [Jesus'] grave was set with the wicked" in fulfillment of this statement.

53:9: "and his grave was set ... with the rich in his deaths"

The burial companions: first the wicked now the rich.

How was Jesus' grave "set ... with the rich in his deaths"?

Christians identify Jesus as the subject of "with the rich in his deaths" to be in conformity with the Gospel of Matthew. It is only in Matthew's narrative that Joseph of Arimathea is identified as a "rich man" (Matthew 27:57) who laid the corpse of Jesus "in his own new tomb" (Matthew 27:60). In Mark he is described simply as "a prominent member of the Council" (Mark 15:43). Luke describes him as "a member of the Council, a good and righteous man" (Luke 23:50). In John he is "a disciple of Jesus, but a secret one" (John 19:38). It is not by chance that Matthew 27:57 specifically identifies Joseph as "a rich man from Arimathea." Given Matthew's propensity for adding biblical allusion to his narrative it is no wonder that he alone adds that Joseph was rich and that he placed Jesus' corpse in his own tomb thereby supposedly fulfilling: "And his grave was set . . . with the rich."

Grave refers to the lands of exile; *rich* refers to the powerful men and institutions of the nations among whom the personified people of Israel are exiled; *deaths* is descriptive of the horrendous violent suffering of exile. The phrase "in his deaths" signifies that the servant experienced literally and figuratively multiple "deaths" in exile.

The character of Joseph of Arimathea was introduced into Matthew's Gospel narrative as a rich man in order to show a fulfillment of Isaiah 53:9, which says that God's servant will be buried "with the rich." This is but one more example of Matthew attempting to introduce supposed biblical "fulfillment of prophecy" into his narrative. The material peculiar to Matthew is a creation of its author's own imagination. It should be emphasized that despite the claim that Jesus was buried in a rich man's tomb he was not buried "with the rich." The Gospels make a point of stating that Jesus alone was buried in the tomb (Luke 23:53, John 19:41). Thus, if Jesus was buried in the new tomb of Joseph then he was buried with neither the wicked nor rich, but alone. Not only was Jesus not buried with the wicked and the rich he was also not the servant.

53:9: "although he had done no violence"

The violent side of Jesus

The Gospels record a number of instances where Jesus *did* commit acts of violence.

- Whip in hand, causing a fracas, he attacked the merchants in the Temple area (Matthew 21:12, Mark 11:15-16, Luke 19:45, John 2:15).

- He destroyed a fig tree for not having fruit out of season (Matthew 21:18-21, Mark 11:13-14).

- He caused the death, by drowning, of a herd of swine by allowing demons to purposely enter their bodies (Matthew 8:32, Mark 5:13, Luke 8:33).

Were Jesus' actions justified?

Biblically, it would not matter if Jesus actions were justified. The question is, "Did this individual literally perform violent acts?"

All New Testament applications of Isaiah 53 to Jesus presume a literal fulfillment. A literal application to Jesus of the phrase "he had done no violence" is not possible. The Gospels inadvertently indicate that forms of violence were perpetrated by Jesus. By the very fact that an *individual* committed violent acts, even if they can be justified, he does *not* qualify as one having done no violence. These are acts of violence under any circumstance and if applied literally to an individual that person could *not* be the fulfillment of verse 9. Jesus' acts of violence demonstrate that he did *not* literally fulfill this description of the servant as prescribed by the New Testament citations of Isaiah 53. On the other hand, Israel as a corporate entity has, in the overall course of its history, sought to avoid violence

Christians provide novel reasons for Jesus' destructive actions, but they still remain acts of violence. All the excuses cannot hide the fact that these violent acts disqualify Jesus from being the servant. One cannot excuse his actions as those of a supernatural being, who allegedly had the authority to do as he pleased. Do what he will, Jesus would still be disqualified from being the servant.

Jesus and his philosophy of violence

Jesus was not adverse to using violence and held no general principle against violent action. If Jesus was truly non-violent he could not have uttered his call to family strife and divisiveness. He proudly avowed that his is a mission which will cause discord and disturb the universal peace and bring war to the world (Matthew 10:34-35, Luke 12:49-53). Jesus called for his opponents to be brought before him for summary execution. He declared: "But these enemies of mine who did not want me to reign over them, bring them here, and slay them in my presence" (Luke 19:27). The use of violence is not always an act of evil. But, in exploring the teachings of Jesus, we are not just dealing with his physical violence, but also with a philosophy of violence.

When one is a teacher, especially when one is considered an authoritative teacher to his followers who's every word has power to transform into actions how one acts is as important as what one teaches. And if you teach and do violent actions—you are violent!

Words of forgiveness or hypocrisy

Could Jesus have preached violence or hated anyone when he spoke words of forgiveness and non-resistance to wickedness? Did he not say: "Love your enemies" (Matthew 5:44, Luke 6:27), "Do not resist him that is wicked; but whoever slaps you on your right cheek, turn to him the other also" (Matthew 5:39) and, alternately: "To him that strikes you on the cheek, offer the other also" (Luke 6:29)? These verses are taken as representative of the extraordinary forgiveness supposedly taught and exercised by Jesus himself.

However, "turn the other cheek" was not practiced by Jesus himself. Jesus, it is said, preached turning the other cheek, loving one's neighbor and praying for them, and forgiving those who wrong you. But, when did Jesus manifest such behavior in his personal relationships, during his lifetime? Was it his cursing of the Pharisees (Matthew 23), his threat of violent retribution on cities that rejected his message (Matthew 11:20-24, Luke 10:13-15), or his condemnation to death of Jews who would not accept him (Luke 19:27)? Jesus himself *never* turned the other cheek. He *never* forgave anyone who rejected his claims. He *never* forgave anyone who wronged or criticized him. He responded to his opponents, not with passive resistance, but by answering criticism with criticism, and by reviling and threatening his adversaries. John's Jesus, when beaten by an officer, instead of offering quietly his other cheek argues with him (John 18:22-23).

Jesus displayed irrational hatred. He condemns the Jewish people for things that happened even before the time of Abraham, their father, saying: "[U]pon you may come all the righteous blood shed upon the earth, from the righteous Abel to the blood of Zechariah son of Barachiah, whom you slew between the Temple and the altar" (Matthew 23:35). The Gospels' Jesus irrationally denounced the *entire* Jewish people for murders neither they nor their fathers committed. He holds them liable for sins in which they could have no part because they were committed even before the birth of Abraham, the progenitor of the nation of Israel.

Instead of forgiving Judas for betraying him, he said: "But woe to that man through whom the Son of Man is betrayed! It would have been good for that man if he had not been born" (Matthew 26:24). What a chance to show the utmost of forgiveness and Jesus missed the opportunity.

Who did Jesus forgive? Jesus only forgave those who wronged others. Whenever an opportunity to personally forgive those who he felt wronged him presented itself he always declined. Where is Jesus' non-violence where is his love and forgiveness of enemies?

Jesus disqualified to be the servant

Don't blame God if Jesus didn't live up to the imaginary Jesus his followers believe in. Perhaps those who believe Jesus was God or authorized by God have no problem with his teachings and actions. However, he still cannot qualify to be the servant of Isaiah 53. If this passage is a literal fulfillment by Jesus then there must be *total* fulfillment by him.

53:9: "neither was there any deceit in his mouth"

A Parable on Deceit

Once upon a time, in a far off city a man entered the city's largest church and announced: "Destroy this church and in three days I will raise it up." Some shrugged their shoulders and said to each other "he's a madman" others just scoffed and said "why is he disrupting the service?" But others said, "You know, we could use a new building and he seems like an honorable fellow." Before you could imagine the last group prevailed. The congregation agreed to destroy the building in anticipation of a beautiful new building ready in three days. When the appointed time for the new building arrived the entire congregation stood waiting but nothing happened, the site remained a ruin. "Where is our new building?" they demanded. "Oh, you misunderstood me," he declared innocently, "I meant that if you executed me, I would be raised up in three days," although he knew all along that they did not understand his true meaning.

- What would you call such an individual?
- Would you call him a liar, a lunatic, or just simply deceitful?
- Do you have any other description you would use to describe such a person?

After thinking about this parable read the following: "[Jesus said to a crowd standing in the Jerusalem Temple:] 'Destroy this Temple, and in three days I will raise it up.' The Jews therefore said, 'It took forty-six years to build this Temple, and will you raise it up in three days?' But he was speaking of the temple of his body'" (John 2:19-21). How fortunate that the Jews did not take him at his word.

The people were led to believe that he meant the Temple in Jerusalem when he actually spoke of "the temple of his body" (John 2:21). John's Jesus certainly knew they misunderstood his meaning. Yet, he did not clarify what he meant. Jesus own secret meaning was clearly hidden from those to whom he spoke. His audience did not infer that Jesus meant anything other than the Jerusalem Temple. What would you call an individual such as Jesus, a liar, a lunatic or just simply deceitful? I know what you could *not* call him - the servant who had no "deceit in his mouth."

The issue of Jesus' deceitful behavior

Is there any indication that Jesus was deceitful to friend and foe alike?

- Empty promises to "believers:"

Jesus said: "Truly I say to you, there is no one who has left house or brothers or sisters or mother or father or children, for my sake and for the gospel's sake, but that he shall receive a hundred times as much now in the present age, houses and brothers and sisters and mothers and children and farms, along with persecutions; and in the world to come, eternal life" (Mark 10:29-30).

He deceived his disciples promising a hundredfold of material possessions ("houses" and "farms") in this life to all who left everything to follow him. It is obvious from Acts and subsequent Christian history that this would not be so. Material comfort does not necessarily come to those who become Christians nor do all find figurative compensation for family among fellow Christians. Persecution is also not the lot of most converts to Christianity. There is no reason to assume that conversion to Christianity brings a hundredfold increase in any of these things or the additional promise of eternal life.

Matthew's Jesus sates: "Truly I say to you, there are some of those who are standing here who shall not taste death until they see the Son of Man coming in his kingdom" (Matthew 16:28). Jesus' disciples must have accepted this statement at face value. Thus, they mistakenly believed his false assurance that the messianic kingdom was about to be established. When the Gospels' Jesus assured his disciples that the end of the world order and his own triumphant return to judge all men would occur before the generation then living had passed away (Matthew 24:34, Mark 13:30, Luke 21:32), he used deceit, for he knew that this was not true. In the alleged post-resurrection era he still is quoted as promising a return in the near future, with its accompanying rewards (Revelation 22:7, 12, 20).

• Deceitful misleading of "unbelievers":

We have seen above how Jesus misled the people who heard him into believing things, which were completely opposite to what he really meant. John's Jesus, speaking in a deceitful manner declared: "Destroy this temple, and in three days I will raise it up" (John 2:19). The people were led to believe that he meant the Temple in Jerusalem when he actually spoke of "the temple of his body" (John 2:21). As we have noted, Jesus' own secret meaning was clearly hidden from those to whom he spoke. Jesus' audience did not infer from his deceptive remark that he meant anything other than the Jerusalem Temple.

- Secret denials:

John stated that when Jesus appeared before the high priest and the elders of Israel he declared that he was never secretive, but had always been open about his mission and its meaning.

> Jesus declared: "I have spoken openly to the world; I always taught in a synagogue and in the Temple, where all the Jews come together; and I spoke nothing in secret. Why do you question me? Question those who have heard what I spoke to them; behold, these know what I said" (John 18:20-22).

A study of the Gospels reveals that this statement was a falsehood. The fact is that Jesus did not want the masses to understand him and deliberately planned that his message be secretive. The Gospels state that on a number of occasions Jesus demanded secrecy. The Gospels indicate that few, if any, people understood the true meaning of Jesus' teachings. Jesus spoke in parables whose meanings were deliberately hidden from those who heard them. The Gospels quote Jesus as saying that he did *not* want everyone who heard him to understand his message and be saved. This is contrary to 2 Peter 3:9, which claims that "The Lord is ... patient toward you, not wishing for any to perish but for all to come to repentance." He is said to have taught his disciples: "To you has been given the secret [*mysterion*] of the kingdom of God; but those who are outside get everything in parables, so that [*hina*] while seeing, they may see and not perceive; and while hearing, they may hear and not understand; lest they return again and be forgiven" (Mark 4:11-12; see also Matthew 13:13-15, Luke 8:10).

Salvation was reserved for the select few

Jesus claimed that he revealed the meaning of his esoteric declarations (the parables) only to his disciples (Matthew 13:10-11; Mark 4:10-12, 34; Luke 8:9-10). Yet even that was untrue. Jesus knew very well that the disciples did not understand everything he told them (Mark 9:32; Luke 9:45, 18:34) and Jesus said and did things

140

secretively so that the multitudes should not understand him. Why the secrecy? Why not a public proclamation instead? Matthew 12:15-21 attempts to show that Jesus' appeal to secrecy was a fulfillment of a prophetic utterance found in a passage in Isaiah (Isaiah 42:1-4). However, the passage can only relate to what Matthew infers by the most farfetched analogy and the use of secrecy would still disqualify Jesus from being the servant. The Gospels' Jesus demanded that his purported messianic identity and/or ability to cure ailments be kept secret by demons (Mark 1:34, 3:11-12; Luke 4:41), his followers (Matthew 16:20, Mark 8:30, Luke 9:21), and those healed (Matthew 8:3-4, 12:15-16; Mark 1:44, 5:43, 7:36; Luke 5:14, 8:56).

Messianic pretensions

The Gospels state that Jesus claimed that he always spoke openly, yet, he never proclaimed himself publicly as Messiah.

According to John, he made a private statement concerning his messianic pretentions to a Samaritan woman (John 4:25-26). But, such news from a Samaritan would not be of any consequence to the Jewish people. When he spoke to Jews his claims were in the form of enigmatic presentations which involved apparent paradoxes regarding the nature and identity of the Messiah; yet they were given without providing a solution (Mark 4:11-12). On a visit to the Temple it is alleged that Jesus was asked to tell "plainly" if he was the Messiah. He parried the question by presenting an ambiguous answer — "I told you but you do not believe" (John 10:24-25).

As we have seen, the Gospels show that he had only given them hints in parables, knowing in advance they would not understand (Matthew 13:13-15, Mark 4:11-12, Luke 8:10). When Peter allegedly declared: "You are the Christ, the Son of the living God" (Matthew 16:16), Jesus gave specific instructions to his disciples. They were to refrain from disclosing his messianic identity — they were to keep it secret (Matthew 16:20). So much for the lie that he spoke openly.

Who allegedly raised Jesus?
- Was it God?

Peter alleges that God raised Jesus from the dead (Acts 2:24; 2:32; 3:15, 26; 4:10; 5:30; 10:40). Paul also agrees with Peter (Acts 13:30, 33,

34, 37, 17:31; Romans 4:24, 6:4, 8:11, 10:9; 1 Corinthians 6:14, 15:15; 2 Corinthians 4:14; Galatians 1:1; Ephesians 1:20; Colossians 2:12; 1 Thessalonians 1:10); Hebrews 13:20 and 1 Peter 1:21 also allege that God raised Jesus up.

- Was it Jesus?

John's Jesus says, referring to his own body: "I will raise it up" (John 2:19). If Peter, et al, are correct than John's Jesus is not only deceptive but a blatant liar.

Lying to Pilate

Did Jesus lead a peaceful group?

According to John 18:36, Jesus said to Pilate: "If my kingdom were of this world, my servants would fight, that I might not be handed over to the Jews." Jesus implies that his followers knew his kingdom was not of this world and would not use violence. But, the truth is that they expected Jesus to restore the kingdom of Israel in a terrestrial sense (e.g., Luke 24:21). Even after his death Jesus' followers are said to have looked forward to a speedy return which would usher in the overthrow of the Roman Empire. His followers are said to ask: "Lord will you at this time restore the kingdom to Israel" (Acts 1:6). Moreover, just a few hours before his meeting Pilate, Jesus had ordered the disciples to buy swords if they had none (Luke 22:36), and the disciples responded by saying that two swords were available (Luke 22:38). Two swords are said to be available, which may be practical for assassination, but not for much else. Soon after this, it is said that Peter cuts off the ear of Malchus, the servant of the high priest, who came to seize Jesus (Matthew 26:51, Mark 14:47, Luke 22:50, John 18:10). Contrary to Jesus' statement that "these know what I said" (John 18:21), Peter did not know or obey that since the kingdom was not of this world he should not fight (John 18:36). But, Jesus knew at his trial that Peter had used violence (John 18:11). Jesus lied and said that his followers would not feel the necessity of acting violently since his kingdom was not of this world. Jesus was aware that his followers would indeed use violence. Yet Jesus persisted in his deceit as he defended himself before Pilate.

A medley of secrets, lies and deception

- Knowing that Elijah must precede the Messiah (Malachi 3:1, 23), Jesus claimed that John the Baptist was Elijah (Matthew 11:10-14, 17:10-13) even though John himself denied any connection with that prophet (John 1:21).

- Jesus' avowal that the Law will exist "until heaven and earth pass away" (Matthew 5:18) is meant to be misleading.

- The Law is only meant to continue for a period of a mere three and one half years at most; that is, the duration of his ministry. Why? Paul alleges that Jesus fulfilled all the Law and the Prophets during the so-called first advent. He says: "For Christ is the end of the Law for righteousness to everyone who believes" (Romans 10:4) and in Hebrews 8:13 it states: "In that he says, a new [covenant], he has made the first obsolete. Now that which is made obsolete and growing old is near vanishing away."

- According to Paul and the author of Hebrews — the Law is over! But Jesus said it will last "until heaven and earth pass away" Did Jesus lie or did they?

- Didn't Jesus deliberately mislead the "thief" when he said: "Truly, I say you, today you will be with me in Paradise" (Luke 23:43)? Jesus did not go to Paradise on that day — he was dead and supposedly rose three days later.

- John relates a conversation between Jesus and his physical brothers prior to the Feast of Tabernacles:

  His brothers … said to him, "Depart from here, and go into Judea … For no one does anything in secret, when he himself seeks to be known publicly. If you do these things, show yourself to the world." For not even his brothers were believing in him. Jesus therefore said to them, "…Go up to the feast yourselves; I do not go up to this feast because my time has not yet fully come." And having said these things to them, he stayed in Galilee. But when his brothers had gone up to the feast, then he himself also went up, not publicly, but as it were, in secret. (John 7:2-10)

- Didn't he instruct the parents of the girl he allegedly revived that they should not inform anyone of what was done? (Luke 8:56).

- Did he not instruct his disciples not to mention that he was "the Christ" (Matthew 16:20)? Yet he declared: "I have spoken openly to the world ... I spoke nothing in secret" (John 18:20). Jesus' actions and instructions say otherwise.

- Matthew's Jesus says to those coming to arrest him: "Day after day I sat in the Temple teaching, and you did not seize me" (Matthew 26:55). On the contrary, John says that on one occasion there were those who wanted to stone him while he was in the Temple, but he "hid and went out of the Temple" (John 8:59). Does anyone doubt that the Temple authorities would want to apprehend and interrogate the person who caused a disturbance in the Temple and seized control of part of it (Mark 11:15-16, 18)?

Did Jesus lie? Did he falsely imply that the authorities never attempted to apprehend him? Or did the evangelist lie? This is from one who said: "I spoke nothing in secret." And this is from one whose followers claim that "neither was there any deceit in his mouth." Jesus' secretive and deceitful behavior further disqualifies him from being the servant.

53:10: "If he would offer himself as a guilt-offering"

The suffering servant as a guilt-offering

Following the initial declaration that it was God's will for the servant to suffer, the verse is written as a conditional statement. *If* condition A is satisfied, *then* the outcome B will occur. That is, the rewards of verse 10 are contingent on the servant's willingness to offer himself as an *asham*, "guilt-offering." In a literal sense the verse says, "If his soul places herself [*tasim*] as a guilt-offering." The *herself* is referring to the soul (*nefesh*) of the servant, *nefesh* being a feminine noun. Grammatically *tasim* could be female third person (she will place, set, put) or masculine second person (you will place), but the female fits best since *nefesh* is a feminine noun. The verse promises the servant poetically that if his soul is willing to offer itself in the service of God as if it were a guilt-offering he will receive rewards. Martyrdom is no stranger to the servant community with many coming to the brink of death and others dying for the *Sanctification of the Name of God*. As the servant's rewards follow after the meeting of the conditional requirements it is a further indication that the servant entity as a whole will not die as an actual guilt-offering.

God does not sin and if He lessened Himself to do so He would not be God. If Jesus was an incarnate part of God he had no free will to sin or choose an evil path. He had no choice but to die and shed his blood for the remission of sin as alleged by the New Testament. Without the choice provided by free will could Jesus do otherwise than carry out the assignment he was programed to do? If an incarnate Jesus had gone against the wishes of the Godhead the cosmic plans for salvation described in the New Testament and developed by later Christian theologians and church councils would have crumbled. In other words, as described in the New Testament, Jesus' incarnate death was not a free will decision on his part but a preprogramed decision decided upon prior to his assuming a fleshly body. However, God's offer is conditional upon a free will acceptance by the servant of his fate here and now on Earth. It is not an offer the personal rewards for which are agreed upon in a previous pre-existence prior to the servant's birth.

Asham requirements

Can Jesus be a guilt-offering who literally takes upon himself the sins of those who trust in him?

The *asham*, as all other sacrifices, must be perfect, without spot, and without blemish (Leviticus 22:19-22). Therefore, the New Testament authors needed to portray Jesus as literally being as "a lamb unblemished and spotless" (1 Peter 1:19) who "offered himself without blemish to God" (Hebrews 9:14). Jesus was none of these so the New Testament authors claimed he was unblemished because he was *sinless*. This conveniently unverifiable contention is not a teaching found in the Jewish Scriptures. There is no proof that Jesus was sinless, there is only the claim that he was.

One must address the fact that human sacrifice is abhorrent to God (e.g., Leviticus 18:21, 20:2-5). Biblical sacrifice is animal specific and is not speaking metaphorically of human self-sacrifice. There is no support in the Jewish Scriptures for a one-time superlative human sacrifice. Jesus' alleged sacrifice is said to have been a literal self-sacrifice of himself (Hebrews 9:26). But, as a human being, he was unfit for sacrificial purposes and no such sacrificial provision is found in the Jewish Scriptures.

According to Paul, the Torah was in effect until Jesus brought it to an end by his blood shed on the cross (Galatians 3:24-25, Colossians 2:14). There is no mention in the Jewish Scriptures of a *perfect human sacrifice* bringing the Law to an end. In any case, under the criteria established by Paul, Jesus was *not* a valid sacrifice under the laws of the Torah. The Torah would be in effect up until the very moment of his death, so his death could not have brought the Torah to an end. Why? As a human he would have been an invalid sacrifice to begin with. Therefore, the effect of Jesus' death on the sacrificial system would have been zero. Outside of New Testament claims the reality is that Jesus' death had *no* salvific function.

Compare the Torah's requirements for the sacrificial offering with Jesus as an alleged offering. The Torah is specific as to the species, age, physical condition, and manner of application of the blood to the altar of the sacrificial animal. All biblical sacrificial offerings have to be physically unblemished with no cuts or deformities. But, nothing is said of it being "sinless." It is an animal, after all. As for physical blemishes, Jesus was circumcised and Paul referred to it as mutilation (Philippians 3:2) and castration (Galatians 5:12). Jesus is also said to have been beaten and whipped prior to his execution (Matthew 27:26, 30; Mark 15:19, John 19:3). Such blemishes would also disqualify an offering.

Making the unsuitable suitable New Testament style

It is alleged that Jesus was spiritually pure and sinless and that his supposed sacrificial death was prefigured in the Jewish Scriptures by images and types (e.g., Isaiah 53, Psalm 22). But who says he was spiritually pure and sinless? Who says his death was prefigured in the Jewish Scriptures? Only the tendentiously self-serving authors of the New Testament and their adherents!

But, why do the New Testament authors make these claims when they are not in the Jewish Scriptures? The answer is clear: How else can they explain Jesus being completely unsuited as a biblical atonement sacrifice other than to go on the offensive and contend that the biblical sacrificial system was a "shadow" which only prefigured him but did not apply to him? Hebrews alleges: "For the Law ... has a shadow of the good things to come [and] not the very form [literally image] of things" (Hebrews 10:1, see also Colossians 2:17). But this is a claim unsubstantiated except in the minds of those who unquestioning accept the New Testament as if it were true.

Bloodshed and vicarious suffering: The Torah view

The blood shed is all-important in the symbolic ritual of animal sacrifice done in the Temple, but forgiveness of sin can be obtained anywhere *without* the sacrificial aspect. The sin-offering can help make atonement by being part of the Temple ritual, but it is *not* required for forgiveness. Only sincere repentance is required. Repentance is a turning point of the heart and mind from sin. This is made clear in Psalms 30:2-3; 40:2, 7 and Micah 6:6-8. Any suffering undergone by the sin-offering either leading up to or at the time of death itself is not what achieves the atonement. Atonement is *never* vicarious. The suffering of one being *cannot* atone for the sins of another (Ezekiel 18:20-22, 26-28). *Neither* the servant, *nor* a sacrificial animal, *nor* Jesus, can literally take on the punishment of another. They need not and they cannot vicariously atone. *Only* the sinner can suffer for, or repent from, *his* sins.

Hebrews claims that Jesus fulfilled that which the animal blood supposedly only foreshadowed (Hebrews 9:12-14). Jesus execution simply does not fulfill fundamental sacrificial requirements set by the Torah. The crucifixion preparatory treatment, the national origins of his executioners, the fact that he was a human being, the geographic location of his death, the lack of a death caused by a literal shedding of blood respectively would render any potential offering as *unfit* for consideration as a fulfillment of a biblically required sacrifice. If the New Testament is a continuation of what Christians call the "Old Testament," it must harmonize with the "Old Testament" — false comparisons will not suffice. The New Testament authors picked and chose what suited them in order to make it seem as if Jesus was a valid sacrifice and that he willingly offered himself as a guilt-offering.

Did Jesus suffer vicariously for the sins of mankind?

Jesus is often portrayed as suffering vicariously for the sins of mankind. No support for such a doctrine is to be found in verse 10. The verse does not say that the servant offered himself on behalf of others. Absolutely nothing is said about offering oneself for other people's sins. The verse says, "If he would offer himself as a guilt-offering," that is, a figurative expression concerning the servant's willingness to devote himself wholeheartedly to the purposes of God in order that "the purposes of the Lord will prosper by his hand." Does the use of the conditional mean that if Jesus is the servant he had a choice? God's promises of reward to the servant are conditional: "If he would ... he shall see...." But, the Jesus of the New Testament did *not* have this option of free will.

If Jesus was part of the Godhead incarnate or a supernatural being sent by God there was no risk of failure and defeat. But, he also did not have a free will choice to abandon his mandate from God. If he was the all-knowing god-man Christian mythology claims him to be when it comes to his alleged mission there could be no question as to whether or not he would fulfill his destiny (cf. Philippians 2:6-8). Risk is something for mere mortals, possessed of free will that despite God's foreknowledge of what choice will be made, are left with the final decision. There should be no need for God to promise a reward on condition that Jesus fulfills His wishes ("If he would"). If Jesus is all that Christianity claims he is, then God knew that this incarnate sinless supernatural being would fulfill all that was required of him right on schedule. If Jesus is part of God then he is ontologically incapable of sin. There was no reason to reward one who is said to be perfection incarnate and an equal part of the triune deity with having children and prolongation of days. It certainly makes no sense to think God would promise to reward such a heaven bound eternal being with having children and prolongation of days. Such things are promised to humans not to one who is supposedly eternal. The very use of the *conditional* shows that verse 10 could not be referring to Jesus.

Self-sacrifice for others or self-promotion for more honors and power?

According to the New Testament, Jesus had specific knowledge of his mission on earth and his destiny in heaven. For example: John's Jesus said: "I ... came down from heaven" (John 6:51) and "I know where I came from, and where I am going" (John 8:14). Matthew's Jesus told his disciples that "he must go to Jerusalem, and suffer many things from the elders and chief priests, and be killed, and be raised on the third day" (Matthew 16:21). It is even maintained that the Pharisees knew of his prediction that "After three days I am to rise again" (Matthew 27:63).

What Jesus supposedly left temporarily in heaven and his alleged additional rewards on his heavenly return are found in Philippians 2:6-11: Before, "He existed in the form of God" (i.e., god-like but not God); after, "God highly exalted him," "bestowed on him the name which is above every name," "every knee should bow [to Jesus] in heaven, and on earth, and under the earth," and "every tongue should confess that Jesus is Lord." Isn't it strange to say that God rewarded part of Himself for doing what he commanded Himself to do? For this increased heavenly reward, it is said, Jesus knowingly gave up a transitory earthly existence devoid of luxury. Where was the sacrifice if he knew exactly what his heavenly rewards would be?

53:10: "he shall see seed"

Zer'a

The expression in the verse is "see seed" (*yireh zer'a*) and appears only here. The absence of a possessive pronominal suffix is a common feature in biblical Hebrew and is understood from the context (e.g., Isaiah 25:11, 59:2, 49:16, 32:11, 33:24, 41:1, 49:22, 65:21). *Zer'a*, refers to actual physical offspring or descendants (Psalms 22:31, Isaiah 54:3). It is never used symbolically in the Jewish Scriptures.

Christians claim that "he shall see seed" is symbolic and refers to the increase in number of those who believe in Jesus. Christians interpret certain verses in the Scriptures (Genesis 3:15, 38:8; Isaiah 1:4, 57:4; Malachi 2:15; Psalms 22:31; Proverbs 11:21) as referring only *symbolically* to "bodily seed." The Christian interpretation is unwarranted, since in each of these verses "seed" is better taken in its usual literal physical sense. For example, Isaiah 57: There the prophet castigates certain individuals (not the nation as a whole) for perpetuating the idolatrous practices of their parents. These verses are a scathing denunciation of wicked offspring who uphold the sinful ways of their parents. Isaiah calls them "**sons** of the sorceress, the **seed** of adulterers and the harlot" (verse 3). He then asks: "Are you not children of transgression, a seed of falsehood?" (verse 4), that is, children of parents who live lives of falsehood. They are what the prophet has earlier termed a "seed of evil-doers" (Isaiah 1:4), that is, children of parents who do evil deeds. The people spoken to in Isaiah 57 were conceived in adultery and harlotry; they are the resultant products of transgression and falsehood. Literally, they are children born as a result of parental transgression, a seed born as a result of parental falsehood. When referring to the sins of the parents, the word *zer'a* is used since they are literally the physical children of these transgressors. But, these same children are also the disciples, *banim* ("sons"), of the sorceress (that is, practitioners of sorcery and divination).

Banim

The word *bein* (literally "son") may figuratively mean "disciples" (2 Kings 2:3, 5, 7, 15). *Zer'a* ("seed") is never used in this sense. For example: "And Abram said: 'Behold to me You have given no seed [*zer'a*], and, see the son [*ben*] of my house is my heir.' And, behold, the word of the Lord came to him, saying: 'This man shall not be your heir, but he that shall come forth out of your own bowels shall be your heir'" (Genesis 15:3-4). *Zer'a* must *always* be taken literally to mean physical descendants. Since *zer'a* refers to one's physical descendants the servant must have children. Since Jesus had no children of his own, the promise that the servant "shall see seed" rules out the possibility that Jesus is the servant.

53:10: "he shall prolong days"

The concept of prolonging of days and that of gaining eternal life:

The differences:

The concept of a prolonged life cannot be treated as the equivalent of eternal life because in an eternal context, time of any duration is of no consequence. Consequently, one cannot speak of an eternal being as having his days prolonged: "Are Your days as the days of man, or

Your years as a man's days?" (Job 10:5). God must be referred to as eternal: "The number of his years is unsearchable" (Job 36:26). He is the first, He is the last, He cannot be anything else. Prolonging the days of one who is already supposed to be eternal would make his life longer than eternity. That is an obvious impossibility. Prolonging of life implies earthly mortality, a cut-off date in the future, while the term eternal life refers to immortality. The phrase "prolonged life" can only relate to the limited bodily existence in this world, and not to the endlessness of eternal life.

Can "he shall prolong days" be applied to Jesus in heaven or on earth? If, after his alleged resurrection Jesus returned to heaven to become an eternal heavenly being again, this stage of his existence cannot be appropriately referred to as prolongation of days. How can such a promise have any meaning for Jesus, if he is viewed as being a supernatural being of divine substance and whose existence is believed by Christians to be eternal? There would be no need for one part of God to assure a fellow member of an eternal triune deity (or a created eternal being) an everlasting life.

"He shall prolong days," can also *not* be applied to the human Jesus, who died young and childless. If the promise of prolonged days is applied to the human Jesus, it is an empty promise. Since the blessings of *seeing children* and *prolonging life* are only appropriate when applied to a mortal man and not to an immortal being, these blessings cannot be applied to the Jesus of Christian theology.

Some Christians argue that "he shall see seed" refers to God seeing the birth of Jesus and "he shall prolong days" refers to God resurrecting Jesus. That would make these two promises into a parenthetical statement having no connection with the conditional nature of the verse. Their argument makes absolutely no sense!

53:11: "From the labor of his soul he shall see; he shall be satisfied."

Christians claim that the life's work of Jesus is reflected in verse 11. Certainly, the Gospels' Jesus was not "satisfied" with what he accomplished during his lifetime; this is indicated by what he said on the cross. There, it is said, he cried out: "My God, my God, why have you forsaken me?" (Matthew 27:46, Mark 15:34). The argument that verse 11 refers to the supposedly heavenly Jesus subsequent to his death, becoming increasingly satisfied as his following grew, is of little help since this verse deals with an earthly being. If Jesus was an equal partner in the triune deity, he would not have had to ask his "Father" to "forgive them, for they do not know what they are doing" (Luke 23:34). He himself would have been able to bear iniquities and forgive sins without invoking the assistance of God the Father. But, then again, the Gospels' Jesus never forgave anyone who he felt wronged him. He only advised others to forgive.

Verse 11 is a continuation of the thoughts expressed in the preceding verse. Thus, the pericope suggests that from the servant's toil and travail on behalf of the purposes of the Lord, "he shall be satisfied" at the outcome of his long struggle. The servant will be pleased with the abundant material and spiritual fulfillments that he will "see" occur.

53:11: "With his knowledge the righteous one, my servant, shall cause many to be just. And their iniquities he shall bear."

God's servant (Israel) will spread the knowledge of His law. God's recognition and acceptance of the faithful servant's many sacrifices made over the centuries of exile become apparent when he is vindicated as righteous and innocent before the nations of the world. Moreover, the servant's actions on behalf of the nations will eventually cause righteousness to spread among them as well. Nevertheless, "their iniquities he shall bear," that is, throughout the centuries, the servant will suffer iniquitous acts perpetrated at the hands of the nations despite all the good he has contributed to the world.

Did the teachings of Jesus uplift the nations? Did they become more just or righteous when they converted (often forcibly) or forced others to convert, many times accompanied by much bloodshed. One can certainly point to righteous deeds done in the name of Jesus. Nevertheless, at the same time horrific harm has been done to large segments of humanity in the name of Jesus. The death toll in bringing the supposed "salvation of Christ" to the world has been staggering.

Countless atrocities have been committed in the name of Jesus by those professing to be his followers. Many who profess Christianity in one of its myriad forms disavow the murderous spreading of

Christianity. But does Jesus only get credit for the good Christians do but is not responsible for the bad? Is there tangible proof to support the claim that Jesus at any time bears the iniquities of anyone? There are certainly many iniquities perpetrated by his followers over the centuries he could start with.

53:12: "I will divide him a portion with the great, and he shall divide the spoil with the mighty"

There is a great divide between truth (Isaiah) and fiction (the New Testament).

To have something or to have nothing that is the question. What portion did Jesus allegedly have and when did he get it? How is a Christian interpretation of "I will divide him a portion with the great, and he shall divide the spoil with the mighty," where the servant receives "a portion with the great" to be reconciled with Daniel 9:26: "And after the sixty-two weeks an anointed one shall be cut off, and he shall have nothing [*v'ein lo*]." The correct rendering of *v'ein lo* is "he has nothing" or "he shall have nothing." Isaiah speaks of the servant whom he repeatedly refers to as Israel and Daniel speaks of "an anointed one" historically identified with the High Priest Alexander Yannai. Christians *incorrectly* identify this anointed one as being Jesus.

Understanding the problem Christians face.

V'ein lo (he shall have nothing) cannot refer to Jesus' situation at or after death, for, unlike mere mortal bodies which decay after death, Christians claim that Jesus rose bodily into heaven, where he sits at the "right hand of the throne of Majesty." *V'ein lo* certainly could not refer to a lack of wealth or followers, for this would not distinguish Jesus from the great majority of the world's population. One who "has nothing" (Daniel 9:26) does not receive "a portion with the great" (Isaiah 53:12), does not rise bodily to heaven (Acts 1:9) and does not sit at the "right hand of the throne of the Majesty" (Hebrews 8:1). It is precisely with his death that Jesus was allegedly able to attain his rewards. From their respective contexts, it is clear that, if applied to the Jesus of Christian theology Daniel 9:26 and Isaiah 53:12 would have to apply to a post-resurrection period, as well as cancel each other out. Therefore, "he shall have nothing" cannot refer to the Jesus of Christian theology. According to Paul, Jesus came into his greatest rewards only after his earthly death, and, indeed, as a result of that death (Philippians 2:5-11) and John's Jesus says that "the Father loves me, because I lay down my soul, that I might take it again" (John 10:17). If verse 12 applies to Jesus, then Daniel's statement, "he shall have nothing," cannot refer to him, for Jesus' rewards could only have been actually guaranteed from the moment he was "cut off." To apply these two verses to one individual is self-contradictory.

Jesus' wealth and power on earth and in heaven

What did Jesus give up in dying a human death? Jesus had no wealth or power as a human being. Because he was allegedly a supernatural being, he could expect, on reassuming his heavenly role, to exercise his power as one-third of the triune deity. Christian theology is saying that Jesus gave up a temporary earthly life as a god-man to return to his role in heaven, where, as part of the triune deity, he reigns as God. Clearly, it is unreasonable to say that Jesus sacrificed himself for the redemption of mankind when, by his actions, he *knowingly* gained more than he lost. As we have seen previously, Paul wrote:

> Jesus Christ, who, although he existed in the form of God, did not regard equality with God a thing to be grasped, but emptied himself, taking the form of a bondservant, and being made in the likeness of men. And being found in appearance as a man, he humbled himself by becoming obedient to the point of death, even death on a cross. Therefore also God highly exalted him, and bestowed on him the name which is above every name, that at the name of Jesus every knee should bow, of those who are in heaven, and on earth, and under the earth, and that every tongue should confess that Jesus Christ is Lord to the Glory of God the Father. (Philippians 2:5-11)

Paul also said of Jesus:

> He [God] raised him [Jesus] from the dead, and seated him at His right hand in the heavenly [places], far above all rule and authority and power and dominion, and every name that is named, not only in this age, but also in the one to come. And He put all things in subjection under his feet, and gave him as head over all things to the church, which is his body, the fullness of him who fills all in all. (Ephesians 1:20-23)

Where is the sacrifice if Jesus came into the world to do certain works knowing that he could not fail and that as a result he would be rewarded for doing what he himself ordained for himself as one-third of the Godhead?

The servant's rewards for faithfulness to God

In verse 12, God speaks of the servant, who, as a result of his selflessness, is willing to give up all that he possesses in the service of God. What is the meaning of sacrifice? This is a crucial question.

The alleged sacrifice of the Christian Jesus is greatly exaggerated. There is a gross misuse of the concept of "sacrifice" where one who is alleged to be a supernatural being knows that by giving up a flesh-and-blood existence, something essentially unimportant to him, he will receive in return a position of eternal exaltation and power. Jesus' death *cannot* be called a sacrifice. On leaving his transitory human lifespan behind him, Jesus, it is alleged, returned to heaven to once more become part of the eternal Godhead in its proper heavenly setting. Is this what Christianity calls "the Lamb of God," a sacrificial offering?

Rewarding one's self for obeying one's self

The biblical sacrifice is an animal slain unaware and unknowing and without reward for the service it provides. Why should Jesus be rewarded for his alleged sacrifice, for doing what he himself, as God, wanted done?

There is no point for God, of whom Jesus is allegedly a part, to say: "I will divide him a portion with the great" as an actual reward to Himself. Such reward can be properly given to one who is all-human, but *not* to one who is at the same time a supernatural being. Indeed, it was not the New Testament human Jesus who is rewarded but the heavenly creature who is said to now sit next to God. Reminder: That which is in any way separate from God is not part of the being of God.

Dividing the spoil with the mighty

Parallel with God's promise to "divide him a portion with the great" is the phrase, "he shall divide the spoil [*shalal*] with the mighty."

The term "the mighty," or "the mighty ones," refers to the mighty nation, the descendants of Abraham (Genesis 18:18). The Hebrew word *shalal*, "spoil," is the term used for booty of war (Genesis 49:27, Numbers 31:11, Isaiah 10:6), and always means physical wealth wherever it is used. In Proverbs *shalal* is used to connote an increase of wealth which does not result from one's personal labor (Proverbs 31:11).

"He shall divide" indicates that the division of the spoils will be done in an orderly fashion by the governing authorities. The entire nation of Israel will share the spoils of war (Zechariah 14:14). "He," that is, Israel as a national unit, will evenly distribute the spoils of war among "the mighty ones," all the Jewish people. It will not just be those who actually fought that will partake in the division of the spoils, but the spoils will be equally shared among all Israel (cf. Numbers 31:27, Joshua 22:8, 1 Samuel 30:24-25).

If Jesus is God, who can be great enough to share the spoil with him? Is it conceivable that one who is God could possibly have only "a portion" comparable to that of mere earthly rulers, or that "he shall divide the spoil" with anyone? Even if this could be rationalized, it would then run counter to what is stated in Psalm 2, which Christians claim refers to Jesus. In that psalm, God offers, to the person in question, the entire earth for a possession (not a portion) and all rulers are told to give homage to that person (verses 10-12). Isaiah 53:12 and Psalm 2 could not literally be referring to the same individual

Jesus and the spoils of war shared with the mighty.

What portion did Jesus share with the great, what spoil did he divide with the mighty? Who are the "great" and who are the "mighty" with whom he supposedly interacted and shared the "spoil"? Where and what is the fulfillment? Is fulfillment left to the "he's coming any day now" second coming farce? Christians, get over it, he's not coming back — not then, not now, not ever.

53:12: "because he had poured out his soul to death"

Many have poured out their soul to death

"Because he has poured out (*'arah*) his soul to death" is the reason the servant will be rewarded. This cannot refer to the Gospels' Jesus if the phrase means to die willingly. Jesus "poured out his soul," that is, died on the cross unwillingly, saying at the last moment: "My God, my God, why have You forsaken me?" (Matthew 27:46, Mark 15:34). According to Matthew/Mark, his last words from the cross expressed a sense of frustration, not obedience.

This final statement from the cross contradicts the assertion that Jesus "learned obedience through what he suffered" (Hebrews 5:8) and that he freely submitted to God's will (Matthew 26:39, 42; Mark 14:36; Luke 22:42).

In those last moments of life, the Gospels say, Jesus expressed himself in such a way that his death *cannot* be considered a voluntary sacrificial death made in response to a call from God.

Jesus went to his death feeling abandoned by God. Jesus' final words on the cross appear in three different forms: "My God, my God, why have you forsaken me?" (Matthew 27:46, Mark 15:34); "Father, into Your hands I commit my spirit." (Luke 23:46); "It is finished!" (John 19:30). Although Luke and John try to give a more positive final statement they are constrained by the earlier Gospels of Matthew and Mark. Only one form out of the three can be Jesus' *last* words or none at all.

Many in the servant community of the people of Israel have poured out their soul to death, some to the brink of death, others dying for the *Sanctification of the Name of God*. In one way or another, the servant community of Israel as a corporate entity has "poured out his soul to death."

53:12: "[H]e was numbered with the transgressors; and he bore the sin of many"

Reviewing the Christian myth of Jesus bearing the sins of transgressors

It is said of the servant, "And he was numbered with the transgressors; and he bore the sin of many," but what assurance is there that it refers to Jesus? While many people throughout history have been "numbered with the transgressors" who can truthfully claim to have borne "the sin of many." In the case of Jesus, there is *no* proof anywhere that he literally "bore the sin of many." This is a contention of Christianity that is based on wishful thinking. He did not fulfill the rest of the servant passage when it comes to things that can be tangibly observed so why should we expect that he fulfilled the non-tangible? There is no tangible proof to support the claim that Jesus at any time bears the iniquities of anyone.

53:12: "[He] made intercession for the transgressors"

Did Jesus make "intercession for the transgressors"? It is said that Jesus in his supposed post-resurrection state intercedes with God on man's behalf and, as heavenly advocate, pleads man's cause before God (Romans 8:34; see also Hebrews 7:25, 9:24; 1 John 2:1). If Jesus is part of a triune deity in which all three beings are in total agreement with each other and of one essence how can he make intercession for transgressors who follow him? The very claim that God (the Father) accepts or rejects Jesus' petition shows a separation of ideation. It shows Jesus to be God's inferior. What is more, an intercessor stands between those he represents and the one receiving the request and deciding on its merit. Jesus would in essence be defense attorney and judge simultaneously. If Jesus is part of a totally synchronized triune deity then there is no one with whom to intercede. But, of course, there is no proof that this intercession is going on. It is solely a non-verifiable contention of certain New Testament authors.

Of God and Israel

As mentioned above a verse by verse explanation of how the people of Israel are the fulfillment the Suffering Servant prophecy can be found in, Gerald Sigal, *Isaiah 53: Who is the Servant?* In answer to those who deny this biblical truth and question how Israel can be called the "righteous one" when the people of Israel have not always obeyed God's commandments God's word declares otherwise. This passage describes the culmination of a long historical period and marks the time of the final redemption from exile. Obviously, if Israel as a nation is repentant there is no problem. But, what if that is not the case and Israel does not fully repent?

It should be noted that God is often merciful and forgiving even when there is an absence of sincere repentance. God declares: "I will be gracious to whom I will be gracious, and will show mercy on whom I will show mercy" (Exodus 33:19). The psalmist writes: "But He, being full of compassion, forgives iniquity, and does not destroy; many a time He turns His anger away and does not stir up all His wrath. For He remembered that they were but flesh; a wind that passes away, and comes not again" (Psalms 78:38-39). The prophet Micah declares: "Who is a God like You that pardons the iniquity, and passes by the transgression of the remnant of His heritage? He retains not His anger forever, because He delights in mercy" (Micah 7:18). Even when Israel is figuratively blind and deaf God still considers the nation as His servant and messenger (Isaiah 42:19). Isaiah records that redemption may be forthcoming even when undeserved, for God's own reasons: "I, even I, am He that blots out your transgressions for My own sake, and will not remember your sins" (Isaiah 43:25; see also Ezekiel 20:14, 22). The prophet informs us that in some cases God's *redemption* precedes Israel's *return*: "Remember these things, O Jacob, and Israel, for you are My servant; I have formed you, you are My servant: O Israel, you should not forget Me, I have blotted out, as a thick cloud, your transgressions, and as a cloud, your sins. Return to Me, for I have redeemed you…. The Lord has redeemed Jacob, and does glorify Himself in Israel" (Isaiah 44:21-23).

God redeems His people even though they do not deserve this redemption according to strict justice. Divine need is the decisive factor and His promises to the patriarchs are unconditional and still binding (e.g., Genesis 17:7). Thus, God declares to the prophet Isaiah: "And your people, they are [as a unit] all righteous" (Isaiah 60:21).

Individually there is no atonement without repentance. However, in the case of Israel, after causing the nation to suffer for her sins, God forgives for His own sake lest the other nations mock Him (Isaiah 43:25). Thus, God's redemption is not always dependent on repentance preceding forgiveness. God considers a forgiven Israel as completely righteous, all past misdeeds forgiven and so to speak forgotten by God. So, although Israel has suffered in the past for its sins at the juncture mentioned in the passage, a new era begins.

In sum, the major issue concerning the suffering servant passage has been the Christian allegation that it refers to Jesus. It should be obvious that the passage does not describe Jesus whatsoever. Although cited by several New Testament authors, as if it referred to Jesus, there is no way of escaping the fact that the opposite is true.

Some Christians realizing that Isaiah 52:13-53:12 refers to Israel but still clinging to the New Testament's identifying this passage with Jesus say its greater fulfillment is Jesus. As we have observed this is not true. Nevertheless, all Jews, good or bad, even Jesus and Paul, are part of the historic national entity of corporate Israel that makes up the servant people of God. As such, what happens to one, be it being "led to the slaughter" or "sharing in the spoils" is considered as if it was experienced by all the people; all Israel is responsible one for the other. The word of God is quite clear as to who is the servant:

> But you, O Israel, My servant, Jacob, you whom I have chosen, offspring of Abraham who loved Me — you who I shall grasp from the ends of the earth and shall summon from among all its noblemen, and to whom I shall say, "You are My servant" — I have chosen you and not rejected you. Fear not, for I am with you; be not dismayed, for I am your God; I have strengthened you, even helped you, and even sustained you with My righteous right hand. Behold, all who become angry with you will be shamed and humiliated; those who fight with you shall be like nothingness and shall perish. (Isaiah 48:8-11)

[1] Origin, *Contra Celsum*, trans. Henry Chadwick, Cambridge: Cambridge University Press, 1965, 1:55 [p. 50].

Chapter 23

THE ANGEL OF HIS PRESENCE
(Isaiah 63:7-10)

Some trinitarians believe that the idea of the existence of three divine personalities active in man's salvation was declared by the prophet Isaiah. He said:

> I will make mention of the mercies of *Y-H-V-H*, and the praises of *Y-H-V-H*, according to all that *Y-H-V-H* has bestowed on us; and the great goodness toward the house of Israel, which He has bestowed on them according to His compassions, and according to the multitude of His mercies. For He said: "Surely, they are My People, children that will not deal falsely," so He was their savior. In all their affliction He was afflicted, and the angel of His presence saved them; in His love and in His pity He redeemed them; and He bore them, and carried them all the days of old. But they rebelled, and grieved His holy spirit; therefore He turned to be their enemy, and Himself fought against them. (Isaiah 63:7-10)

An examination of this passage will show that it describes God's special relationship with Israel, acting as Israel's savior and redeemer in times of affliction. It does not at all contain any reference or implication concerning a division in His unity. The phrase "angel of His presence" refers to the angel, which God chooses in any given incident to do His bidding.

Basing themselves on the Hebrew, which literally translated reads "angel of His face," some trinitarians argue that this proves that the angel is a being in God's likeness. They then infer that this angel is synonymous with the "angel of the Lord," who, they claim is the second member of the Trinity. To say that the angel is a being in God's likeness is an obvious distortion of the phrase because "of His face" is used in a possessive and not a qualitative sense. Furthermore, the term "face" (*panim*) is never used for *tselem*, "likeness" or "image." *Panim* is used here to mean "presence" (cf. Genesis 4:16; Isaiah 59:2;

Jonah 1:3, 10). In this passage, "angel of His presence" is simply the angel whom God appoints as His emissary to act as the representative of His presence in the cause of Israel.

Some trinitarians allege that the phrase "and grieved His holy spirit" (verse 10) indicates that the "holy spirit" is a separate conscious personality. How else, they ask, could it grieve? An impersonal manifestation cannot grieve! The fact is that "and grieved His holy spirit" is a figure of speech for the sorrow God felt at the children of Israel's rebelliousness. Its usage is parallel to such statements as: "He tried my patience"; "He hurt my feelings"; "He broke my spirit"; "He broke my heart." "Patience," "feelings," "spirit," and "heart" are not entities in themselves and neither is "holy spirit." The verse does not indicate that the holy spirit refers to a separate personality within the Godhead.

Chapter 24

THE LORD IS OUR RIGHTEOUSNESS
(Jeremiah 23:5-6)

In their effort to substantiate the belief in a triune deity, Christians have alleged that a prophecy given by Jeremiah supports their contention. The prophet declares:

> Behold, the days are coming says the Lord, that I will raise up for David a righteous branch, and he shall reign as king and prosper, and shall execute justice and righteousness in the land. In his days Judah will be saved, and Israel will dwell securely. And this is his name by which he will be called: "The Lord is our righteousness." (Jeremiah 23:5-6)

Christians argue that only God could properly bear the name *Y-H-V-H tsidkeinu* — "The Lord is our righteousness." However, names are often given to human beings, and even to inanimate objects, with the intention of expressing honor to God (e.g., Exodus 17:15, Jeremiah 3:17). It is not at all strange to find biblical names which incorporate the divine name within them. In Jeremiah 23:5-6, the name is there to tell us why the Messiah's rule will be just and equal for all, the source of the Messiah's righteousness is God. "The Lord is our righteousness" indicates that God will direct His Messiah's every step. The inclusion of God's name signifies the total submission of the Messiah's every action to the will of God. *The Lord is our Righteousness* is not an everyday name, but a descriptive title disclosing the level of honest judgment and compassion the Messiah will dispense as God's wholehearted representative. That this is not an ordinary given name is seen in that when a biblical personality has a name which contains the word *Y-H-V-H*, the full name of God is never included in the person's name. Most often the name takes the shortened form *y-a-h* (e.g., Isaiah, "God is Salvation"; Zechariah, "God Remembers"), or some other shortened form of the name, such as, *y-h* (e.g., Joshua, "Help of God"; Jehoshaphat, "God has Judged"). Nowhere are all

163

four letters, *Y-H-V-H* found together in that form in a name given to a human being for everyday use. The bearer of the title *The Lord is our Righteousness* is imbued with the renown and reputation of God but he is not God or part of God. He will in a very real and concrete way emulate the full meaning of the righteousness of God expressed in this name. We find that the name chosen in the Bible for a child is often descriptive of the parents' wishes or expectations for the personality that is to mature. This is also evident in the renaming of adults in the Bible, e.g., Jacob becoming Israel (Genesis 35:10). The name (or title) "the Lord is out righteousness" is one given to the Messiah when he is already a mature adult, not one given to him at birth.

The Messiah will be a visible testimony of God's activity as were the prophets, and like them he is not part of the Godhead. The name explains the very character and essence of the one bearing the name as being totally in sync with God's righteousness. By no means is there the slightest hint that the Messiah's being is of divine origin.

Chapter 25

A WOMAN ENCOMPASSES A MAN
(Jeremiah 31:22)

"A woman encompasses a man"

Christians offer a tendentious interpretation of the verse: "For the Lord has created a new thing on the earth: a woman encompasses a man" (Jeremiah 31:22). The noun *neqevah* ("woman") does not mean virgin per se and the verse says nothing of conception, pregnancy, or birth. *Neqevah* is used in the Bible in reference to any woman, virgin or not (Leviticus 27:4-7; Numbers 5:3, 31:15; Deuteronomy 4:16). Any discussion that suggests this verse is speaking of conception by a virgin has no biblical support; and more specifically that this verse predicts the birth of Jesus from a virgin is completely fallacious. In both instances neither context nor language usage justifies a connection with the birth of Jesus.

The metaphorical language found in verse 22 reverses the roles of a man and woman during courtship. It is customary for a man to go after and court a woman. Now, the woman shall go after the man, that is to say, that previously God courted Israel calling upon the nation to love Him. Israel (depicted here as a woman) will now court God (depicted here as a man). Thus, the verse exclaims that the children of Israel shall return to the Lord, their God, and He will redeem them.

The claim that this verse alludes to the birth of Jesus from a virgin is completely unfounded. The story of the virgin conception was an unknown and alien concept to the proto-Christian community. Even Paul, known for his overzealous imagination never mentions a miraculous birth for Jesus. Mark, the earliest of the canonical Gospels, also makes no mention of a virgin conception. Christians assign meanings and interpretations to words that have absolutely no basis in fact. A study of the relevant texts shows that neither context nor language usage justifies the Christian position.

The biological process by which the Messiah will be born will *not* differ from the natural method of human reproduction; he will not be born of a woman without a man's intervention. In what way will the Messiah differ? He will descend paternally from a valid regal line of the house of David and Solomon respectively. No one else will have a right to the throne. He will differ biologically, not through manner of conception, but through a specific Davidic ancestry.

Chapter 26

A NEW COVENANT WITH ISRAEL
(Jeremiah 31:31-34)

Jeremiah declares:

> Behold, the days come, says the Lord, that I will make a new covenant
> with the house of Israel, and with the house of Judah; not according
> to the covenant that I made with their fathers in the day that I took
> them by the hand to bring them out of the land of Egypt; forasmuch
> as they broke My covenant, although I was a lord over them, says
> the Lord. But this is the covenant that I will make with the house
> of Israel after those days, says the Lord, I will put My law in their
> inward parts, and in their heart I will write it; and I will be their God,
> and they shall be My people; and they shall teach no more every man
> his neighbor, and every man his brother, saying: "Know the Lord";
> for they shall all know Me, from the least of them to the greatest of
> them, says the Lord; for I will forgive their iniquity, and their sin will
> I remember no more. (Jeremiah 31:31-34)

Christians believe that the term "new covenant" means the
implementation of a new religious obligation in the form of a new
covenant, which is to take the place of the old. This new covenant
they allege is *Christianity* in the particular form to which they
personally adhere. In truth, Jeremiah's prophecy says nothing of a
new covenant that will supersede the Torah or contain any changes in
God's commandments to Israel.

What Jeremiah declares is that God will establish a new covenant
with Israel that unlike the old will be faithfully observed by Israel,
because it will become innately part of their being. God will then
grant them freedom from subjection to their foes (Leviticus 26:44).
God is to confer upon Israel a new covenant of protection, one
which will never be broken by them once they are restored to their
homeland.

There is no reason to assume that the term "new covenant" means

167

that there is a change in the eternal Torah. It is rather a reaffirmation of the commitment to the Torah given at Mount Sinai. It will resemble the covenant made by King Josiah to observe the Torah, which took place during the lifetime of Jeremiah: "And the king stood on the platform, and made a covenant before the Lord, to walk after the Lord, and to keep His commandments, and His testimonies and His statutes, with all his heart, and all his soul, to confirm the words of this covenant that were written in this book; and the people stood to the covenant" (2 Kings 23:3). But, unlike this pledge to adhere to the covenant which, though well-intentioned did not last very long, the one Jeremiah speaks of will be everlasting.

The prophet stresses the covenantal nature of the relationship between God and Israel. But, now, there is an emphasis on the permanent faithfulness that will occur on the part of Israel which will allow for God never having to neglect or forsake His people. The concept that the ancient divine law will be renewed as an everlasting inscription upon their hearts that will never be forgotten is *not* confined to Jeremiah's prophecy alone. The same prophecy is similarly found in Ezekiel:

> And I will give them one heart, and I will put a new spirit within you; and I will remove the stony heart out of their flesh, and I will give them a heart of flesh; that they may walk in My statutes, and keep My ordinances, and do them; and they shall be My people, and I will be their God. (Ezekiel 11:19-20)

The covenant made at Mount Sinai is ageless and is never to be superseded. It may be renewed and reinvigorated but never superseded by a *new covenant* that is the antithesis of the Mosaic Law. Thus, it is declared:

> And yet for all that, when they are in the land of their enemies, I will not reject them, neither will I abhor them, to destroy them utterly, and to break My covenant with them; for I am the Lord their God. But I will for their sakes remember the covenant of their ancestors, whom I brought forth out of the land of Egypt in the sight of the nations, that I might be their God: I am the Lord. (Leviticus 26:44-45)

Jeremiah reasserts this message:

> Behold, I will gather them out of all the countries, to which I have driven them in My anger, and in My fury, and in great wrath; and I will bring them back to this place, and I will cause them to dwell safely; and they shall be My people, and I will be their God; and I will give them one heart and one way, that they may fear Me forever; for the good of them, and of their children after them; and I will make an everlasting covenant with them, that I will not turn away from them, to do them good; and I will put My fear in their hearts, that they shall not depart from Me. Yea, I will rejoice over them to do them good, and I will plant them in this land in truth with My whole heart and with My whole soul. For thus says the Lord: Just as I brought all this great evil upon this people, so will I bring upon them all the good that I have promised them. (Jeremiah 32:37-42)

The author of Hebrews totally disregards the plain meaning of the prophetic message reiterated throughout the Scriptures. He alleges: "In that he says, a new covenant, he has made the first obsolete. Now that which is being made obsolete and growing old is near to vanishing away." This is a total contradiction of the biblical teaching which states: "The works of His hands are truth and justice and His precepts are sure. They are established forever and ever, they are done in truth and uprightness" (Psalms 111:7-8); "The grass withers, the flower fades; but the word of our God shall stand forever" (Isaiah 40:8). The scriptural message is clear: Gods enactments are eternally valid and immutable (see also, Genesis 17:7, 13, 19; Psalms 105:8-10; 1 Chronicles 16:13-18).

It is obvious that "new covenant" does not mean that there is a "replacement covenant." The use of the word "new" accords with biblical poetic style to express a reinvigorating or renewal of that which is already in existence. Thus Isaiah could record God's words, "For, behold, I create new heavens and a new earth" (Isaiah 65:17) and yet this does not contradict, "And the earth abides forever" (Ecclesiastes 1:4); God is speaking metaphorically of His reordering of that which already exists. There is no literal new heaven and earth. So too Jeremiah's "new covenant" is not to be viewed as a replacement of the existing covenant, but merely as a figure of speech for the reinvigoration and revitalization of the old covenant.

Jeremiah records God's words to His chosen people:

> And you shall say to them: Thus says the Lord, the God of Israel: Cursed be the man that does not hear the words of this covenant, which I commanded your fathers in the day that I brought them forth out of the land of Egypt, out of the iron furnace, saying: Listen to My voice, and do them, according to all which I commanded you; so shall you be My people, and I will be your God. (Jeremiah 11:3-4)

The people of Israel possess a God given timeless covenantal relationship — an old covenant yet a new covenant — everlasting in its nature.

Chapter 27

DOES HOSEA 1:7 MENTION TWO DIVINE PERSONALITIES?
(Hosea 1:7)

Some Christians contend that two divine personalities appear in Hosea 1:7: "But I will have mercy upon the house of Judah, and will save them [Israel] by *Y-H-V-H* their God [*'Eloheihem*]." The claim is made that if one should promise another that he will do a certain work by a third person, it would be quite evident that the one who promised the work is different from the one through whom he does it. Hence, the conclusion that the Lord who speaks is different from the Lord who actually delivers Israel. But this is an inconclusive argument, as it is not unusual for God to speak of Himself in the third person (e.g., Genesis 18:19; Exodus 3:12, 24:1; Numbers 19:1-2; Zechariah 1:12-17).

If "the Lord their God" means, as Christians say, "the Lord their Gods," it would have to refer to all three members of the Trinity. Under the circumstances, then, which member of the Trinity made the promise? It must simply be God speaking about Himself in the third person. Furthermore, if we look carefully at the Hebrew text, we will discover that the particular names of God are used advisedly, as each carries a definite meaning bearing on the overall idea of the verse. Accordingly, it should be rendered: "But I will have mercy upon the house of Judah, and will save them by means of [Myself] the Lord of Mercy [*Y-H-V-H*], their God of Justice [*'Eloheihem*]." For the divine name *Y-H-V-H* represents God's quality of mercy, i.e., the God of Mercy, and *'Elohim* represents God's quality of justice, i.e., the God of Justice.[1] Not by weapons of war did God save Judah, but by using His own weapon, "an angel of the Lord,"[2] to inflict punishment on Judah's enemies.

[1] See Rashi, Genesis 1:1 as based on *Bereshit Rabbah* 33:4 and *Sifre* (*Parashat Va-etchannan* 27 — on Deuteronomy 3:24).

[2] See 2 Kings 19:34-35.

Chapter 28

Did Hosea Mention a Second Coming of Jesus?
(Hosea 5:15)

The prophet Hosea declares: "I will go and return to My place until they feel guilt and seek My face; in their trouble they will earnestly seek Me" (Hosea 5:15). In the course of his message of rebuke for apostasy, Hosea stresses the necessity for Ephraim and Judah to first return to God through their own conscious decision before He will grant relief from their affliction.

Disregarding context, many Christians interpret Hosea 5:15 as a prophesy dealing with circumstances necessary to inaugurate the alleged second coming of Jesus. As Christians explain this verse, the Jewish people must first accept Jesus as their messianic lord and savior before he can return a second time. This interpretation is belied by events surrounding the prophecy. What makes this interpretation even more ludicrous is that it blames the Jews for the failure of Jesus to return.

Interestingly, this Christian interpretation of the prophecy is even shown to be incorrect by Paul's teachings. He says, that Israel as a nation will accept belief in Jesus, not through their own efforts but through the direct intervention of Jesus *after* his alleged return. Paul supports his position by citing Isaiah 59:20-21, with a number of critical variations. He writes, "and thus all Israel will be saved; just as it is written: 'The Deliverer will come *from* Zion, he will remove ungodliness from Jacob. And this is My covenant with them, when I take away their sins;" (Romans 11:26-27). The Hebrew text of Isaiah 59:20-21 reads in translation:

> And a redeemer will come *to* Zion, and to those that turn from transgression in Jacob, says the Lord. And as for Me, this is My covenant with them, says the Lord; My spirit that is upon you, and My words which I have put in your mouth, shall not depart out of

your mouth, nor out of the mouth of your seed, nor out of the mouth of your seed's seed, says the Lord, from henceforth and forever.

The Hebrew text of Isaiah 59:20 agrees with Hosea that the people must first repent. Redemption will come to those who have first turned away from transgression: "And a redeemer will come to Zion, and to those that turn from transgression in Jacob." Thus, even without taking the context of the verse in Hosea into account the verse itself does not agree with Paul's claim that Jesus will initiate the conversion of Israel as a nation *through his direct intervention*. Paul changed Isaiah's "a redeemer will come *to* Zion" to "a Deliverer will come *from* Zion" and Isaiah's "*and to those that turn* from transgression in Jacob" to "*he will remove* ungodliness from Jacob." The latter wording agrees with the Septuagint as it appears in modern versions.

The prophet's words are unmistakable in their message that Israel must of their own volition return to God before He will intervene to save them from all that they suffer. There will be no direct divine intervention forthcoming to begin the process of repentance — it must begin with the sinner. As we see, even the New Testament does not take Hosea's words as a referral to a second coming of Jesus.

Chapter 29

CALLED OUT OF EGYPT
(Hosea 11:1-2)

Hosea 11:1-2: When Israel was a child, then I loved him, and out of Egypt I called My son. The more they [the prophets] called them, the more they went from them. They sacrificed to the Baalim, and offered to graven images.

As we have seen Matthew relates real or fictitious events in the life of Jesus to passages from the Bible. For example, Matthew 2:15 claims that the child Jesus was literally brought by Joseph and Mary out of Egypt to fulfill the supposed prophecy: "Out of Egypt have I called My son" (Hosea 11:1).

For clarification it needs to be understood that Matthew assumes that Jesus' parents were in permanent residence in Bethlehem prior to Jesus' birth. Consequently, he says nothing of their needing to travel to Bethlehem because of a census and Jesus is not born in a manger (Luke 2:7) but in a house (Matthew 2:11). Supposedly divinely forewarned of Herod's malevolent intentions the family flees to Egypt (Matthew 2:14). Herod's alleged slaughter of children — an event not recorded in any other first century C.E. source is an historical difficulty that overshadows Matthew's birth narrative. The author's contemporary, the Jewish historian Josephus, wrote extensively about Herod's cruel deeds. It seems highly unlikely that if a slaughter of babies had taken place near Jerusalem (Bethlehem is six miles away), Josephus would not have heard about it and used it as an example of Herod's heinous crimes.

In contrast to Matthew's version of events, Luke has the family in Jerusalem thirty-three days later seemingly in no hurry to leave (Luke 2:22, cf. Leviticus 12:1-8). In Matthew the family flees to Egypt. At a later date, after receiving news of Herod's death the family is said to return in fulfillment of another alleged prophecy "that was spoken by the Lord through the prophet might be fulfilled, saying, 'Out of

Egypt I called My son' (Matthew 2:15). Matthew takes Hosea 11:1b out of context. He cannot use the verse in context for the prophet continues: "The more they [the prophets] called them, the more they went from them. They sacrificed to the Baalim, and offered to graven images" (Hosea 11:2). Hosea speaks out against the stubborn idolatry of the northern kingdom of Israel, especially Ephraim, despite God's loving concern manifested by the Exodus from Egypt. Matthew takes Hosea's words that address contemporary issues leading to the northern kingdom of Israel being exiled by the Assyrians, selects what suits him and turns it into a prophecy to occur in the distant future. But, of course, for Matthew the literal fulfillment has already come through his own application of the select text to Jesus. He could not consider the full context as applying to Jesus, Mary and Joseph for then it would describe Jesus and his family as stubborn idolaters.

The contexts of Hosea's verse shows that the prophet's reference is to the Exodus, and to an unfaithful Israel, not, as Matthew contends, to a faithful Jesus. Those who accept Matthew's claim that Hosea's words *literally* foreshadow a future event in the life of Jesus must contend with the immediately following verse, which states that "The more they [the prophets] called them, the more they went from them. They sacrificed to the Baalim, and offered to graven images."

Chapter 30

BORN IN BETHLEHEM
(Micah 5:1)

Micah 5:1 states: "But you, Bethlehem Ephratah, who are little to be among the thousands of Judah, out of you shall one come forth to Me that is to be ruler in Israel; whose goings forth are from of old, from ancient days."

Except for the birth reference found in Luke (2:4-7) everything points to Jesus being from Nazareth. In any case, being born in Bethlehem is of questionable value in establishing messianic credentials for Jesus. So many essential qualifications, as found in the Prophets, were not fulfilled by Jesus that having been born in Bethlehem would be of no consequence whatsoever.

Christians go further than simply saying that the Messiah has to be born in Bethlehem. They claim that the Messiah is shown in this verse to be an uncreated, eternal being that would be physically born. This interpretation is to be found in the King James Version and in many other Christian renderings, but by no means in all. It renders this verse as "But thou, Bethlehem Ephratah, though thou be little among the thousands of Judah, yet out of thee shall he come forth unto me that is to be ruler in Israel; whose goings forth have been from old, from everlasting."

Interestingly the Hebrew text says literally: "from you to Me will come forth" not "from Me to you." This shows that the Messiah is not conceived and born in some supernatural way as generated from God to someone or someplace. He who is to be the Messiah will come out of the Davidic heritage originating in Bethlehem to become worthy of the office by coming close to God.

How should one render the Hebrew phrase *miqedem mi-yemei 'olam.* The first word, *mikedem*, means "from of old," "from antiquity" (cf. Micah 7:20). The next two words indicate a period in the indeterminate distant past, "from the distant past," "from ages ago," "from eternity."

The problem here is to determine what the word *'olam* means in the context of verse 1. In most cases it means "eternal," but in many cases it has the meaning "for a long time" (either in the past or in the future). The prophet uses the word *'olam* in other contexts as well. In Micah 2:9, *'olam* may mean "forever," or an "indefinite long period into the future." In Micah 4:5 the phrase *l'olam va'ed* means "forever and ever" and in 4:7 the phrase *ve'ad 'olam* means "even forever." However, in Micah 7:14 the phrase *kimei 'olam* is used in a definitely non-eternal sense, "as in the days of old [*'olam*]." Therefore, there is a degree of uncertainty in the precise meaning within the context of Micah 5:1.

This verse refers to the Messiah, a descendant of David. Since David came from Bethlehem, Micah's prophecy speaks of Bethlehem as the Messiah's place of origin. The text does not necessarily mean the Messiah will be born in that town, but that his family originates from there. From the ancient family of the house of David will come forth the Messiah, whose eventual existence was known to God from the beginning of time.

The prophet does not speak of a preexistent Messiah, but of one who is, so to speak, contemplated in the mind of God. This is what is also meant in the *midrashim* which speak of the Messiah as being born or originating before the creation of the world. Thus, we find the statements: "The Fathers, Israel, the Temple, and the name of the Messiah arose in the thought [of God] to be created"[1] and "You find that at the very beginning of the creation of the world, the king Messiah had already come into being, for he existed in God's thought even before the world was created."[2] It should be noted that the Jewish Scriptures intimate that souls have an independent existence that precedes that of the person's birth (Jeremiah 1:5). If that is the case, the soul of the Messiah exists even before his body does, as all other souls do.

In sum, the Messiah is "from ancient days" in the sense that he was created "in God's thought." The Messiah is not a preexistent being, but that he eventually will play a role in Israel's future is a thought contemplated by God. This will someday be actualized in the wholly human Messiah whose every action is foreseen in the mind of God.

[1] *Bereshit Rabbah* 1:4.

[2] *Pesikta Rabbati*, "I even I, am He that comforts you," 33.6.

Chapter 31

YOUR KING IS COMING
(Zechariah 9:9)

The prophet Zechariah declares: "Rejoice greatly, O daughter of Zion, shout, O daughter of Jerusalem; behold, your king is coming to you, he is just and has been saved, humble, and riding upon an ass, even upon a colt the foal of a she-ass" (Zechariah 9:9). The Synoptic Gospels say that this prophecy was fulfilled when Jesus sent two of his disciples to fetch the animal that was to carry him into Jerusalem (Matthew 21:2-7, Mark 11:2-7, Luke 19:30-35). The Gospel of John claims that Jesus found the animal on his own. He writes, "And Jesus, finding a young ass, sat on it; as it is written: 'Fear not, daughter of Zion; behold, your King comes sitting on a she-ass's colt'" (John 12:14-15). Only one version can be correct, although both can be wrong.

Matthew has an interesting variation in his narrative, which brings up the question: Did Jesus enter Jerusalem riding on one animal, as in the three other Gospels or on two animals, as in the Gospel of Matthew? Matthew writes:

> [Jesus said] to them: "Go into the village opposite you, and immediately you will find a she-ass tied and a colt with her; untie them, and bring them to me. And if anyone says something to you, you shall say, 'The Lord needs them'; and immediately he will send them." Now this took place that what was spoken through the prophet might be fulfilled saying: "Say to the daughter of Zion, behold your King is coming to you, gentle, and mounted upon a she-ass, and upon a colt, the foal of a beast of burden." And the disciples went and did as Jesus had directed them, and brought the she-ass and the colt, and put upon them their garments, and he sat upon them. (Matthew 21:2-7)

Matthew ignores that synonymous parallelism is a common feature of biblical poetry. As a result, he gives a misreading of the prophecy, which is as if the prophet was referring to someone riding two animals. But, the fact is that the parallel structure of biblical poetry is a poetic device that calls for repetition of an idea or fact. However, this does not mean there is an actual duplication that is to be taken literally. Zechariah's prophecy mentions only the riding of one male animal. The prophet's statement, "riding upon an ass, even upon a colt the foal of a she-ass," expresses the same event in different words. Matthew creates an imaginary fulfillment of a prophecy that never existed in the first place. He thinks that two different animals are involved and so has the disciples bring two, a she-ass and its colt. Therefore, he writes, "Behold your King is coming to you, gentle, and mounted upon a she-ass, and upon a colt, the foal of a beast of burden. And the disciples ... put upon them their garments, and he sat upon them."

Matthew's Jesus came to Jerusalem riding astride both animals, one being male and the other female respectively. A rather uncomfortable fulfillment but all the more a miracle as they would be of different sizes. Each animal, we are told, was covered by the garments of Jesus' disciples, which shows that "he sat upon them" refers to the animals not the garments. The mention of the garments is incidental to the narrative. Those who accept such alleged fulfillments of prophecy must do it on faith alone, as they lack a basis in in historical fact.

Chapter 32

WHO WAS PIERCED?
(Zechariah 12:10)

Christians have argued that the prophet Zechariah is speaking of Jesus when he declares: "And they shall look to Me whom they have pierced; then they shall mourn for him, as one mourns for an only son" (Zechariah 12:10). They equate the "Me" with the "him" of verse 10 and connect both to Jesus at his supposed second coming. At that time, they expect the Jews will repent their allegedly having caused his death. Grammatically, the "Me" and the "him" cannot refer to the same individual.

The author of the Gospel of John realized the untenability of the claim that Zechariah's prophecy referred to Jesus. John changed the wording of verse 10 to make it conform to his belief. Thus, he wrote: "They shall look upon [*him*] whom they have pierced" (John 19:37). Actually, there is no "him" in John's text. Compare this with the citation based on verse 10 found at Revelation 1:7: "Every eye will see him, everyone who pierced him." In Revelation the predicted looking to the one who was pierced is interpreted of the second coming of Jesus. But in John 19:37 the piercing is interpreted of the piercing of Jesus' side with a soldier's lance after his death and here Zechariah is expressly quoted, albeit with the change from "me" to "him."

John's wording not only disagrees with the Masoretic[1] text but also is not in agreement with the Septuagint. The Greek interpretative reading found in the Codex Vaticanus and most other Septuagint manuscripts, "they shall look upon Me, because they have danced insultingly [=mocked],[2] matches the "to me" reading of the Hebrew text. The Greek of the Vienna Codex (5th-6th centuries) is much closer to a literal rendering of the Masoretic text.

But, let us look at the context of John's statement. John writes: "The [Roman] soldiers therefore came … [and] one of the [Roman] soldiers pierced his [Jesus'] side with a spear.… For these things came to pass, that the Scripture might be fulfilled, 'Not a bone of him shall be broken.' And again another Scripture says, 'They [the Roman soldiers] shall look on him whom they [the Roman soldiers] pierced'" (John 19:32-37). Both of these supposed fulfillments of Scripture have an immediate final fulfillment in the mind of the author of John. It is the Roman soldier who pierces the body and he and his fellow soldiers supposedly fulfill the Scripture. There is not the slightest hint of a future fulfillment following an alleged second coming of Jesus. The original commandment concerning the paschal lamb given to the Israelites reads, "They shall leave none of it until morning, nor break a bone of it" (Numbers 9:12). In the Gospel of John, this Torah commandment given to the Israelites becomes a prophecy fulfilled by the Roman soldiers! So too, Zechariah's words spoken concerning God's saving the Jewish people from their enemies is totally reinterpreted to find fulfillment in the contemporary actions of the Roman soldiers! The author of John attaches no significance to verse 10 as providing evidence for the supposed deity of Jesus or a future fulfillment.

The sentence structure in Zechariah 12:10 may appear confusing to those reading this verse in translation. However, it must be remembered that we are dealing here with an English rendering of biblical Hebrew, which has its own particular grammatical rules and usages. The translation "look to Me whom they have pierced" is correct. The relative clause "whom they have pierced" is in apposition to "Me," the spokesman of the passage. The Hebrew word, *et*, that introduces the clause marks it as the object of the verb "look to"; the Hebrew word *'asher* is always a relative pronoun in that context, and never the conjunction "because." It should also be noted that the Hebrew clause "they have pierced" lacks the pronominal suffix "him."

Let us look at this verse in context. In Zechariah 12, we are told that God will defend His people and destroy their enemies. On that day:

> [T]hey [the nation of Israel, i.e., the house of David and the inhabitants of Jerusalem, mentioned at the beginning of verse 10] shall look to Me [God] whom they [the nations, spoken of in verse 9, that shall come up against Jerusalem] have pierced; then they [Israel]

shall mourn for him [the slain of Israel as personified by the leader of the people, the warrior Messiah who will die in battle at this time].

Of course, God cannot literally be pierced. The idea of piercing God expresses the fact that Israel stands in a very special relationship to God among all the nations of the earth. God identifies with His people to the degree that He takes part figuratively in the nation's destiny. To attack (pierce) Israel is to attack God. That is why God says: "Me whom they have pierced" even though it is the people of Israel and not God who is actually "pierced." Accordingly, Isaiah says of God's relationship to Israel: "In all their affliction He was afflicted" (Isaiah 63:9), and in Psalms 83:2-6 we see that the nations which hate God manifest that hatred by seeking to destroy the Jewish people. God's presence in history is *revealed* in the continued survival of the Jewish people. There are many biblical passages which show that God identifies Himself with Israel (e.g., Jeremiah 12:14, Isaiah 49:25, Exodus 23:22, Zechariah 2:12-13).

As stated above, the Gentile nations shall look to God, whom they have attacked by the persecution, death and general suffering they inflicted on the nation of Israel ("him"), whose dead will be mourned by the surviving Jewish people. The rabbis of the Talmud saw this suffering personified in the leader of the people, the warrior Messiah, the son of Joseph (a descendant of Joseph's son Ephraim), who will be slain at the time discussed in verse 10 (B.T. *Sukkah* 52a). All of the nation's dead will be mourned, but the mourning over the death of the warrior Messiah symbolizes the collective grief as the people mourn for the fallen of Israel.

Zechariah 12:10 does not equate Jesus with God in any way, nor does it say anything of a return by Jesus, or a mourning by the nation of Israel over his death.

---

[1] Apparently to avoid what seems to be a reference to a "piercing" of God some later Hebrew manuscripts underwent scribal emendation so as to read "look to *him* whom they have pierced," rather than "look to *me* whom they have pierced." Initially, these late Jewish manuscripts show this in the marginal notes (*kere*), but eventually in some manuscripts the change was made directly in the body of the text itself. However, the oldest and best Hebrew manuscripts read "me" rather than "him."

[2] This may reflect a misreading of the Hebrew root *dqr*, "to stab," "to pierce," as

deriving from the root *rqd*, "to skip about." In Hebrew the *dalet* and the *resh* are very similar

Chapter 33

THE COMING OF ELIJAH
(Malachi 3:1, 23-24)

Did Elijah come and we didn't recognize him?

The prophet Malachi declares:

> Behold, I send you My messenger, and he shall clear the way before Me; and the Lord, whom you seek will suddenly come to His Temple; and the messenger of the covenant, whom you delight in, behold, he comes, says the Lord of hosts. (Malachi 3:1)

> Behold, I will send you Elijah the prophet before the coming of the great and terrible day of the Lord. And he shall turn the heart of the fathers to the children, and the heart of the children to their fathers; lest I come and smite the land with utter destruction. (Malachi 3:23-24).

The Jesus of the Synoptic Gospels applies these verses to John the Baptist. He considers Malachi's prophecies concerning Elijah, the forerunner of the Messiah, as completely fulfilled in John. He not only believed this but also believed that Elijah had returned in the person of John. When asked: Why then do the scribes say that Elijah must come first" (Matthew 17:10), Jesus replied: "Elijah, indeed, is coming and will restore all things," that is, before the arrival of the Messiah (Matthew 17:11). He then continues: "But I am saying to you Elijah has already come" (Matthew 17:12). This is stated in Mark as: "But I say to you Elijah, also, has come" (Mark 9:13).

According to these Gospels, Jesus did not say that Elijah would come in the future.

He explained the prophecies as *showing* that "Elijah, indeed, does come first and restore all things" (Mark 9:12). As Matthew and Mark narrate the story, it was Jesus' understanding that Elijah must precede the arrival of the Messiah and that Elijah has already come. What makes these statements most significant is that Jesus links John the

Baptist with Malachi 3:1 (Matthew 11:10-11, Luke 7:27-28). The New Testament's Jesus contends that Elijah has already come in the actual person of John, thus fulfilling Malachi 3:23. But, the identification of John the Baptist with Elijah is totally rejected by John the Baptist himself (John 1:21). According to the Gospel of John, when asked, "Are you Elijah?" John answered, "I am not." To the question, "Are you the Prophet?" his answer was, "No."

Wishing will not make it so

Some Christians insist that what Jesus meant was that John the Baptist was not actually Elijah but only represented him in regard to Elijah's "spirit and power" (Luke 1:17). But, if that were true the text would read "like Elijah," or "similar to Elijah." Instead, the Hebrew text of Malachi 3:23 reads, *hinnei 'anochi sholeiach lachem 'et 'Eiliya hanavi'* ("Behold, I will send you Elijah the prophet"). The participle *'et* is placed before the direct object of a verb if the object it indicates is definite. Elijah is a proper noun and is regarded as definite. The presence of *'et* emphasizes that the individual who is to appear will be Elijah. Thus, the allegation that John the Baptist simply represented Elijah in spirit and power does not satisfy Malachi's prophecy, as it does not agree with the plain meaning as defined by the grammatical usage of the participle. In any case, Jesus himself said that John the Baptist was Elijah in the flesh and not merely in the spirit. Jesus said of John while the latter was alive: "And if you care to accept it, he is Elijah who is intended to come" (Matthew 11:14). After John was executed, Jesus said of him: "But I am saying to you Elijah has already come, and they did not recognize him" (Matthew 17:12). Jesus did not differentiate between Malachi 3:1 and 3:23. Thus, he identified John as the "messenger" and announced that "he is Elijah."

Evidence that demands to be heard

There are details of evidence that disagree with an identification of John as only in the spirit sand power of Elijah and not bodily. Elijah's return is to be bodily not just in spirit. This is implicit in the fact that in leaving this world he was taken up bodily (2 Kings 2:11). There would have been no need for Elijah to ascend to heaven bodily if only his "spirit and power" were going to return. In addition, even the John the Baptist of the Gospels does *not* claim that he is Elijah in spirit. When he was asked who he was, John allegedly replied: "I am a voice of one crying in the wilderness, 'Make straight the way of the Lord,' as said the prophet Isaiah" (John 1:23). John is not identifying himself with Elijah since this verse from Isaiah is taken from a prophecy foretelling the return of the Jewish people from exile and there is nothing to link it to the supposed mission of John as the forerunner of the Messiah. The exile of the Jewish people was not terminated during John the Baptist's lifetime. In view of John's emphatic denial of having any connection with Elijah (John 1:21), it is obvious that *either* Jesus or John was in error about the role of the latter.

Who was in error?

Some Christians say that Elijah will come just before Jesus' second coming, but it is obvious from the Gospel's Jesus that he expected Elijah in his own lifetime. If John was Elijah in *any* form he failed in his God given commission. The biblical mandate for the forerunner of the Messiah includes ushering in an era of perfect peace and harmony between fathers and their children, ending all discord and strife between them. Malachi says clearly: "And he shall turn the heart of the fathers to the children, and the heart of the children to their fathers."

According to Luke, John's mission was supposed to be "to turn the hearts of the fathers back to the children, and the disobedient to the attitude of the righteous; so as to make ready a people prepared for the Lord" (Luke 1:17). John the Baptist did not accomplish this task as he had little impact on his generation. Jesus explained his own function as the exact reverse not only of Elijah's mission but of John's as well. He said:

> Do not think that I came to bring peace on earth; I did not come to bring peace, but a sword. For I came to set a man against his father, and a daughter against her mother, and a daughter-in-law against her mother-in-law. (Matthew 10:34-35)

> I have come to cast fire upon the earth; and how I wish it were already kindled! But I have a baptism to undergo, and how distressed

I am until it is accomplished! Do you suppose that I came to grant peace on earth? I tell you, no, but rather division; for from now on five members in one household will be divided, three against two, and two against three. They will be divided, father against son, and son against father; mother against daughter, and daughter against mother, mother-in-law against daughter-in-law, and daughter-in-law against mother-in-law. (Luke 12:49-53)

Undoubtedly, Malachi 3:1 and 3:23-24 refer to the actual return of Elijah immediately preceding the Messiah's arrival. Since Elijah did not come during Jesus' lifetime (although he claimed John the Baptist was Elijah) it is obvious that he could not be the Messiah.

Chapter 34

YOU ARE MY SON
(Psalms 2:7)

Psalms 2:7

The concept of physical sonship with God the Father is not found in biblical theology or in first century Judaism. What is found is the biblical concept of the covenantal relationship whereby Israel or an individual within that nation is metaphorically adopted as God's son. One does not need to undergo a supernatural conception to be declared "son of God" in a Jewish context.

In the Christian search for biblical proof of the belief in Jesus as the "Son of God," proof has often been found where none exists by violating the integrity of the plain meaning of scriptural passages. Prominent among these is Psalms 2:7, wherein it is stated: "The Lord said to me: 'You are My son, this day I have begotten you.'" An examination of the context will show that this verse refers to the metaphoric father-and-son relationship between God and David. The king is not divine by nature, rather he is elected to a special relationship with God (metaphorically a father-son relationship; cf. Psalms 89:36). A similar relationship later existed between God and Solomon (2 Samuel 7:14; 1 Chronicles 22:10, 28:6). This special relationship is not to be taken in a literal sense. We can only speak of God metaphorically, as for example, "mouth of God" (2 Chronicles 35:22), "the eye of the Lord" (Psalms 33:18), "the ears of God" (2 Samuel 22:7), and the like. It is in a similar metaphorical sense that the verse speaks of the son of God, or the sons of God, for whoever carries out the will of God is called "son," as the son carries out the will of the father. It is for this reason that the text says, "You are My son, this day have I begotten you" (Psalms 2:7), and it states in similar fashion, "Israel is My son, My first born" (Exodus 4:22). To be singled out for God's special favor as an individual or as a whole people is called, in the Scriptures, "to beget" (Deuteronomy 32:18). David, on his ascension to the throne, was declared to be begotten of God.

The title of son is given to all those who enjoy a special relationship with God (Exodus 4:22, Hosea 2:1). David becomes the son of God *ex officio*. Similar hyperbolic language is found in Psalm 110, a psalm that portrays the Davidic king enthroned at the right hand of God, reigning in Zion as God's earthly representative. In all of these cases, the language of poetic hyperbole should not be construed to mean that the king (messiah) is regarded as a divine being.

Christians may argue that the references to sonship are typologies pointing to the existence of an actual divine sonship embodied in Jesus. But this argument is obviously based on purely subjective reasoning, with no facts from the Jewish Scriptures to give it support. Psalms 2:7 could not at all refer to Jesus. The verse says: "The Lord said to me: 'You are My son.'" Why would God have to inform Jesus, a fellow member of the Trinity, of the exact nature of their relationship? The verse then continues: "this day I have begotten you." If Jesus is God, how can he be begotten? Are we to presume that this statement was made on the day of Jesus' incarnate conception, and that God spoke to the fertilized egg? Moreover, should we presume that this fertilized egg had the ability to answer God, as is implied in verse 8? There, God states: "Ask of Me, and I will give the nations for your inheritance, and the ends of the earth for your possession." Would Jesus, if he was a member of the Trinity, with all its implications, have to make this request of God? Did Jesus have to ask for these or any other possessions? If he were God, the heavens and the earth and all that they contain are already his possessions. Furthermore, if Jesus had the ability to understand God's statement on the very day of his conception, it would seem incongruous for the New Testament to describe him as "increasing in wisdom and in physical growth with both God and men" (Luke 2:52). This offer by God would have had no meaning since Matthew 20:28 and Mark 10:45 say Jesus came to serve, not to be served. Did God make an empty offer? If the statement, "This day I have begotten you" was made to Jesus at a date later than the day of his conception, and is thus figurative in meaning, he is then not distinguished from all the others who are in the "sonship of God."

According to the New Testament accounts, Jesus certainly did

189

not have an earthly kingdom during his lifetime. If this is supposed to occur during a second coming, then we come to a further problem. It is alleged that at that time Jesus would be coming back not in an earthly state, but exalted and as God. That being the case, he would not have to ask for either "inheritance" or "possession." Actually, verse 7 does not mean that David was to inherit literally "the ends of the earth." It is an obvious hyperbole, the true meaning of which is, a large expanse of territory, and can only apply to a human being that, unlike God, or allegedly Jesus, does not possess all of creation. Similar hyperboles can be found in the Scriptures, for example, "There was *no* end to his treasures ... and there was *no end* to his chariots" (Isaiah 2:7), and David, who never left the vicinity of the Land of Israel, says: "From the end of the earth I will call you" (Psalms 61:3).

A related statement parallel to that of Psalms 2:7 is found in Psalms 89:28: "I will also appoint him firstborn, the highest of the kings of the earth." Since the latter verse clearly refers to the actual person of David, and not to any typological messiah, as is evident from verses 4, 21, 27, 36, and 37, there is good reason to assume that Psalms 2:7 refers to King David. There is no doubt that when the true Messiah comes he will rule the nations, as can be seen from Isaiah 11, and we do not have to seek out proof where none exists. Psalm 2 is a historical psalm and in its plain meaning does not speak about the messianic age. Nevertheless, there are Jewish sources which give this psalm a messianic context, especially midrashic literature. The messianic interpretation of Psalm 2 occurs in the late Midrash *Tehillim*, but there "sonship" is metaphorical, "as when a master says to his slave, 'you are my son'" (Psalms 2:7). It is simply an expression of endearment.

Chapter 35

DO HOMAGE IN PURITY
(Psalms 2:12)

"Do homage in purity"

In Psalms 2:12 it is stated: "Do homage in purity [*nash-ku bar*], lest He be angry, and you perish in the way." The Christian rendering of the Hebrew phrase *nash-ku bar* as "kiss the son" is based on a misinterpretation. The meaning of the Hebrew word (*bar*) is "pure" or "clear." Only in Aramaic does it have the meaning of "son (of)." However, in Aramaic, *bar* is used only as a construct "son of" (Proverbs 31:2; Ezra 5:1-2, 6:14), whereas the absolute form of "son" in Aramaic (which would have to be used in verse 12) is *ber'a* – "the son". Thus, according to the Christian conception, the verse should have read *nash-ku ber'a*, "kiss the son," not *nash-ku bar*, "kiss the son of." Even though "son" could refer to David in verse 12, it is not the proper translation. There is no compelling reason to employ an Aramaism in view of the use of the Hebrew noun *bein*, "son," in verse 7. The phrase is best rendered as, "do homage in purity," because kissing is generally an expression of homage, as found, for example, in 1 Samuel 10:1: "Then Samuel took the vial of oil, and poured it upon his head, *and kissed him.*" *Bar*, meaning "purity," occurs in the phrase "pure in heart" (Psalms 24:4, 73:1). The intention implied in verse 12 is: with sincerity of heart, acknowledge me, David, as God's anointed, and thereby avoid incurring God's anger. Thus, the Hebrew phrase *nash-ku bar* simply means "do homage in purity," in the sense of expressing sincere loyalty.

There is a misconception that states that the Jewish biblical commentator, Ibn Ezra, explained *nashku bar* as "kiss the son." As such, his commentary is incorrectly rendered as: "'Serve the Lord' refers to the Lord, while 'kiss the son' refers to his anointed one, and the meaning of *bar* is like [the meaning of *bar* in the phrase] 'what, my son [*beri*], and what, son of my womb [*bar bitni*, Proverbs 31:2]? And thus it is written, 'You are My son' [Psalms 2:7]. And it is the

191

custom of the nations in the world to put their hands under the hand of the king, as the brothers of Solomon did [see 1 Chronicles 29:24], or for the servant [to put his hand] under the thigh of his master [see Genesis 24:2], or to kiss the king. And this is the custom until today in the land of India."

It is improbable that Ibn Ezra would have explained the word *bar* by appealing to the Aramaic word *bar*, "son of," which being in the construct state would, in any case, be incorrect grammatically. Of course, there is the possibility that because of the proximity of the phrase, "you are My son," there was an impetus to make a linguistic equation between the *bar* in the phrase *nashku bar* with the Aramaic word, *bar*. Indeed, there are some Jewish commentators who use a midrashic approach rather than citing the plain meaning and therefore render *bar* in this context as "son." But this would not be consistent with the exacting exegesis associated with Ibn Ezra. More than likely, it is the common understanding of what he wrote that is incorrect. The key to a proper understanding of his commentary is found in his reference to Proverbs 31:2; at that verse, a "son" is referred to. But, in this totally Hebrew passage the words *beri* and *bar* appear and are commonly rendered as if derived from the Aramaic for "my son" and "son of" respectively. However, as the 19th century commentator Meir Leibush Malbim explains, Proverbs 31:2 should be explained in terms of a son who is held in great esteem and designated, using the Hebrew, as *bar*, "chosen" or "beloved" (see Song of Songs 6:9; Psalms 65:14 — in the sense of purified). This noun is from the Hebrew verb form *barar*, "select," "choose," "cleanse," "purify," "sift." Hence, the verse should read, "What, my chosen one [*beri*], and what, beloved one of my womb [*bar bitni*]. Returning to Ibn Ezra's words, we should render them as, "'Serve the Lord' refers to the Lord, while 'kiss [or, "do homage to"] the chosen [or, "beloved"] one' refers to his anointed one, and the meaning of *bar* is like [the meaning of *bar* in the phrase] 'What, my chosen one [*beri*], and what, beloved one of my womb [*bar bitni;* Proverbs 31:2]? And thus it is written, 'You are My son' {Psalms 2:7]. Literally rendered, Ibn Ezra is saying *nashku bar* means "kiss the chosen [beloved] one," that is, give homage to he who is called "My son" [*bini*] as mentioned in verse 2.

For the Jewish proto-Christian community, who had known Jesus and his family he was a human being, a great teacher, one who was a "son of God" through fulfillment of mission. This notion developed in Hellenistic Jewish-Christian circles into identification with the divine Logos (Word) concept familiar from the writings of Philo.[1] But, Jesus was still not divine in the ontological sense that developed in later Christianity.

All Israel are considered to be the children of God,[2] "Israel is My firstborn son" (Exodus 4:22, Hosea 2:1) and David and Solomon as personifications of that ideal are specifically designated as sons of God. Of David it is written: "The Lord said to me: 'you are My son, today I have begotten you'" (Psalms 2:7) and of Solomon, God says, "I will be to him for a father, and he shall be to Me for a son" (2 Samuel 7:14). Whether or not one gives these verses a messianic significance or not, it is clear that in the biblical setting neither Israel nor these two monarchs are to be regarded as God's sons in the sense of a union between a woman and a manifestation of God, that is, a miraculous conception. Rather the significance of this designation is specifically because they are the chosen of God. The same may be said of the Messiah as well; he is to be regarded as God's son only in the fact that he is the chosen of God. With the stories of the virgin conception of Jesus in the respective Gospels of Matthew and Luke the figurative idea of being God's son is transformed so as to refer literally to one's being physically God's son from conception in the Hellenistic sense. However, even in the New Testament itself, this meaning of divine sonship from conception is contradicted. As seen above, for Mark divine sonship was bestowed upon Jesus at his baptism. For Paul, whose writings antedate those of the Gospels, Jesus is God's son not from birth or baptism, but from his alleged resurrection at which time he supposedly entered this special relationship. Paul declared Jesus to be "the son of God with power by the resurrection from the dead" (Romans 1:4, see also Acts 13:33 where Psalms 2:7 is applied to the resurrection). With time, Christian theology made the significant reverse transformation from "son of God" to "God the Son," the second person of the Trinity.

[1] According to Philo's Logos notion, it was the Logos that mediated the action of

God in this material universe: in creation, providence, and salvation. Philo saw this as the force of rationality and physical and moral order. The means through which God brings about the reordering of the disordered and sinful.

[2] The use of the masculine in this case includes females as well.

Chapter 36

MY FLESH DWELLS IN SAFETY: A RESURRECTION FANTASY

(Psalms 16:9-10)

My flesh dwells in safety

The Masoretic text of Psalms 16:9-10 reads:

Therefore my heart is glad, and my glory rejoices; my flesh also dwells in safety. For You will not abandon my soul to the nether-world; neither will You allow Your faithful one to see the pit.

However, while the Masoretic text renders the Hebrew word spelled *shin-vav-hay* as "pit" the Septuagint Greek renders it as "corruption," "decay." The difference is the result of choosing a different set of vowels. The author of Acts claims that this passage is a prophecy of the alleged resurrection of Jesus. Thus, in a fictive speech based on the Septuagint rendering he has Peter state:

He [David] saw beforehand and spoke concerning the resurrection of the Christ, that neither was he forsaken in Hades nor did his flesh see decay. (Acts 2:31)

The author of Acts then quotes Paul as stating:

That He raised him up from the dead, no more to return to decay, He has spoken in this way: "I will give you the holy and sure things of David." Therefore He also says in another psalm: "You will not allow Your loyal one to see decay." For David, after he had served the purpose of God in his own generation, fell asleep, and was laid among his fathers, and did see decay; but he whom God raised did not see decay. (Acts 13:34-37)

This misuse of Psalms 16:9-10 is a desperate attempt to explain the disappearance of Jesus' body.

But, if the psalmist's words are to be used as an explanation of what happened to the entombed physical remains of Jesus, there is no reason for not applying the statement: "My flesh also dwells in safety" to his entire lifetime as well. The Hebrew verb *yishkon*, "dwells," appears in the imperfect tense, which denotes incomplete action. It is used to express a continuation of an action that starts at a point in time and continues on into the future. Did Jesus' body "dwell in safety," never seeing any form of "corruption," that is, decay, as implied by the statements attributed to Peter and Paul in Acts? If we apply the words, "my flesh also dwells in safety," to Jesus the god-man, then what happened to his foreskin after his circumcision (Luke 2:21)? Did it ascend to heaven, or did it decompose as with any human piece of flesh? Did his umbilical cord ascend as well? During his lifetime what happened to his hair, nails, and blood shed from wounds? Did the cells of his body die as in ordinary human beings? If his body did not function in a truly human way, he could not be truly human as well as truly God. Yet, if his body functioned exactly in a human way, this would nullify any claim to divinity. It would be impossible for any part of God, even if incarnate, to decompose in any way and still be considered God. By definition, not mystery, the everlasting, one God, in whole or in part, does not die, disintegrate, or decompose: "For I the Lord do not change" (Malachi 3:6). Did Jesus' flesh dwell in safety after his death? 1 Peter 3:18 states that Jesus was "put to death in the flesh, but made alive in the spirit." 1 Corinthians 15:44-45 claims Jesus was "raised a spiritual body," that is, he "became a life-giving spirit." No mention of the survival of the flesh is alluded to. Obviously, even according to the New Testament, Jesus did not fulfill the psalmist's statement, "My flesh also dwells in safety."

Note that Jesus' foreskin was considered one of the most precious relics of the Middle Ages — and at one time there existed at least eighteen of them in Europe. One was on display at the Church of the Prepuce (Calcata, Italy), which became a shrine for women who could not conceive; viewing the holy foreskin was said to bring fertility.

Physical or spiritual body?

What does the New Testament claim happened to the corpse of

196

Jesus? Jesus is said to have been resurrected, to have entered into another kind and level of existence, one in which he will never again die. The New Testament authors are ambivalent on the subject of whether Jesus was resurrected with a physical body or only as a spirit. What was the state of the returned Jesus? The early church could not agree as to what was his post-resurrection nature: Did he undergo a "physical" or a "spiritual" resurrection? Disputes in early Christian literature show that Christians accepted disparate understandings of Jesus and his alleged resurrection. The earliest Christian teachings did not uniformly stress that Jesus rose with a physical body.

For our discussion, the crucial time period is at the moment the alleged resurrection took place. However, we must take into consideration the nature of the alleged later appearances as well. Luke and John write in their respective Gospels that Jesus appeared, on occasion, after the resurrection in a physical body. John illustrates this by having Jesus order Mary Magdalene to stop touching him (John 20:17). By this he wishes to show that the body of Jesus was, after the resurrection, a tangible object. John continues in this manner when he writes that Thomas was instructed by the resurrected Jesus to touch him.

> And after eight days again his disciples were inside and Thomas with them. Jesus came, the doors having been shut, and stood in the midst, and said: "Peace be to you." Then he said to Thomas: "Put your finger here, and see my hands, and take your hand and thrust it into my side." (John 20:26-27)

While nothing is mentioned of his actually touching Jesus, the reader is left with the impression that what Thomas discerned was the physical nature of Jesus. John does not indicate whether the apparition actually looked like Jesus.

Luke states emphatically that Jesus was not a spirit. He writes that when Jesus allegedly appeared in Jerusalem to the eleven apostles they imagined that they were seeing a spirit. They were then instructed to look at his hands and feet. "'See my hands and my feet, that it is I myself; touch me and see, for a spirit does not have flesh and bones as you see that I have.' And when he said this he showed them his hands and his feet" (Luke 24:39-40). Luke claims that Jesus appeared in an actual physical body, without clearly indicating whether it was the same body as he had before his death. Identification was to be made not by his facial features but by his wounds. The evangelist then states that Jesus, as further proof of his physical state, partakes of their meal (Luke 24:41-43). Luke suggests that a definite physical resurrection took place. The implication of his words is that whereas a spirit is not a tangible object, which one is able to touch, the post-resurrection Jesus was an actual physical being that could be touched and was even capable of consuming food. Alternately, Luke may be saying that Jesus is not simply an intangible spirit but, rather, a "divine being," which could metamorphose from his "spirit" self to assume a solid material form that could be touched or partake of food.

Whatever Luke or John may have believed about the tangibility of Jesus' body when he allegedly appeared to his followers, the respective epistles attributed to Peter and Paul state emphatically that Jesus did not rise in a physical body. Paul explicitly denies that the resurrection body is physical. Instead, he said, it is spiritual (1 Corinthians 15:12-57). In Paul's explanation of the nature of the body at the time of resurrection, he denies the physical resurrection, saying that the "natural body" is buried, but what is raised is a "spiritual body" (1 Corinthians 15:44). There is a transformation from a dead physical body to a living spiritual one. This he applies not just to ordinary human beings, but even to Jesus. Although Paul refers to the post-resurrection Jesus as a "man" in 1 Timothy 2:5, he obviously does not mean that Jesus is a physical man. Paul emphatically declares the risen Jesus to be spirit, not flesh: "The last Adam [literally "man" in Hebrew] became a life-giving spirit" (1 Corinthians 15:45). Accordingly, Paul's resurrected Jesus was not a man in the physical sense, but rather, a spiritual man. The author of the First Epistle of Peter states that the change from flesh to spirit occurred at the moment of resurrection. He states that Jesus was "put to death in the flesh, but made alive in the spirit" (1 Peter 3:18). The epistles attributed to Peter and Paul provide information, which is in direct contradiction to the claim that Jesus rose in a physical body from his tomb.

Paul, in referring to the alleged resurrection of Jesus, does not mention an empty tomb, but says Jesus "was buried and rose again." To say Jesus "was buried and rose again" is different from saying, "And they found the tomb empty." The first may mean that Jesus was dead and that his spirit rose from his body that remained stationary in the tomb. The second statement says that something happened to the corpse of Jesus. Paul writes, "For I delivered to you as of first importance what I also received, that Christ died for our sins according to the Scriptures, and that he was buried, and that he was raised on the third day according to the Scriptures" (1 Corinthians 15:3-4). There are some that understand this passage to mean that Paul is teaching a physical resurrection. But, this approach ignores what Paul says in the rest of the chapter, especially verses 35-50. As we have seen, there Paul explicitly denies that it is the physical body that is raised; rather, it is the spiritual body that is raised. Does Paul believe in a physical resurrection? Not according to his own testimony.

Some Christians attempt to harmonize the differences of opinion among the New Testament authors by conjecturing that Jesus had a "glorified" physical body. Therefore, they claim, he could enter locked rooms, appearing and disappearing at will. Others take the view that God disposed of the physical body of Jesus without resorting to the process of decay. Both Peter and Paul propagate a belief that Jesus' physical body was not preserved for use by the resurrected Jesus. While they do not speculate as to how the physical body was disposed of, neither do they mention a "glorified" physical body. In fact, what they teach is quite contrary to this belief. Paul believes that Jesus had a "body of glory" (Philippians 3:21) but does not state that it was a physical body. He argues that Jesus received a spiritual body at his resurrection (1 Corinthians 15:44-49). Paul definitely rules out a physical resurrection in any form for Jesus when he states: "Flesh and blood cannot inherit the kingdom of God; nor does the perishable inherit the imperishable" (1 Corinthians 15:50).

Whether a "physical" or "spiritual" resurrection is contended both views present problems for Christian theology. The author of Hebrews writes that Jesus "offered one sacrifice for all sins for all time" (Hebrews 10:12). This sacrifice was "the offering of the body of Jesus Christ" (Hebrews 10:10). To this John's Jesus adds, "I am the living bread that came down out of heaven, if any one eats of this bread, he will live forever; and the bread also which I will give for the life of the world is my flesh" (John 6:5). Accordingly, the New Testament's Jesus could not take back his fleshly body, even as part of a resurrection. To do so would mean taking back the offering given but once as the supreme atonement sacrifice. Taking back his sacrificed fleshly body in resurrection would cancel out the original offering made at the crucifixion for all sins. Jesus' death is considered as a literal not metaphorical sacrifice presented to God, the Father. Therefore, Jesus could not have risen in the body offered as a sacrifice to God, the Father, as it was no longer his. Did God, the Father, return his body to him? If so, what sort of a sacrifice would that be? After all, Jesus is allegedly an equal partner of a triune Godhead who supposedly predicted his own resurrection (Matthew 16:21). Surely, he also knew whether as part of the divine drama he would get his sacrificed fleshly body returned to him. A physical resurrection of Jesus' pre-crucifixion fleshly body would have profoundly negative christological implications. It would show that Jesus' death was not a sacrifice. He knew what to expect. He gave up nothing, neither his life nor his body. Both, the New Testament maintains, were returned to him in some form or other, along with enormous universal power (Philippians 2:8-11).

Could Jesus have risen in either a completely different material body or in an immaterial body possessing the properties of an angelic being which could metamorphose itself from a "spirit" into a solid material form that could be touched (Genesis 32:24-26) or partake of food (Genesis 18:1-18)? These related theories contain respectively inherent problems. If Jesus' body ceased to be material and later became material again, then it was not the identical body that was crucified. Unless Jesus rose in the same physical body in which he died it is not the unique resurrection described as exclusive to him. It would not matter if the pre-resurrection and post-resurrection bodies show continuity of person and personality but discontinuity in the relationship of the resurrected body to the pre-death physical body. That is understandable and expected for ordinary human beings whose bodies undergo decay and disintegration into the environment. The New Testament also declares that God did not permit Jesus' fleshly body to undergo decay. The author of Acts, in Acts 2:26-27, applies the Septuagint rendering of Psalms 16:9-10 [verses 8-11 in some versions] to Jesus. This author claims that Jesus is saying that his "flesh" has hope because God will not leave his soul in Hades nor allow him to undergo decay. The author's meaning is that Jesus' body and spirit would not remain separated, but, through the resurrection, "he was neither abandoned to Hades, nor did his flesh suffer decay" (Acts 2:31). If Jesus arose in an immortal spiritual body, but not with the identical form and the actual substance of his mortal body, it renders his resurrection as outside the New Testament understanding that Jesus' body would not decay or disintegrate in any way. There would be no empirical proof of continuity, as there is no actual total physical identity, between the pre-resurrection and post-resurrection Jesus. In sum, continuity of physical likeness, of itself, without continuity of physical substance, is no basis for establishing that the resurrection of Jesus occurred since his body was not supposed to decay or disintegrate. For the same reason, a claim of resurrection in an invisible, immaterial body is unverifiable and is not, in actuality, a resurrection of a dead body.

Christian denominations and sects have always differed on whether Jesus rose from the grave in the same physical body that died on the cross. Some hold that the post-resurrection Jesus was in a different mode of existence, which involved one or more different bodies being utilized. According to this view, there was a discontinuity in the relationship of the physical body to the resurrection body. It is maintained that the continuity between the pre- and post-resurrection state of Jesus was person and personality and not material. Others argue that it is necessary for the very same physical, material body that died to have been raised from the dead. They maintain that if Jesus' body changed into an invisible, immaterial one then what occurred was annihilation, not resurrection. It is also claimed that if there is no numerical identity between the pre- and post-resurrection body, then what occurred is not a resurrection of the same body, but rather a reincarnation into another body. In general, the problem stems from the unclear and divergent views already found in the early church and reflected in the New Testament. However, all these speculations are in vain since Jesus was never resurrected to begin with and therefore never appeared to anyone after his death.

The New Testament does not provide any proof for the allegation that either a physical or spiritual resurrection of Jesus ever took place. Although Peter states: "This Jesus God resurrected, of which we are all witnesses" (Acts 2:32), absolutely no one saw the alleged resurrection take place, in any form whatsoever. At best, the only statement that can be made is that the body was missing. Nothing definite can be said concerning its final disposition at the time of the supposed resurrection. All the information concerning this non-event is derived from the New Testament. The New Testament, while not consisting of contemporary documents, is the earliest and only source of information on the subject of *the resurrection of Jesus*. However, it lacks the necessary factual information to allow one to learn about the final disposition of the physical remains of Jesus. Paul, the earliest New Testament author, not only has a list and sequence of resurrection stories that differ from the Gospels, but also does not even mention the claim of the empty tomb. If true, the empty tomb would be the only public, visible evidence by which to claim that resurrection took place. All alleged sightings of a risen being were said to be appearances to select followers of Jesus. Moreover, the New Testament authors often explicitly indicate that the alleged post-resurrection appearances were sightings of individuals who did not look or sound like Jesus. Jesus' disciples and the early Christian community simply did not really know what had happened to the remains of their crucified leader.

To be blunt, an empty tomb does not prove that a resurrection occurred. Moreover, materialization in an unrecognizable form does not prove a bodily resurrection occurred. The original body could have disappeared in any number of ways and the appearances could have been of someone else. There is no way to verify empirically that Jesus was resurrected unless he was materially resurrected in the same physical body in which he died and was buried. Yet, as we have seen above, this was impossibile according to the New Testament theology by which Jesus' fleshly body is offered as a permanent sin offering.

The psalmist's words can only make sense if they are a poetic reference to David's gratitude to God for watching over him throughout his life, rather than to a resurrected body of a divine being. There was nothing in Jewish Scripture or tradition about a resurrected Messiah, only the resurrection of all men for the last judgment (Daniel 12:2, Isaiah 26:19) and certain individuals on occasion (2 Kings 4:32-37, 13:21). Resurrection, which is a restoration of physical life, relates only to human beings; it cannot apply to spirit immortals. Jesus' alleged resurrection would be relevant only if he was wholly human to begin with. Resurrection, being a phenomenon relating to restoration of physical existence to a dead human being, can only be claimed if Jesus was and remained no more than a man. Of what miraculous significance does resurrection have to one already possessing a divine eternal nature in the first place? Springing back to life, if death can be inflicted on such a one, is to be expected. What was the state of the returned Jesus? The early church could not agree to his post-resurrection nature: Did he undergo a "physical" or a "spiritual" resurrection, or none at all?

Chapter 37

THE CRUCIFIXION OF JESUS AND PSALM 22
(Psalm 22)

Finding the Jesus who never was

The early church used the Jewish Scriptures to augment the little they knew of the circumstances surrounding Jesus' death. To this end they made use of Psalms 22:2, 19. Later Christians sought further confirmation of their claims by expanding their citations from this psalm. The historical Jesus was of little interest to that part of the church that had not known Jesus the man personally. What interested this faction was how to show Jesus as the messianic savior raised from the dead to bring salvation to those who believed in him. He was no longer simply Jesus the Messiah; he now was *the risen Christ*, the supernatural savior. Consequently Paul wrote:

> He died for all, that they who live should no longer live for themselves, but for him who died and rose again on their behalf. Therefore, from now on we recognize no man according to the flesh; even though we have known Christ according to the flesh, yet now we know [him thus] no longer. (2 Corinthians 5:15-16)

The *Christ* of the flesh, the historical Jesus, was of no significance to Paul and his teachings prevailed. Consequently, when the churches he founded sought to gain converts they could not rely on actual historical data concerning the life of Jesus. They sought to apply what they read in the Jewish Scriptures, mostly in their Greek rendering, to his life as if he was the fulfillment of those readings. It really did not matter since his actually earthly existence was of little importance.

For Christians Psalm 22 became a foreshadowing of the crucifixion of Jesus. The typological approach to sacred scripture was not unknown among Jews, but it became the characteristic Christian method of reading and understanding the Jewish Scriptures.

It was common for Christians to believe that the Jewish Scriptures contained hints and allusions that foreshadowed events in the life of Jesus. Events in the life and death of Jesus were created to reflect the foreshadowing *found* in biblical verses (e.g., virgin conception, resurrection). Other typologies were used to prove later Christian beliefs and practices (e.g., the Trinity, Eucharist). Typologies were found in such biblical figures as Adam, Joseph, Moses, and David who were said to prefigure Jesus. One could supposedly see common parallels in the lives of these biblical personalities and that of Jesus. The typological approach was seen by Christians as confirmation that God had prearranged events in the so-called *Old Testament* as forshadowings of events occurring in the New Testament. This notion is expressed in the Latin saying: *Quod in vetere latet in novo patet* ("What is hidden in the Old [Testament] is made explicit in the New"). Therefore, it comes as no surprise that Psalm 22 should be seen as just such a prefiguring of the crucifixion. However, when this claim is carefully scrutinized the interpretation's validity must be rejected.

"My God, my God, why have you forsaken me?"

There are several versions recorded by the evangelists as to what were Jesus' last words from the cross. Mark, followed generally by Matthew, gives this account:

> And at the ninth hour Jesus called out with a loud voice: "Eloi, Eloi, lama sabachthani?" which is translated: "My God, my God, why have you forsaken me?" And some of the bystanders having heard it were saying: "Behold, he is calling for Elijah." And someone ran and filled a sponge full of sour wine, put it on a reed, and gave it to him to drink, saying: "Let us see whether Elijah will come to take him down." And Jesus uttered a loud cry, and expired. (Mark 15:34-37)

Jesus' cry of anguish: "My God, my God, why have you forsaken me?" is the second verse of Psalm 22. But why should Jesus have expressed this sentiment? Why should he have thought of himself as separated from God at the very moment when, according to Christian theology, he was fulfilling God's plan? Luke and John omit this cry in their crucifixion accounts, and instead, imply that Jesus himself was in complete control of the event. According to Luke, Jesus' final cry was: "Father, into your hands I commit my spirit" (Luke 23:46), words taken from Psalms 31:6. John also views the crucifixion not as abandonment by God, but as the conclusion of Jesus' alleged divine mission, in which he peacefully surrenders his soul to God. Thus, John writes: "He bowed his head and gave up his spirit" (John 19:30).

Christians, attempting to explain Jesus' feeling of abandonment, as recorded by Matthew and Mark, contend that in reality he had in mind, not only the despairing words with which Psalm 22 opens, but also the trusting words with which this psalm ends. But this argument from silence amounts to putting words in Jesus' mouth. Whether Jesus knew the theme of the entire psalm is of no consequence. What matters is that he allegedly only made use of the opening words of a psalm, to express his despair and failed to continue with the concluding words of the psalm expressive of hope and trust in God. Furthermore, it makes little sense to see in Psalm 22 prophecies depicting the agony felt by Jesus at his crucifixion. Are we to believe that Jesus, who is supposed to be a supernatural being that is part of the Godhead and God's only begotten son, fell into deep depression and anguish because God refused to help him in his hour of need? Why should he offer prayers to be saved from a fate that he was knowingly supposed to endure in order to redeem all humanity from the power of sin? How could Jesus have entertained the thought that God forsook him if by his allegedly preplanned divinely ordained death humanity was supposedly given its only means of attaining salvation? If, as the Gospels assume, Jesus knew and predicted long in advance the events surrounding his death and if these events were neither a surprise nor a defeat but a working out of a divinely designed plan, then what sense does it make for Jesus to complain: "My God, my God, why have you forsaken me?" It is precisely to be killed that he allegedly became incarnate. Earlier, in Gethsemane, Jesus is alleged to have prayed that God should spare him from having to undergo his bitter fate. However, Jesus added that not his will, but his "Father's" will, should be done (Matthew 26:36-45, Mark 14:32-41, Luke 22:41-44). Why did Jesus give vent to feelings of despair and failure when he supposedly knew that he was really acting out a preordained cosmic plan? John wrote: "After this, Jesus, knowing that all things had already been accomplished, in order that the Scripture might be fulfilled, said: 'I am thirsty'" (John 19:28). Despite this claim, Jesus obviously had neither foreknowledge nor control of events.

If Jesus, in those last agonizing minutes, truly felt personally abandoned, his mission coming to grief, then he could *not* be the messiah that Christian theology believes him to be. Having been foretold in Psalm 22, the messiah of Christian mythology would have known that death by crucifixion was essential to his mission. If he knew this, then his words of despair were deceptive, something unbefitting to a supernatural being called the Son of God.

Psalm 22 does not apply to the life of Jesus. Jesus' life ends disappointedly, whereas the psalmist, after metaphorically describing his trials and tribulations, concludes on a positive note. Jesus takes *no* such positive position. If he literally fulfilled all of Psalm 22, the logical order of development would be for depression to give way to joy as he realized God's purpose had been attained through his act of sacrificial death.

"Like a lion"

Although the psalm gives no indication that it is describing this mode of death, Psalm 22 has become, for Christianity, a major source for defining the agony of the crucifixion process.[1] In particular, verse 17b [16b in some versions] as found in most Christian Bible translations, is most frequently cited as a prooftext. This despite the fact that there never is any direct citation of this verse in the New Testament. Christians render verse 17b as "they pierced my hands and my feet." But, who says this is the meaning of the psalmist's words? The Christian rendering is neither in any Hebrew manuscript nor is it to be found in the Septuagint as it is often alleged.

The controversy surrounding verse 17b begins with the question: Is the disputed word read as in the Masoretic text, *ka-'ari* ("as a lion"), with the Hebrew letters *kaph/'aleph/resh/yod* or is to be read as in the Greek Septuagint as if presumably derived from the verb, *karah*, "to dig," with the Hebrew letters *kaph/resh/heh*, but omitting the *'aleph* (and translated as "pierced" in Christian Bibles)? Hebrew manuscript support for rendering the word in question as derived from the Hebrew verb root *kaph/resh/heh* is thought by some scholars to be found in a manuscript fragment of Psalm 22 from the Dead Sea Scrolls (4QPs[f]).[2] This fragment does not contain an *'aleph* but contains the reading *kr* with the remaining letter or letters missing and which some scholars reconstruct by adding a *vav*. It is the oldest known, but not the best Hebrew manuscript of Psalm 22.[3] The incorrect spelling is most likely due to a defective manuscript, a similar error is found in the Septuagint reading.

As stated above, most Christian Bibles render verse 17b as: "They pierced my hands and my feet." This supposedly follows the Septuagint, the Greek biblical text used by the early Christians. The Septuagint's rendering is assumed by Christians not only to be dependent on understanding the Hebrew as derived from the verb "to dig [soil]" but, in addition, to have the meaning "to pierce [the flesh]." However, the reading they propose, *karu*, "they dug," is not trouble-free. If it is assumed that the root of this Hebrew word is *krh*, "to dig," then the function of the *'aleph* in the word *ka-'ari* is inexplicable since it is not part of the root. As we have seen, *karah* consists only of the Hebrew letters *kaph/resh/heh*, whereas the word in the Hebrew text, *ka-'ari*, consists of *kaph/'aleph/resh/yod*. Moreover, the verb *krh*, "to dig," does not have the meaning "to pierce." *Karah* refers to the digging of the soil, and is *never* applied in the Scriptures to the piercing of the flesh (cf. Genesis 26:25, Exodus 21:33; Numbers 21:18; Jeremiah 18:20, 22; Psalms 7:16, 57:7). The verb *krh* is also used figuratively in Psalms 40:6, with the meaning "to open," or "to unclog" (that is, "to dig out") the ears.

There are a number of words which are used in Hebrew for piercing the body: *ratz'a*, to pierce, to bore with an awl (Exodus 21:6); *dakar*, to pierce (Zechariah 12:10, Isaiah 13:15); *nakar*, to pierce, to bore, to perforate (2 Kings 18:21). This last word is used in a very significant sense in the last verse cited: "It [the reed] will go into his hand and pierce it." Any of these words would be far better suited for use in this passage than one that is generally used to denote digging the soil. In New Testament references to the crucifixion, we find: "They will look upon him whom they pierced [*ekekentesan*]" (John 19:37) and "those who pierced [*ekekentesan*] him" (Revelation 1:7). In both examples, the Greek verb is *ekkenteo*, "to pierce" and not the

Greek equivalent of the Hebrew *krh*, *orusso*, "to dig" as for example in "dug in [*oruxen*] the ground" (Matthew 25:18).

The translator into the Septuagint Greek most likely had a defective Hebrew text before him that had dropped the *'aleph* and had an extended *yod* which appeared to be a *vav* and so he read the text as *krv*. We can assume this because it is more likely that a scribe for some reason left out the letter *'aleph* than that he inadvertently inserted one. In addition, confusion over whether a letter is a *yod* or *vav* is common

The Septuagint renders the controversial word into the Greek as *oruxan*, "they dug." Indeed, the Septuagint consistently translated *karu* as *oruxan* wherever it was mentioned in that work. *Only* in Psalm 22 did Christian versions of the Bible render *oruxan* as "they pierced." In *all* other citations of this word it was rendered "to dig." Perhaps the translator of the Septuagint conflated this word at Psalm 22 with the thought "they *dug* their nails (claws) into me," "they *dug* into my flesh," or simply translated the text before him without bothering to analyze it. In either case, neither the Hebrew nor the Greek words mean or justify the later Christian interpretative rendering, "they pierced."

We must also consider that while there are some Hebrew verbs that have an *'aleph* intrusion in some forms of the verb, there is *no* example of this occurring in the verb *krh*.[4] Advocates of the Christian reading have no example of *'aleph* intrusion into *krh* and can only point to verse 17b in trying to establish their case. This leaves their argument as mere speculation with absolutely *no* proof to support their allegation. The presence of the *'aleph* in those verb forms where it appears may simply be orthographic variations reflecting variant dialect pronunciation in the Hebrew spoken in different parts of *'Eretz Yisrael* that made their way into the biblical text but which are no longer discernible in Hebrew speech. In any case, the presence of the *'aleph* makes the Christian position all the more dubious.

One textual emendation suggested by some scholars involves determining the last letter as either *yod* as found in most manuscripts (viz., *ka'ri*, "like a lion") or *vav* as found in some variant manuscripts (viz., *ka'aru*, "they made ugly," "they disfigured") and then using both words. The authoritative manuscripts have a *yod* as the final letter.[5] The Hebrew verb *kaph/ 'ayin/resh* (alternately spelled *kaph/ 'aleph /resh*), "to be ugly," "to be disfigured" is *not* found in the Jewish Scriptures. It has been suggested that at one time both these readings were in the text as *ka'ari ka'aru*. This would produce through word play an added force to the imagery: "Like a lion they tore [disfigured] my hands and my feet." Paronomasia (impossible to reproduce in translation) is a common feature found throughout the biblical text—cf. Isaiah 10:30; Jeremiah 2:12, 48:2; Joel 1:10; Micah 1:10; Habakkuk 2:18; Zephaniah 2:4; Psalms 40:4, 147:16; Lamentations 4:18. It is conjectured that because of their similar spellings one word or the other was dropped from the verse through scribal error.[6]

Some scholars say the spelling *ka'aru* is found in a 1st/2nd century C.E. manuscript from Nachal Chever (5/6 Hev Ps). Typical of the tendentious claims made by those advocating the Christian reading of verse 17b is the following: "Psalm 22 is a favorite among Christians since it is often linked in the New Testament with the suffering and death of Jesus. A well-known and controversial reading is found in verse 16, where the Masoretic text has 'Like a lion are my hands and feet,' whereas the Septuagint has 'They have pierced my hands and feet.' Among the scrolls the reading in question is found only in the Psalms scroll found at Nahal Hever (abbreviated 5/6HevPs), which reads: 'They have pierced my hands and my feet'!"[7] This reading as a *vav* is also found in several medieval manuscripts (but is not rendered as "pierced"). This may reflect an initial scribal error which misread the *yod* as a *vav* simply extending the vertical component of the letter *yod* to form the letter *vav*. The error was then perpetuated in one sub-family of manuscripts. On the other hand, the presence of the *vav* may be due to a deliberate scribal emendation elongating the *yod* thinking it corrected a common error and thus supposedly restored a smoother reading through the verb *kaph/ 'aleph/resh/vav*. If used in the context of verse 17b, *ka'aru* should be rendered as a causative with the vocalization, *ki-'aru*, "they made ugly," "they made repulsive," "they caused to be disfigured."

There is nothing in the Nachal Chever manuscript nor the Septuagint to indicate that either *k'arv* or a conjectured *krv* (4QPs^f)

was understood or should be understood to mean "pierced." Let us examine the rendering of *k'arv* by scrutinizing the manuscript more closely. The difference between a letter *yod* and a letter *vav* is that the vertical length of the *vav* is longer. A comparison of these two letters as they appear on the fragment show them not to be uniform in the respective length of the vertical line as needed for either a *yod* or a *vav* and in some cases the verticals are of equal size. Thus, it is unclear as to which of the two is meant by merely looking at the letter. Add to this that there is no three-letter Hebrew root verb that has a silent *aleph* as its second letter. The outcome is that rendering the word in question as "pierced" is totally incorrect.

In Aquila's Greek rendering of verse 17b, we find the Greek word *eschunan* = *ki'aru*, "they have made ugly," "they have made repulsive," and "they caused to be disfigured."[8] It is not known if Aquila used a manuscript containing the combination of Hebrew letters *kaph*/*'aleph*/*resh*/*vav* or if he used this Greek verb in his translation because *k'rv* (alt. *k'rv*) has a phonic resemblance to *k'ari* and a meaning that can elucidate the sense of the verse. That is, the phonic similarity of the word *k'ru* with that of *k'ri* coupled with its meaning of disfigurement may have lent itself to his exposition of the text. Considering the early date of Aquila (2nd century C.E.), his Hebrew text would not have contained any vowel marks. Therefore, if *k'rv* was in his text, the vocalization of this word would have been based on oral tradition and he most likely read it as the causative, *ki-'aru*, "they made ugly," or "they caused to be disfigured." Aquila's Greek text is an important factor in trying to reconstruct not only the wording of verse 17b in the Hebrew manuscript he used but also in understanding his interpretation of that reading. His rendering has an affinity with Rashi's interpretation of the verse based on the reading *ka-'ari* ("as a lion"): "As if crushed by the mouth of a lion are my hands and my feet." The element of disfigurement is emphasized as the result of the lion's actions. Aquila's manuscript may also have read *ka-'ari* and he arrived at his rendering of verse 17b through a similar understanding of the context as that found in the later commentary of Rashi (11th century).

Some Christians cite the lack of a verb in 17b. However, the verb in 17b is to be understood as already expressed in the first part of the verse: "For dogs have encompassed me; a company of evildoers have enclosed me." Thus, when the psalmist complains that his enemies are like "the lion," the missing words are understood, and it is to be read, in effect: "Like the lion [they are (gnawing) at] my hands and my feet." This is the clearest exposition of the text. Rashi's interpretation of the verse — "As if crushed by the mouth of a lion are my hands and my feet" — is similar in thought to the one offered here though differently stated. The tendentious Christian translation, "They pierced my hands and my feet," is based on Christian theological assumption. It has to do with a mode of suffering, but does not address the literal text of verse 17b. Too be blunt, neither one of the proposed verbs ever means "bore," or "pierce."

The Masoretic text has a *qamatz* (vowel sound) under the *kaph* in *ka-'ari*, this results from an assimilated definite article. Thus, the literal translation is "Like *the* lion" (cf. Isaiah 38:13). While in English, a noun used in a general sense is recognized by having no article, neither definite nor indefinite, in Hebrew, as well as in many other languages, such nouns take the definite article. For example, "Work is good for man" in Hebrew would be "*The* work is good for man." (cf. Amos 5:19, literally: "As if a man did flee from *the* lion" with its English translation, "As if a man did flee from *a* lion").

Examining Psalm 22, we find that verses 17, 21, and 22 express parallel thoughts. In verse 17, the psalmist speaks of "dogs" and "the lion," which are metaphoric representations of his enemies. In verses 21 and 22 respectively, he beseeches the Almighty to save him "from the dog's paw" and "from the lion's mouth." This parallel structure adds to the understanding that the correct interpretation of verse 17b involves comparing the psalmist's enemies to certain animals. Furthermore, the psalmist uses an elliptical style. Ellipsis is an apt rhetorical device for a composition in which extreme suffering and agony is described. A person in this condition does not normally express his feelings in complete sentences. Such a person is capable of exclaiming only the most critical words of his thoughts and feelings. Hence, the psalmist wrote: "Like a lion ... my hands and my feet!" Similarly, in verse 2 we find broken phrases rather than whole sentences: "Far from helping me ... the words of my cry." Hence, we see that the Masoretic text is not in need of emendation. Its grammatical awkwardness is by design. It imitates a person's reaction on being attacked by a lion. Pinned to the ground by a lion one is not worried about grammatical correctness but gripped by an encompassing terror he cries out in panic and pain.

Some Christians have questioned why when the word *lion* is mentioned in other verses in Psalm 22 the word *'aryeh* is used instead of *'ari*? But, both are synonymous Hebrew words for "a lion" and can be used interchangeably. Perhaps it was due to the psalmist's poetic style that he interchanges them. Christians have also asked: Why would the psalmist write "the lion" when the enemy in the context of the psalm is mostly in the plural: verse 7—"the people," verse 8—"all they," verse 13—"bulls," verse 17—"dogs," verse 22— "wild oxen"? These Christians miss the point of the psalmist intent. "The lion" is not a reference to a particular lion, but is speaking of the inherent behavior of lions to which the psalmist compares his enemies' behavior. "They" behave like "the lion," and so "Like the lion, they are at my hands and my feet (verse 17b) ... save me from the lion's mouth (verse 22a)."

The metaphorical terminology the psalmist uses to express his mental anguish in physical terms is comparable to similar usage found in Jeremiah 23:9, where the prophet exclaims: "My heart within me is broken, all my bones shake; I am like a drunken man, and like a man whom wine has overcome."

"They divide my clothes"

Psalms 22:19 (18 in some versions) reads: "They divide my clothes among them, and for my garment they cast lots." A misunderstanding by the author of the Gospel of John influenced the way he applied this verse to his version of the division-of-the-clothing episode (John 19:24; cf. Matthew 27:35, Luke 23:34). He misinterpreted the Hebrew parallelism as referring to two separate acts. In biblical poetry, which is often based on parallel structure, the repetition of an idea does not indicate its duplication in reality (cf. Zechariah 9:9). John states that the soldiers divided Jesus' garments among themselves. However, they could not divide the inner garment, which was seamless—

so they cast lots for it. John writes: "They said therefore to one another: 'Let us not tear it, but let us decide by lot whose it will be'; that the Scripture might be fulfilled: 'They divided my outer garments among themselves, and for my apparel they cast lots'" (John 19:24). Evidently, John created this legendary crucifixion event to meet what he believed to be a messianic requirement of Psalm 22. In this way, the crucifixion tradition was rounded out to agree with what John thought was the prophetic message of this psalm.

[1] The graphic language of suffering found in Psalm 22 has been used to describe the suffering of Israel as expressed by messianic suffering and in a more universalistic sense exemplifying the distress of the righteous individual generally. The interpretation of select verses from Psalm 22 alluding to the sufferings of the Messiah are found in *Pesikta Rabbati*, Piska ("section") 36.2 (verse 16) and Piska 37.1 (verses 8, 14-15, 16). Dated by some scholars to the second or third century and by others to the sixth or seventh century, they are the only instance in rabbinic literature of such an interpretation of the psalm. The following interpretations are given: "It was because of the ordeal of the son of David that David wept, saying *My strength is dried up like a potsherd* (Psalms 22:16)" (Piska 36.2); "Why does the verse speak twice of mercy: *In mercy I will have mercy upon him* ["Ephraim, our true Messiah"]? One mercy refers to the time when he will be shut up in prison, a time when the nations of the earth will gnash their teeth at him every day, wink their eyes at one another in derision of him, nod their heads at him in contempt, open wide their lips to guffaw, as it is said *All they that see me laugh me to scorn; they shoot out the lip, they shake the head* (Psalms 22:8); *My strength is dried up like a potsherd; and my tongue cleaves to my throat; and you lay me in the dust of death* (Psalms 22:16). Moreover, they will roar over him like lions, as is said *They open wide their mouth against me, as a ravening and roaring lion. I am poured out like water, and all my bones are out of joint; my heart is become like wax; it is melted in my inmost parts* (Psalms 22:14-15)" (Piska 37.1).

The goal of the homiletic interpretation of biblical verses is to reveal a deeper meaning and a wider application of the words and spirit of the Jewish Scriptures. For example, Psalm 22 is about David and his tribulations. David faced many difficulties including a revolt led by one of his own sons. Reading the psalms one is struck by David's expressions of emotion concerning these difficulties and his unwavering faith that God would always stand by him. Although the psalm addresses David's hardships, the *midrash* finds a hint to Esther in the words of this psalm. To understand what relationship the *midrash* is pointing out, we must look at the psalm itself. In this psalm, David covers three subject areas: (1) That enemies surrounded him (for example, in verse 8, 13, and 14). (2) His depression in feeling abandoned (verses 2, 3). (3) His strong faith and calls to praise God (verses 5-6, 24-27). The *midrash* sees reflected here the same emotions that Esther must have felt when faced with the destruction of her people. Although she was queen, she felt surrounded by those who would kill her. She is fearful and depressed as she stands in the hall waiting to see if the king will extend his staff and accept her (and not kill her). By attributing these emotions to Esther, the *midrash* is showing that the psalm has a universal aspect that applies to many people in many situations.

We see similarities between the life situation of a biblical character and another person. The verses that refer to this biblical personage can be applied metaphorically to the other person who is in the same situation. We see this with Esther, who was in a similar position to that of David in Psalm 22. Thus, verses are applied to other people because of the similarities of their situation but always as metaphor.

Rabbi Joseph Soloveitchik writes: "Rabbi Joshua ben Levi quoted a verse from Psalm 22, the famous prayer of an individual in distress, forsaken and abandoned: 'My God, my God, why have You forsaken me?" This psalm reflects the cry of total despair, the shriek of a frightened, lonely child who has suddenly discovered that his or her mother is gone. According to our tradition, Esther recited this psalm on her way to the inner court of Ahasuerus. In a word, it is the psalm of a person who has lost almost all hope and, out of the depths of despair, petitions the Almighty. From this psalm, Rabbi Joshua ben Levi inferred that one must read the Megillah at night as well as in the daytime, for the prayer of the lonely, forsaken person is without pause or stop. He cannot help himself but pray.

In other words, the reading of the Megillah was equated by Rabbi Joshua ben Levi with the offering of a prayer to the Almighty from the straits of distress, addressing a petition to Him from the depths of agony and misery." (Joseph Soloveitchik, *Days of Deliverance: Essays on Purim and Hanukkah*, edited by Eli D. Clark, Joel B. Wolowelsky, Reuven Ziegler, Jersey City: Ktav Publishing House, 2007, p. 2).

[2] 4QPs^f is written in a late Hasmonean semicursive script dating to about 50 B.C.E. This is the only Dead Sea Scroll that preserves text from Psalm 22 (verses 4-9, 14-21).

[3] 4QPs^f is on plates 13 and 14 as published in E. Ulrich (ed.), *Discoveries in the Judaean Desert: Psalms to Chronicles*, Vol. 16, Oxford: Clarendon, 2000, pp. 85-89. Verse 17 is on line 25. The *kaf* is flaked at the top and the last letter or letters is missing.

[4]Examples of *'aleph* intrusion in verb roots: *la'at* ("he covered") from *lut* (2 Samuel 19:5), *ve-yanei'tz* ("and it shall blossom") *hiphil* from *natzatz* (Ecclesiastes 12:5), *ra'amah* ("she shall be lifted up") from *rum* (Zechariah 14:10).

[5] See the Leningrad Codex. The Leningrad Codex, named for the city where it has resided since the mid-19th century is the oldest complete Hebrew Bible in existence. Dating to 1010, the text derives from the work of five generations of the Ben Asher family of Masoretes, who lived from the sixth to the early tenth century in Tiberias. However, the Leningrad Codex is not the finest example of their work, that distinction belongs to an earlier manuscript called the Aleppo Codex, which dates a century earlier then the Leningrad Codex. Psalm 22 is missing in the Aleppo Codex.

The Aleppo Codex, housed in a synagogue in Aleppo, Syria, was partly destroyed by fire during anti-Jewish riots in 1947 before the surviving pages were smuggled to Jerusalem. For a list of manuscript variations of this word see the apparatus in R. Kittel, *Biblia Hebraica*, Stuttgart: Deutsche Bibelgesellschaft, 1997, p. 1104.

[6] See Christian D. Ginsberg, *Introduction to the Massoretico-Critical Edition of the Hebrew Bible,* (reprint) New York: Ktav Publishing House, 1966, pp. 968-972.

[7] Martin Abegg Jr., Peter Flint, and Eugene Ulrich, eds. and trans., *The Dead Sea Scrolls Bible: The Oldest Known Bible*, San Francisco: HarperSan Francisco, 1999, p. 519.

[8] Later manuscripts of Aquila's rendering have *epedasan*, "bound" (aorist tense of *pedau*, "bind," "to shackle," "fetter"). Symmachus used the phrase *hos zatountes dasai* ("those who seek to bind"). The *Peshitta*, the Syriac rendering influenced by the Septuagint, has the word *baz'u*, "they have dug." The Latin Vulgate rendering first used the word *foderunt*, "they have dug" (c. 387). A later revision (c. 391) read *vinxerunt*, "they have bound," but this reading was rejected and the earlier version, *foderunt* was reinstated.

Chapter 38

A FRIEND'S BETRAYAL
(Psalms 41:10)

New Testament authors attempt to legitimatize the claims they make on behalf of Jesus by referral to biblical verses. Psalms 41:10 (verse 9 in some versions) reads: "Even my own familiar friend, in whom I trusted, who did eat my bread, has lifted his heel against me." The Gospel of John has Jesus use the last half of this verse to predict that Judas will betray him. It states: "He who eats my bread has lifted up his heel against me" (John 13:18). The biblical citation is not used in a homiletic sense, but supposedly finds historic fulfillment in this application to the betrayal of Jesus by Judas. Herein we find an example of one of the great lapses in the general claim that Jesus "fulfilled" biblical prophecy. In an historic context it is the plain meaning of a verse that needs to be considered if one is to speak of actual prophetic fulfillment and not merely a similarity of circumstances. In such a case, the full verse and, in fact, the entire context should be viewed as one integral unit.

Had the author of John considered the contents of the full verse or, indeed, the entire psalm it would have disrupted his perception of Jesus as a sinless, all-knowing, miracle-working celestial being come to earth. Jesus, it is alleged, had the all-knowing insight afforded him by his supposed divine status to see fulfillment of this verse in his life. What is more, John's Jesus would have the foreknowledge of the traitorous role Judas would play in the unfolding of events leading to his passion. But, if that is correct, then Jesus would not be telling the truth in calling Judas by the psalmist's words "familiar friend" (literally "the man of my peace"). In addition, Jesus would be lying when, again, he referred to Judas in the words of the psalm, as one "in whom I trusted." With the supernatural qualities attributed to Jesus he would have known that Judas could not be trusted and that eventually he would betray Jesus..

Psalms 41:10 addresses the feelings of betrayal at the hands of a

217

trusted friend. It expresses the sorrow one feels when one who is close to you betrays your trust. But, if Jesus was who the author of John claims, then he knew the heart of Judas long before they even met. John's Jesus is even said to have known that Judas was about to betray him. Thus, he says to Judas, "What you do, do quickly," as Judas leaves to inform Jesus' enemies of his whereabouts. (John 13:27).

There is one more significant point that must be addressed. This psalm is a complete unit recording one individual's feelings, not random statements collected together. Therefore, it rightly must be understood as applying in its entirety to one individual. But, then consider this, verse 5 (verse 4 in some versions) says, "As for me, I said: O Lord, be gracious to me, heal my soul; for I have sinned against You." If applied to Jesus, it would be tantamount to an admission to his being a sinner against God. To think that Jesus is the fulfillment of part of verse 10, but not of the entire verse is simply deluding oneself. There is no honest way to consider any part of this psalm as a prophecy of the betrayal of Jesus without considering that he was also a sinner.

Chapter 39

THE KING OF ISRAEL
(Psalms 45:7-8)

Psalms 45:7-8 reads: "Your throne, God [*'Elohim*], is for ever and ever; a scepter of equity is the scepter of your kingdom. You have loved righteousness, and hated wickedness; therefore God [*'Elohim*], your God [*'Elohecha*], has anointed you with the oil of gladness above your fellows." In particular, we are interested in the literal text of Psalms 45:7a which states, "Your throne God [*'Elohim*] is forever and ever." The overall context shows that an earthly king of Israel is being addressed. As a result, some Christians ask, "How is it possible that an earthly king is called *'Elohim*? Tendentiously, presupposing this to be a messianic passage, they then contend that verse 7a actually points to the Messiah as a divine king, and then draw the conclusion that it refers to Jesus. But, these Christians ignore the poetic symbolism expressed in verse 7a. The Davidic king is the earthly ruler of God's people. In that capacity he is God's surrogate, the representative of the actual and eternal king of Israel, Israel's Divine Ruler. Thus, it is said: "Solomon sat upon the throne *of the Lord* as king, in place of his father, David, and he was successful" (1 Chronicles 29:23). Verse 7a, "Your throne, God [*'Elohim*], is for ever and ever," is a parenthetical statement placed in the text to explain why verse 8b says, "therefore God [*'Elohim*], your God [*'Elohecha*], has anointed you." As an ideal, the earthly king of the house of David is rewarded because he has "loved righteousness, and hated wickedness" (verse 8a); this will, of course, someday include the Messiah. Yet, whoever the reigning king may be, the throne still belongs to the eternal God of Israel. The Davidic throne is God's throne on earth. Kings of the house of David rule by God's permission and are His representatives. Therefore, verse 7a is to be understood as an acknowledgement made to God but addressed to God's surrogate. The reigning king is told, in effect, "Your throne is God's forever and ever." And, today, although this earthly kingship is temporarily suspended it is, nevertheless, God's "for ever and ever."

Chapter 40

MIXED-UP DRINKS
(Psalms 69:22)

The Gospel authors often employed scriptural verses out of context in order to support their claim that Jesus is the central theme of the Bible. Sometimes there are subtle contradictions in their respective narrations that show the fictive origins of their assumptions. For example, Psalms 69:22 (verse 21 in some versions) states: "They put poison into my food; and in my thirst they gave me vinegar to drink." Ignoring context and word meanings Matthew writes that while Jesus was being crucified, "They gave him wine to drink mingled with gall, and after tasting it, he was unwilling to drink" (Matthew 27:34). This author used the Greek word *khole* ("gall"), the same term employed by the Septuagint version of Psalms 69:22.

Mark reports this alleged scriptural fulfillment as follows: "And they tried to give him wine mixed with myrrh; but he did not take it" (Mark 15:23). This account differs from that found in Matthew in that it mentions myrrh not gall. Some Christians attempt to harmonize these two contradictory versions by maintaining that the "poison" or "gall" referred to was myrrh. But, the psalmist was not randomly using a word but was precise in his terminology. The psalmist choice of words is *ro'sh*, "poison" or "gall," and not the word *mor*, "myrrh." *Ro'sh*, is usually rendered as "poison" or "gall," but more precisely may have referred to hemlock, colocynth, or the poppy (opium). The exact identification of this poisonous plant has been lost. *Ro'sh* is employed in several ways in the Bible: as a poisonous plant (Lamentations 3:5, 19); poison or venom (Deuteronomy 32:33), Job 20:16); or poisonous water (Jeremiah 8:14, 9:14, 23:15). It is also used in a figurative sense for the perversion of justice (Hosea 10:4, Amos 6:12) and for describing apostasy (Deuteronomy 29:17). In order to reconcile the two Gospel texts listing "gall" or "myrrh" respectively, some Christians propose the solution that the drink contained both gall and myrrh. Nevertheless, there is no denying that *ro'sh* and *mor* are simply not the same substances. In fact, myrrh, although bitter tasting, is not poisonous and is even used as an ingredient in medication.

Was verse 22 fulfilled in an episode involving Jesus? When was poison (gall) put into Jesus' food? Does the "wine mingled with gall" or the "wine mixed with myrrh" qualify as the poison put into "my food" or the "vinegar [given] to drink" spoken of by the psalmist? Was Jesus given food at his execution? The simple truth is that there is no comparison between the psalmist's words and the Gospel claims of fulfillment of Scripture during the crucifixion of Jesus.

Chapter 41

IS GOD SITTING NEXT TO HIMSELF?

(Psalms 110:1)

Who's your daddy?

On the basis of Mark 12:35-37, Christians ask: "If the Jewish Messiah is not the Son of God, how do you answer Jesus' question?"

> The Messiah is the Son of David. Yet David calls him "Lord." How can David call the Messiah "Lord" if he is David's descendant?

Some Christians answer that the Messiah is David's descendant according to his humanity and David's Lord according to his divinity — he is God come down from Heaven and incarnated as a human being. To assert divine sonship is a wild assumption neither explicit or implicit in the text.

The assumption that Jesus' question has any validity is incorrect to begin with. The Christian answer presupposes a dual nature for Jesus that is not justified. If he is God's literal son, as Christians believe, then he cannot be Joseph's literal son. If he is Joseph's literal son, then he is not God's literal son. Additionally, adoption would still not give Jesus the required genetic lineage, since, kingship is passed down paternally. It is also interesting to note that the New Testament makes no claims or even mention of Mary being a descendant of King David.

Y-H-V-H and 'adoni

It is a Christian contention that several verses in Psalm 110 show that the Messiah will not only be greater than David but must also be a divine being. Psalms 110:1 states: "A Psalm concerning David. *Y-H-V-H* says to my master ["lord"]: 'Sit at My right hand, until I make your enemies your footstool.'" There is no problem with accepting that one's descendants can rise to a more exalted position than we possess at present. There is no problem with David accepting that the Messiah will be greater than he is. But, there is nothing in this verse to show that David is referring to the Messiah when he writes *'adoni*, "my master," "my lord." Moreover, there is nothing in David's words to indicate that the individual he refers to as "my master" is a divine being. David *concerning* himself wrote Psalm 110 poetically in the third person. There are several midrashic explanations of this psalm. They are *not* meant to be taken literally, but are homiletic presentations concerned with spiritual lessons to be learned from this text. As such, they do not concern our study of the literal meaning of the psalmist's words.

Christians explain this verse based on New Testament exegesis. Mark's Jesus says:

> How is it that the scribes say that the Christ is the son of David? David himself said by the Holy Spirit; "The Lord [*ho kyrios*] said to my Lord [*kyrio mou*], 'Sit at My right hand, until I put your enemies beneath your feet.' David himself calls him 'Lord,' how is he then his son?" (Mark 12:35-37)

Mark's rendering, as in the Septuagint of Psalms 110:1 (LXX: 109:1), uses the Greek word *kyrios*, "lord," twice in the sentence, and the Christian translations into English capitalize the initial letter of the word to read "Lord" in both instances. In the Greek text, the initial *kyrios* is a reference to "the Lord" (*Y-H-V-H*). The second *kyrios*, renders *'adoni*, "my master," "my lord," which according to Mark's understanding refers to "the Christ". That is, the Greek, *kyrios*, is used to render two separate and distinct Hebrew words in the Greek translation. The confusion it creates in Greek does not exist in the Hebrew original. In Mark's exposition of the text he has Jesus distance the Messiah from a Davidic descent.

Being politically correct

Why does he question how the Messiah could be the son of David yet David calls him "my Lord" thus giving him more honor than conventional courtesy would demand of elders to their descendants? The Gospel of Mark was as much a political apologia as a religious one. Writing in the aftermath of the Roman-Jewish War, Mark found it undesirable to portray Jesus as a Davidic descendant. The Romans were very much aware that for decades the focus of Jewish aspirations centered on the establishment of a religio-political kingdom of God governed by the messianic descendant of David. Therefore, when Mark wrote his Gospel, he felt that claiming Jesus was a descendant of David was not in the best political interests of the Christian community. This denial that the Messiah must be of Davidic descent is highlighted by the fact that Mark gives no Davidic genealogy for Jesus, as we find in Matthew and Luke.

Attributing the questions of Mark 12:35 and 12:37 to Jesus, Mark derides the scribes and their teachings concerning the Davidic descent of the Messiah who he calls "the Christ." This particular discussion, if it ever took place, uses Psalms 110:1 to argue against a Davidic descent for the Messiah. As such, Mark's Jesus not only distances himself from Jewish beliefs, but also assures the Roman authorities that he does not have a physical connection with the rebel-supported house of David. Mark's negative attitude toward Judaism was part of an apologetic intended to show the Romans that the Jews who revolted against Rome were also hostile to Jesus. Mark was trying to exclude Christians from Roman anger toward the Jews.

Who did David write about?

In rendering Psalms 110:1 as, "the Lord said to my Lord" Christians argue that it shows Jesus is greater than David and is the Messiah. Some maintain that the verse even implies that he is of divine origin as well (see Matthew 22:42-45, Mark 12:35-37, Luke 20:41-44, Acts 2:34-36, Hebrews 1:13). Yet, a careful examination finds their claims to be totally without merit. Since *le-David*, in verse 1, does not always mean "written [composed] by David," but sometimes "concerning David" or "in the style of David," it cannot be said with certainty that the preposition *le*, often translated "of," actually indicates "composed by David." Additional investigation is necessary in order to understand its meaning as governed by the context of this psalm. Psalm 72 was written by David "for," or "concerning," Solomon (cf. verses 1 and 20), yet the Hebrew contains an introductory phrase similar to the one found in Psalm 110. The introductory statement, *li-Shlomo*, stresses that the psalm is "concerning" Solomon rather than that it is by Solomon. In 2 Samuel 22:51 and Psalms 144:10, David speaks of himself in the third person. Accordingly, there is every indication that David wrote this psalm and that the proper translation of verse 1 is: "A Psalm concerning David. *Y-H-V-H* says to my master ['*adoni*]: 'Sit at My right hand, until I make your enemies your footstool.'" This psalm is written from the perspective of the individual who is going to recite it. From this perspective, David, as king, is appropriately referred to as "my master," or "my lord" (cf. "my lord the king," "our lord David," "my lord" — 1 Kings 1:1-31). The claim that David is actually (or also) referring to the Messiah by the phrase "my master" is not found in the text. The New Testament's messianic interpretation of this psalm, of course, connects it to Jesus. This interpretation is faulty in light of other christological claims.

God cannot be separate from Himself

The privilege of sitting at the right hand is a mark of distinction (1 Kings 2:19). The terminology "sit at My right hand" is used here as an idiomatic expression showing God's favoritism toward David. When God invites David to "sit at My right hand," it is to show the privileged position enjoyed by David in his relationship with God. It is not to be taken as literally indicating anyone actually sitting at God's right hand. Similarly, in "until I make your enemies your footstool," the description is of the subjection of David's enemies as an expression of God's will. The use of the term "footstool" is clearly a metaphoric expression of subjection. It is a hyperbolic statement not inclusive of all David's enemies. This poetic style never intends its meaning to be in absolutes; rather it shows the overall triumph experienced by David in subduing his enemies with the help of God.

Role confusion

In the Christian sources, does the name of God (*Y-H-V-H*), translated as "the Lord" in many English versions of Psalms 110:1, refer to "God the Father" or to "God the Son' or does it refer inclusively to all three members of the Trinity? Christians are divided on the answer. But, let us examine this Christian controversy in more detail. Concerning the word *'Eloheinu* ("our God"), which appears in the *Shem'a*, "Hear, O Israel, the Lord [*Y-H-V-H*] our God, the Lord [*Y-H-V-H*] is One ['*Echad*]" (Deuteronomy 6:4), most Christians maintain that it connotes a plurality and should be understood in its literal sense as "our Gods," but in the sense of a "triunity." For this reason, they often interpret the verse as: "Hear, O Israel, the Lord our Gods, the Lord is a compound unity."

From this Christian interpretation of the *Shem'a*, it follows that "the Lord" (*Y-H-V-H*) could not refer to either "God the Father" or "God the Son" alone, but must refer to all three members of the Trinity as a whole. This being the case, how is it possible for Christians to maintain that the phrase "to my lord" in the verse: "The Lord [*Y-H-V-H*] says to my lord [*'adoni*]: 'Sit at My right hand'" (Psalms 110:1) refers to Jesus? If "my lord" refers to the second member of the supposed Trinity, Jesus, then who is the first "Lord," mentioned in the verse? If "the Lord" (*Y-H-V-H*) in the *Shem'a* is a "triunity" united in the divine name, that is, "the Lord [*Y-H-V-H*] is our Gods," the first "Lord" in Psalms 110:1 must also refer to the united Trinity. If this is so, then the phrase "to my lord" automatically excludes Jesus, who allegedly is already included in the first part of the verse, "the Lord."

Some Christians in desperation attempt to evade this problem by insisting that *Y-H-V-H* can refer to any part of their three-fold deity. But, then how does one identify "the Father" as differentiated from "the Son" or "the Holy Spirit"? In any case, if the second "lord," supposedly Jesus, is sitting next to the first "Lord," the triune godhead or two-thirds of it, or any aggregate of it, he cannot be part of it. That which exists outside of God cannot be God. The author of the Letter to the Hebrews takes the term "sitting" literally when he says, "When he [Jesus] had made purification of sins, he sat down at the right hand of the Majesty on high" (1:3); "We have such a high priest, who has taken his seat at the right hand of the throne of the Majesty in the heavens" (8:1). This remains an unsubstantiated claim.

The implied answer

Mark's Jesus is not citing Scripture for the view that the Messiah is the son of David, but is said to refer to the unanimous view of "the scribes" that this is the teaching of Scripture. Is he rejecting this view of the "scribes" (Mark 12:35), when he poses the question: in what sense is the Messiah the son of David if he is also, as Psalms 110:1 shows, David's lord? Is he indirectly and allusively intimating his own messianic claims? Whether Jesus actually had this discussion with the scribes is a matter of conjecture. However, this episode is used by Mark to further disassociate Jesus from any connection with the House of David. In any case, the implied answer need not be that the Messiah's real origin is heavenly and divine. It need be only that the Messiah is not simply another king in succession to David, like the rest of the kings of Judah, but a greater figure, through whom the kingdom of God will come.

Chapter 42

WHO IS MELCHIZEDEK?
(Psalms 110:4)

"A priest forever"

Psalms 110:4 states, "You are a priest forever after the manner of Melchizedek." God considers David as being in special service or servant capacity to Himself. This is expressed by the term "priest" being applied to David. However, he was not a priest in the manner of the priesthood of Aaron, but rather a priest of God, "after the manner of Melchizedek." Genesis 14:18 describes Melchizedek as "king of Salem and "priest of God Most High." Melchizedek and David each ruled his people in accordance with God's will as so to speak a priest-king.

The Hebrew term *le'olam*, commonly rendered in English as "forever," is not necessarily always synonymous with "eternal." It is frequently used with the meaning "for a very long time," or "for an indefinite period," or, as in the verse under discussion, to indicate the normal life-span of an individual (cf. Exodus 21:6). The analogy between Melchizedek and David focuses on the king's priestly role, it does not imply that Melchizedek was an eternal priest. Thus, "You are priest forever" means that David discharged certain priestly functions during his lifetime. We are informed that, on occasion, David wore the sacerdotal ephod (2 Samuel 6:14), "offered burnt-offerings and peace-offerings before the Lord" (2 Samuel 6:17-18) as was the right of all Israelites to do themselves or through a priestly surrogate and blessed the people (2 Samuel 6:12-19). That is David helped officiate in some capacity, but was not a priest in accordance with the Aaronic priesthood of the Torah. He was, as it were, a priest in the sense of a non-Torah dispensation, as was Melchizedek.

At the dedication of the Temple, Solomon led the ceremony, offered sacrifices and prayers on behalf of the people (1 Kings 8).

It is not farfetched to expect that the Messiah, when he comes, will exercise certain "priestly" prerogatives in the manner of David. But, this is not the same as the tendentious claims made by the author of the Letter to the Hebrews. In his interpretation of Psalm 110 the author of Hebrews alleges that Jesus is the subject of this psalm and is literally an eternal priest "according to the order of Melchizedek" (Hebrews 6:20). From this claim some Christians surmise that the priest-king was a manifestation of the pre-incarnate Jesus in human form.

The author of Hebrews says referring to Melchizedek, priest-king of Salem:

> Without father, without mother, without genealogy, having neither beginning of days nor end of life, but made like the Son of God, he abides a priest perpetually. (Hebrews 7:3)

The Scriptures contain no such misleading information. The absence of any reference to Melchizedek's descent does not justify the extreme statement that he had "neither beginning of days nor end of life." There is absolutely no biblical foundation for such a conclusion. Moreover, Melchizedek cannot be identified as an earlier manifestation of Jesus as some Christians allege. If he was "made like the Son of God," he could not actually *be* "the Son." However, "having been made like the Son of God, he remains a priest perpetually" is asserting that Melchizedek did not just typify Jesus, but was something more than a mere mortal. It appears that the author of Hebrews gives Melchizedek an existence not possible for a human being. If Melchizedek, without father, mother or genealogy, has "neither beginning of days nor end of life" and has "been made like the Son of God," he must be an eternal being. But, at the same time, he could not be the pre-incarnate Jesus of Christian mythology.

The speculation of some Christians that Melchizedek was an angel is untenable. According to the author of Hebrews, Melchizedek could not have been an angel since angels are created beings and, as such, have a "beginning of days." In Hebrews, Melchizedek is said to be without "beginning."

Elevated to the status of a divinity, Melchizedek is lifted to a level equal to the members of the Trinity. Thus, he becomes a fourth member of the Christian godhead, thereby replacing the Trinity with a Quaternary. This addition of Melchizedek to the Christian godhead to form a Quaternary, rather than a Trinity, is the only conclusion to be drawn from the information provided by the author of Hebrews.

Unlike Melchizedek, Jesus had a father, Joseph, a mother, Mary and a genealogy, as found in Matthew and Luke. Most significantly, the New Testament says that Jesus also had a beginning in time. According to Revelation, he was the first thing created by God, that is, "the beginning of the creation of God" (Revelation 3:14) and Matthew speaks of the "birth of Jesus Christ" (Matthew 1:18).

Since Melchizedek is said to have been "made like the Son of God," he could not be identical with Jesus who the New Testament calls "the Son of God" (e.g., Matthew 14:33). To be made like something does not mean it is that thing. Instead, it merely has certain similar characteristics.

There are Christians who believe that Melchizedek was a manifestation of God in human form, but then, how could God the Father, be "made like the Son of God"? God cannot be made like anyone, nor can a father be considered to have been made like his son. Obviously, Melchizedek must be a completely distinct individual, different from either God or Jesus.

The author of Hebrews does not merely say that Melchizedek's genealogy, father, and mother were not recorded in the Bible, but that he *never* had any ancestry, which an actual human being would have. Following the information found in the Letter to the Hebrews, what kind of being could he be? As indicated, Melchizedek is said to be without beginning and Jesus is said to have had a beginning. Therefore, while the two might have been conceived by some Christians as similar in some way since it is said that Melchizedek was "made like the Son of God," the two represent two independent beings. They are said to be "made like" each other, which means they are not one and the same. What results is a fourth member of the Christian godhead. As mentioned above, what the author of Hebrews creates is a Quaternary instead of a Trinity.

The Aaronic priesthood and the "order of Melchizedek"

The author of Hebrews has misconstrued Psalm 110 as a reference to Jesus. The biblically unsound arguments presented are vain attempts to prove that Jesus was more than a mere mortal. It is maintained that Jesus did not have the Aaronic priesthood, but did possess the Melchizedek priesthood and thereby could offer up himself as a sacrifice.

The claim that Jesus held a priesthood "according to the order of Melchizedek" is irrelevant to any discussion of sacrifice made under the Torah. It is the Torah that Jesus is said to have fulfilled and nullified by offering up himself (Hebrews 7:27). The so-called "better covenant" (Hebrews 7:22) allegedly instituted by Jesus and its accompanying everlasting Melchizedek priesthood have to do with Christian beliefs concerning Jesus after his death. A non-Aaronic order of priesthood has no relevancy to the requirements of the Torah. Moreover, what are the ordinances of the priestly "order of Melchizedek"?

The New Testament Jesus is a fraud

The New Testament claims that Jesus fulfilled and nullified the law by offering up himself as a sacrifice. According to the description it provides, this came about in a manner that runs counter to the Torah. Yet, the claim is made that everything Jesus did was in accordance with the Torah. This is a New Testament conundrum. To the rest of us, it is obvious that this New Testament claim has no basis in fact.

Concerning the Messiah, God says:

> And I will set up one shepherd over them, and he shall feed them, even My servant David; he shall feed them, and he shall be their shepherd. And I the Lord will be their God. And My servant David prince among them; I the Lord have spoken. (Ezekiel 34:23-24)

The Lord (*Y-H-V-H*) alone will be worshiped as God, while the Messiah, as the servant of God, lives with the people. God and the Messiah are not and cannot be equals, for it is God alone who gives the Messiah power to rule in that capacity as His appointed servant.

Chapter 43

WHAT IS HIS NAME?
(Proverbs 30:4)

Christians argue that Proverbs 30:4 is a prooftext for the divine origin of Jesus. But, who says this passage is messianic and who says that even if it were that it refers to Jesus? Their allegations are self-serving presumptions not based on what the text actually says. Admitting to a self-deficiency in wisdom and understanding, Agur, the son of Jakeh, puts forward a set of rhetorical questions, the answers to which he feels all who seek knowledge should possess. He writes:

> Who has ascended up into heaven, and descended?
> Who has gathered the wind in his fists?
> Who has bound the waters in his garment?
> Who has established all the ends of the earth?
> What is his name, and what is his son's name, if you know? (Proverbs 30:4)

One who knows the answer to these questions possesses the fundamentals of all knowledge.

The first question, "What is his name?", is answered in the Bible, where we see that only God, the creator of heaven and earth, is in complete control of the forces of nature. The second question, "What is his son's name?" is also answered by examining the biblical record, the source of all true knowledge. There we find verses that show conclusively that Israel as a national entity is called the "son of God." For example, "Israel is My son, My firstborn" (Exodus 4:22); "You are the children of the Lord your God" (Deuteronomy 14:1); and "It will be said of them: 'You are the children of the living God'" (Hosea 2:1). The biblical record is clear in stating that Israel is the name of God's son, His firstborn. The Bible also teaches that David and Solomon were considered in a filial relationship with God (Psalms 89:27-28; 1 Chronicles 22:10, 28:6). This will also be true of the future Messiah because he like David and Solomon will be the representative personification of Israel as a whole. But, it is Israel as a national unit that is the sole bearer of the title of the "son" or "firstborn" of God.

Some Christians propose that Israel's filial relationship with God points to what they claim is a greater relationship between God and Jesus. But, who says there is a special filial connection between God and Jesus? Who says this interpretation is right? It is based like so many other claims made on behalf of Jesus, on preconceived tendentious views rather than objective truth derived from the biblical record. The Messiah when he comes will in a figurative sense enter into the "sonship" of God, an honor he will share with all of God's chosen servants.

Chapter 44

ONE LIKE THE SON OF MAN
(Daniel 7:13-14, 27)

Christians often cite Daniel 7:13-14 as proof that the Messiah is to be a divine being. The text reads:

> I saw in the night visions, and behold, there came with the clouds of heaven one like a son of man, and he came to the Ancient of days, and he was brought near before Him. And there was given him dominion, and glory, and a kingdom, that all the peoples, nations, and languages should serve him [*shaltaneih*]; his dominion is an everlasting dominion, which shall not pass away, and his kingdom that which shall not be destroyed.

Some Christians maintain that since "one like a son of man" comes with the clouds of heaven and receives worldwide authority and obedience it is clear that he is more than merely human. Other Christians mistranslate *shaltaneih*, "serve him," as "worship him" to indicate that he is recognized as divine.

Daniel 7:27 reads:

> And the kingdom and the dominion, and the greatness of the kingdoms under the whole heaven, shall be given to the people of the holy ones of the Most High; their kingdom is an everlasting kingdom, and all dominions shall serve and obey them.

We see that in both Daniel 7:13-14 and 7:27 the terms "one like a son of man" and "the people of the holy ones of the Most High" refer collectively to the people of Israel who will receive worldwide authority and obedience. Rabbinical exegesis applied the term "one like a son of man" to the Messiah, but not as a divine or semi-divine being. There is nothing in Daniel's visionary experience to indicate that "one like a son of man' is a divine being. This is a visionary experience and as such the reality of the arrival of the true Messiah when he comes, as with any visionary experience, need not conform to the vision's details.

The "people of the holy ones [alt. "holy exalted ones" — because *elyonim* is also plural] of the Most High" refers to the faithful core of the Jewish people (see Psalms 34:10, 16:3; Daniel 8:24). God acts through His people who may therefore be called "holy exalted ones," the name used elsewhere in Daniel to describe celestial beings. In the vision, the people of the holy exalted ones of God are represented by one like a *man*, that is, *man* is representative of the collective people of Israel. The emphasis is on heavenly power which acts through the faithful Jews as contrasted with the power of chaos which acts through the kingdoms of this world.

Chapter 45

THE SEVENTY WEEKS OF DANIEL 9:24 -27

Part 1

LIARS FOR JESUS

There a problem with Christian interpretative credibility. I am referring to those Christians — theologians, laymen, missionaries or would-be missionaries who know what the original language texts actually say but who distort their meaning through deliberate mistranslations and the like because they feel it's more important that people believe in Jesus as their Messiah and Savior than know that such beliefs are based on falsehoods. Special note should be taken of those Christian Bible translations that deliberately craft their renderings of important texts to hide the true meaning in order to manipulate Jewish and Gentile readers alike into believing the translator's preconceived theological beliefs.

As it is, all scriptural reference said to be messianic are interpretations, whether Jewish or Christian. So why do we say Christian interpretations are dishonest, don't they have a right to their own opinion? They have a right to their own opinion, but have no right to manufacture false *facts*. Daniel's Seventy Week's is among the passages most abused by Christians in their attempt to prove Jesus is the Messiah. Who says Daniel 9:24-27 is a messianic passage pinpointing the Messiah's arrival and why do they say it? For centuries Christians have offered explanations of Daniel 9 based on manipulation of the text through fallacious translations, ignoring what the text actually states, and by providing erroneous computations to arrive at pre-selected years that coincide with the life of Jesus. When all else fails, they resort to accusing the Jews of altering the Hebrew text. A charge made all the more despicable by their own alterations of the text in translation.

Many of the most vocal Christian interpreters of the Seventy

Weeks passage follow the inaccurate speculative computations of Robert Anderson and/or Harold Hoehner that state that only the decree of Artaxerxes Longimanus explicitly gives permission for the rebuilding of the city of Jerusalem.

Anderson's attempt to explain the angel's message is ingenious, but totally incorrect. His assumptions work out only to the extent that he chose dates that fit in with his notion concerning the number of days involved in a sixty-nine week period. Moreover, he uses an unnatural unit of time — years of 360 days. This is based on the assumption that there is something called a "prophetic year" and that it contains 360 days. Despite Anderson's claims it is not known in what year the crucifixion took place, an essential factor in verifying his assertions. According to some calculations, the 32 C.E. date for the crucifixion would mean that Jesus' execution took place on either a Sunday or a Monday. Additionally, it cannot even be said with any certainty that Jesus' entry into Jerusalem, just a few days before his crucifixion, is what is meant by "until one anointed, a prince." Indeed, if his calculations coincide with dates of his own choosing this proves nothing about the actual dates on which the events took place. Anderson takes subjective assumptions and makes objective conclusions based on them, without any justification for doing so. His calculations are for naught. An in-depth study of Daniel 9:24-27 yields information which demolishes Anderson's claim that Gabriel's words refer to Jesus. Based on the evidence: Anderson's faulty reasoning in establishing a starting date, his assumption that there is one, not two anointed ones mentioned in this passage and his not realizing there is no zero year between B.C.E and C.E. dates go to show that his calculations are proved incorrect. Harold Hoehner uses Anderson's method but not his dates to establish an alternate chronological time frame for Jesus' alleged fulfillment of Daniel 9. As a result, he too is incorrect.[1]

This passage is one of the most contested passages among Christians themselves. The inter-Christian antagonism goes beyond differences of interpretation and is often accompanied with vitriolic attacks and accusations of heresy. There are a plethora of Christian interpretations of the Seventy Weeks prophecy that differ fundamentally with each other. They are all "carefully" crafted to give the desired results sort after. The often irreconcilable and conflicting interpretations are nothing short of bordering on theological anarchy. Suffice it to say that the Jewish Scriptures are overwhelmingly supportive of the decree of Cyrus as the edict allowing for the rebuilding of the city of Jerusalem (see Isaiah 44:28, 45:13; Zechariah 1:16; Ezra 6:14).

In conversation with missionaries and would-be missionaries concerning this passage, Jews do not have to explain or defend Jewish interpretations of the Seventy Weeks. The whole purpose of the Christian conversation is to show that Jesus is the subject of the passage. They often appeal to non-literal Jewish renderings that seem to support some Christian contentions, but such translations have no relevance to the discussion. The Jewish response need not be to show a better translation or interpretation but rather to show why a simple reading of the original *Hebrew text* indicates that it cannot refer to the Jesus of Christian theology. In reading the Christian translation of this passage, one must ask, "Are we looking at as literal a rendering as is possible or one dependent on preconceived Christian traditions and views that are not supported by the text?" And, yes, we desire the same standard from Jewish translations as well!

The plain reading of a scriptural text is always to be sought in order to understand it in its literal sense. Translation by its very nature often involves interpretation. Nevertheless, it is no excuse for renderings to deliberately champion preconceived theological doctrines. It is a matter of one's self-serving opinion in contrast with the simple facts delineated in the text. In the Seventy Weeks passage Christian translations read too much christology into the literal text to justify their translation of key words and phrases. But does that mean the interpretation is wrong? One should not confuse *translation* with *interpretation*. Take, for instance, the use of the Hebrew word *mashiach* in verses 25 and 26. All agree that the word means *an anointed one* in and by itself, but what does it mean in the context of this passage? Does it have reference to two separate anointed individuals, to one anointed individual not specifically named in the text, specifically to the Jewish Messiah and by further Christian inference to Jesus?

What can we learn from the literal text itself and what is actually in the realm of interpretation? Is there justification for reading too much into the text by translating it as "the Messiah" (or "Messiah") with all its implications (expressed in the use of the definite article and the capitalization) as opposed to the literal "an anointed one" (or even "the anointed one" as in some Jewish renderings)? Is there justification for mistranslating *v'ein lo* as "but not for himself," even for those who, while admitting the phrase means "he shall have nothing," nevertheless give the mistranslation as a legitimate alternative? They have no justification because they reluctantly acknowledge the correct meaning while advocating the counterfeit translation in practice.

In spreading the Christian message, they disregard the proper translation, and combine the dishonest renderings of "the Messiah" and "but not for himself" to wrongly show that this passage is a prophecy foretelling the *Messiah's* atoning death. The text implies neither a reference to the Messiah *par excellence* nor to his undergoing an *atoning death*. Christian translators cannot be forgiven for seeking to obscure the text and falsely create the impression that it says that the Messiah is referred to in this passage and that it moreover, declares he will die an atoning death for others. Some Christians, in defense, say the translators merely sought to bring the true meaning out even more clearly than the original text intended. Such misrepresentation and defense we call *lying for Jesus*. They are true disciples of Paul who declared: "What then? Only that in every way, whether in pretense or in truth, Christ is proclaimed; and in this I rejoice. Yes, and I wll rejoice" (Philippians 1:18).

It simply will not do to assume, as some Christians do, that verse 26 speaks of the death of the Messiah, and that Christian Bible translations are fully justified in explaining Daniel 9:24-27 in Messianic terms. Rendering "anointed" as *Messiah* in this context and the implications of the word Messiah generally is making an interpretative judgment about the meaning of the text, whether a specific figure is identified as Messiah or not. To deny the literal text that identifies two different *anointed ones* living hundreds of years apart and to render the text corruptly by omitting the definite article before "threescore and two weeks" in verse 26 in order to support a theological belief is simply dishonest. There is no textual reason for capitalizing the initial letter of the word *mashiach* in translation or pretending there is a definite article before it and then to render it as *the Messiah* (verse 25); neither is there justification for the deletion of the definite article before the mention of sixty-two weeks (verse 26). These are beliefs that should be properly confined to footnotes and not to a rendering of a scriptural text that millions rely on as being "the literal word of God" (e.g., the KJV renders *mashiach* as "anointed" throughout its entire translation except in two places Daniel 9, verses 25 and 26).

Where do these mistranslations lead? Two words in verse 26: *v'ein lo*, are translated dishonestly to encapsulate what Christians consider the supposed central purpose of Jesus' mission. The mistranslation is completely transparent to anyone knowing the Hebrew language, of which we presume the translators had knowledge. There is no other explanation for their rendering then it is disingenuously used to support a belief that Jesus had to die for the sins of mankind. Some Christians point to this phrase as the clearest support from the Jewish Scriptures for the claim that Jesus died as a sacrifice for others. The irony of the matter is that Daniel's text makes no such connection.

Getting past the Christian references to an imaginary "prophetic year" of 360 days and the manipulating of dates and numbers that add up to conflicting and competing calculations developed in the imagination of Christian apologists let us see what the text actually says. When approached by Christians with this passage the discerning reader should ask: Why do Christians put definite articles before "an anointed one" and "a prince" respectively, in verse 25, when none is indicated by the Hebrew text? Why do Christians ignore the *'atnach* (punctuation/cantilation corresponding to a semi-colon) positioned between the "seven weeks" and the "sixty-two weeks," in verse 25 that significantly divides the two periods and indicates that there are two anointed ones referred to in the verse? Why do Christians disregard the definite article before the "sixty-two weeks" mentioned in verse 26 that emphasizes the division in the sequence? Why do Christians ignore that verse 26 speaks of a second "anointed one" coming "after the sixty-two weeks"? Why do Christians mistranslate *v'ein lo*, "he shall have nothing" (in reference to the second anointed one's condition after death) obscuring its implicit denial of any reference to the Jesus of Christian theology?

If Daniel 9 pinpoints the coming of Jesus as the Messiah down to the exact date, then why is there no clear reference to this passage in the New Testament? There are no calculations in the New Testament that would show Jesus' contemporaries that the long-awaited Messiah has come. In particular, there are no calculations in the New Testament to support an alleged connection between the Seventy Weeks and contemporary Christian claims. Where are the apostles to proclaim: "Jews of Jerusalem, get out your quill and parchment and do the calculations!"? Where in the New Testament is Peter or Paul to cry out that the dates are all there and that it all adds up to Jesus, according to the Scriptures? The silence is not deafening, it is revealing of the fraudulent Christian misuse of this passage.

The conclusion arrived at by answering these questions honestly is straightforward and to the point: this passage does not speak of Jesus. Moreover, it is not a messianic passage and certainly finds no fulfillment in the life and death of Jesus.

Part 2

THE PASSAGE: VERSE BY VERSE

The decree

> Verse 24: Seventy weeks are decreed upon your people and upon your holy city, to terminate the transgression, and to make an end of sin, and to forgive iniquity, and to bring in everlasting righteousness, and to seal vision and prophet, and to anoint the Holy of Holies.

Verse 24 contains six phrases directed solely for "your people and upon your holy city" (that is, the Jewish nation and Jerusalem) whose respective content is to find fulfillment in the seventy weeks period if another period of exilic punishment is to be avoided: (1) to terminate the transgression (2) to make an end of sin (3) to forgive iniquity[2] (4) to bring in everlasting righteousness (5) to seal vision and prophet (6) to anoint the Holy of Holies.

As we shall see, much was accomplished toward fulfilling these goals, but total compliance was not realized. The results of falling

241

short were already expected and foretold in the passage (verses 26-27).

The transgression

Special attention is given to the most grievous of sins from which so many other sins and their inevitable punishments originate. In this period the centrality of the Jerusalem Temple is to be recognized by the people in both word and deed as the cessation of rampant idolatry of previous centuries takes place. While individuals and even groups of Israelites may be led astray, there will no longer be that pervasive idolatry which ate away at the national fabric of both the southern kingdom of Judah as well as the northern kingdom of Israel.

The angel declares the great changes that need to be accomplished during this period. Thus is terminated *ha-pesh'a* "the transgression," the rebelliousness against God manifested in the corrosive idolatry of the First Temple period, the root cause of Israel's punishment (see Daniel 8:13 where *ha-pesh'a* is used of heathen objects of worship). *Ha-pesh'a* is written with the definite article to indicate the specific transgression of idolatry that distinct from all other sins is given specific attention. Historically, it finally ceased as a major internal threat to national existence. It was terminated not in the sense of ceasing to exist altogether, but in the sense that it is reduced in form and size and confined to a minority of apostates. *External attempts* at imposing idolatry will be met with contempt, defiance, and actual physical resistance by the masses of the nation. *Internal attempts* to impose alien teaching will lead to eventual expulsion and/or disappearance from the national body.

Sin and iniquity

Chatat, "sin" (that is, inadvertent sin), and *'avon*, "iniquity" (that is, intentional sin), are not written with the definite article as they refer to sins for which there was ongoing ability to obtain forgiveness throughout this period by recourse to the divinely ordained system of atonement. Under this system sincere repentance represented by remorse and confession in prayer was coupled with a sacrificial offering in the Temple. Most sins then and now could be atoned for anytime through sincere prayer alone. Despite the vicissitudes and dangers to the future existence of the Jewish people during these "troubled times" (verse 25), an intensification of adherence to Judaism takes place. As a result, there is nothing that can destroy the remnant's loyalty to the God of Israel in future periods of persecution and exile, which were to follow.

Everlasting righteousness of the Torah

It is a time "to bring in everlasting righteousness" through the promulgation of the Torah, both Written and Oral. Torah law is the spiritual system of the commandments by which God judges His people. The Torah, God's righteous law, is of unchanging character, undiminishing vitality, and never-ending validity. It is therefore everlasting, outlasting even the Temple. By its vitality the Torah shows the way for forgiveness from sin even when the Temple may lie in ruin and provides the means by which the Jewish people could remain strong and rise again. In this sense, the Second Temple era was a preparation for the bitter exile to follow the Temple's destruction.

The end of vision and prophet

The phrase "to seal [*lachtom*] vision and prophet [i.e., prophecy]" refers to the fact that the prophetic era during which time God made His will known to and through the prophets by means of visions and oracles (see Numbers 12:1-8, Deuteronomy 16:18) came to an end during this period. The cessation of prophecy is not to be taken in a negative sense but is to be viewed simply as the culmination of one mode of God's relationship with His people. "To seal" is not in the sense of "shutting up" or "sealing away," but of confirmation of something "finished," "completed." The prophetic task was not simply to foretell future events. Its main feature was decrying idolatry and social and moral failings and bringing the nation close to God. All that needed to be said was to be found in the recorded prophets. While much was accomplished toward this end the accompanying failures would eventually lead to exile once more.

Anointing the Holy of Holies

The expression "and to anoint the Holy of Holies" refers to the reestablished Second Temple (Ezekiel 46:12) and the office of high priest (1 Chronicles 23:13).[3] With all the tremendous positive strides made during the Second Temple period a national and spiritual disunity prevailed. Temple expansion by the cruel Herod the Great, an avarice priestly hierarchy starting with the Hasmoneans debased the priesthood and its function impeding the termination of sin and iniquity through corrupt practices. At a time when Jerusalem was surrounded by the Romans internecine deeds weakened the defenders of Jerusalem. Sectarian groups arose during this period endangering the spiritual welfare of Israel.

The vision expresses succinctly the ideal expectation God desired of the returnees from exile. At the same time, it indicates that this ideal would not find its complete fulfillment and that once more the nation would go into exile. The irony of this exile would be that the greatest tormentors of the Jewish people were a metamorphic offshoot deriving from one of the sects of this period — the followers of Jesus of Nazareth.

Was Jesus the awaited Messiah coming to save his people and, as claimed, the whole of mankind? Is it true that the Seventy Week passage predicts the coming of Jesus as Messiah? The Seventy Week passage does not make any predictions about Jesus. Even if one assumed for a moment that the passage was messianic in content it would still not refer to Jesus. Israel waits for the arrival of the true Messiah but the negatives that could be found in the national milieu do not indicate that it needed the intrusion of this false messianic personality called Jesus of Nazareth. Christian interpretations strain at credulity in attempts to identify this passage with Jesus, but these attempts do not remain true to either the biblical text or historical data found in secular sources.

Let us review the six expectations of verse 24 and see if they have any fulfillment in the life and death of Jesus.

- *to terminate the transgression*: What transgression was terminated by Jesus? Some of the most heinous transgressions of the basic requirements God desires of mankind have been perpetrated by those who in one form or another give their spiritual allegiance to Jesus. In fact, many of those nefarious deeds were done to "glorify" Jesus. So, how did he terminate the sinful behavior of countless millions of treacherous followers? It does not matter if

Jesus would approve of their behavior or if one says they were not his true followers. What matters is that in respect to this divine pronouncement Jesus failed to fulfill its requirements.

- *to make an end of sin*: Attempts are made to identify Jesus with the fulfillment of these divine pronouncements through unverifiable claims to his conquering sin and the like. Perhaps most glaring in terms of non-fulfillment is the claim that Jesus brought an end to sin, as if the world has seen the end of sin and unrighteousness; certainly not among those who venerate him as a god. Did Jesus terminate idolatry among those who eventually accepted him as part of God or did those who became his followers accommodate many of their old beliefs to the new? Local gods and spirits became saints to be venerated, pagan religious holidays became Christian holy days and even the very concept of a triune god incorporates pagan thought. Indeed, the Protestant Reformation did not cleanse itself of pagan influence.

- *To forgive iniquity*: It is said that Jesus made the necessary one time offering that would be the basis upon which iniquity could be forgiven. Christians claim one's sins are forgiven on accepting Jesus as sin bearer and repenting past sins entitling the person to eternity in heaven. Outside of the claims made on behalf of *Jesus the savior god* no proof exists that this is the fate of the repentant sinner. There is absolutely no proof other than Christian claims to support the allegation that Jesus "having offered one sacrifice for sins for all time, sat down at the right hand of God" (Hebrews 10:13).

- *to bring in everlasting righteousness*: Where is the everlasting righteousness supposedly brought by Jesus? Some Christians say that this refers to the alleged second coming of Jesus. It is very convenient to say anything not fulfilled refers to the future. But since his fulfillment record is at absolute zero there is not much sustainable promise in saying it is a future event.

- *to seal vision and prophet*: Did Jesus "seal vision and prophet"? Some Christians say Jesus sealed both "vision and prophet" indicating that this method of revelation and the "Jewish dispensation" ceased with his death, that is, this refers to the fulfillment of prophecies in Jesus. Once again, claims are made that Jesus fulfilled prophecy but such allegations are made on flimsy arguments. It is claimed that he fulfilled all the visions and prophecies of the Jewish Scriptures. Some supposedly relate to his person and office; others to his coming into the world, the time, place and manner of it; others to what is portrayed as his "great work of redemption and salvation"; and others to his alleged miracles, sufferings and death, and the fantasy of glory that should follow; all which is said to have been fulfilled although one sees no tangible change in the world to support Christian allegations. Some say "to seal up the vision and prophet" means that the prophets were until John the Baptist, and then vision and prophecy were to cease. Therefore, since the times of Jesus; there has been no prophet among the Jews. Jesus is then the last and greatest prophet of all, with a full revelation of the divine will, and no other is to be expected. Needless to say, reading the New Testament one finds that events are often remodeled to fit into the life of Jesus sometimes completely disregarding the original intent of the biblical reference. Therefore, the argument that Jesus fulfilled prophecy is far from the truth. Some Christians say Jesus brought the era of "vision and prophet" to an end being the last of the prophets. However, the New Testament authors claim that Christian prophecy continued. For example, "the four virgin daughters [of Philip the evangelist] who were prophetesses" (Acts 21:8-9) and "a certain prophet named Agabus" from Judea (Act 21:10).

• *to anoint the Holy of Holies*: Some Christians say this term refers to Jesus in one way or another by ascribing to him fanciful attributes: anointed priest of a special non-Aaronic order, priestly officiant in a heavenly temple and the list goes on. They imagine Jesus to be the Prophet, Priest, and King of mankind. Others refer it to an anointing of a future earthly temple following a second coming of Jesus. Some refer it to the anointing of a most holy person, namely Jesus, while others refer it to the church and its membership (confined of course to "true believers" as defined by the particular advocates of this interpretation). There is an interpretation that says the phrase refers to the holy of holies in the so-called heavenly New Jerusalem established after a second coming of Jesus. This would then be one more pronouncement not fulfilled by Jesus and consigned to a future fantasy. Other theories have also been suggested. What this tells us is that although some might show outward confidence in their claims, they just do not know the answer.

It is said that when Jesus supposedly ascended to heaven every one of the six objectives to be accomplished had been fulfilled. It is said he fulfilled all of the prophecies of the Jewish Scriptures. Well, except for those he is going to fulfill when he comes back, whenever that's supposed to happen. A review of the supposed fulfillments finds he fulfilled nothing.

It is obvious that Jesus did not fulfill any of the six expectations of verse 24, despite the strained unverifiable explanations given as Christians struggle to connect Jesus to a fulfillment of Daniel 9. Some Christians admit they do not understand the prophecy but insist it must refer to Jesus. Interestingly, the very fact that the nation of Israel did not fully fulfill God's desires was part of the prediction of events expressed in verses 26-27 that lead to renewed exile. This passage falls within the parameters of the historically verifiable with the *last* phrase, (*until decisive destruction shall be poured out upon that which causes desolation*) falling outside the seventy weeks. That last phrase awaits the great fulfillment when the Temple is once more rebuilt as indicated at the end of verse 27.

There is no room for speculations of a future fantasy fulfillment by a failed false messiah.

God's promises to national Israel (and be very clear, that is precisely what is stated in the Seventy Weeks passage) are irrevocable eternal declarations - the endless covenantal promises of the God of Israel who declares the eternality of His promise (Jeremiah 33:19-26). A promise and covenant that no man can rent asunder; nor deviant religious, political, or cultural systems destroy; nor Gentile dispersion, religious intolerance and expulsion, persecution, Crusade, inquisition, pogrom, Holocaust or Jihad, nor ceaseless Gentile trampling upon this holy people's divine rights and mandate ever succeed in annihilating.

The first anointed one

> Verse 25. Know therefore and understand that from the going forth of the word to restore and to build Jerusalem until an anointed one, a prince, shall be seven weeks; then for sixty-two weeks it shall be built again, with broad place and moat, but in troubled times.

Verse 25 delineates the time between the commencement of the Seventy Week period and the appearance of "an anointed one." Starting with "the going forth of the word to restore and to build Jerusalem," in 586 B.C.E., the first sequence of seven weeks (forty-nine years) culminates with Cyrus, the *anointed one* (see Isaiah 45:1). It is this Gentile ruler of the Persian Empire who decreed that the Jews might return to their native land and rebuild their Temple. God declares concerning Cyrus: "[H]e shall build My city, and he shall let go My captives, not for price nor reward" (Isaiah 45:13, see also Ezra 1:1-4).[4]

Following these forty-nine years is a period of "troubled times" lasting sixty-two weeks or 434 years. During these years many enemies will arise seeking to annihilate the Jewish people either physically or spiritually, or both, and to hinder Jerusalem from taking its rightful place as the spiritual center of the nation of Israel. At the instigation of the enemies of the Jews, the building of the Second Temple was halted for some time, but Jerusalem, which expresses physically the heartfelt spiritual yearnings of the Jewish people "shall be built again." As a result, the rebuilding of the Temple once more commenced in approximately 520 B.C.E. and was completed in 516 B.C.E. Jerusalem is to be economically and physically strong, as indicated by "broad place and moat," despite all adversaries. "Broad place" refers to the main square of the city where the population assembled to conduct social, judicial, and business affairs and "moat" refers to the city's defenses. The length of the Second Temple period was 589 years.[5]

The year 516 B.C.E. ends the seventy years of captivity. Although Jews had been returning to their homeland for approximately thirty years the people were not truly free until they were able to complete the rebuilding of the Temple; only then was it considered the end of the desolation of Jerusalem.

According to the text punctuation, the seven weeks of years and the sixty-two weeks of years are not meant to be added together into one combination of sixty-nine weeks. As a result, we see that there are two different *anointed ones* spoken of in this passage. This, as we shall see, is confirmed in verse 26, which describes what happens specifically during the sixty-two weeks of years. It is alleged by some Christians that the Jews (alt. the rabbis) deliberately inserted the *'atnach* in the accented Hebrew text of this verse after "seven weeks," thereby dividing it from the "sixty-two weeks (434 years) as a deliberate effort to make it appear as if the text did not refer to the time of their so-called messiah's coming. The reason these Christians give for this alleged action was the Jewish rejection of Jesus and was used to obscure his advent as the Messiah. The Christian argument is important to understand as it reveals the fallacy inherent in their exposition of the text and the truth of the Jewish understanding of the angel's words.

But, what happens if one disregards the punctuation and simply looks and the consonantal text of this passage? The proof that the *'atnach* (expressed as a semi-colon) is used properly in verse 25 is found in verse 26. There it says that "after *the* sixty-two weeks an anointed one shall be cut off." What sixty-two weeks is the verse referring to in emphasizing the number by placing the definite article before it? It must be the sixty-two weeks referred to in verse 25. But, why does verse 26 specifically divide off these sixty-two weeks? In so doing, it provides proof that the anointed one of verse 24 could not be the same person as that of verse 26 who was destined to live sometime *after* a further sixty-two weeks (434 years) from the lifetime of the first anointed one. Therefore, Christians are incorrect in alleging that only one anointed one is mentioned in the passage and they are also wrong in giving either anointed one the singular messianic identification as the long awaited Messiah. Yes, there are disagreements among Jewish commentators as to who these two individuals are but on the basis of the textual evidence we can be certain that it does not refer to Jesus.

The second anointed one

Verse 26.   And after the sixty-two weeks an anointed one shall be cut off, and he shall have nothing; the people of a leader who is to come shall destroy the city and the Sanctuary; and its end shall be with a flood; and until the end of war desolations are determined.

Verse 26 is concerned with events that are to take place *after* "the sixty-two weeks." It is only *after* the sixty-two weeks that an anointed one is cut off and no mention is made of how long after this will occur. That is all that can be derived from the text. As previously mentioned, the presence of a definite article before the mention of sixty-two weeks shows that there is a separation between the seven weeks and the sixty-two weeks. This emphasis necessitates a grammatical division represented by a semi-colon in the rendering of verse 25 to show that there is a division between the seven weeks and the sixty-two weeks. The resultant span of years makes it impossible for the two mentions of "anointed one" to refer to the same individual.

In this time segment two events are mentioned. First, after a sixty-two week period (434 years) of "troubled times" in which Jerusalem "shall be built again, with broad place and moat" "an anointed one shall be cut off." Obviously, this anointed one is not to be identified with the anointed one of verse 25. The time differential is just too great. Second, this verse mentions the fate of "the city and the Sanctuary" (that is, Jerusalem and the Temple), which are to be destroyed by "the people of the leader who is to come" as if by a devastating flood (cf. Nahum 1:8). Although "desolations are determined" while the war is still in progress it is seen from verse 27 that this verdict was put into full effect at the war's end. That is, its fulfillment did not end with the war but continued into the future with further negative decrees and persecutions seeking to destroy the Jewish people.

The first seven weeks of the seventy week period ends in 537 B.C.E. with Cyrus the *anointed one* who issues the decree allowing the Jews to return from exile. The second segment of sixty-two weeks in length, covered by verse 26, culminates in 103 B.C.E. (586-49-434=103 B.C.E.). Verse 26 indicates that "after sixty-two weeks an anointed one shall be cut off." This "anointed one" is the High Priest Alexander Yannai (reign: 103-76 B.C.E.) who came to power just at the end of the sixty-two week period in 103 B.C.E. and was the last of the important Hasmonean leaders.[6] There is nothing unusual in referring to a high priest as an *anointed one*, since he was anointed on assuming that position. Alexander Yannai also held the position of king, a position formalized by anointing.

The phrase "after sixty-two weeks" indicates the time frame during which the "anointed one shall be cut off," that is, suffer *karet*, "excision." Alexander Yannai is not "cut off" immediately after sixty-two weeks, but through the actions of his reign he was to have this final judgment following his death. From this we see a further indication that there are intervals between the specific identifiable time periods. The penalty accompanying *karet* is here aptly described as "to have nothing," or "be no more." That is, he will have no reward after death.

This punishment is given to Alexander Yannai infamous for his unjust, tyrannical, and bloody rule.[7] He is notorious for his violent animosity directed against the Pharisees and his brazen rejection of the Oral Law.[8] For example, Josephus records that Alexander Yannai fought against the Pharisees for six years, "and ... slew no fewer than fifty thousand of them."[9] He also "ordered some eight hundred of the Jews to be crucified, and slaughtered their children and wives before the eyes of the still living wretches."[10]

Verse 26 shows when Alexander Yannai, the "anointed one," would assume power and what kind of punishment would be meted out to him for his transgressions against God. Alexander Yannai's sons and grandsons continued his unmitigated lust for power and thereby finalized the demise of the Hasmonean dynasty. The fate of these three generations may be expressed by the psalmist's words: "But transgressors shall be destroyed together; the future of the wicked shall be cut off" (Psalms 37:38)[11]

The second part of verse 26 is a sweeping historical synopsis of events leading to the destruction of the Second Temple. This is the tragedy encapsulated "and the people [the Romans] of the leader [Pompey] who is to come, shall destroy [under Titus]" that is, the years 63 B.C.E. to 70 C.E. The encounter with the destructive forces of the Roman Empire did not begin with the Jewish Revolt but go back to Pompey's attack on Jerusalem and the Temple.

But, of course, our discussion is not solely centered on a Jewish understanding of verse 26. Christians maintain that the anointed one of verse 26 refers to Jesus. However, "he shall have nothing" contradicts the Christian claim that Isaiah 53:12, "I will divide him a portion with the great" refers to Jesus. According to Christian theology, Jesus in his pre-incarnation state existed in heaven where he was *rich*, so-to-speak, in that as one-third of the Godhead (or divine being) he possessed the entire universe and beyond and all it contains. In his supposed incarnate existence he was born into a poor family of humble means (except for the gifts of the magi–Matthew 2:11). At his death he was still poor and had a small group of followers. It is only subsequent to his death that it is said that he gained rewards and honors for his alleged sacrifice (Philippians 2:8-11).

Yes, rather strange that a part of the Godhead needed to reward and honor himself for doing what he himself desired to be done. Now read carefully what verse 26 says of the second anointed one: "an anointed one shall be cut off, and he shall have nothing." This anointed one will be "cut off," that is, die. The emphasis is not on what this anointed one possessed at death, but on what he had following his death. In death he will have nothing. It is not merely at the moment of death that he will have nothing. The future tense, "he shall have nothing," shows that the heavenly judgment rendered the individual spoken of is devoid of any reward after death. Does this describe the Jesus portrayed by Paul or is there another Jesus?

The words "he shall have nothing" (*v'ein lo* —9:26) are incorrectly translated by the King James Version (and many other Christian translations) as "but not for himself." The reason for this deliberate mistranslation is to give biblical support for the Christian contention that Jesus died for humanity's sins. This phrase should be translated as "he has nothing [following *karet*]" or "he shall have nothing." There are those Christians who for tendentious reasons maintain that this phrase has both meanings. For example, *The Holy Bible: New International Version*, renders the Hebrew as "cut off and will have nothing" in the main text but in the apparatus has "or *off, but not for himself.*"[12] The latter rendering cannot be supported grammatically. Indeed, a number of modern Christian translations recognize the untenability of the "but not for himself" rendering and do translate the phrase correctly, without any explanations to the contrary. Unfortunately, millions of Christians rely totally and without question on the King James Version and other Bible translations containing this and other erroneous Christian renderings and are thereby deceived.

With the clear distinction between the seven weeks and the sixty-two weeks established, the following questions must be asked: Are these sixty-nine weeks to be simply taken together and added consecutively without interruption as found in most Christian translations, leading many to assume only one anointed individual is mentioned? Could their separation instead signify a time-gap between them and the presence of two separate anointed ones? There is nothing to indicate that such a gap between the first seven weeks and the next sixty-two weeks would constitute any violation of the text. In fact, a gap between these two periods is the only explanation to account for their separation.

Christians tend to combine the seven week unit and the sixty-two week unit and contend that according to the passage only one anointed one is referred to and he comes after the period of 483 years. They then assume that that individual is the Messiah par excellence. Although some Christians admit there are two separate anointed individuals most combine the two mentions of "an anointed one" and refer to the combination in one way or another as a reference to Jesus. Nevertheless, it is clear from the text that the time intervals make it impossible for there to be only one anointed. Christian explanations (and there are several in conflict with each other) violate the plain meaning of the Hebrew text as it is grammatically constructed.

The last week and its aftermath

> Verse 27. And it [the Roman government] shall make a strong covenant with many for one week; and during half of the week it [the Roman government on account of its successful military campaigns] shall cause sacrifice and meal offering to cease; and upon the wing of abominations shall be that which causes desolation; and that until decisive destruction shall be poured out upon that which causes desolation.

Verse 27 focuses in on what the Romans will do at the end of the

Second Temple period.

Thus, the prophetic text presents a broad sweep of the historical period from the end of Jewish political sovereignty, which is marked by the Roman entrance into the Temple (63 B.C.E.) until the Temple destruction in 70 C.E. Verse 27 continues the presentation of verse 26. This verse also concerns itself with the last seven years of the Second Temple's existence. The verse terminates with the promise that at some indeterminate time beyond the Seventy Weeks the last of the abominations set up on the Temple Mount by the Gentiles will be destroyed.

While the last week does not run consecutively with the rest of the time period there is no break prophetically, but rather a logical transition occurs between the time of Alexander Yannai ("after sixty-two weeks") and the last week of years. This is because Alexander Yannai's actions ushered in events, which eventually led to the "last week." The week is considered as following directly on, and as a consequence of, Alexander Yannai's reign and the advent of Roman domination (as already announced in verse 26). That is, the seventieth week was the direct result of events generated by the reign of Alexander Yannai, which opened the door for Roman rule and its accompanying problems. The text does not require that the last week run consecutively with the sixty-two weeks. It will come "after the sixty-two weeks," but not necessarily immediately following that period of time. However, it does necessitate a unity of events requiring this seven-year period to take place within the period of the Second Temple and, indeed, be the last seven years of that period. Christian interpretations, which place the seventieth week beyond the year 70 C.E. and especially those that place that last seven years in the remote future, violate the cohesiveness of the passage. This passage is a self-contained time capsule of Jewish history.

Alexander Yannai was the last of the powerful Hasmonean rulers. At his death he left a power vacuum, only filled for a time by his wife Salome Alexandra (76 B.C.E. - 67 B.C.E.) who succeeded him as ruler of the kingdom. Her death ushered in a period of incessant fighting between their two sons for the throne. Neither one was capable of sustaining the power built up by their forebears. Aristobulus II reigned from 67 - 63 B.C.E. after having driven his older brother, Hyrcanus II, from the throne (67 B.C.E.). Aristobulus was in turn forced out after Pompey laid siege to the Temple Mount, and after three months captured the Temple area (63 B.C.E.). Thus, began the period in which "the people [the Romans] of the leader [Pompey] who is to come shall destroy" (9:26). The year 63 B.C.E. marked the end of Judea's political independence.[13]

As we see, a chain of events is set in motion following the ascendancy of Alexander Yannai and intensifies following his death, which eventually brought Roman hegemony over Judea and culminated in the destruction of the Temple. The Second Temple's fate is sealed at a definitely designated time from the destruction of the First Temple. The culmination of the Second Temple period at the terminus of the last week gives a capsulated picture. The last week represents the bitter outcome of Roman rule up to the destruction in 70 C.E. In Daniel's Seventy Weeks events progress immediately from the historical situation "after the sixty-two weeks" directly to the culminating cataclysm which is to come within a few generations. As the Seventy Weeks era started immediately following the First Temple's destruction so it is reasonable to assume that it ends with the Second Temple's destruction. It makes for a cohesive period despite the apparent hiatus before the last week.

In the seventieth week spoken of in verse 26 "the people[14] [the Romans] of the leader [Pompey] who is to come" (63 B.C.E.) will eventually destroy Jerusalem and the Temple under the leadership of Titus (70 C.E.). In this phrase, referring to the initial event and the concluding event that mark this period we have a summary of the entire period between 63 B.C.E. and 70 C.E. Verse 27 then relates how "it" ("the people" is a collective singular; or "he," Titus) will *higbir b'rit*, "make a strong covenant," that is, the Romans will consolidate their forces and those of allied national groups.

The Romans were ever vigilant against a Jewish insurrection. Tenacious in their loyalty to ancestral beliefs and customs Jews presented Rome with a unique security problem, once their religious sensibilities were aroused. Moreover, there was the Jewish refusal to practice the formalities of state worship. This inevitably brought the charge of disloyalty, from their detractors, especially among the Hellenized Gentile communities. Judea showed the least appreciable increase in Romanization or Hellenization of customs of any region under Roman control. To the Roman administrative officials, accountable for the security of Judea and surrounding regions, there was little, if any, admiration for this situation. They sided with those Hellenized Gentile groups who for the most part dutifully complied with Roman desires. Thus, was forged the compact that in the seventieth week, increasingly aligned Rome with local allies, consisting of several national groups, against Judea and the Jews of the surrounding region. This is the compact that was strengthened over the course of the seven years of the last week. These Hellenized national groups are collectively referred to as *rabim*, "many" (verse 27). Specifically, the term *rabim*, "the great ones," may be a reference to the national group leaders (cf. Isaiah 53:12). *Rabim*, "great ones" may also include those Jews who conspired with the Romans against their own people. Josephus and Tacitus both write of the Greeks, Syrians, and Nabataean Arabs joining the Romans in the murder, destruction, and plundering of the Jewish population. Josephus reports that after Vespasian was appointed commander his son, Titus, went to Syria "where he concentrated the Roman forces and numerous auxiliary contingents furnished by the kings of the neighboring districts."[15] Tacitus writes that the Roman legions, which Titus mustered for the siege of Jerusalem were "accompanied by twenty cohorts of allied troops and eight squadrons of cavalry, by the two kings Agrippa and Sohemus, by the auxiliary forces of king Antiochus, by a strong contingent of Arabs, who hated the Jews with the usual hatred of neighbors, and, lastly, by many persons brought from the capital and from Italy by private hope of securing the yet unengaged affections of the Prince."[16]

Before the First Jewish Revolt, the Roman garrison in Judea consisted only of auxiliary units recruited from the non-Jewish population of the region.[17] The ruins at the site of the Jewish city of Gamla situated in the Golan, near the Sea of Galilee, affords further evidence of the Roman use of national auxiliary troops in their war against the Jews. The extensive variety of arrowhead types found at the site reflect the participation of "auxiliary units composed of different ethnic groups from the East who were excellent archers" to make up for the Roman's own lack of archery skills. "[E]ach of the different ethnic units seems to have used differently shaped arrowheads as well as the 'standard' Roman issue."[18]

Even before the war began the Roman administration gave support to the Greek and Syrian population of the region in and around Judea. These communities, whose status had declined during the period of Hasmonean rule, had under Roman rule increased in power at the expense of the Jewish population. Furthermore, they became a privileged class. The local Roman forces were recruited mainly from the Hellenized cities such as Samarian Sebaste and Caesarea. Josephus writes that the Greeks of Caesarea had "the support of the military; for the troops stationed here were mainly levied by the Romans from Syria, and were consequently always ready to lend aid to their compatriots."[19] This tension acquired increased significance during the decades immediately preceding the revolt, when more and more members of the Greek element rose to even higher positions in the Roman administrative hierarchy. Once appointed, these officials naturally tended to support the citizens of the Greek towns, and it was no coincidence that Florus, the worst procurator, was a Greek from Asia Minor. In fact, what precipitated the revolt were the anti-Jewish policies of the Greek citizens of Caesarea who in 66 C.E. obtained from Nero the administration of the government of that city;[20] and the decrees of Florus who not only confiscated a large sum of money from the Temple treasury but ordered his soldiers to plunder and massacre part of the city of Jerusalem.[21]

The question may be asked: Why does the last week start with Albinus (62-64 C.E.)? Certainly such procurators as Cumanus (48-52 C.E.) and Felix (52-60 C.E.) were ruthless in their dealings with the Jews. Not only did Cumanus massacre Jews in Jerusalem but he also condoned attacks on Jews by Samaritans. In consequence of the latter action, he was subsequently banished. For his part, Felix also favored the Samaritans as against the Jews. Of Felix, Tacitus writes that he "exercised the power of a king in the spirit of a slave.[22]

Albinus, however, was even worse. Josephus reports that under "The administration of Albinus ... there was no form of villainy which he omitted to practice."[23] Josephus writes further "from this date were sown in the city [Jerusalem] the seeds of its impending fall."[24] He then declares that Albinus' "successor, Gessius Florus [64-66 C.E.], made him appear by comparison a paragon of virtue. The crimes of Albinus were, for the most part, perpetrated in secret and with dissimulation; Gessius, on the contrary, ostentatiously paraded his outrages upon the nation, and, as though he had been sent as hangman of condemned criminals, abstained from no form of robbery or violence."[25]

The phrase *ve-chatzi sh'vu'ah yash-bit*, "and during half of the week" must be understood both from a grammatical and historical perspective. Since the abolition of the sacrifices and the meal offerings did not just end for a period of three and one-half years but, in fact, for a longer period, down to our own days, this phrase cannot be translated as if they were abolished for only that one-half week period. The usual rendering gives the impression that sacrifices and meal offerings were abolished for only a one-half week period, that is, three and one-half years, and implies that they ceased for only that time and were reinstated afterwards. Rather, the abolition came about over the span of the entire three and one-half year period. This is seen from the grammatical construction of the phrase. To express this fact the *vav*, due to its multi-purpose nature, should be rendered "and during." This is made even more necessary by the nature of the *hiphil* construction of *yash-bit*. With any verb denoting "cessation," "destruction," and the like, such as, *yash-bit*, "to cause to cease," "abolish," unless explicitly indicated by the context that it is for a limited time, it is to be assumed that the cessation is to last for an indefinite period of time. In this case, the verb *yash-bit* implies that the changed condition is to continue on throughout the post-Second Temple era. Thus, the rendering is, "and during half of the week it [the Romans or "he" referring to Vespasian in particular] shall cause sacrifice and meal offering to cease." That is, the sacrificial system will cease to be carried out over the period of one-half of the week or three and one-half years, not in one stroke, but by cumulative events over that span of time.

Vespasian decided that the best way to proceed with the war would be to first take the rear — the Galilee and Golan — and only then to attack the center of the rebellion — Judea and its capital, Jerusalem. In the spring of 67 C.E. Vespasian began his military campaign by entering Galilee. The Romans systematically took city after city and village after village. Within a short time the Romans occupied almost the whole country, including the coastal plain and the transjordanian area. Vespasian himself, at the head of the main force, conquered northern Judea, and in 68 C.E. joined up with the column that had subdued the transjordanian area. He then began systematically to subdue one district of Judea after another, with the aim of isolating Jerusalem. "Vespasian ... succeeded within the space of two summers in occupying with his victorious army the whole of the level country and all the cities, except Jerusalem."[26] This reconquest came to a halt in 69 C.E. because of troubles in Rome which eventually culminated in Vespasian being proclaimed emperor and departing for that city. In the early spring, just prior to Passover, of the year 70 C.E., Titus began his siege operations. His assault against the city was completed approximately five months later, in late summer.

Not at once did "sacrifice and meal offering" stop. The cessation of daily sacrifices occurred over the course of the three years that Vespasian tightened the ring around Jerusalem[27] and the five months that elapsed between Titus' assuming his father's command and his establishing himself in Caesarea.[28] During this time, the last three and one-half years, it became more and more difficult to bring sacrifices and meal offerings to the Temple. The sacrificial infrastructure began to break down although Jerusalem itself remained unconquered. Finally, even the daily sacrifice, the *korban tamid* had to be suspended on the seventeenth of Tammuz 70 C.E., for lack of lambs with which to perform the ceremony.[29] That does not preclude the possibility that some sacrifices continued intermittently until the final destruction on the ninth of Av.

After the night comes the dawn

Daniel's text is followed by a simple but poignant statement concerning the post-destruction status of the Temple Mount under the control of various Gentile groups during the indeterminate period which will eventually be followed by the building of the Third Temple.

Once the seventy weeks have passed, "upon the wing[30] of abominations [that is, upon the elevated place of the Temple Mount on which there are detestable things] shall be that which causes desolation." The Temple Mount, the elevated place referred to metaphorically as "wing" will, after 70 C.E., be a place of detestable things, abominations, that is, Roman pagan,[31] Crusader[32] and Islamic shrines and mosques will be built on it. During the Crusader occupation of Jerusalem (1099-1187), the Islamic shrine, the Dome of the Rock, was converted into a Christian church. This appalling situation will last "until decisive destruction shall be poured out upon that which causes desolation," that is, until the last desolator, that of Islam, will also be removed from the Temple Mount.

"Wing" may have additional significance in that the Roman Empire had as its symbol the eagle that appeared on the legion standards along with the image of the emperor and were an object of worship; the heathen temple Hadrian built on the Temple Mount was dedicated to Jupiter whose messenger was also the eagle; and Saladin (12th century), the most famous Muslim conqueror of Jerusalem, had a golden eagle on his flag.

According to the text, without the Temple, the mount is considered desolate and that any alien buildings occupying this site are considered desolators, that is, "that which causes desolation," whose very presence on the sacred site causes one to be appalled.

The Christian delusion

What is the major flaw in the Christian evaluation of New Testament texts without even considering any other relevant material?

- The texts all predict these events to happen contemporary with that first generation of followers of Jesus and not in the distant future.

- Christians can delude themselves and attempt to delude non-Christians with various "Jesus is coming soon" slogans. They can reinvent and reinterpret to their hearts content but it is over, the time has passed and Jesus never came back and according to their own scriptures never will.

[1] For an in depth review of Anderson's and Hoehner's chronology errors, see Gerald

Sigal, *The 70 Weeks of Daniel (9:24-27)*, Xlibris: Bloomington, IN., 2013.

[2] The technical term employed, *viz. kapper*, means "atone for" when used of the priest, and "absolve" or "forgive," when used, as here, of God.

[3] The term *Kodesh kadashim* ("holy of holies") is used in the Scriptures in a variety of ways, of material objects particularly sacred to God and of sacred places including the *Devir* or innermost shrine of the Temple. Thus, it refers to the altar (Exodus 29:37, 30:10), the holy objects of the Holy Place or Temple (Numbers 18:10; Ezekiel 43:12, 45:3; 48:12; Daniel 9:24), the holy incense (Exodus 30:36), the showbread (Leviticus 24:9), the priestly portion of peace offerings (Leviticus 2:3,10; 6:10; 10:12), the sin offerings (Leviticus 6:18, 22), offerings in general (Leviticus 21:22; Numbers 18:9; Ezekiel 42:13, 44:13 Ezra 2:63; Nehemiah 7:65; 2 Chronicles 31:14), the Holy Place of the Tabernacle or Temple (Exodus 26:33-34; 1 Kings 6:16, 7:50, 8:6; Ezekiel 41:4; 2 Chronicles 3:8, 10).

[4] A talmudic passage (B.T. *Megillah* 12a) discusses Cyrus' role in Jewish history:

Rav Nachman bar Rav Chisda expounded: "What is [the meaning of that] which is written: 'So says God to His anointed, to Cyrus, whose right hand I have held' [Isaiah 45:1] — Was Cyrus [actually anointed with the oil used to anoint kings from the House of David, that he should be called the] 'anointed one'? — Rather, [Scripture means that] the Holy One, Blessed is He, said to the Messiah: I complain to you about Cyrus. I had proclaimed: 'He shall build My House and gather My exiles.'"

This talmudic passage explores the meaning of "Thus said God to His anointed, to Cyrus," *limshicho l'choresh*). Rav Nachman explains that *limshicho* refers to the Messiah, so that *limshicho* and *l'choresh* are not connected and should be translated as, "Thus said God to the Messiah concerning Cyrus." Rashi explains that the *trope* (the Masoretic cantillation), of the word *limshicho* is a *zarka*, which is generally followed by a word with the *trope* of *segol*, which shows that the words are connected. However, in this verse the word *l'choresh*, which follows *limshicho* does not have a *segol*, showing that the words are not connected in translation. Nevertheless, the absence of the *zarka-segol* sequence does not definitively show that the two words are not connected. In any case, in our discussion the verse needs to be understood in its historical context as differentiated from its midrashic usage. In mishnaic narrative we often encounter God and the Messiah in dialogue. This is not an indication of a preexistent messianic being. It is an expositional device employed by the Sages to convey a scriptural message to their audience.

[5] It should be noted that during this period, conventional historians list more than ten Medeo-Persian kings who ruled for 207 years, commencing in 539 B.C.E. and ending with Alexander's conquest in 332 B.C.E. These kings include Cyrus, Cambyses, Darius I, Xerxes I, Artaxerxes I, Darius II, Artaxerxes II, Artaxerxes III, Arses, and Darius III. Artaxerxes is compounded from *arta*, "great," and *khsathra*, "kingdom," and is used like the Egyptian name "pharaoh" to describe the kings of Persia. The Old Persian form of Xerxes's name was "Khshayarsha," a name

very similar to that of Ahashverosh. Biblical references to Persian kings are only concerned with those monarchs having an impact on the Jewish people.

[6] The Hasmonean dynasty ended in 37 B.C.E. with the execution of the last Hasmonean king, Mattathias Antigonus, by the Romans. Antigonus' sister held Hyrcania, a fortress in the Judean desert, for another five or six years (Josephus, *Jewish Wars* I. 19. 1 [364].)

[7] Alexander Yannai came to power *after* the culmination of the sixty-two weeks and is obviously the *second anointed one*. Calculating according to *Seder Olam Rabbah* an alternate *anointed one* is suggested. According to *Seder Olam Rabbah*, the First Temple was destroyed seventy years before the Second Temple was built, and the Second Temple, which was destroyed in 70 C.E., stood for 420 years. Accordingly, the First Temple was destroyed in 421 B.C.E. (not 420 — there is no zero year between 1 B.C.E. and 1 C.E.). This means that the first seven weeks ended in 372 B.C.E. (during the reign of Cyrus). The second segment of the Seventy Weeks period, sixty-two weeks in length, covered by verse 26, culminates in 62 C.E. (421-49-424=62 C.E.). The seventieth week would end in 69 C.E., followed by the Temple destruction. There are a number of questions concerning the accuracy of the *Seder Olam Rabbah* calculations.

According to this reckoning, the first "anointed one" mentioned is Cyrus. The second "anointed one" who verse 26 says will be "cut off" "after 62 weeks," that is, suffer *karet*, "excision," is the High Priest Ananias (Chanin). He was appointed high priest by Herod of Chalcis in 47 C.E., deposed by Agrippa II in 59 C.E., and killed by the Sicarii at the outset of the rebellion against Rome. He continued to wield considerable power after being replaced as high priest, "using his wealth to attract those who were willing to receive bribes" (Josephus, *Jewish Antiquities* XX. 9. 4 [213]). Of the post-62 C.E. period Josephus writes: "Now the high priest Ananias daily advanced greatly in reputation and was splendidly rewarded by the goodwill and esteem of the citizens; for he was able to supply them with money: at any rate he daily paid court with gifts to Albinus and the high priest. But Ananias had servants who were utter rascals and who, combining operations with the most reckless of men, would go to the threshing floors and take by force the tithes of the priests; nor did they refrain from beating those who refused to give. The high priests were guilty of the same practices as his slaves, and no one could stop them. So it happened at that time that those of the priests who in olden days were maintained by the tithes now starved to death" (*Jewish Antiquities* XX. 9. 2 [205-207]; see also T.B. *Pesachim* 57a: "Woe to me because of the house of Boethus ... For they are High Priests and their sons are [Temple] treasurers and their sons-in-law are trustees and their servants beat the people with staves."). "An anointed one shall be cut off" may in a sense refer to the anointed priesthood officiating in the Temple generally. In any case, Ananias exemplified those in the priesthood who through injustice grew wealthy in this world, disgraced the Temple and the priestly office, and caused needless hardship and death. As a result of his actions in this world there was nothing for him in the next world.

According to the calculation based on *Seder Olam Rabbah*, the second part of verse 26 describes the most crucial event occurring following the sixty-two weeks (that ended in 62 C.E.), the destruction of the city of Jerusalem and the Second Temple, "and the people [the Romans] of the leader [Pompey] who is to come, shall destroy" that is, the year 63 B.C.E. and subsequently.

"To him [the priest] who performed the libation they used to say, 'Raise your hand!' for on one occasion he poured it over his feet and all the people pelted him with their *etrogim*" (Mishnah *Sukkah* 4:9). Josephus (*Jewish Antiquities* XIII. 13. 5. [372]) identifies the offending priest as Alexander Yannai.

[9] *Jewish Antiquities* XIII. 13. 5. [373].

[10] *Jewish Antiquities* XIII. 14. 2. [380]. This atrocity may be alluded to in the Qumran commentary on the Book of Nachum (4Qp Nah 2:13) which states: "[S]uch a thing has never before been done in Israel, for the Scripture [Deuteronomy 21:23] designates a man hung up alive as a reproach to God."

[11] The early Hasmoneans called themselves mere custodians of the throne until the coming of the Messiah and the restoration of the Davidic monarchy. Once power was consolidated in their hands, they ruled without restraint.

[12] *The Holy Bible: New International Version*, Grand Rapids, Mich.: Zondervan, 1978.

[13] Beginning in 67 B.C.E., Alexander Yannai's children Hyrcanus II and Aristobulus II engaged in a bitter civil war for the throne. Hyrcanus sought the assistance of Pompey, then in Spain. Pompey supported Hyrcanus who he recognized as the weaker of the two rivals and thus more controllable by Rome. This proved to be the case when in 63 B.C.E. Hyrcanus opened the gates of Jerusalem to Roman soldiers. Absalom, Aristobulus' uncle, resisted the Roman's, and took refuge on the Temple Mount. The Romans took the Temple area after a three-month siege and Pompey is said to have entered the Holy of Holies. Hyrcanus was rewarded by being granted the high priesthood and leadership of the nation. The Hasmonean dynasty continued for two more decades, but Judea's independence was, in essence, lost on that day.

[14] See 2 Samuel 10:13 and Ezekiel 30:11 where "the people" is used in the sense of a body of troops.

[15] Josephus, *The Jewish War* III. 1. 3. [8].

[16] Tacitus, *History* V. 1; *The Jewish War* III. 4. 2. [64-69].

[17] After suppressing the revolt the Tenth Roman Legion remained to take care of Roman security needs in the Land of Israel.

[18] Danny Syon, "Gamla — Portrait of a Rebellion," *Biblical Archaeology Review* (18), January/February 1992, p. 31.

[19] *The Jewish War* II. 13. 7. [268].

[20] *The Jewish War* II. 14. 4-5. [284-290].

[21] *The Jewish War* II. 14. 6, 9. [293, 305].

[22] *History* V. 9.

[23] *The Jewish War* II. 14. 1. [272].

[24] *The Jewish War* II. 14. 1. [276].

[25] *The Jewish War* II. 14. 2. [277].

[26] *History* V. 10.

[27] "Vespasian, the Caesar who came and besieged Jerusalem for three years" (B.T. *Gittin* 56a).

[28] *The Jewish War* IV. 11. 5. [658]-V. 1. 1 [1].

[29] Mishnah *Taanit* 4:6; *The Jewish War* VI. 2. 1. [94] (See text correction of "for lack of *men* ceased to be offered" to "for lack of *lambs* ceased to be offered" in Josephus, *The Jewish War*, trans. H. St. J. Thackeray, Loeb Classical Library, Cambridge, MA: Harvard University Press, 1961, vol. 3, p. 403n.)

[30] "Wing" refers metaphorically to an elevated position, here, in particular, to the Temple Mount.

[31] Dio Cassius, the third-century C.E. Roman historian writes: "At Jerusalem, Hadrian founded a city in place of the one that had been razed to the ground, naming it Aelia Capitolina, and on the site of the temple of the god he raised a new temple to Jupiter" (Dio Cassius, *Roman History* 69. 12. 1, trans. E. Cary, in the Loeb Classical Library, London: Heinemann, 1925, vol. 8, p. 447). The "temple of the god" is a reference to the Jewish temple that had stood on the Temple Mount.

It may be that the Roman abomination placed on the Temple Mount was not a pagan temple as related by Dio Cassius but statues. The earliest Christian pilgrim to Jerusalem who has left a record of his journey is the Pilgrim of Bordeaux, who came to the city in 333 C.E. He makes no mention of a Roman temple. Instead, he writes that "two statues of Hadrian stand there [on the Temple Mount] and, not far from them, a pierced stone to which the Jews come each year" (Pilgrim of Bordeaux, *Itinerarium Burdigalense* (*Corpus Christianorum, Series Latina* [CCL] 175, ed. P. Geyer and O. Cuntz [Turnout: Brepols, 1965]), trans. Wilkinson, *Egeria's Travels*, p. 157.). It is unlikely that this Christian pilgrim would have failed to mention a Roman temple if one stood on the Temple Mount at the time of his visit.

[32] The *Templum Domini* of the Franks.

PART 2
THE NEW TESTAMENT

Chapter 46

DIVERGENT TRADITIONS
(Matthew 1:1-23 – 2:23, Luke 1:26 –3:38)

Some first century Christians felt a need to address the problem of providing a Davidic ancestry for Jesus thereby justifying claims that Jesus was the Davidic Messiah. This resulted in at least two separate Davidic genealogies for Jesus being independently produced. Both are extensively imaginary and each mostly in disagreement with the other; they now appear in the respective Gospels of Matthew and Luke. The two dissimilar lists of paternal ancestors for the supposed virginally conceived Jesus are no small miracle in themselves.

The narratives describing events surrounding the birth of Jesus represent two quite distinct and divergent traditions and are, for the most part, irreconcilable. Nevertheless, the conception and birth stories in Matthew and Luke reveal both common themes as well as wide divergence. Similarities in the birth stories suggest the possibility that they both used some common core source. The widespread divergence, however, suggests that the respective Gospel authors were also dependent on other sources available to each alone or that each author's work reflects his own imaginative thoughts, which were used to satisfy a preset theological agenda. The claim of some Christians that the differences can be accounted for by assuming that Matthew was written from Joseph's point of view and Luke was written from Mary's is simply unsupportable. It is most unlikely that Mary would not recall or think insignificant the visit of the Magi or the flight into Egypt and that Joseph would not recall or think insignificant the visit of the shepherds, the birth in the stable, or the journey to Bethlehem to be enrolled on the tax list. Would they not recall that following the birth of Jesus they fled to Egypt (Matthew) or leisurely set out for Nazareth (Luke)?

The shared material common to both Matthew and Luke may show a common core source for the claim of a virgin birth, but does

266

not prove the historicity of either birth narrative. In both Gospels the parents of Jesus are named Joseph and Mary, and they are engaged but have not yet begun living together as man and wife[1] when Mary became pregnant (Matthew 1:18; Luke 1:27, 34). In both, the authors try to prove that Joseph is of Davidic descent (Matthew 1:16, 20; Luke 1:27, 32; 2:4). Although the details differ, both contain an angelic announcement about the child who is to be born (Matthew 1:20-23, Luke 1:30-35). Both allegedly claim that the conception of the child is not accomplished through sexual union between Joseph and Mary (Matthew 1:20, 23, 25; Luke 1:34). Instead, it results from an action involving a spirit originating from God with Mary (Matthew 1:18, 20; Luke 1:35). Although directed to a different person in each, an angelic pronouncement that the child's name is to be Jesus is found in both Gospels (Matthew 1:21, Luke 1:31). In both Gospels an angelic pronouncement proclaims Jesus to be savior (Matthew 1:21, Luke 2:11). Both Gospels agree that the birth of Jesus in Bethlehem (Matthew 2:1, Luke 2:4-6) is related chronologically to the reign of Herod the Great (Matthew 2:1, Luke 1:5). Finally, both agree that Jesus, Joseph and Mary lived in Nazareth (Matthew 2:23, Luke 2:51). This list may seem to show that there is substantial agreement between the two birth narrative traditions. However, the list of different and contradictory material is much longer and more significant.

When did Joseph and Mary wed? Are the Gospels in disagreement as to when they come to live together? Matthew writes: "And Joseph arose from his sleep, and did as the angel of the Lord commanded him and *he took along the woman of him*; and he did not know her until she gave birth to a son, and he called his name Jesus (Matthew 1:24-25)." English translations loosely render the critical words "he took along the woman of him" as, for example, "he took her as his wife," "he took his wife to himself," "he took his wife home." There is an ambiguity as to whether the word *woman* here refers to an individual who has undergone the full marriage ceremony or to one who is still in the engagement stage of the Jewish marriage ritual. Luke writes that Joseph came to Bethlehem "in order to register, along with Mary, who was engaged to him, and was with child. And it came about that while they were there the days were completed for her to give birth" (Luke 2:5-6). According to Luke, Joseph and Mary were *not* married when they arrived in Bethlehem. Matthew never mentions Joseph and Mary travelling to Bethlehem and it appears that they reside there. However, Luke is clear that they were not residents of Bethlehem (Luke 2:7). Matthew's angelic visitation and Joseph's "taking of" Mary occurs at the beginning of the pregnancy. Luke's mention of them still being engaged occurs shortly before Mary gives birth. Were Joseph and Mary married when Jesus was born (Matthew?) or were they still engaged (Luke)?

Luke presents a totally different genealogy from Joseph back to David, which has only the names Shealtiel and Zerubbabel in common with that given by Matthew. Luke traces Jesus' genealogy all the way back to God through Adam (Luke 3:38) while Matthew begins the genealogy with Abraham (Matthew 1:2) and brings it forward to Jesus. Matthew traces the lineage through David's son Solomon (Matthew 1:6ff); Luke allegedly traces the lineage from David's son Nathan (Luke 3:31). Luke lists Heli as Jesus' grandfather (Luke 3:23); Matthew gives the name of Jesus' grandfather as Jacob (Matthew 1:16). Following the genealogies, the differences between the two Gospels' birth narratives multiply. Luke alone relates the story of Zechariah and Elizabeth and the birth of their son, known as John the Baptist (Luke 1:5-25). Luke devises a census to bring Joseph and Mary to Bethlehem (Luke 2:1, 2), while Matthew assumes that they live in Bethlehem in a specific and known house over which a star stops (Matthew 2:9). Matthew alone records the story of Joseph, Mary and Jesus fleeing into Egypt to escape Herod the Great and because he considered Bethlehem to be their home he includes a story to explain why they move to Nazareth (Matthew 2:21-23). Matthew has nothing about a stable, an angelic chorus, and shepherds; Luke knows nothing of a star in the east, magi who come bearing gifts, and King Herod's order to slaughter the male babies in Bethlehem and its environs. Luke contains poetic pieces unknown to Matthew. For his part, Matthew collects what he considers prooftexts taken from the Jewish Scriptures to support his account of Jesus' birth.

Matthew records a tumultuous sequence of events following the birth of Jesus while Luke records the family calmly performing the circumcision on the eight day and presentation in the Jerusalem Temple on the fortieth day (Luke 2:21ff.). Luke records a non-eventful return trip to Nazareth, which this Gospel considers the trio's hometown (Luke 2:39). The sequence of events would be impossible if the trio fled into Egypt following the birth, as Matthew relates.

Those who believe in a virginal conception may be divided into two groups: those who say Jesus is part of a triune god and those who say he is a celestial being created by God. In either case, a Jesus who receives his human nature from Mary and his supernatural nature from the "Holy Spirit" would, in fact, be neither fully human nor fully divine. Despite the claims made in post-New Testament creedal formulas that alleged Jesus was fully human as well as fully God, a virginal conception would restrict Jesus' humanity in order to make room for his alleged divinity. Divine incarnation through virginal conception resulting from an encounter with "holy spirit" would, if it were to occur, produce a divine-human hybrid. Virginal conception makes Jesus less than fully human. Indeed, is one truly human who has no free will? To refuse negative temptation because of a choice made freely is not the same as refusing temptation because of an inherent inability to choose evil.

There is no way of knowing what Matthew and Luke thought concerning the mechanism of human reproduction. There were a variety of views on the subject of human reproduction in antiquity. Nevertheless, although the two virginal conception stories differ in some details they seem to follow Aristotle's view of human reproduction. Aristotle explained the male and female contributions in procreation by means of his usual distinction between form and matter. The mother provides all the *matter* from which the embryo develops, but this purely passive matter needs the active principle of the semen (which does not become part of the embryo) to give it form and movement.[2] It is not difficult to see how, in a modification of the Aristotelian account of reproduction the divine creative activity could substitute, in the virginal conception, for the male role, but without needing to create any of the material of Jesus' humanity that derived entirely from Mary. Thus, the body of Jesus was considered thoroughly human though it housed a supernatural being.

God can create a human being from either a man or a woman, as in the case of Adam or from a man without a woman, as in the case of Eve, which could also provide for a Davidic ancestry through the male line. As such, what was the need for a virginal conception? Why was it alleged that God chose a method of conception so riddled with the myths of pagan idolatry? Some Christians conjecture that Jesus could be free of what they call original sin only by means of a virginal conception while others allege that the so-called "divine person of the Son" could only take human nature by means of a virgin conception devoid of sexual desire or union.

It is our intention to investigate those passages in the Jewish Scriptures and the New Testament that Christians use to support their claim that Jesus was virginally conceived, that he was an incarnate celestial being and that he was a Davidic descendant. In the New Testament, Jesus is a unique being, chosen by God, sent into the world by God and raised from the dead by God. However, he is never God Himself, although he is invested with quasi-divine attributes. As Christianity developed, the trinitarian belief in a triune God prevailed, mostly through violence against those who held other views about Jesus' origins.

---

[1] Engagement in Judaism is as binding as marriage. It requires formal dissolution to undo such a commitment. In ancient times the period of formal engagement lasted for an extended interval. Today engagement takes place just prior to the wedding ceremony to avoid the possibility of dissolution.

[2] For an account of Aristotle's view, see A. Preus, *Science and Philosophy in Aristotle's Biological Works*, Hildersheim: Georg Olms Verlag, 1975, pp. 52-63.

Chapter 47

THE BIRTH OF THE JESUS MYTH
(Matthew 1:1-16, Luke 3:23-38)

Section 1: LINEAL DESCENT

Privileges of biological bloodline

Before investigating if Jesus fulfilled the Jewish Scriptures the first question that should be asked is, "Did he have the proper biological lineage to actually be the Messiah[1] and thereby inherit the throne of David?" If he did not fulfill this basic necessity as biblically prescribed, no further claims made on behalf of Jesus will be of any consequence. Therefore, all responses to Christians should begin with the investigation of claims to the proper biological descent from David and Solomon, as befits the true Messiah. If Christians can satisfactorily answer the problems such an investigation engenders then, and only then, can they proceed to discuss other matters pertaining to their allegations. If they cannot properly answer these problems there is really no point in continuing any conversation with them.

Is it possible to know with any certainty if the historical Jesus was a direct descendant of David? There is no inherent contradiction in the claim that the historical Jesus was a Davidic descendant. Actually, many of his contemporaries could also make that claim. Yet, Davidic descent alone does not, in its own right, qualify one for the messianic office. This study will investigate the messianic claim made on behalf of Jesus by reference to the respective genealogies found in the Gospels of Matthew and Luke. These two genealogical listings are theological documents that obscure rather than clarify the question of whether the historical Jesus was of Davidic descent. However, these two genealogies do show themselves respectively unsuitable for establishing a legitimate claim to the messianic office.

In any discussion involving biblical genealogy it is important to recognize that lineal descent through the male biological bloodline plays a decisive role in God's determination of who shall be chosen to do certain works on His behalf. For example, when Abraham thought that his faithful servant would be his heir, God informed him instead: "This man shall not be your heir; but he that shall come forth out of your own bowels shall be your heir" (Genesis 15:4).

Many biblical events indicate that certain privileges were restricted to descent through the male biological bloodline. The incident regarding the succession to Zelophehad's estate by his daughters (Numbers 27:1-11, 36:1-12) shows that, a daughter is entitled to her father's physical property and that the lineal privilege of tribal affiliation is not inherited through the maternal side. The latter is passed on exclusively through the paternal line (Numbers 1:18). That is why Zelophehad's daughters are bidden to marry within the tribe of Manasseh, their father's tribe. In that way their children, inheriting lineage from their respective fathers would also be members of the tribe of Manasseh rather than of another tribe, and so keep their inheritance within the domain of Manasseh (Numbers 36:5-12).

Some Christians point to 1 Chronicles 2:34-41 as representative of a genealogical listing through the female line. They overreact to these verses. In this passage Sheshan's daughter and a number of male generations descended from her are listed. Of course, everyone has a genealogy through both his/her father and mother. But, while incidentally linking the genealogy to Sheshan this particular genealogy is specifically traced back to Jarha, the husband of Sheshan's daughter, as it is stated in the text: "So Sheshan gave his daughter to Jarha his servant for a wife; and she bore him Attai" (verse 35). "Jarha his servant" is the progenitor of this family line for "she bore him Attai."

The problem with Zelophehad and Sheshan was one in which their natural line of succession was disrupted by the lack of male heirs. However, in the case of the Messiah, this problem will not arise because there will never lack a man to sit on the throne of David (Jeremiah 33:17-22, 1 Chronicles 17:11).

An occurrence of interest to our discussion involves "the children of Barzillai" (Ezra 2:61, Nehemiah 7:63). While the name of "the children of Barzillai" was derived through the honoring of the illustrious father of a maternal ancestress who was not a priest, the family genealogy was traced through the priestly paternal ancestor. This shows clearly that lineage was a privilege passed on exclusively through the male line. No matter how illustrious a maternal ancestress or her father may have been, lineal privilege was still determined through the paternal side.

In his attempt to secure the throne for himself, Jehoram killed all his brothers and some of the princes of Israel (2 Chronicles 21:4). Later, when his widow, Athaliah, sought to secure the throne for herself after the death of their son, Ahaziah, she limited herself to the killing of the king's sons, evidently because the female line had no legal right of succession. Thus, Jehosheba, a royal daughter and sister to Ahaziah, could save Joash and hide him in the Temple where her husband was a priest (2 Kings 11:1-3, 2 Chronicles 22:10-12). If Jehosheba had sons they presented no threat to Athaliah. Although descended from Solomon on their mother's side they were priests, that is, of the tribe of Levi. It becomes evident from this incident that, similar to the priesthood, the right to the throne was passed on exclusively through the male line.

These events indicate that the rights of lineal privilege, that is, tribal affiliation, priesthood, or kingship are passed on exclusively through the male line. The daughter of a priestly family could not participate in the service of the Temple. Similarly, a princess of the house of David could not aspire to be appointed queen of Israel by virtue of her lineage. For this reason, it was not necessary for Solomon's sisters to pledge allegiance to his reign and authority, as it was for his brothers (1 Chronicles 9:23-24). If a princess of the house of David married a prince of that family, the male children born to them would inherit privileges regarding ascendancy to the throne solely through their father. That is why it is stated: "There shall not be cut off to David a man to sit upon the throne of the house of Israel" (Jeremiah 33:17).

God's promises

What does the Bible have to say concerning the lineal descent of the Messiah, the son of David? The Scriptures teach that the Messiah will inherit his lawful and legal right to kingship through the ancestry of his biological father. Explicit in this evidence is the fact that God's promised Messiah must be a male heir of not only David:

> For thus says the Lord: There shall not be cut off to David a man
> to sit upon the throne of the house of Israel.... If you can break
> My covenant with the day and My covenant with the night, so that
> there should not be day and night in their season; then may also My
> covenant be broken with David My servant, that he should not have
> a son to reign upon his throne.... So will I multiply the seed of
> David My servant. (Jeremiah 33:17-22)

but specifically of Solomon as well:

> When your [David's] days are fulfilled, and you shall sleep with your
> fathers, I will set up your seed after you, that shall proceed out of
> your body, and I will establish his kingdom. He shall build a house
> for My name, and I will establish the throne of his kingdom forever.
> I will be to him for a father, and he shall be to Me for a son; if he
> commits iniquity, I will chasten him with the rod of men, and with
> the stripes of the children of men, but My mercy shall not depart
> from him, as I took it from Saul, whom I put away before you. And
> your house and your kingdom shall be made sure forever before you:
> your throne shall be established forever. (2 Samuel 7:12-16; see also
> 1 Chronicles 17:11-14, 2 Chronicles 7:17-18)

> And of all my sons — for the Lord has given me many sons — He
> has chosen Solomon my son to sit upon the throne of the kingdom
> of the Lord over Israel. And He said to me: "Solomon your son,
> he shall build My house and My courts; for I have chosen him to be
> for a son, and I will be to him for a father. And I will establish his
> kingdom forever, if he be constant to do My commandments and
> My ordinances, as at this day." (1 Chronicles 28:5-7)

> And David the king said to the entire congregation: "Solomon my
> son, who alone God has chosen." (1 Chronicles 29:1)

> [A]s the Lord lives, who has established me [Solomon], and set me on
> the throne of my father, and who made me a house, as He promised.
> (1 Kings 2:24)

In obedience to God's decision to establish Solomon as king the

Scriptures state:

> And all the princes, and the mighty men, and all the sons likewise of king David, submitted themselves to Solomon the king. (1 Chronicles 29:24)

God declares that under no circumstances would He take the throne away from Solomon as He took it from Saul. "If he [Solomon] commits iniquity I will chasten him with the rod of men, and with the stripes of the children of men, but My mercy shall not depart from him, as I took it from Saul ..." (2 Samuel 7:14-15). How did God take the kingdom from Saul? The right to the kingship terminated with Saul's death. No son of Saul ever sat on or had a right to the throne. But Solomon's descendants, with the exception of one branch of the family, would never lose their right to the throne. The punishment for disobedience would be chastening at the hands of men but not the termination of all monarchical right. It is God's unconditional promise that the posterity of David, specifically that of Solomon, will possess the kingship forever. God assures that there will always be a male of paternal Solomonic descent with the right to reign upon David's throne.

The biblical text differentiates between two components of Davidic kingship: the throne of Israel and the throne of Judah. The extent of Davidic kingship is dependent on behavior. God promises David that "There will not be cut off from you a man before Me sitting on the throne of Israel only if your sons keep their way, to go before Me as you went before Me" (1 Kings 8:25). Davidic dynastic rule has an element of conditional kingship only insofar as the throne of all Israel is concerned. The promise of unconditional possession is restricted to the throne of Judah. David, Solomon, Rehoboam ruled a united kingdom which included all the tribes of Israel. Under Rehoboam, the Davidic dynasty lost its rule over all the northern tribes. This was possible because the promise to David had both conditional and unconditional elements. The special relationship of David and his successors to God and the divine promise that his dynasty has an eternal right to rule were not conditioned on fidelity to God by the successors of David. No matter how they behaved the

Solomonic branch of the Davidic dynasty would always possess the throne of Judah, but would not necessarily rule all the tribes of Israel.

> And the Lord said to Solomon: "Forasmuch as this has been in your mind, and you have not kept My covenant and My statutes, which I have commanded you, I will surely rend the kingdom from you, and will give it to your servant. Notwithstanding in your days I will not do it; for David your father's sake; but I will rend it out of the hand of your son. But I will not rend away all the kingdom; but I will give one tribe to your son, for David My servant's sake and for Jerusalem's sake which I have chosen." (1 Kings 11:11-13)

> [F]or thus says the Lord, the God of Israel: "Behold, I will rend the kingdom out of the hand of Solomon, and will give ten tribes to you [Jeroboam] — but he shall have one tribe, for My servant David's sake."[2] (1 Kings 11:31-32)

Although the biblical text says it was Solomon who was to be left with but one tribe it was not he who actually lost the northern tribes, but his son Rehoboam. The kingdom of Judah was to be Solomon's possession in that the throne of Solomon was continued through his descendants. This is a further indication that it was the Solomonic branch of the Davidic family, which was to inherit and possess forever the Davidic throne. The Solomonic branch was to possess the throne of united Israel, that is, Israel and Judah, only on condition that its kings obey God. Although division of the kingdom did take place that condition was not to last forever (1 Kings 11:39, Jeremiah 33:17).

In taking the throne of Israel, consisting of the ten tribes, away from the Davidic dynasty and giving it to Jeroboam, God declares through the prophet Ahijah, "I will give Israel to you [Jeroboam]. And I will for this afflict the seed of David, but not forever" (1 Kings 11:38-39). Ahijah says that the Davidic dynasty's loss of the throne of Israel is temporary. Although presently unoccupied the complete Davidic throne, that is, of Judah and of Israel, is eternally available to a Davidic descendant through Solomon.

Concerning the Davidic kingship the psalmist records:

Forever will I keep for him My mercy, and My covenant shall stand fast with him. His seed also will I make to endure forever, and his throne as the days of heaven. If his children forsake My law, and do not walk in My ordinances; if they profane My statutes, and do not keep My commandments; then will I visit their transgression with the rod, and their iniquity with strokes. But I will not break off My mercy from him, nor will I be false to My faithfulness. My covenant I will not profane, nor alter that which has gone out of My lips. Once I have sworn by My holiness: Surely I will not be false to David; his seed shall endure forever, and his throne as the sun before Me. It shall be established forever as the moon; and be steadfast as the witness in the sky. (Psalms 89:29-38)

Having firmly established this throne with David and with Solomon, God made it absolutely clear that His promise is for a continuous, unbroken right to the throne throughout all generations. The sins of the kings could not change it. The promise stood and still stands immutable. When Solomon sinned, his kingdom was destined for division, but the Davidic kingship of Solomon's descendants was not terminated (1 Kings 11:11-13); when subsequent kings of the Solomonic branch of the house of David sinned the kingship was threatened with suspension, not with abolition. The division of the kingdom and the loss of the throne are temporary, not permanent losses, "And I will for this afflict the seed of David, but not forever" (1 Kings 11:39). It is true that Solomon and many of the kings of Judah provoked God's displeasure through their sins, but the legal right to the throne was never taken away from his branch of the house of David. The phrase "the seed of David," when referring to kingship, can only refer to that one branch of David's family that possesses that throne. Maimonides expresses this biblical teaching as follows: "Part of this article of faith [that is, the belief in the Messiah] is that there can be no king for Israel except from the house of David and through the seed of Solomon alone; and whoever opposes this family denies God, may He be blessed, and the words of His prophets."[3] Even today, there is a descendant of Solomon who is the legal heir to the Davidic throne. Although he is personally unaware of his regal heritage, God knows his ancestry. With the arrival of the messianic age, God will send Elijah the Prophet to restore the genealogical records of Israel and redeem God's pledge for the reestablishment of the Davidic throne (Malachi 3:1, 24; cf. Ezekiel 47:13-23).

The royal lineage of the house of David was defined still further by the elimination from the right to the throne of the descendants of Jehoiakim. Jeremiah states:

> Thus says the Lord: "Write this man childless ['*ariri*], a man that shall not prosper in his days; for no man of his seed shall prosper, sitting upon the throne of David, and ruling anymore in Judah." (Jeremiah 22:30; see also Jeremiah 36:30)

Those Christians who argue that Jesus had a legal right to the throne of David through Joseph, as recorded in Matthew's genealogy, although he was not Joseph's biological son, cannot ignore this curse on Jehoiakim. Jehoiakim was to be considered "childless," although he was not literally childless, because neither he nor any of his descendants would have any legal right to inherit the throne of David.[4]

There are some Christians who assert that the Jewish sources indicate that the curse placed on Jehoiakim (Jeremiah 36:30) and his son Jehoiachin (Jeremiah 22:30) was rescinded. This, however, does not seem to be the case. A *midrash* informs us that: "He [God] said about Jeconiah [he is also named Coniah and Jehoiachin]: 'For no man of his seed shall prosper' [Jeremiah 22:30] and it says; 'I will overthrow the throne of kingdoms, and I will destroy the strength of the kingdoms of the nations.... In that day, says the Lord of hosts, will I take you, Zerubbabel, My servant, the son of Shealtiel, says the Lord, and will make you as a signet' [Haggai 2:22-23]. Thus was annulled that which He had said to his forefathers: 'As I live, says the Lord, even if Coniah the son of Jehoiakim king of Judah were the signet upon My right hand, yet I would pull you off from there [Jeremiah 22:24]."[5] The reference to Zerubbabel "as a signet" contrasts with the use of "signet" when applied to his grandfather, Jehoiachin. The signet was the seal with which the bearer sealed documents in his name. As such, the wearer carefully guarded it. God says here that even if Jehoiachin were such a signet upon His own hand He would still discard him. However, of Zerubbabel God says that He would carefully look after him as one normally does with a signet.

The forceful removal of Jehoiachin, portrayed in Jeremiah 22:24, is explained in the subsequent verses as pertaining to the exiling of Jehoiachin's family: "And I will give you into the hands of those who seek your life, and into the hands of those of whom you are afraid, even into the hand of the Chaldeans. And I will cast you out and the mother who bore you, into another country, where you were not born; and there you will die. But as for the land to which they desire to return, there they will not return" (Jeremiah 22:25-27). While these verses denote exile, the statement in Haggai 2:23 concerning Zerubbabel signifies restoration from exile. Accordingly, we may surmise that there was sincere repentance on the part of, at least, some of Jehoiachin's family while in exile. As a result, God forgave them. This repentance and the subsequent forgiveness enabled Zerubbabel to return from the Babylonian exile. However, since Zerubbabel ruled with the limited powers of a governor, not as king, it suggests that what was annulled was, as indicated by the *midrash*, only the enforcement of the exile of Jehoiachin's descendants. The specific curse that "no man of his seed shall prosper, sitting upon the throne of David, and ruling anymore in Judah" (Jeremiah 22:30) still applied. Neither biblical, talmudic, nor midrashic sources state explicitly that the curse was ever rescinded.[6] Even if the curse of Jeremiah 22:30 had been removed from Jehoiachin's descendants, its cessation would still not give Jesus any right to the Davidic throne if, as Christian doctrine claims, Jesus was not the biological son of the Joseph recorded in Matthew's genealogical listing.

Matthew's genealogy seems to give Davidic lineage to Jesus through Joseph who, however, is called "the husband of Mary," not the father of Jesus. The author of Matthew states: "And Jacob begot Joseph the husband of Mary, of whom was born Jesus, who is called Christ" (Matthew 1:16). In this verse, the Greek word that is translated as "whom," (*hes*) is in the feminine gender. Matthew emphasizes Mary as the mother of Jesus, and while he does not say it directly, his wording has been taken by Christians to imply here that Joseph is not biologically connected with Jesus' birth. However, if the genealogy is traced solely through Joseph as explicitly stated in

279

Matthew 1:16, then the statement made in Matthew 1:1: "The book of the genealogy [*Biblos geneseos*][7] of Jesus Christ, son of David, son of Abraham" is false since the genealogy which follows would not be connected to Jesus in any way whatsoever if Joseph is not his father. The biological determination of lineal privilege means that even if Joseph married Mary after she conceived but prior to Jesus' birth, Jesus could still not obtain a legal right to the Davidic throne through Joseph. Again we see that lineage can only be passed on through the bloodline of the father.

Some Christians have contended that the prediction with reference to Jeconiah's offspring meant no more than none of his descendants would occupy David's earthly throne. The supposed heavenly messianic throne has not been prohibited. But, if Jeconiah's descendants are prohibited from ever occupying the earthly throne of David how much more unworthy would descent from Jeconiah render such individuals if it came to occupying a *supposed* heavenly throne? Moreover, if Jesus was not the biological son of Joseph then the argument allowing for the occupation of a heavenly throne as opposed to being prohibited from an earthly throne is a moot point.

Mary's fiancé, Joseph, is alleged to have been a descendant of Jehoiakim (Matthew 1:11-12, Luke 3:27, cf. 1 Chronicles 3:16-17) and so was disqualified from any legal right to inherit the Davidic kingship. Joseph could not pass on what he did not possess, even to a biological son, much less to one who is his foster child. Possession of the Davidic throne was restricted to Solomon and his male descendants, but no further restriction was placed on the acquisition of the throne except for that placed on the particular branch of the family consisting of Jehoiakim's descendants. As a result, there are many legal claimants to the throne by virtue of Solomonic descent other than through Jehoiakim from whom God's choice for the royal successor to the Davidic throne will come: "As the host of heaven cannot be numbered, neither the sand of the sea measured, so will I multiply the seed of My servant David" (Jeremiah 33:22). Consequently, only those of Solomonic descent, of which there surely are many who are not the descendants of Jehoiakim, are qualified to sit on the throne of David. In no way can the Jesus of Christian theology qualify for that position.

Biblically, one cannot receive lineal privileges, that is, tribal affiliation, priesthood or kingship, except through the male bloodline of one's biological father. As such, the Messiah must be a direct descendant of David and Solomon through the male bloodline of his own biological father. The one exception to this rule is the denial of the throne of David to the descendants of Jehoiakim. By the alleged virginal conception of Jesus, as portrayed in the Gospel narratives, Jesus lacked an actual human father through whom he could acquire the male lineal bloodline of the Solomonic descendants of David. This is significant because no messianic claimant other than one who is a Solomonic descendant of David can fulfill God's promise. But, the questions may be asked: "Cannot God, if He so desires, do otherwise than what He promised to David and Solomon? Could He not, if He willed it, make Jesus the Messiah without benefit of a proper Davidic ancestry, especially if Jesus is His own son?" The answer to these questions forms the foundation of God's relationship with man: God does not lie or break His promises. A divine promise, once made, is irrevocable; what God declares will occur as He has stated (Psalms 89:35-36). Therefore, the answer to these two questions is a resounding negative.

Section 2: THE CONFLICTING GENEALOGIES OF MATTHEW AND LUKE

There are extensive disagreements and numerous historical improbabilities in the only two Gospels that posit a Bethlehem birth: Matthew and Luke. The most serious doubts about the historicity of the respective birth accounts in these two Gospels become known as we compare the two texts. They are not complementary, filling in the gaps in each other's narratives, as is often assumed by Christians. They are, instead, irreconcilably different accounts from beginning to end. Both accounts explain that Jesus was born to the "virgin" Mary and Joseph in Bethlehem and grew up in Nazareth, but that is all they share. The respective narratives indicate that their authors knew nothing of the circumstances surrounding Jesus' birth. The difficulty in accepting these accounts is most acute in that the Gospels differ in their respective presentations of Jesus' genealogy through Joseph

(Matthew 1:1-17, Luke 3:23-38). Consequently, the fundamental questioning of the historical reliability of the genealogies cannot be avoided.

From Abraham to David the two genealogies agree, for both follow the biblical text (Ruth 4:12, 18:22; 1 Chronicles 2:1-14). Then the differences appear. This leads to four basic problems with the assumption that both lists are historically accurate. (1) From David to the exile Matthew traces the line of descent through the Solomonic succession of the kings of Judah while in Luke the lineage is said to be traced through David's son Nathan; (2) the two lists meet again in Shealtiel and Zerubbabel, but give Shealtiel different fathers (Matthew 1:12, Jeconiah, cf. 1 Chronicles 3:17; Luke 3:27, Neri); (3) from Zerubbabel to Jesus both lists diverge completely, continuing through two different sons of Zerubbabel (Matthew 1:13, Abiud; Luke 3:27, Rhesa, who in 1 Chronicles 3:19-30 does not appear among the sons of Zerubbabel), until the two lines meet again in Joseph, but differ in the names of Jesus grandfathers: according to Matthew 1:16 he is called Jacob, but in Luke 3:23, he is called Heli; and (4) the number of names from Solomon to the exile in Matthew is fourteen in Luke twenty (Nathan through Neri, inclusive), while from the exile to Jesus in Matthew there are thirteen generations, in Luke there are twenty-one. There are, of course, other differences as well, but the four basic problems have been of greatest concern for Christian scholars.

The genealogical record of the Davidic dynasty found in the Gospel of Matthew is not taken from the Jewish Scriptures. The genealogy is artificially constructed out of three groups of supposedly fourteen names each, taken principally from Genesis, Ruth, 2 Kings, and 1 Chronicles. The list of names beginning with Abiud in Matthew 1:13 is not found in the Jewish Scriptures. It is not a historical document but a contrived list compiled in an attempt by its author to show that "all the generations from Abraham to David are fourteen generations; and from David to the Babylonian exile are fourteen generations; and from the Babylonian exile to the Christ are fourteen generations" (Matthew 1:17). However, when one counts the generations listed in the first and third sections of the genealogy one finds that the number of generations do not coincide with Matthew's claim in verse

17 that each section contains fourteen generations.[8] In Matthew 1:2-17, the number of generations in each block are actually 13, 14 and 13 instead of the three 14-generation blocks claimed. Only forty-one names are listed.

The first section can only contain the stated amount if one counts Abraham as the fourteenth generation despite the fact that this is not consistent with the way Matthew constructs his genealogical list. The first generation actually given is that of Isaac, that is, "Abraham begot Isaac" (Matthew 1:2). Examining the construction of the rest of the list one can see that Isaac is the first generation given. To include Abraham's generation the text would have to read, "Terah begot Abraham, and Abraham begot Isaac."

Only in the second section, from David to the Babylonian exile, are there fourteen generations but this is only achieved by omitting four generations (Ahaziah, Joash, Amaziah, and Jehoiakim). There were actually eighteen not fourteen generations of kings of Judah in the period between David and the exile. In the Greek text of Matthew 1:8, it is written, "and Asap begot Josaphat, and Josaphat begot Joram, and Joram begat Ozias." This genealogical version agrees with the genealogical order found in the Septuagint, the Greek version of the Bible, with the exception of the name Asaph being substituted by Matthew for that of King Asa of Judah. (Some Christian, English versions substitute the name Asa in accordance with the Jewish Scriptures.) Matthew's list is not in accord with the Jewish Scriptures, which state that Asa's son was Jehoshaphat, Jehoshaphat's son was Joram, Joram's son was Ahaziah, Ahaziah's son was Joash, Joash's son was Amaziah, and Amaziah's son was Azariah (Uzziah) (1 Chronicles 3:10-11). In verse 10, Matthew's Greek text substitutes the name Amos for that of King Amon of Judah (1 Chronicles 3:14). (Some Christian versions in English substitute the name Amon in accordance with the Jewish Scriptures.)

The third section, from the Babylonian exile to Jesus, contains only thirteen generations. Unlike the first section, where some Christians explain the missing fourteenth generation by including the unlisted generation of Abraham the appeal to the preceding generation cannot be used in the last section. In the third section one cannot resolve the discrepancy by referring to the generation of the first person named in this section, Jechoniah, because his generation is already mentioned as the last of the second section. "Josiah begot Jechoniah and his brothers at the time of the Babylonian exile." After the Babylonian exile Jechoniah begot Shealtiel (Matthew 1:11-12). Matthew records that "Josiah begot Jechoniah." Josiah was actually the grandfather of Jechoniah (Jehoiachin, alt. Jeconiah, Coniah). Jehoiakim was the son of Josiah and the father of Jechoniah. While this manner of expressing relationship is not unusual, it is significant here in regard to Matthew's claim to a threefold division of fourteen generations each. This further deletion of a generation from the monarchial period brings the total to four generations omitted by the author of Matthew in his fruitless quest to achieve three sections of fourteen generations each.

In Matthew 1:5 its author writes, "Salmon begot Boaz by Rahab." It is virtually certain that Matthew is referring to the Rahab who appears in the events surrounding the conquest of Jericho (Joshua 2:4-5). However, the claim that Boaz was the son of Rahab is not supported by any text in the Jewish Scriptures. This is not surprising since Rahab lived approximately two centuries before Boaz's time.[9] This reference to Rahab, as the mother of Boaz, is an inaccuracy in the genealogy of Jesus as found in the Gospel of Matthew.

For unofficial purposes, it was not necessary to name every link in the line of descent when giving one's genealogy. However, if Matthew is presenting us with an official record of the genealogy of Jesus, it is sadly wanting. The rationalization that he excluded evil ancestors, besides it being pure speculation, is hardly acceptable, because an official record is no place for playing favorites. Matthew's genealogical listing is inaccurate and, consequently, devoid of any worth.

Neither is Luke's genealogy of Jesus problem-free, even where it appears to agree with the Jewish Scriptures. Luke inserts a second "Cainan" (the first being the son of Enos [Enosh], who is called Kenan in Genesis 5:9-14 and 1 Chronicles 1:2) between Arphaxad (Arpachshad) and his son Sala (Shela) (Luke 3:35-36). Cainan (Kenan) is not found in this position in the Hebrew text (Genesis 10:24, 11:12; 1 Chronicles 1:18, 24). Furthermore, Luke's additional use of this name is found neither in the Samaritan Hebrew text of Genesis nor in any of the *targumim*. It is found only in the Septuagint. Evidently, Luke inserted the name Cainan between the names Sala and Arphaxad based on the Septuagint version.[10] The discrepancy among the genealogies in Matthew, Luke and the Jewish Scriptures are symptomatic of a major difference between Judaism and Christianity. The New Testament authors accepted the Greek Septuagint version, or a similar Greek text, rather than the Hebrew text, as their major biblical source. As a result, Jews and Christians *do not* use the same biblical text. This is a fact, which often leads to conflicting conclusions as to the meaning of the Scriptures.

There are even greater discrepancies when one compares the respective genealogies of Luke and Matthew. Luke lists seventy-seven names[11] compared with Matthew's forty-one. The names appearing in the two genealogical listings differ more often than not. These two Gospel authors cannot even agree on the name of Jesus' grandfather! What little agreement there is between the two lists is mainly to be found in the period between Abraham and David. The most notable exception to genealogical agreement found in this period occurs over a point of great confusion in the manuscript tradition regarding the names between Hezron and Amminadab. There the Greek text of Matthew 1:3-4 has Aram, while the Greek text of Luke 3:33 has Admin and Arni. Matthew's Aram (so also in the Septuagint, but Ram in the Jewish Scriptures) is attested to, in its Hebrew form, by Ruth 4:18-19 and 1 Chronicles 2:9-10; no such evidence exists to support Luke's listing of Admin and Arni. (Some Christian renderings into English substitute Ram for Arni in order to make it conform to the Jewish Scriptures or omit one or both names.)

In the period between David and the Babylonian captivity the two genealogies are totally different, agreeing only on David. Luke has twenty-one names, compared with Matthew's fifteen; of Luke's twenty-one names only David and Nathan are found in the Jewish Scriptures.

In the period between the Babylonian captivity and the birth of Jesus, Matthew's list contains thirteen names and Luke's list contains twenty-two names. They agree only in the first two, Shealtiel and

285

Zerubbabel, and in the last two, Joseph and Jesus. Of all the names listed for this period in both genealogies only Shealtiel and Zerubbabel are mentioned in the Jewish Scriptures. It is through Zerubbabel that both Matthew and Luke trace Jesus' descent from David, yet neither genealogical listing contains the descendants of Zerubbabel listed in 1 Chronicles 3:19-24 nor do they agree with each other.

Christians face a serious problem in that although both evangelists trace Jesus' genealogy through Joseph, Luke's list of Jesus' ancestors is very different from the list given in Matthew. In total, while Matthew enumerates forty-one generations from Abraham to Jesus, Luke counts forty-six generations in what is basically a different genealogy. The problem is not difficult to see. For example, Luke states: "And Jesus began to be about thirty years old, being, just as was supposed, the son of Joseph, the son of Heli, the son of Matthat, the son of Levi, the son of Melchi ... the son of Nathan, the son of David." In Matthew, where the origin of Joseph is traced back to Solomon, the son of David, the enumeration of the ancestors closes in the following manner: "and Eliud the father of Eleazar, and Eleazar the father of Matthan, and Matthan the father of Jacob, and Jacob the father of Joseph the husband of Mary, of whom Jesus was born, who is called Christ" (Matthew 1:15-16). From this inconsistency the question arises as to who was the husband of Mary. Was it Joseph, the son of Heli, the son of Matthat, as Luke proposes; or was it Joseph, the son of Jacob, the son of Matthan, as Matthew supposes?

Luke or his sources rejects a genealogy reckoned through the royal line of the Davidic kings of Judah. Rather than enumerating the royal succession from David to the exile, as does Matthew, Luke proceeds from David to his third son, Nathan (2 Samuel 5:14; 1 Chronicles 3:5, 14:4), and from him through a series of unknown names up to Shealtiel and Zerubbabel and from them, again through a series of unknown names, to Joseph. This deviation from the kings of Judah not only rejects the royal line, but also fails to incorporate any biblical genealogical data between Nathan and Zerubbabel. Thus, Jesus is alleged to be the Davidic Messiah, but not through biblical royalty. This genealogy may record the opinion held by some that the curse of God on Jeconiah in Jeremiah 22:24-30 made it impossible for the

Messiah to descend from the royal line of the kings of Judah (not considering that the royal line did not go exclusively through Jeconiah). Consequently, it may be conjectured, they affirmed that the Messiah would descend from Nathan probably based on the mention of the "house of Nathan" in Zechariah 12:13. Luke's genealogy, it would be assumed, incorporates the alleged succession through Nathan to the throne of David, which was based on the curse of God on Jeconiah. Nevertheless, the fact that the royal line would have had several Solomonic branches other than the descendants of Jeconiah negates the need to imagine a succession to the throne through Nathan.

Why does Luke's genealogy trace Jesus' descent from Nathan *through Zerubbabel?* In the section of Luke's genealogy between David and Jesus the line of descent from David is traced not through Solomon and his descendants, the kings of Judah, but through Nathan, a son of David by Bathsheba. Nathan is barely mentioned in the Jewish Scriptures (2 Samuel 5:14; 1 Chronicles 3:5, 14:4). The names of Nathan's alleged descendants listed in Luke's genealogy are not found in any biblical genealogy. In addition, Luke's genealogical list makes Shealtiel and Zerubbabel descendants of David through Nathan. The inclusion of Zerubbabel and his grandfather Shealtiel, who are descendants of Solomon only goes to highlight the artificiality of Luke's genealogical listing. Zerubbabel is frequently called the son of Shealtiel in the Jewish Scriptures (Ezra 3:2, 8; 5:2; Nehemiah 12:1; Haggai 1:1, 12, 14; 2:2, 23). Only once, in the Davidic genealogy, found in Chronicles 3, is he given a more detailed lineage, as the great-grandson of king Jeconiah (1 Chronicles 3:16-19). Specifically, this genealogy lists Shealtiel's son Pedaiah as the father of Zerubbabel. The brevity of the Chronicler's style makes this relationship difficult to follow. However, for the purpose of this study, establishing that Shealtiel and Zerubbabel are descendants of Solomon is sufficient. It makes the point that a satisfactory explanation of the alleged line of Jesus' descent from David in Luke's genealogy must include not only why the line is traced from Nathan but also why it is traced from Nathan through Zerubbabel whose lineage is traced to Solomon.

How does one explain Luke's listing the descent of Zerubbabel from Nathan rather than from Jeconiah and the kings of Judah? It has been suggested that Jesus' descent from Nathan was postulated to circumvent the prophecy of Jeconiah which predicted that no descendant of king Jeconiah would ever sit on the throne of David (Jeremiah 22:30). If Zerubbabel was in fact descended from Nathan rather than Solomon, the Chronicler is recording incorrect information. However, Luke's genealogical listing, tracing Zerubbabel's descent from Nathan the son of David, is biblically unsupportable. Luke's genealogy is totally inadequate for establishing a right to the Davidic throne. In order to be exempt from the curse placed on Jeconiah and his descendants, the Messiah could be descended from any of the previous kings of Judah except Jehoiakim (Jeconiah's father) on whom a similar curse had been laid (Jeremiah 36:30). The notion that the messianic genealogy has to bypass the whole royal line from Solomon onwards is baseless. God's promises were made not only to David, but to Solomon as well. God never overthrew the royal line of Solomon outside of Jeconiah's descendants. In addition, the Gospel of Luke provides no explanation of why the alleged line from Nathan to Jesus should pass through Zerubbabel who is a descendant of Solomon.

Luke's genealogical listing that claims Zerubbabel's descent from Nathan, the son of David implies the point at which a previously non-royal Davidic line acquires the right of succession to the throne of David. It also indicates that it was from the descendants of Zerubbabel that the promised restoration of Davidic rule over Israel could be expected. But, it is wrong on both points.

Luke's claim that Zerubbabel was descended from David's son Nathan is historically implausible. It may be the result of a concern to derive the messianic line from a Davidic branch other than Solomon's to disassociate Jesus from the misdeeds of some of the kings of Judah. The mention of "the house Nathan," a prominent family in post-exilic Jerusalem (Zechariah 12:12) may have played a role in the formation of Luke's genealogical list. But, there is no conclusive evidence that the members of the house of Nathan of this verse are descendants of David's son Nathan. It has been suggested that this is established by the parallel between, on the one hand, the house of David and the house of Nathan, and on the other hand, the house of Levi and the

Shimeites (verse 13). The latter are a subdivision of the tribe of Levi (1 Chronicles 23:7-11), and so the house of Nathan it is contended must be a subdivision of the house of David. Nevertheless, without further confirmation, the connection remains speculative. In any case, it would have no bearing on the present discussion. The Gospel of Luke makes no connection between the "house of Nathan" and the genealogical listing.

Whatever its origins, Luke's genealogy of Jesus that is traced back to Nathan is an artificial construction. It gives Jesus an ancestry that would circumvent the problem caused by the curse on Jeconiah's descendants, but creates new problems for claiming a messianic lineage for Jesus. As already indicated, Nathan's descendants were of Davidic ancestry, but not members of the royal family entitled to kingship. They simply could not inherit the throne. Whether the names in the genealogy are actually descendants of Nathan cannot be proven by reference to a biblical genealogy, and is, in any case, immaterial. As it stands, this lineage, with its connection to Zerubbabel is a purely artificial construction.

Some Christians, recognizing the futility of attempting to establish Jesus' right to the throne of David through Joseph's genealogy, as found in Matthew, have resorted to an alternative tactic. Acknowledging Matthew's genealogy as a disqualified lineage, they justify its usage through subterfuge. It is claimed that Matthew's purpose was not to show the regal line of Jesus' descent through Joseph. These Christians maintain that the purpose of Matthew's genealogy is to show why Jesus could not inherit the throne of Israel, if he were really Joseph's son. Thus, they assert Matthew presents this genealogy to show that Joseph and his progeny are disqualified from inheriting the Davidic throne. However, since the genealogy is followed by the presentation of the virgin conception it is claimed that this is Matthew's solution to the problem of the disqualification through descent from Jechoniah, son of Jehoiakim. If this were the case, Matthew has defeated his own purpose by not making his point clear. Indeed, even if his intention was as portrayed by this argument what has he accomplished? The hypothetical reasoning attributed to Matthew by which he presents Joseph's ancestry in order to show that it has no legal right to the throne is simply too farfetched. In so doing, Matthew would destroy the only possibly viable claim to Davidic ancestry that he presents on behalf of Jesus. No comparable right to the throne is even attempted through a maternal lineage. On the contrary, Matthew gives every indication that he is presenting the paternal lineage as a messianic lineage qualifying Jesus not disqualifying Joseph. This is readily seen in his opening remark with its specific emphasis, "The book of the genealogy of Jesus Christ, son of David, son of Abraham" (Matthew 1:1). Matthew has every reason to qualify Joseph because upon him rests Jesus' own genealogical qualifications. The intent of Matthew's genealogy is the establishment of Jesus' right to the throne through that specific lineage. The Christian claim by which Matthew rejects Joseph's lineage is inventive, but is an argument born of futility unacceptable on New Testament evidence alone. Theological speculations will not suffice; assumptions do not make for doctrinal truth.

Was Mary of Davidic descent?

Christians, unable to reconcile a virgin conception with a Davidic descent for Jesus through Joseph, who they claim was not his biological father, are forced to think of Mary as being of Davidic descent. Tertullian proposed the theory that Matthew gave the genealogy of Mary and Luke that of Joseph.[12] Tertullian says that Matthew traced the origin of Jesus from Abraham to Mary,[13] Jesse being the root (*radix*) of David's stem, Mary a shoot from this root (*virga ex radice*), and her son the flower from this shoot (*flos ex virgo*),[14] and that Paul, when saying that Jesus was born from the seed of David according to the flesh (Romans 1:3), really means according to Mary's flesh from the seed of David: *Ergo ex Mariae carne est dum ex semine David*.[15] This solution is at odds, however, with the text of Matthew 1:16, which does *not* say, "and Jacob begot Mary of whom Jesus was born."

Luke's matrilineal explanation for the existence of two divergent genealogies was first proposed by Annius of Viterbo (c. 1490).[16] He assumed that Matthew's genealogy traces the lineage of Jesus through Joseph while the one in Luke traces it through Mary.[17] Since his time there have been a number of attempts to identify Matthew's list with Joseph's genealogy and Luke's list with Mary's genealogy. This conclusion is reached, some maintain, because of the emphasis on Joseph in Matthew's discussion of the events surrounding the birth of Jesus, as compared with Luke's emphasis on Mary, in his version of the events surrounding the birth.

Those Christians who maintain this position hold that Luke's genealogical listing (Luke 3:32-38) refers to Mary, although the text makes no such claim. It is alleged that Luke 3:23 gives Mary's lineage but that Joseph is called the son of Heli in accordance with Jewish legal custom; this means he was the son of Heli because he was the husband of Heli's daughter.[18] Yet, Christians cannot substantiate their contention from Jewish sources. Joseph is not the son-in-law of Heli in Luke's genealogy. This is because no such Jewish legal custom of substituting the husband's name for that of his wife in the latter's genealogy ever existed. Christians fabricated this spurious claim in order to extricate Christian belief from the theological morass created by the variant genealogies.

Both solutions violate the Jewish principle that descent is reckoned only through the male line: "The family of [one's] father is called [one's] family, the family of [one's] mother is not called [one's] family" (B.T. *Baba Batra* 110b). This does not mean that a woman's genealogy could not be presented. In the non-canonical Book of Judith, we find the genealogy of the heroine going back to the patriarch Israel (8:1). If Matthew, therefore, had wished to show the genealogy of Mary as "a daughter of David," he could have done so, but that alone would not have made Jesus "a son of David."

On the one hand, many Christians explain the variant genealogies by claiming that Luke follows the ancestry of Mary, making Jesus a biological descendant from David's son Nathan (Luke 3:31). On the other hand, they claim that Matthew derives Jesus' legal right to the throne of David by descent from David's son Solomon (Matthew 1:6) through Joseph, who they allege was the legal father of Jesus. This solution is, at bottom, inadequate and cannot be taken seriously: a genealogy traced through the mother is not the norm in biblical or post-biblical Judaism. Deriving the right of kingship through Mary, as it is alleged Luke has, is contrary to the biblical provisions governing royal succession. Deriving the right of kingship through Joseph as

Jesus' foster father, as Matthew has, is not in accordance with the biblical view that the rights of royal succession are determined through paternal biological descent and not through adoption or foster care. In fact, since a descendant of Solomon through a non-disqualified family branch can only inherit the Davidic throne, Luke's lineage through the non-royal family of Nathan is irrelevant whether it is that of Joseph or Mary respectively. Moreover, an added problem for Luke's genealogy is that there is no line of descent from Nathan that goes through Zerubbabel.

Let us examine in more detail the Christian contention that assumes Luke does not give Joseph's genealogy, but, rather, Mary's genealogy. This notion holds that Heli died with no sons and that Mary became his heiress. Joseph's name is substituted for Mary's by virtue of his marriage to her, which supposedly made him heir of Mary's father Heli. This would appear to preserve the name of a man who dies leaving behind daughters but no sons. In this case, the process is accomplished by Joseph's becoming identified with Mary's paternal lineage. Joseph is included in the genealogy, although the genealogy is really Mary's. It is maintained that the genealogies of Matthew and Luke diverge from David only because Matthew traces the Davidic descent of Joseph, and Luke the Davidic descent of Mary (with Joseph's name substituted). But, it should be noted that in the classical example of an occurrence of a man who dies leaving behind daughters but no sons, that of Zelophehad (Numbers 27:1-11; 36:1-12), none of his sons-in-law are recorded as being inserted into his line of descent as a substitute for a daughter's name. In effect, Zelophehad's tribal line of descent stops with his death. Moreover, there is no indication in the Jewish Scriptures that a custom of inserting a son-in-law's name into a father-in-law's genealogy ever existed.

There is no genealogical record in the Jewish Scriptures, which refers to a man as the son of his father-in-law. Saul's words: "Is this your voice, my son David?" (1 Samuel 24:17) cannot be cited as a prooftext that a son-in-law was considered equal to a son. One is often addressed as "my son" by way of affection or endearment, for example, Joshua 7:19; 1 Samuel 3:6, 16; 4:16. This is especially true when an older person is addressing a younger person whom he loves. Such was the case with Saul, who had love for David, as stated: "and he [Saul] loved him [greatly]" (1 Samuel 16:21). But David always remained the "son of Jesse" and was never referred to or considered the "son of Saul."

Unraveling Joseph's Genealogy

In any genealogical record, Joseph's own paternal ancestry would have to be given not that of his father-in-law. Luke's naming of Heli rather than Jacob, as Joseph's father is simply a variant tradition. Heli is not on the list because he is thought to be Joseph's father-in-law. It is inconceivable (in the patriarchal society in which Jesus was born) that Joseph would have adopted the genealogy of his father-in-law in lieu of that of his own father. In fact, Luke makes it quite explicit that he is tracing Jesus' descent through Joseph's ancestry (Luke 3:23, 4:22). For Christians to propose their forced interpretation is an act of sheer desperation.

It has been contended that proof that Heli (Luke 3:23) is actually Mary's father can be found in the Jerusalem Talmud: "He saw Miriam the daughter of Eli in the shadows." R. Lazar bar Josah said that she was suspended by the nipples of the breasts. R. Jose ben Chanina said that the hinges of hell's gate were stuck in her ear …. He said to them: 'How long will this punishment last?' They answered him: "Until Shimon ben Shetach will come." (J.T. *Chagigah* 2:2). On the basis of its context, there is no ground to consider this passage as referring to the mother of Jesus, or her father, whatever his name may have been. Jesus is not mentioned or even alluded to in the text. Furthermore, there is no reason whatsoever for assuming that the rather common Hebrew names of Miriam (Mary) and Eli (Heli) here refer to New Testament characters. There is absolutely no substantive evidence to link Mary the mother of Jesus to this talmudic passage. Any suggestion that this reference is to the mother of Jesus must remain an unfounded conjecture.

A literal translation of the Greek found in Luke 3 says: "Joseph of the Heli of the Matthat of the Levi of the Melchi … of the Judah of the Jacob of the Isaac of the Abraham of the Terah." It is clear from the context that the Greek "of the" is to be rendered "son of." In fact, if Luke was listing Heli as Joseph's father-in-law then this entire genealogy must be a list of father-in-laws since the Greek word *tou*, "of the" is used throughout this genealogical listing. It would certainly be a unique genealogy, which lists the patriarchs as in-laws, rather than as fathers and sons. We may therefore conclude that the meaning of Luke 3:23 is that Joseph was the son of Heli and not his son-in-law, as some Christians would have us believe. To say otherwise is a mere supposition.

There are some Christians who claim that the Hebrew language has no expression for in-law relationships. As a result, it is claimed that when a man and woman married, the girl's father legally became his father, and he legally became his wife's father's son. This, they say, is the relationship that Luke describes. Joseph was the "son-in-law" of Heli, a relationship that was properly expressed by calling him the "son" of Heli. The argument is based on the incorrect assumption that there are no expressions for in-law relationships in Hebrew. But, that is totally incorrect as can be seen from such references as "father-in-law," *chotein* (Exodus 18:1); "her mother-in-law," *chamotah* (Ruth 2:18); "his son-in-law," *chatano* (Judges 19:5); "your daughter-in-law," *kala-tehcha* (Genesis 38:24); "your sister-in-law," *ye-vim-teich* (Ruth 1:15). In any relationship between in-laws one cannot impart one's own genealogy upon another to replace the genealogy received biologically.

When desperation sets in

The Gospels do not show that Mary was a descendant of David. They claim that Joseph belonged to the house of David (Matthew 1:6, 16; Luke 1:27, 2:4, 3:23), but nothing of a like ancestry is indicated for Mary. Matthew and Luke would certainly have unequivocally mentioned a Davidic ancestry for Mary if they thought it would enhance their claims. In fact, there is no New Testament evidence to support the contention that Mary was of Davidic descent. We simply do not know what any New Testament author thought of Mary's tribal or family lineage. Some Christians claim that women's genealogies never appear in Jewish literature, but this is contrary to the evidence of the non-canonical Book of Judith 8:1, 9:2, which gives the lineage of Judith.

Christians claim that the Davidic descent of Mary is implied in the Gospel of Luke (1:27, 32, 69; 2:5) and that it may be inferred from such passages as Romans 1:3, 2 Timothy 2:8, and Hebrews 7:14. As a result, they insist that not only Joseph, but Mary as well, was of Davidic descent. However, a careful study of the passages cited reveals that none of them gives any indication that Mary is of Davidic descent. They are actually further proof that there are absolutely no references to Mary's ancestry to be found in all of the New Testament.

Luke 1:26-27 states: "In the sixth month the angel Gabriel was sent from God to a city of Galilee named Nazareth, to a virgin betrothed to a man whose name was Joseph, of the house of David; and the virgin's name was Mary." Some Christians would like to understand "of the house of David" as a reference to Mary while others take it as a reference to both Mary and Joseph. Grammatically, Luke's phrasing favors a reference solely to Joseph as being, "of the house of David." Firstly, this phrase comes immediately after the name Joseph. Secondly, if Luke intended to refer to Mary he would not have needed to reintroduce her as subject in the next clause ("and the virgin's name was Mary"). That is, the repetition of the noun "virgin" would not have been necessary at the end of the verse if Mary had just been referred to in the previous clause. If "of the house of David" referred to Mary, the wording would be, "to a virgin betrothed to a man whose name was Joseph, of the house of David, and her name was Mary."

Christians have maintained that the repetition of the word "virgin" instead of the use of the simple pronoun "her," is due to Luke's desire to emphasize Mary's virginity. They also assume that since Mary is the central character in the narrative the three phrases: "betrothed to a man whose name was Joseph," "of the house of David" and "the name of the virgin was Mary" are all descriptions of Mary. These explanations are not sufficient to dismiss the obvious fact that a simple reading of the text yields the words, "of the house of David," as a reference here to Joseph. Elsewhere, Luke refers only to Joseph as being of Davidic descent. For example, in Luke 2:4 he maintains that Joseph went to Bethlehem "because he was of the house and lineage of David," not "because they were" or "she was" and in Luke 3:23 it is Joseph whose genealogy is traced to David. It is in connection with Joseph's genealogy, not Mary's, that such statements as, "and the Lord God will give him the throne of his father David" (Luke 1:32) and "And He raised up a horn of salvation for us in the house of David His servant" (Luke 1:69) are made on behalf of Jesus.

Christians have a serious problem if the phrase "of the house of David" does not apply to Mary. Without this application of the phrase to Mary there is absolutely no New Testament evidence to support the contention that she was of Davidic descent. The argument advanced by some, that Joseph, a Davidic descendant, would have married only within his own tribe and house is at best wishful thinking. Eusebius held that Mary's lineage, though not given, was also through David, claiming that according to the Torah people had to marry within their own tribe. He wrote: "Mary, also, at the same time, as far as can be, is evinced to be of the same tribe, since, the Mosaic law did not permit intermarriages among different tribes. For the injunction is, to marry one of the same kindred, and the same family, so that the inheritance may not be transferred from tribe to tribe. And this may suffice, also, on the present point."[19] He does not cite his authority. It is probably Numbers 36:6-12, which contains a commandment requiring a female to marry within her own tribe under certain circumstances. The function of this commandment is to keep the female's inheritance within her tribe when she has no brother to inherit her father's landed property. This related to the division of the land when Israel entered Canaan following the exodus from Egypt. After the Babylonian captivity and the fragmentation of the tribes, it is extremely doubtful that conditions allowed for the practice of this specific commandment especially in the first century of the Common Era in Judea and Galilee. In fact, a general prohibition against tribal intermarriage cannot be assumed in either biblical or post-biblical times on the basis of Numbers 36:6-12. For example, David, who was of the tribe of Judah, married Michal, the daughter of Saul, who was of the tribe of Benjamin.

The view of Mary's ancestry espoused by Eusebius makes a number of unfounded assumptions. He assumes that Mary was of the tribe of Judah; that she was specifically of the Davidic family; that she had no brothers to inherit her father's landed property; and that an intertribal marriage prohibition was in effect in the first century of the Common Era in Judea and Galilee. All these assumptions must remain in the realm of pure speculation, as they are not confirmed or even implied by the sources. Interestingly, Julius Africanus, as quoted by Eusebius (with no objection), also held that Matthew's and Luke's respective genealogies were through Joseph: "As Joseph, then, is our proposed object, we are to show how it happened that each is recorded as his father; both Jacob as deduced from Solomon, and Heli from Nathan; also, how it happened that these two, Jacob and Heli, were brothers; and moreover, how the fathers of these, Matthan and Melchi, being of different families, are proved to be the grandfathers of Joseph."[20]

Intermarriage between the tribes was perfectly permissible according to the Law. Yet, on the basis of the assumption that Joseph would only marry within his own tribe, some Christians conclude that Mary went to Bethlehem in order to register as a Davidic descendant. However, Luke 2:5 shows that Mary went to Bethlehem not because she was of Davidic descent but because "he [Joseph] was of the house and family of David" (Luke 2:4) and she accompanied him. Any suggestion that it offers proof of her own ancestry would necessitate an impossible situation. If Mary also went to Bethlehem to register as a Davidic descendant it would suggest that engaged and even married couples who were not of the same familial ancestry would have to go in opposite directions in order to register for the census mentioned in Luke 2:1-3. Luke 2:5 offers no intrinsic evidence for the assumption of a Davidic ancestry for Mary.

"As was supposed"

Basing themselves on Luke 3:23, which literally reads: "And Jesus began to be about thirty years old, being [the] son, just as was supposed, of Joseph, of the Heli" Christians claim that Matthew gives Joseph's genealogy through his father, Jacob, and that Luke gives Mary's genealogy through her father (or grandfather), Heli. They reason that this must be the case since in Luke's list Joseph's name appears without the Greek article — "of Joseph," not "of the Joseph," — while every other name on the list has the definite article, that is, "of the Heli of the Matthat ... of the Adam." It is claimed that this lack of the definite article places Joseph in a category separate from all the other names. He is not properly part of the genealogy, and is mentioned only parenthetically. Accordingly, it is maintained, his name belongs within parenthesis and the reading of Luke 3:23 should be: "Jesus ... being [the] son (as was supposed, of Joseph) of the Heli, of the Matthat." The idea to be conveyed, the exponents of this exegesis assert, is that while Jesus was thought of as the son of Joseph he was really descended through Mary whose paternal lineage is traced back through Heli, who they claim was her father or grandfather. This would make Jesus the son, that is, grandson or descendant of Heli. Heli is understood to be the progenitor of Mary, not of Joseph. But this is not what Luke's text says. He emphasizes "[the] son ... of Joseph" as a unit of identification essentially inseparable. The addition of *hos* ["just as," "as"] ["was supposed," "was thought," "was the opinion"] is an affirmation, not a denial, of this point. The opinion that Jesus was the biological son of Joseph, *hos enomizeto*, "just as was supposed" was the belief of those who were the source of this information. To this was added on the virgin conception story, while keeping the earlier venerated tradition within the narrative. However, there is absolutely no indication from the text, or anywhere else, that Luke's genealogical list refers to Mary's lineage rather than to Joseph's. If the claim of those who hold "of Joseph" is part of the parenthetical statement were true, then, *huios*, "son," would not be needed in the sentence, but would be expressed in the phrase *tou Heli*, "of the Heli." The text would then read: *Iesous ... tou Heli*, "Jesus ... of the Heli," that is, "Jesus, son of Heli." Since this is not the case, the proponents of the view under discussion parenthesize "of Joseph" unnecessarily. A further variation of this notion is the placing of "son," as well, within the parenthesis. However, this would still not negate the fact that Luke's sources consider Jesus to be the biological son of Joseph "just as was supposed." The author of Luke included this belief despite the inclusion of the virgin conception story as well.

What did Luke or his source mean by "just as was supposed"? He claimed to have collected information "handed down to us" from several sources and maintains that he "investigated everything carefully" (Luke 1:1-3). This would seem to show that he was dependent on one of these sources for the genealogical listing that appears in the Gospel of Luke. Accuracy aside, what we must question here is the meaning of this phrase. Does it mean that Jesus was the biological son of Joseph? Does it mean Jesus was Joseph's legal heir? Does it mean the lineage was that of Jesus but not through Joseph but through Mary? The phrase *hos enomizeto* is an editorial comment, which shows an awareness of the difficulty of tracing Jesus' descent from Joseph while at the same time claiming that a virgin conception and birth took place. It shows uncertainty with the virgin conception tradition and its inherent contradiction of Jesus' genealogical descent through Joseph.

A closer look at Luke's genealogy of Jesus

A perusal of the text of Luke 3 shows the entire birth narrative of Luke 1 and 2 to be an interpolation into the text of the overall narrative. Perhaps the author of Luke wrote his narrative in more than one version with Luke 1 and 2 being part of a later version. The genealogy most likely originally stated Joseph was the father of Jesus and either Luke or a later redactor interpolated the virgin conception story into the text. In its earlier form, the story the author of Luke inherited assumed Joseph was Jesus' father. It stresses that Mary is engaged to a man named Joseph, a descendant of David (Luke 1:27). This is followed by the angel's declaration that Jesus will possess "the throne of his father David" (Luke 1:32). Joseph's Davidic lineage in chapter one is directly connected to the Davidic genealogy of Joseph in chapter three. David is said to be Jesus' ancestor because he is Joseph's ancestor. The story's denial of the virgin conception is disguised by Mary's question concerning the prediction of her imminent conception: "How can this be, since I know no man" (Luke 1:34). There is, however, implicit evidence that virgin conception is a later addition to the story. The multi-layered dating process that begins chapter 3 (3:1-3) and the inclusion of a genealogy awkwardly after rather than before the birth story are evidence that this Gospel originally started with chapter 3 rather than chapter 1. An emphasis on the father-son relationship of Joseph and Jesus expressed as "as was supposed" was part of the genealogical listing from a pre-Gospel source which denied the virgin conception and which was retained when the virgin conception narrative was added to the Gospel of Luke. As it is presented in Luke, the text states that those listed in the genealogy are supposed to represent Joseph's ancestry. In whatever sense the author himself thought Jesus to be virginally conceived he nevertheless was reluctant to change the genealogy he received which stated that Jesus was Joseph's son "as was supposed."

In no way does this verse connect Heli and Mary in a father-daughter relationship. Mary is not mentioned at all in connection with the genealogy, relegating to conjecture the claim that Heli is her father or grandfather. To revise the text so as to exclude Joseph leaves Jesus fathered by Heli, but does not establish a lineal connection between Heli and Mary. This revision of the text causes more problems for Christian theology than it solves. For Luke, Jesus' genealogical listing of ancestors begins with "of Joseph," with *Iesous ... huios ... Ioseph*," Jesus ... son ... of Joseph," considered as a unit of son-father identification. This identification shows that the following genealogical listing is of a paternal descent. In Luke 2:36 the literal Greek word order is, "And was Anna prophetess, daughter of Phanuel out of tribe of Asher." "Anna ... daughter of Phanuel" is the unit of daughter-father identification, and it is this unit which, despite any further identification or information, is "out of tribe of Asher." So too, it is "Jesus ... son ... of Joseph" who Luke declares is "of the Heli of the Matthat."

In the Greek text, Joseph's name occurs without the article prefixed; every other name in the series has the definite article. The definite article before each name listed in the genealogy, except that of Joseph, serves a vital function. The article is included with all the fathers' names in order to emphasize to the reader that these names are to be understood as being in the genitive case (that is, expressing possession). This inclusion is made necessary because these names are non-Greek in origin, and, as a result, do not decline in Greek to indicate the genitive case. Since they are indeclinable their grammatical relation to another word is not always clear without an added article. The article, which might otherwise be left out, is included in order to show that each noun with which it is connected is actually a genitive and thus a new name in the list of genitives. The article is unnecessary before the name of Joseph because this name follows and depends upon *huios*, "son." That is, *huios* expresses sufficiently the son-father relationship between Jesus and Joseph. To indicate the son-father relationship in the rest of the list, something is needed, and *tou*, "of the," serves that purpose. *Tou* should be taken throughout the genealogy in its obvious sense of referring to a "son" not "grandson." Moreover, in two of the three places where Jesus is called "son of Joseph" in the New Testament (Luke 4:22, John 6:42, John 1:45), "Joseph" appears without the definite article (Luke 4:22, John 6:42).

Although Luke 3:23 literally rendered from the Greek states that Joseph is the son of Heli, some Christians cannot admit to such on understanding of this verse. It would defy Christian theology. Therefore, they opt for a different construction, which is based on a rather forced exegesis of this verse. Accordingly, they favor adding the words, "Jesus was the son" before every proper name in the list. The term "son," then, has the connotation of "descendant." This interpretation assumes that Heli was the father of Mary, the mother or Jesus, and hence Jesus' actual grandfather through his mother. Adopting this view removes the difficulty for those anxious to uphold Christian theology rather than the plain meaning of the text. The assumption is that Luke desires to give the actual genealogy of Jesus and enumerates the persons from whom Jesus is descended through Mary. It is alleged that Luke mentions Joseph, but immediately removes him from the genealogy with the statement that it was only through error that he was considered as being the father of Jesus. The conclusion these Christian exegetes would have the reader believe is that the author of Luke does not present the genealogy of Joseph, at all, but that of Mary, and that in no way is he saying that Joseph was the son of Heli.

But, if Luke records Mary's lineage why did he not somehow include her name within his version of the genealogy? Some Christians have pointed out that women were rarely included in Jewish genealogies. And although giving her descent, Luke conforms to Jewish custom by not mentioning Mary by name. But, it should be noted that although rare, a woman may, at times, be included within a genealogical listing (1 Chronicles 4:3, Judith 8:1) or in conjunction with her father's name (2 Kings 23:1), or identified as the mother of her sons with no mention of their father's name (1 Samuel 26:6; 2 Samuel 2:13, 18; 2 Samuel 14:1, 18:5; 1 Chronicles 2:16). Indeed, precisely what Jewish custom was the author of Luke conforming to in not mentioning Mary by name within the context of a formal genealogy?

Certainly, in such a unique case as that of a birth due to a virgin conception, giving the physical matrilineal descent of one who had no human father, starting with the mother's name would be in order. If Luke was giving Mary's lineage rather than Joseph's he was not confined to rigid traditional motifs, even when giving a formal genealogical listing of ancestors. In fact, the genealogical lineage found in Luke departs from customary genealogical listings by starting with the name Jesus and then listing ancestors rather than starting in the past and ascending to the name Jesus. And in such an unusual case as a birth resulting from a virgin conception was precedent even needed? Luke did not have to leave doubt as to the daughter-father relationship between Mary and Heli if such existed. Luke could easily have included her name if his intent was to give Mary's genealogy rather than that of Joseph's. As we see above, there was precedent for inclusion of Mary's name in conjunction with her father or within the context of a genealogical record if she actually was the daughter or granddaughter of Heli and precedent, as well, for not mentioning her husband. How much more so if he is not the child's father? Luke had mentioned a number of times in the first two chapters of his Gospel that Mary was the mother of Jesus. But, a Jewish genealogy includes the name of the father, grandfather, great-grandfather, and so on. Even if Joseph is only mentioned because of a common mistake, which attributed the fathering of his wife's child to him, it does not establish a line of descent between Mary and Heli. This is because of the significance of the literal reading of the text, which makes Joseph the father, as was commonly thought. The alleged common supposition does not just extend to naming Joseph as the father, but proceeds to give his own genealogy as well. Mary's genealogy is not mentioned at all.

Wishful thinking

A comparison of the texts involved demonstrates that the matrilineal explanation is nothing but wishful thinking. Matthew 1:15-16 speaks of "Matthan the father of Jacob, and Jacob the father of Joseph," whereas Luke 3:23 says, Jesus "being [the] son, just as was supposed, of Joseph, of the Heli, of the Matthat." The attempt at a matrilineal explanation is simply untenable according to Greek grammatical construction. To reach a matrilineal conclusion, in Luke 3:23, Greek grammar is stretched beyond what is possible. To read Luke 3:23 to mean that Jesus "was [the] son (as was the supposed, of Joseph) of the Heli, of the Matthat" or "was ([the] son, as was supposed, of Joseph), [Jesus was the son] of the Heli, [Jesus was the son] of the Matthat" in order to bypass Joseph is to render the Greek in a very unnatural and forced way. In addition, it must be emphasized that there is no New Testament text, which links Mary to Luke's genealogy. It is clear from the respective texts that both genealogies claim to be genealogies of Jesus through Joseph. The ancient and modern attempts to explain one or the other listing as Mary's genealogy have all failed.

An explanation for the divergent genealogies, which maintains that both genealogies are through Joseph, alleges that one traces the lineage back through Joseph's father, and that the other traces back through Joseph's mother. The maternal genealogy, however, drops the name of Joseph's mother and instead starts with her father. It is asserted that the genealogy in Luke is through Joseph's father and that the genealogy in Matthew is through Joseph's maternal grandfather.

That Matthew's version of the genealogical listing should delete Joseph's mother is not considered inconsistent. He leaves out a number of individuals in his listing in order to reach a desired structural symmetry. According to those who maintain this position, it is not unreasonable that Matthew might leave out the name of Joseph's mother in order to attain this structural format. In addition, Matthew's genealogy lists four women — Tamar, Rahab, Ruth, and Bathsheba — a fact that it is felt supports the view that this is a woman's genealogy.

The notion that Joseph's maternal genealogy is recorded in

Matthew is flawed. Does the mentioning of women support the belief that this might be a woman's genealogy? In each of the four instances where women are mentioned in Matthew's genealogy the man by whom she conceived is still the primary focus of what is a consistently paternal lineage. If women are mentioned why was Joseph's mother, who is so crucial in establishing this notion, not mentioned? There was no need to leave out Joseph's mother's name since formulating Matthew's desired structural format did not depend on the inclusion or deletion of female names. However, there was every reason not only to include her name among those women mentioned but also to give it primacy if a choice had to be made. The name of Joseph's mother, which would supposedly provide the needed linkage between Matthew's Jacob (supposedly Joseph's grandfather) and Joseph's supposed father, Luke's Heli, is not even hinted at. It is obvious that the claim that one genealogy is Joseph's paternal lineage and one is Joseph's maternal lineage has no textual support. Above all, Joseph's maternal lineage would not provide Jesus with a biblical right to the throne of Israel.

What did Paul have to say?

Paul's statement: "His son, who was born of the seed of David according to the flesh" (Romans 1:3) has been cited as proof that Mary must have been a descendant of David. Yet, Paul was not stating that Mary was of the house of David. Matthew's and Luke's genealogies are listings "of the seed of David according to the flesh" through Joseph. There is no reason to assume otherwise than that his assertion of a Davidic descent for Jesus refers to Joseph rather than Mary.

Paul's writings do not deny a belief that Jesus was conceived in the natural manner. There is no claim made that Jesus was the son of God as a result of a union of the "Holy Spirit" with Mary. Independent of Paul, the Hellenistic synthesis occurred that produced the notion of a virgin conceived god, a scriptural promised god, in the manner of pagan mythology. Paul considered Jesus to be a preexistent incarnate angelic being who is, as such, God's son in the sense that "he is the image of the invisible God, the firstborn of all creation" (Colossians 1:15). In his earthly existence he "was born of the seed of David according to the flesh." Paul did not consider Jesus to be part of God in the trinitarian sense. According to Paul, Jesus attained to a significantly higher position in God's universe by his suffering the agonies of death on the cross (Philippians 2:6-11). Apparently, such suffering could not be undergone by an angelic being but could be by a human being. As a reward for his sacrifice, Paul declares, God bestowed upon Jesus the status, "Son of God" "by the resurrection" (Romans 1:4) not at the time of his conception. Paul declared that Jesus' exalted position was granted to him by God (Philippians 2:9), not that it was naturally his as one would expect if Jesus was truly God. Jesus had to earn it even considering his angelic preexistence. There is no reason to believe otherwise than that Paul considered Jesus to be the biological son of both Joseph and Mary. In all of his writings, Paul never mentions either Joseph or Mary by name and shows no interest in them. As with Romans 1:3, "born of the seed of David," so too 2 Timothy 2:8, "descendant of David," and Hebrews 7:14 "descended from Judah," refer to Jesus' ancestry. There is no mention if this royal claim came through his mother's or father's side of the family. These phrases simply declare nothing other than a pre-Gospel acceptance of a Davidic descent for Jesus.

You can't pass on what you never possessed

The fact remains that in their respective Gospels, Matthew and Luke are quite clear in stating that the genealogies given are those of Joseph. Throughout the Gospels, Jesus is explicitly referred to as the son of Joseph (Luke 3:23, 4:22; John 1:45, 6:42). One redactor of the Gospel of Luke emphasizes this point when he declares that Jesus was the actual son of Joseph, "just as was supposed" (Luke 3:23). If Joseph was not the biological father of Jesus, then the Gospels tell us nothing about Jesus' ancestry except that his mother's name was Mary. Even with Joseph as his biological father, it is quite impossible to verify either variant genealogical version.

As mentioned above, some Christians base their conclusion that Luke's genealogical record is that of Mary's familial line on the emphasis given to Mary in the early chapters of that Gospel's narrative. This is in comparison to the scant references made concerning Joseph. However, this conclusion is unwarranted. A distinctive feature of Luke's account is the prominent position generally given women (chapters 1; 2; 7:11-13; 8:1-3; 10:38-42; 21:1-4; 23:27-31, 49). Certainly, given this feature, Mary, as the mother of Jesus, would be prominently portrayed. However, women's role in Luke's Gospel, as well as in Acts, is subordinate to the role assigned males whether in the pre-Christian history or nascent Christian community. Women exercise no leading function. Therefore, it should not be expected that in the recording of lineal descent Mary's lineage preempts that of Joseph. Mary's prominence is based on, and restricted to, her being the mother of Jesus. No special formulation was concocted to allow for her genealogy to be presented. Lineal descent is reserved in Luke's narrative for Joseph as it is the normal procedure to list genealogy through the paternal line. The reason Luke's genealogical listing differs from that of Matthew's account is due to variant traditions within the primitive Christian community. There is no reason to assume that Luke lists Jesus' maternal lineage.

Luke's genealogical listing explicitly traces a Davidic descent for Joseph and, despite later Christian speculation, there is no evidence that Mary was of Davidic descent as well. The contention that Mary was of Davidic descent results from the realization that it is impossible to reconcile a Davidic descent for Jesus through Joseph with the claim that Joseph was not his biological father. But, even if Luke did refer to Mary's genealogy as some Christians contend, God's promise to pass on the hereditary right to the throne solely through male descendants of Solomon would disqualify Jesus from succession to the throne of David through his mother's family. Mary could not pass on what she did not possess. No descendant of any other son of David but Solomon (with the exception of Jehoiakim's Solomonic line) is fit to sit upon the throne of David.

Luke's genealogy of Jesus is ultimately traced back to David's son Nathan, who is of no consequence in determining succession to the royal throne of Israel. Consequently, the descendants of David's son Nathan, as presented in Luke's genealogical listing (Luke 3:31), are resolutely excluded from the right to David's throne. As shown above, only Solomonic descendants of David may sit on the throne. Thus, claiming Jesus to have been a descendant of David's son Nathan renders him unqualified to sit upon the throne. God promised that royal succession will take place only through Solomon's male descendants, yet not of Jehoiakim's seed. Therefore, the Messiah must be of a specific Solomonic descent. Since Shealtiel and Zerubbabel are descendants of Jehoiakim, their appearance in Luke's record automatically nullifies any claim to the throne by the use of this record. Moreover, since Matthew's genealogy of Jesus is said to be traced through a foster father who was a member of this same disinherited branch of Solomon's descendants, it too is of no consequence. This is all in accordance with the prophecy of Jeremiah — no descendant of Jehoiakim will sit on David's throne (Jeremiah 36:30). In order to be exempt from the curse on Jehoiakim and his descendants, the Messiah must be descended from any of the previous kings of Judah. There is no need for the Messiah's genealogy to bypass the whole royal line from Solomon onwards. It is thus clear that Jesus could not inherit the throne of David by use of either evangelical record. Furthermore, claiming a virginal conception for Jesus denies him any paternal biological connection with the house of David. The result is that while it is impossible to verify the Davidic descent of Jesus outside of the New Testament, it is equally impossible to verify that alleged descent by reference to that record.

Christians are faced with the problem that the very genealogical evidence that the New Testament presents traces Jesus' ancestry through Joseph, who Christian theology declares, was not the actual father of Jesus. The genealogies allegedly tracing Joseph's lineage and the claim that Jesus was conceived through a holy spirit (Matthew 1:18, Luke 1:35) are mutually exclusive. Tracing the genealogies through Joseph either shows him to be the biological father of Jesus, or these genealogies are totally meaningless for establishing a Davidic ancestry for Jesus. If Jesus was conceived of a holy spirit, offering Joseph's lineage is of no consequence whatsoever. There is no question of legal paternity verses natural paternity involved. Even if Joseph had had a proper claim to the throne, which, according to both variant genealogies he did not have, and had acknowledged Jesus as his legal son rather than as his natural son, to whom he wished to pass on the right to Davidic kingship, God would have had to overrule him. It would not be Joseph's prerogative to decide to bestow Davidic kingship upon a non-Davidic descendant. God would overrule such a decision, as it would violate His respective promises to David and Solomon. Christians may propose clever classifications to legitimize a non-biblical father-son relationship between Joseph and Jesus, which seemingly entitles the latter to use Joseph's genealogy. In fact, however, Joseph could not be the adoptive father of Jesus, for no such legal concept existed in Jewish law, nor would such a designation entitle one to assume a lineage not that of one's own biological father. If Joseph is to be called the legal father of Jesus, it can only be in the sense that he acknowledged the duty to care for him as a foster father. But his legal obligations exclude and, indeed, prohibit the application of a genealogy to Jesus, which, according to the New Testament is not his to begin with.

An alternative explanation of the divergent genealogies claims that Matthew's genealogy is that of Mary through her father and that Luke's genealogy is that of Joseph through his father. To reach this conclusion the adherents of this solution to the problem must insist that the rendering "husband" in Matthew 1:16: "And Jacob begot Joseph the husband [*andra*] of Mary ..." is a mistranslation. The word rendered "husband" is the Greek word *andra*, from the root word *aner*, "man." Even though *aner* is also rendered as "husband" in a number of contexts (e.g., Mark 10:2; John 4:16-18; Romans 7:2-3; 1 Corinthians 7:2-4; Galatians 4:27; 1 Timothy 3:2, 12; Titus 1:6) or as an engaged or future husband (e.g., Matthew 1:9, Revelation 21:2) they insist that "husband" is not its meaning in Matthew 1:16. They claim that the proper rendering of Matthew 1:16, would read that Joseph is the *aner*, the "man" of Mary. They then connect "the man" not with Joseph the husband of Mary but with the father of Mary who they claim also was named Joseph. *Andra*, they claim, should be rendered Mary's "man" or more specifically Mary's "father" rather than her "husband": "And Jacob begot Joseph the father of Mary." Hence, they say Mary's father's name was Joseph, and Mary's husband's name also was Joseph. There is no New Testament substantiation for the rendering of *andra* as "father." However, there is ample New Testament substantiation for rendering this word as "husband."

Interestingly, even the relatives of Jesus mentioned by the church fathers in their writings as claiming Davidic ancestry (some in later centuries *specifically* using Matthew's genealogy), are *all* on Joseph's side of the family. There is never any mention of Mary's side of the family joining the church much less taking a leadership position. After all, supposedly they were the blood relatives of Jesus, not Joseph's family. Nevertheless, it is Joseph's side of the family that is said to take an active and prominent leadership role in the church. It is Simeon, second head of the Jerusalem church (after James) that Hegesippus says was son of Cleophas. According to Hegesippus, Cleophas was the brother of Joseph, the husband of Mary.[21]

Even if Matthew records Mary's genealogy, Jesus would still not be entitled to the throne of David. She still would not have inherited the throne, which is only promised through the male progeny of Solomon, that is, it is passed on from father to son but not through a daughter. Thus, if Mary's father would have been in direct line to inherit the throne and he had no sons, on his death, neither Mary nor her son would inherit that right. The next in line to inherit the throne would be one of her father's male paternal relatives other than her son. Most likely one of Mary's uncles or cousins would be so designated, for God has promised that there would always be a male heir to the throne. To base Jesus' right to the Davidic throne on the claim that Matthew's genealogy is that of Mary is in essence an exercise in futility. Matthew's entire list of names following that of Jehoiakim is of individuals disqualified to sit on the throne of David because of their particular ancestry.

If a Jewish child, conceived of a non-Jewish father (as Christian theology claims for Jesus), inherited his mother's lineage in lieu of a paternal Jewish lineage this would do Jesus absolutely no good insofar as a claim to the Davidic throne is concerned. At most, if such a lineage were possible, he would have his mother's tribal affiliation but no right to ancestral privileges, such as priesthood or kingship, as these are patrilineal privileges. Certainly the disqualifications inherent in the respective genealogies are still relevant, even when these genealogies are maternal in origin. If Matthew's Gospel actually records Mary's genealogy, then Christian theology must contend with the disqualification of Jehoiakim's branch of the Davidic family.

If, on the other hand, Luke's Gospel records Mary's genealogy, then, Christian theology must contend with the problem of lineal descent from Nathan, the son of David, a Davidic branch devoid of monarchical rights. The respective genealogical listings given by Matthew and Luke diverge after Solomon and Nathan. The alleged names of Nathan's descendants in Luke's genealogy are not derived from any genealogy found in the Jewish Scriptures. However, it does include Zerubbabel and his father Shealtiel. Thus, the two genealogical lists briefly reunite with the mention of Shealtiel and his son Zerubbabel.

Zerubbabel is frequently called the son of Shealtiel in the Jewish Scriptures (Ezra 3:2, 8; 5:2; Nehemiah 12:1; Haggai 1:1, 12, 14; 2:2, 23). Only once, in the genealogy of the house of David in 1 Chronicles 3, is he described as the grandson of king Jeconiah (1 Chronicles 3:16-19). In fact, this genealogy makes Shealtiel, Jeconiah's eldest son, the uncle of Zerubbabel, whose father is said to be Jeconiah's third son Pedaiah. This difference has sometimes been explained by levirate marriage. Matthew's genealogy of Jesus follows Chronicles, making Shealtiel the son of Jeconiah (Matthew 1:12), but Luke ignores Chronicles and makes Shealtiel and Zerubbabel descendants of David through Nathan. Clearly, a satisfactory understanding of the line of Jesus' descent from David as proposed in Luke's genealogy must explain not only why the line is traced from Nathan but also why it is traced from Nathan through Zerubbabel.

The two genealogies diverge once more after Zerubbabel, with neither genealogy agreeing with the other, or with the Book of Chronicles (1 Chronicles 3:17-19). The overlapping of these two genealogies, however, is crucial for exposing their inconsistencies and the uselessness of their claims. The assumption that Mary's tribal lineage is represented in either Matthew's or Luke's genealogy is without foundation. In fact, her tribal lineage is not mentioned in the New Testament. But, even assuming that Mary's genealogy is recorded by either Matthew's or Luke's genealogy and that that genealogy devolved upon Jesus, he still remains unqualified to attain the messianic office. The disqualifications inherent in the respective genealogies show that Jesus simply cannot sit on the throne of David.

The claim that Jesus had a legal right to the throne is an absurdity born of desperation. The attempt at legitimizing that claim is made because without that right he could not be the Messiah and all further Christian theological allegations concerning his person are in vain.

Matthew and Luke considered it important to present their respective ancestries for Jesus despite the admonition of Paul, who being aware of the utter improbability of the claims made by some of his followers concerning Jesus' antecedents and conception, advised the faithful "not to occupy themselves with myths and endless genealogies which give rise to speculations" (1 Timothy 1:4; see also Titus 3:9). However, since the virgin conception myth and the variant genealogies now hold prominent positions in the Gospel narratives of Matthew and Luke as well as in Christian theology they simply cannot be ignored as Paul recommended.

Christians contend that since there is no record that Jesus' opponents questioned the claim of Davidic descent, this claim must never have been contested by them. This, of course, overlooks the possibility that any documentation of such questioning was either successfully suppressed by the church or lost. Indeed, who says it was even considered an issue during Jesus' lifetime or during the years of the early church? Due to the later Gospel claims, Jews began to question Jesus' paternity, even if there is no specific polemic known that attacks his alleged Davidic descent. In fact, the very nature of a charge of paternal impropriety would, in itself, strongly question the Davidic descent of Jesus as, for example, the statement found in the Gospel of Luke that "Mary was engaged to him [Joseph], and was with child" (Luke 2:5).[22]

The New Testament references to Jesus as "son of David" (Matthew 9:27; 12:23; 15:22; 20:30-31; 21:9, 15; Mark 10:47-48; Luke 18:38-39) offer no substantiation of the claim that he is indeed of Davidic lineage let alone that he has the right of royal succession. They are isolated references which are an outgrowth of the Christian belief that Jesus as the Messiah must also be "the son of David." It is no wonder, then, that such references would occur in the New Testament tradition. However, the tradition is based on theological speculation, not historical fact. The independent development of the two divergent genealogical lists of Matthew and Luke show an attempt to give credence to this speculative theological tradition.

The virgin misconception

The introduction of the virginal conception complication into the story still necessitated adherence to the early tradition of paternal descent from David through Joseph. As a result of this already strongly implanted tradition, Joseph's alleged genealogy is given, in two widely divergent forms. The ascendancy and final domination of the virgin conception doctrine within the church meant attributing virgin conception to Mary without explanation of how Joseph's lineage played a role in Jesus' background. The problem was simply glossed over by the Gospels caught between these two theological speculations. It was left for later generations to reconcile these genealogies with the notion of a virginal conception. But, in actuality, this reconciliation never occurred. The fact is that the respective genealogies found in Matthew and Luke are a contradiction of the virgin conception doctrine. Attempts to prove the authenticity of the genealogies and the virginal conception stories are unconvincing and strained. The contradictions between Matthew 1 and Luke 3 make impossible the belief that both genealogies are the result of accurate genealogical records. It is highly improbable that either list preserves the family records of Joseph (or Mary). The New Testament genealogies reflect early Christian belief in Jesus' Davidic descent but are not actual family genealogies.

---

[1] "Messiah" (*mashiach*) in its Greek translation, *christos*, is used most often in the New Testament, but sometimes *messias* (John 1:41, 4:25) is used. In Paul's letters, *christos* is used as if it were not a title but part of Jesus' name: "Jesus Christ." But, what did the title "Messiah" mean to Jesus' contemporaries in the Land of Israel? In the Jewish Scriptures, three groups of people were anointed: prophets, priests, and kings. The term as used here centers on the third of these. It refers to one, chosen by God, who is a physical descendant of King David through his son Solomon and was thereby the Davidic Messiah.

The early church redefined the title "Messiah." They defined it as referring to a miracle-worker and prophet, who becomes, after his death, the heavenly Lord, "Jesus Christ," who will return at the end of days.

[2] The tribes of Benjamin and Simeon that formed the southern kingdom with the tribe of Judah were too insignificant in number and influence to be specifically

referred to as tribes. Of course, the tribe of Levi was scattered throughout the tribes. Lost were: Reuben, Issachar, Zebulon, Gad, Asher, Dan, Naphtali, the two half-tribes of Manasseh, and Ephraim.

[3] Maimonides, *Commentary on the Mishnah*, Sanhedrin, chap. 10. s.v. "The Twelfth Article of Faith." See also Negative Commandment 362 in Maimonides' *Sefer HaMitzvot*: "There may be no king over any believer in the Torah of Moses, our teacher, except from the descendants of David and Solomon."

[4] Some Christian scholars maintain that Jeconiah was condemned to childlessness in Jeremiah 22:24-30. He then allegedly adopted Shealtiel who according to Luke 3:27 is the son of Neri, an alleged descendent of David through Nathan. But, there is no evidence to support this conjecture.

[5] *Bamidbar Rabbah* 22:20.

[6] A *midrash* says, "[A]nd from whom [what descent] will be born [the Messiah]? From Zerubabbel" (Tanchuma, *Toledot* 14). Midrashic exegesis may contain valid historical and theological information but may also be purely speculative as in this midrashic text.

[7] The opening expression of Matthew, *Biblos geneseos*, is found in the Septuagint version of Genesis 2:4, where it means "history of the origins," and Genesis 5:1, where it means "a record of the genealogy." The latter rendering appropriately translates *Biblos geneseos* as used in Matthew's introduction to verses 2-16.

[8] Some Christians are of the opinion that fourteen may simply be based on the numerical value of the Hebrew letter in the name David (*DVD* = 4+6+4). If true, it need not indicate that the genealogy or its prototype was at some point written in Hebrew or Aramaic. It may be that a bilingual author was aware of the numerical value of the Hebrew/Aramaic name *DVD* and compiled the genealogy in Greek involving a calculation based on the numerical value of the Hebrew name *DVD* occurring in a Greek transliteration.

[9] The name Rahab occurs only in the Book of Joshua. There is no biblical connection between Rahab and the tribe of Judah or the ancestry of David. According to T.B. *Megillah* 14b Rahab married Joshua, who was of the tribe of Ephraim.

[10] The following texts and versions omit the name Cainan: (1) all the passages in the Hebrew text (Genesis 10:24, 11:12-13; 1 Chronicles 1:18, 24); (2) the Samaritan text of Genesis; (3) 1 Chronicles 1:24 in the Septuagint; (4) the *targumim* of Jonathan and Onkelos; (5) the Syriac Version; (6) the Latin Vulgate; and (7) Codex Bezae on Luke 3:36. But those which do mention Cainan are: (1) nearly all the Greek manuscripts of Luke 3:36; (2) the Septuagint of Genesis 10:24, 11:12-13; 1 Chronicles 1:18; and (3) the Book of Jubilees.

[11] The figure of seventy-seven names is found in most but not all manuscripts of the Gospel of Luke. Some have fewer names, ranging from seventy-two to seventy-six. Modern editions of the Greek New Testament have seventy-seven names. The

name Jesus (Joshua) occurs in forty-ninth as well as seventy-seventh position (from Adam) and suggests that the seventy-seven name list was a deliberately composed one, not an accident of the transmission of the text.

[12] Tertullian discusses Jesus' descent in his book, *On the Flesh of Christ* (20-22).

[13] Tertullian, 20. 2.

[14] Tertullian, 21. 5.

[15] Tertullian, 22. 6.

[16] I. Howard Marshall, *The Gospel of Luke*, Grand Rapids: Eerdmans. 1978, p. 158.

[17] A.T. Robertson, *A Harmony of the Gospels*, New York: Harper, 1950, pp. 261-262, lists eleven Christian scholars, among whom is Martin Luther, who accept this explanation.

[18] According to Christian tradition Mary's parents were named Joachim and Anna.

[19] Eusebius, *Ecclesiastical History* 1. 7.

[20] Eusebius, 1. 7.

[21] Eusebius, 3.11, 3.32, 4.22.

[22] One Christian author that questions the paternity of Jesus is Jane Schaberg (*The Illegitimacy of Jesus*, San Francisco: Harper and Row, 1987).

Chapter 48

ADOPTION AND THE RIGHTS OF ROYAL SUCCESSION
(Matthew 1:1)

In Matthew 1:1, Jesus is called "the son of David." The Gospel's author also reports a number of times (e.g., 9:27) that other people, too, addressed him as such. However, as we have seen, Christians take this Gospel's account of Jesus' birth (1:18-25) as an explicit denial that Joseph was the biological father of Jesus (1:16, 1:20). The inherent contradiction in the claim that Jesus is the son of David by virtue of Joseph's Davidic lineage is glossed over. Joseph, it is said, treated Jesus as if he were a son of his own, the people in Nazareth knew him as "the son of the carpenter" (13:55) and as a consequence Jesus is for Matthew a son of David as well. Thus some Christians argue that Jesus was therefore the adopted son of Joseph. But, there is no reliable evidence at all for the existence of adoption, in the post-Exilic period in the Land of Israel. Nevertheless, when Matthew's Gospel circulated in the Greco-Roman world, the story was certainly understood as implying adoption, which was a common practice in the Empire.

There are no biblical statutes discussing the rights and privileges of an adoptee or a foster care child. Adoption, the legal transference of a child to a family or individual to which it did not belong by birth is not provided for in Jewish law. Nevertheless, one can safely presume that such children were raised by others and often treated as one would treat one's own biological children. One might bestow on such a child love and affection and physical and economic benefits but that child is not legally entitled to succeed to its adopted or foster father's lineage. Just as adopted or foster children do not inherit hereditary diseases from their adopted or foster parents; neither can they inherit privileges that are based solely on a biological bloodline. Neither adoption nor foster care can affect the consequences of the blood relationship between a child and its biological parents.

If Jesus was not the biological son of Joseph, he must then be considered his foster child, since adoption did not exist as a legal concept in Jewish law. This would apply even though Joseph was married to the biological mother of the child.

As Christians explain it, Jesus is the "son of David" not through physical begetting, but through acceptance by the Davidic descendant, Joseph.[1] To this end, use is incorrectly made of Mishnah *Baba Batra* 8:6: "If one says, 'This is my son, he is to be believed.'" (This refers to biological kinship.) These Christians conclude that according to Jewish law, Jesus was a descendant of David through a process of acknowledgment. As such, it is contended that Joseph was the father of Jesus, not in a biological sense but in terms of legal paternity — adoption —whereby his acceptance of the child Jesus as his own son is what made him the father. It is said that by naming the child, Joseph acknowledged Mary's child as his adopted son, thereby assuming public responsibility for him. They construe this to mean that by accepting the child as his own, Joseph gives Jesus a Davidic genealogy. Thus, Davidic descent is said to be transferred not through biological paternity but through legal paternity.

This explanation is total fantasy. It misses the point that Joseph and Jesus are still not biologically of the same lineage. Legal paternity is not biological paternity, and what Christians allege is that Joseph was Jesus' legal father, not his biological father. They also assume that there were no other legitimate biological contenders for the throne except Joseph. Even presuming that Joseph was in direct line to inherit the throne of David and wanted to recognize Jesus as not only his son but as his firstborn heir to that kingship what would God's response be? Would God disregard His own promise that it would be the actual physical descendants of David through the male line of Solomon that would always be heir to the throne (Jeremiah 33:17-22, 2 Samuel 7:12-16, 1 Chronicles 28:5-7, Psalms 89:29-38)? We can be confident that God would be true to his word and fulfill the promise literally. God would know that Joseph's acknowledgment, if it actually was ever given, could never fulfill the word of God.

In a vain effort to buttress their contention that Joseph adopted and thereby transferred his lineage to Jesus some Christians appeal to Judges 17:7: "And there was a lad from Bethlehem in Judah [in contrast to Bethlehem of Zebulon (Joshua 19:15)] of the family [or clan] of Judah; and he was a Levite, and he sojourned there." He then left Bethlehem "and came to the hill country of Ephraim" (Joshua 17:8). This otherwise unidentified young man is identified with "Jonathan, the son of Gershom, the son of Manasseh" (Judges 18:30, cf. *Baba Batra*). The suspended letter in the name Manasseh, as found in the Hebrew text, indicates that it is really Moses who was "the father of Gershom" (Exodus 2:22). According to one explanation, the alteration was made out of respect for Moses, so as not to associate his name with a grandson who was involved with idols. Without the *nun* the word spells *Moshe* (Moses).

So why is Gershom's son Jonathan described as a Levite from the family of Judah? Some Christians come up with a totally convoluted answer. The fantasy they weave goes something like this: They surmise that Jonathan's biological father who is not mentioned in the text was from the tribe of Judah. This anonymous person is said to have died at which time Gershom married Jonathan's widowed mother and took Jonathan as his adopted son. This it is claimed explains why Judges 17:7 describes Jonathan as a Levite from the family of Judah. His biological father, it is claimed, was from the tribe of Judah, but his adopted father was a Levite.

Having established a nonexistent biblical precedent to satisfy themselves, Christians using this argument say it provides evidence that a child's adopted father can determine his tribal affiliation. This is, they claim, because when Gershom supposedly married Jonathan's mother and took her child into his home, the boy was incorporated into Levi, Gershom's tribe. They then apply this fanciful explanation to Joseph, Mary and Jesus.

The literal reading of the text gives an insight into contemporary living conditions among the Levites. They did not all live in Levitical cities but were scattered throughout the tribal territories. The phrase "of the family [or clan] of Judah" with an *'atnach* under Judah acting as a semicolon is a further description of the location of Bethlehem. The young man is not being described as being Judean or adopted by a Judean family but describes where he served as a Levite.

The Talmud states that "If anyone brings up an orphan boy or girl in his house, the Scripture accounts it as if he had begotten him" (B.T. *Megillah* 13a, *Sanhedrin* 19b). The two parties enter into a personal relationship, which does not include the adoption by the child of the foster father's lineage, which can only be obtained biologically. Although Joseph and Jesus might be considered father and son respectively, there would be no blood or legal ties between them. Under the Jewish law which governed the lives of Joseph and Jesus at the time of the latter's birth, Jesus might be called Joseph's son, but certainly not the son of David. Joseph might give the child his name, but not his alleged Davidic heritage. Let us not overlook the fact that God's promise was biological. He promised David and Solomon actual physical descendants through the male line to be heirs to the throne of David. What Christians advocate does not provide a biological male descendant through the paternal line, and would violate God's promise. Besides, since when do Christians recognize the validity of the Oral Law? Is it only when it can be twisted to suit their purposes?

As mentioned above, formal adoption was not a Jewish custom. However, it was a Roman one. A Roman citizen might accept a child who was not his own by birth into his family and give him his name by a formal legal act, attested by witnesses. The son thus adopted had, in all matters, the rights and privileges pertaining to a child who entered the family by birth. Although there was no formal adoption among the Jews as there was among the Romans, one could be recognized as a foster child, as in the case of the informal adoption of Esther by Mordecai: "And he brought up Hadassah, that is, Esther his uncles' daughter; for she had neither father nor mother ... and when her father and mother were dead, Mordecai took her for his own daughter" (Esther 2:7). Nevertheless, she is described as: "Esther, the daughter of Abihail the uncle of Mordecai, who had taken her for his daughter" (Esther 2:15). She is still formally the daughter of her biological father, Abihail. A further practice that needs to be mentioned is that of adopting slaves as sons, which was a common practice in the Middle East. As such, they had inheritance rights, though not above those of natural children of the father. When childless Abram thought that his servant, Eliezer of Damascus, would be his heir God said to him: "This man shall not be your heir; but he that shall come forth out of your own bowels shall be your heir" (Genesis 15:4). It must be emphasized that no matter what customs prevailed among other nations, within the nation of Israel lineal privileges belonged solely to the natural children biologically connected to the father (Numbers 1:2-4).

[1] There are Christians who allege that Jesus could claim Davidic descent through his mother's genealogy. However, there is no explicit or implicit proof in the New Testament for their contention.

Chapter 49

DID JOSIAH FATHER CHILDREN
AFTER HE WAS DEAD?
(Matthew 1:11-12)

Matthew writes that "Josiah begat Jeconiah and his brethren, about the time they were carried away to Babylon. And after they were brought to Babylon, Jeconiah begat Shaltiel, and Shaltiel begat Zerubbabel" (1:11-12). This is historically incorrect and even well-beyond the twisting of the biblical record we have come to expect from the author of the Gospel of Matthew. He overlooks that Josiah (died c. 610/609 B.C.E.) was dead many years before the exile that Matthew is referring to (586 B.C.E.). Well, a Christian might say, perhaps Matthew is referring to an earlier exile and its deportees that occurred shortly after the death of Josiah.

Let us get the history sorted out. Josiah was the father of Jehoiakim who was the father of Jeconiah. Jehoiakim was twenty-five years old when he began to reign (2 Kings 23:36), following his father's death. Jehoiakim reigned for eleven years to 598 B.C.E. and was succeeded by his son Jeconiah (also known as Jehoiachin and Coniah), who reigned for only three months. Jeconiah was eighteen years old when he began to reign (2 Kings 24:8). Accordingly, Jeconiah was seven years old when Josiah died. This does not fit into any claim that "Josiah [or Jehoiakim] begat Jeconiah and his brethren, about the time they were carried away to Babylon." There was no exile to Babylon around the time Josiah died

Chapter 50

RACHEL WEEPING FOR HER CHILDREN
(Matthew 2:16-18)

The author of Matthew writes:

> Then when Herod saw that he had been tricked by the magi, he became very enraged, and sent and slew all the male children who were in Bethlehem and in all its environs, from two years old and under, according to the time which he had ascertained from the magi. Then that which was spoken of through Jeremiah the prophet was fulfilled, saying: "A voice was heard in Ramah, weeping and much wailing, Rachel weeping for her children; and she refused to be comforted, because they were no more." (Matthew 2:16-18).

This author uses Jeremiah 31:15 as a prooftext that Rachel wept for the allegedly slain children of Bethlehem. (It is strange that such an outrageous act is neither mentioned by the historian Josephus or in any rabbinic sources.) Let us examine Jeremiah's statement within its context. The prophet states:

> Thus says the Lord: A voice is heard in Ramah, lamentation, and bitter weeping, Rachel weeping for her children; she refuses to be comforted for her children, because they are no more. Thus says the Lord: Refrain your voice from weeping, and your eyes from tears; for your work shall be rewarded, says the Lord; and they shall come back from the land of the enemy. And there is hope for your future, says the Lord; and your children shall return to their own border. I have surely heard Ephraim bemoaning himself: "You have chastised me, and I was chastised, as an untrained calf; bring me back and I shall be restored, for You are the Lord my God. For after I was turned, I repented, and after I was instructed, I smote upon my thigh; I was ashamed, and also humiliated, because I bore the disgrace of my mouth." (Jeremiah 31:15-19)

321

A perusal of the prophet's statement within its context shows that verse 15 is a poetic expression of excruciating grief that serves as an introduction to the actual prophecy itself. It is not part of the prophecy per se. Its subject is not slain children, but rather captive children.

The exiled northern Israelite tribes are collectively called by the name Ephraim, the leading northern tribe. Ephraim was the son of Joseph, whose mother was Rachel. If verse 15 was meant to be connected with the alleged massacre of the innocent children of Bethlehem, it would not have been Rachel weeping, but Leah, the ancestress of the tribe of Judah, in whose tribal area that town is located.

In Matthew's use of typology, nothing matters except convincing his audience that the Scriptures point to Jesus being the Messiah. Throughout his Gospel he alludes to biblical verses as if they verified his beliefs about Jesus. A closer look at what Matthew says shows how dishonest his methodology is. The fact is that Matthew is not providing a typology, but as he says, "that which was spoken through the prophet was fulfilled."

In other words, he is saying the alleged slaying of the children of Bethlehem was the literal fulfillment of Jeremiah's lament. According to Matthew, the alleged slaying of the children of Bethlehem was an actual fulfillment of the prophet's words; and that is sheer nonsense.

Chapter 51

THE NAZARENE
(Matthew 2:23)

Matthew writes: "And he [Joseph, along with Mary and Jesus] came and resided in a city called Nazareth, that what was spoken through the prophets might be fulfilled: 'He will be called a Nazarene'" (Matthew 2:23). But, there is not one prophecy in the Jewish Scriptures, which predicts that the Messiah will be called a Nazarene. Furthermore, there is no prophecy indicating that the Messiah will be an inhabitant of Nazareth. In fact, the town of Nazareth is never mentioned in the Jewish Scriptures.

Christians suggest that Matthew is giving a summary of what he claims the prophets were saying about the Messiah, not quoting from a particular prophet. According to those holding this view, Galilee was a region that was looked down upon and Nazareth, in particular, was a place held in low-esteem and contempt. Thus, Nazareth, they say, was considered the worst of the worst. They cite Nathanael's comment to Philip: Can any good thing come out of Nazareth?" (John 1:46). And that comment being from one living in Galilee! The Christian contention being that the term "Nazarene" was a disparaging remark, voicing contempt of anyone residing in Nazareth. As such, it would point to the Christian portrait of the Messiah as being of humble origins and despised status, one who is "despised and rejected of men" (Isaiah 53:3). It is to this that these Christians say Matthew is referring, although there is no record of Nazareth or its inhabitants being singled out for contempt.

Of course, Christians have to explain away Matthew's non-existent prophecy. But, consider that it is exactly in Galilee that the Gospels claim Jesus was best known and had his greatest following and most faithful adherents. It is in Galilee that Luke says: "[N]ews about him spread through all the surrounding district. And he began teaching in their synagogues and was praised by all" (Luke 4:14-15). Indeed, if Nazareth was such a terrible place why is Jesus surprised "and wondered at their unbelief" (Mark 6:6); rejection should have been expected.

The fact is that the prophets do not predict that the Messiah will be "despised and rejected." What is more, the prophets say nothing of his residing in a town considered the most despised and rejected in all of Galilee by even those living in that same region. Jesus is never called a "Nazarene" as a form of contempt, so where is the fulfillment of this so-called messianic prophecy?

Some Christians argue that Matthew is alluding to Isaiah's description of the Messiah as a *netzer*, "shoot," that is, a new, flourishing growth from the Davidic line. The prophet declares: "And there shall come forth a shoot out of the stock of Jesse, and a branch out of his roots shall bear fruit" (Isaiah 11:1). But, Isaiah never claims that the Messiah will be called *netzer*.

It has also been suggested that Matthew is intimating that the Messiah will be a Nazarite (Numbers 6:1-21), but nowhere in the Jewish Scriptures is it stated that the Messiah will be a Nazarite. In fact, the New Testament never makes the claim that Jesus was a Nazarite. One of the vows of the Nazarite is to abstain from the drinking of wine. Matthew's Jesus implies that he did drink wine previous to his statement at the Last Supper: "I will not drink of this fruit of the vine from now on until that day when I drink it new with you in my Father's kingdom" (Matthew 26:29). A further sign of the untenability of this exegesis is that the spellings of the words Nazarite, *nazir*, and Nazarene, *notzri*, are not the same in Hebrew. It is futile to try to identify *notzri* with *netzer* or *notzri* with *nazir*, for there is no basis upon which to make any connection. There is no reason to take seriously Matthew's attempt to show fulfillment of prophecy in the life of Jesus.

Chapter 52

THE POOR MEMORY OF JOHN THE BAPTIST

(Matthew 3:11, 13-17; Mark 1:7-11; Luke 3:16, 21-22; John 1:26-34)

Matthew writes:

> "As for me [John], I baptize you in water for repentance, but he who is coming after me is mightier than I, and I am not fit to remove his sandals. He will baptize you with holy spirit and fire…." Then Jesus came from Galilee to the Jordan to John in order to be baptized by him. But the latter tried to prevent him, saying: "I have need to be baptized by you, and you are coming to me?" But Jesus answering said to him" "Let it be so now, for in this way it is fitting for us to fulfill all righteousness." Then he permitted him. After being baptized Jesus immediately came up from the water; and behold, the heavens were opened up, and he saw God's spirit descending like a dove, coming upon him. And behold, a voice out of the heavens, saying: "This is My Son, the beloved, in whom I am well pleased." (Matthew 3:11, 13-17)

All four canonical Gospels claim that when Jesus came to be baptized by John the Baptist, the latter realized that Jesus was greater than he was (Matthew 3:11, 13-17; Mark 1:7-11; Luke 3:16, 21-22; John 1:26-34). At first John hesitated to baptize Jesus, but after being reassured that it was proper, he complied with Jesus' request. As Jesus was being baptized, the Synoptic Gospels allege that the spirit of God descended upon Jesus in the form of a dove. According to the Synoptic Gospels, this was witnessed solely by Jesus. The Gospel of John claims that John the Baptist also saw the spirit of God descend upon Jesus in the form of a dove (John 1:32-34). To give any benefit of doubt to the Fourth Gospel, it comes as no surprise that having witnessed this event John the Baptist felt that Jesus was superior to himself and called Jesus "the Son of God" (John 1:34) and "the Lamb of God" (John 1:36). This leads Andrew to exclaim to his brother

Simon (Peter), "We have found the Messiah" (John 1:41). As the story unfolds in the Gospel of John, there is no doubt that in John's mind Jesus was the Messiah.

Shortly after the baptism episode, John the Baptist was imprisoned by Herod Antipas. According to the Gospels of Matthew and Luke, while in prison John forgot what he had said, seen and heard just a short time before. The authors of these two Gospels state that while in prison, John was visited by his disciples, who informed him of Jesus' accomplishments. His response was to send two of his disciples to inquire as to whether Jesus was the Messiah (Matthew 11:2-3, Luke 7:19-20). How could John have forgotten so quickly who Jesus was? Did he not identify Jesus as the "Lamb of God" before the assembled throng at the Jordan River (John 1:29)? It would have been impossible for John to forget who Jesus was had he actually witnessed the spirit of God descending upon him and heard the accompanying heavenly affirmation of Jesus' chosen position, as recorded in the Fourth Gospel. Who could ever forget such a sight? Yet, the John the Baptist of the Synoptic Gospels did forget. Is it not strange that he had to ask his disciples to verify who Jesus actually was?

Apparently, the John the Baptist of some New Testament sources was not at all aware as to Jesus' significance (Matthew 11:3, Luke 7:19). They report that John had to be convinced once again of who Jesus was supposed to be, despite all that he had supposedly witnessed and said at the Jordan River. There is no indication in the Gospels that John underwent any torture while in prison which might have impaired his memory. As the story is told, John was in complete mental control of himself when he sent his disciples to Jesus. It would also be expected that his disciple were at the Jordan River and heard what John said concerning Jesus on two consecutive days (see John 1:29-34 and 1:35-36). Surely, before his imprisonment John informed at least some of his disciples about Jesus, and the word would then have spread to all of them that he had met the Messiah at the Jordan River. According to the Fourth Gospel, two of John's disciples on hearing him refer to Jesus as the "Lamb of God" went off to follow Jesus (John 1:35-37). Why did the John the Baptist of the Gospels of Matthew and Luke need a new confirmation of something that had earlier been shown so clearly to him?

Chapter 53

SON OF GOD
(Matthew 3:17, Mark 1:11, Luke 3:22)

Son of God as used in the Gospels

Based on the birth narrative myths found in Matthew and Luke, Christians think that the term "son of God" when it appears in the Jewish Scriptures refers to the offspring of a union of God with a virgin. The notion taught leads them to imagine that God's holy spirit fertilized a human ovum with, for want a better term, *divine sperm*. This is a story that fits the birth motifs of Greek mythology. When Gentiles became Christians, they may have understood the concept of "son of God" as it was used in pagan mythology where gods have sexual relations with human females and sire hybrid children combining human and divine attributes. No Jew faithful to biblical teachings and concepts would use "son of God" in such a literal sense of a human being. In conformity with biblical teachings, there was no Jewish expectation that the Messiah or anyone else would be God's son in the sense of having been conceived by God's holy spirit without a human male parent. The first Jewish followers of Jesus, if they called him "son of God," would have envisioned a person standing in a special relationship to God, who chose him to accomplish a task of great importance. Jesus, for them, would be a special "son of God," one of a nation of "sons of God." But, even they would not have considered him to be a literal son of God.

God's irrevocable promise is for the Messiah to be one of the male descendants of David and Solomon, not His own literal son, that is, according to Christian theology, one-third of Himself. All Jews are "sons of God" (the term, better rendered as "children of God," is inclusive of males and females). To Jews, the term "sons of God" had nothing to do with an unnatural conception and being a hybrid offspring, half-human half-divine or fully-human fully-divine. For Jews, the expression, "sons of God," when applied to human beings, is applicable to those especially called and designated by God for a particular task, that is, humans with special standing before God. Certainly the idea that "son of God" meant that God was personally involved in some sort of a conception process with Mary has no basis in biblical thought. "Son of God" is also a confused term in respect to the trinitarian Godhead. Having separated himself from himself the Christian god stands in a separate relationship to himself (Matthew 24:36, Mark 13:32, Acts 1:7). Was Jesus his own father? Was Jesus "son of God, the Father? Or, was he, as Matthew and Luke maintain, the "son of holy spirit"?

The Gospels refer to Jesus as "son of God," in contexts other than the birth narratives (Luke 1:35). In the variant stories of Jesus' baptism, a dove descends and a voice from heaven declares directly to Jesus, "You are My beloved son" (Mark 1:11, Luke 3:22). In Matthew 3:17 the voice speaks of Jesus in the third person, "this is My son." These stories are based on Psalms 2:7 where God declares to David, a normally conceived human being, "You are My son." Apparently, Mark's statement, "You are My beloved son," is meant as a declaration of adoption; God supposedly established a special relationship with Jesus at the time of his baptism. In contradistinction, Paul writes that Jesus was declared to be "son of God in power" by his supposed resurrection, not at the time of his conception (Romans 1:4). This shows that in Paul's view, the application of "son of God" to Jesus was not dependent on the claim of a virgin conception. A heavenly voice is said to proclaim, "This is My beloved son" in the transfiguration episode (Mark 9:7); demons call Jesus "son of God" (Mark 3:11, Luke 4:41); in the temptation episodes as described in the Gospels and Luke the devil addresses Jesus as the possible son of God ("if you are the son of God" — Matthew 4:3-7, Luke 4:3-9); at Jesus' supposed Jewish trial the high priest asks him if he is "son of God" (Matthew 26:63; alternately "son of the Blessed" (Mark 14:61); and the centurion who witnesses Jesus' death exclaims that Jesus was "son of God" (Mark 15:39, Matthew 27:54). The only passage that might infer that Jesus was something other than simply human is the high priest's question at the *Jewish trial* — "Are you the Christ, the son of the Blessed [that is, God]," since the high priest follows the question by exclaiming, "blasphemy," when Jesus does not repudiate the title. With the exception of the *Jewish trial* usage of the term it apparently is used to convey the notion that Jesus had a special relationship with God as manifested in the power to exorcise. The designation of Jesus as "son of God" denotes his alleged sharing in the power and authority of God the Father (Matthew 11:25-30). Nevertheless, it does not necessarily follow that Jesus was originally thought to be the literal incarnate son of God by those who first applied this phrase to him.

Mark places a major emphasis on Jesus' alleged divine sonship. His public career is presented as beginning with the declaration at the baptism, "You are My beloved son, in you I am well pleased" (Mark 1:11) and ending with the idol worshiping centurion's declaration at the cross: "Truly this man was a son of God [*huios theou*]" (Mark 15:39). Mark employed a literary convention that was familiar to his Gentile audience. A heavenly figure becomes "son of God" incarnate, but not at birth. In fact, Mark's story of Jesus' life contains no mention whatsoever of his conception or origin.

According to the Synoptic Gospels, it is not Jesus' Jewish disciples who first call him "son of God," but demons (Mark 5:7, Matthew 8:29, Luke 8:28; Mark 3:11, Luke 4:41). Matthew's version of Jesus' walking on water is the only passage in that Gospel in which his disciples allegedly say that Jesus is the "son of God" (Matthew 14:33). In contrast, Mark states that following Jesus' supposed walk on water "their heart was hardened" (Mark 6:52). Luke does not mention this story at all. One cannot conjecture from alleged demonic cries that Jesus' contemporary followers thought him to be "son of God." The verse from Matthew is actually evidence only of the author's own view, since it is simply a revision of Mark.

At some point, the Hebrew phrase "son of God" was applied to Jesus. To this, some Christians added the belief that although conceived naturally he was an angelic being. As Mark expresses the concept of Jesus as "son of God," Jesus receives the title only at his baptism. There is no indication in Mark that Jesus was in any way "son of God" before his baptism. Certainly, his mother's response to his public displays belies any claim that he was "son of God" from the womb (Mark 3:21, 32; Luke 2:48-50).

Apparently, Mark believed in the preexistence of an angelic being that existed in some indeterminate form before it came to earth and entered the mature physical body of Jesus. Thus, the parable of the vineyard presents Jesus as God's "beloved son" sent to Israel (Mark 12:1-11). Nevertheless, Mark does not explicitly explain how and when this preexistent being became the incarnate Jesus. Mark's narrative contains no birth story and implies that Jesus became "son of God" at his baptism, at which time his sins were forgiven him (Mark 1:4-9). Apparently, at that time he was infused with the spirit of this preexistent being and God validated this spirit transference. Mark describes this occasion: "And immediately coming up out of the water, he [Jesus] saw the heavens opening, and the spirit like a dove descending upon him" (Mark 1:10).

Matthew and Luke later took a different approach. They inserted birth narratives into their respective revisions of the Gospel of Mark. Independent of each other they developed nativity narratives based on legends already circulating about the manner of Jesus' conception and birth: he was the son of God because God's "holy spirit" impregnated his mother. The resulting narratives present legends basically irreconcilable with each other. Matthew, directing his Gospel toward Jews as well as Gentiles, presented what was supposed to be the biblical basis for the virgin conception doctrine (Isaiah 7:14). Luke, writing for a predominantly Gentile audience, provides no biblical basis for his version of the virgin conception doctrine. According to both descriptions of events, a holy spirit emanating from God impregnated a virgin. The child of this union is the incarnate "son of God." However, the details surrounding this event differ greatly between the two Gospels.

Luke traces the genealogy back not to Abraham, as in the Gospel of Matthew, but to Adam, son of God. Luke's genealogy running *backwards* from Jesus to God has no parallel in the Bible or in rabbinic literature; no genealogy begins with or culminates with the naming of God. This suggests two diametrically opposite views of the function of Luke's genealogy. On the one hand, the concept of Jesus as son of God does not express preexistence as an angelic being or a physical (or metaphysical) relationship between Father and son, but merely indicates a human lineage that ultimately, like all humanity,

331

goes back to Adam and to his Creator. Consequently, the genealogy shows in what sense Jesus is derived from God. There is no idea of preexistence; there is no idea of a physical divine nature in the title of "son of God." On the other hand, while this may have been acceptable christology to early Jewish followers of Jesus it was not the intention of Luke when he recorded the genealogy for the benefit of Christians with pagan origins. For them, Jesus as "son of God" by virtue of his descent from Adam, the son of God *par excellence*, constituted a close parallel with the Hellenistic and Roman attempts to prove the "divinity" of heroes and emperors by tracing their lineage to a "god."[1] Luke would have been aware that such a genealogy would have special significance to his Gentile readers. Even if Luke's source of the genealogy was of Jewish origin, it may have been a Hellenistically influenced Jewish source. There is also the possibility that Luke arranged the order of the genealogy going from Jesus to God in order to establish a "divine" sonship.

"Son of God" speculations were used as a means of making Jesus more attractive to the pagans, who were familiar with the birth myths of gods and heroes born of the union of a god with a virgin. From this pagan origin derived the virginal conception story found in the Gospels' of Matthew and Luke respectively. The son of a deity, enters the world as a man to perform acts of salvation, and then returns to heaven. In Greek, such a figure was called a *soter*, "savior," and the declaration of his coming was called "gospel" or "good news" (*eua*[n] *ggelion*).

In opening his Gospel, Mark uses the formula: "[The] beginning of the good news of Jesus Christ [*Arche tou euaggelion*], [the] son of God [*huiou theou*]" (Mark 1:1). Some manuscripts omit the words, "son of God." The question of interpolation into the text of this title cannot be given a definitive answer. There are nine other instances in which Mark depicted Jesus as God's son (Mark 1:11; 3:11; 5:7; 9:7; 12:6; 13:32; 14:36, 61; 15:39). "Son of God" is an important theme in this Gospel and affords an indication of the general plan of its author. Apparently, its occurrence at the beginning of the Gospel (1:1) is balanced with its appearance at the end (15:39) where the centurion confesses that Jesus is a "son of God." It is possible that "son of God" was accidentally omitted in some manuscript transmissions because the two previous words (*Iesou Christou*) have the same endings. However, it is also possible that a later interpolator saw an opportunity to achieve a more balanced text by the addition of "son of God" to Mark 1:1.

At first glance, it would appear that Mark and Matthew record a profession of faith by a Roman centurion in Jesus as "son of God." But, second thoughts dispel this notion. The expression *huios theou* (Mark 15:39), alternately *theou huios* (Matthew 27:54), "a son of God," "son of a God," "God's son," is anarthrous (that is, it does not have the definite article before either noun).[2] Does the centurion's statement mean something less than "the son of God?" Is there a significant difference between the presence of the definite article and its absence in understanding the Synoptic Gospels' presentation of the relationship between Jesus and God? Apparently not, they recognized a unique sonship, even if they disagreed on when he attained this relationship. This relationship between Jesus and God is expressed both with and without the definite article by the Synoptic Gospel authors. Matthew has Jesus' disciples call him God's son [*theou huios*]" (anarthrous 14:33) after the walking on the water, and later Simon Peter calls Jesus "the son of the living God [*ho huios tou theou tou zontos*]" (arthrous 16:16) at Caesar Philippe. In these verses Matthew used the anathrous and arthrous expressions interchangeably. Certainly, this author was not merely having the disciples state, "You are a son of God, like other human beings," after claiming they saw Jesus walk on water and calm the storm. In Luke 1:32, 35, it is claimed that the angel Gabriel told Mary that Jesus will be called "son of the Most High" and "son of God." The article is lacking but undoubtedly the titles are used in an exclusive sense of meaning unparalleled by previous definitions. These citations give the reader some indication of how the Synoptic Gospel authors thought the title "son of God" related to Jesus.

What did the centurion in Mark (Compare with Matthew's account of a group of soldiers stationed with the centurion at the cross.) mean in declaring Jesus "son of God"? Did he come to a realization that Jesus was the son of the one true God because he was a good or holy man and therefore a son in that sense, or did he consider Jesus a divine hero in the Hellenistic sense and therefore the physical son of God? If the episode is historical and the centurion spoke this sentence, what language did he speak? Did the centurion speak in Latin where there is no definite article [*filius Dei*],[3] or Greek? Did a miraculous profession of faith, as understood by later Christian theology, take place at the cross or was he thinking in terms of pagan mythology?

The major difference between Mark's Jesus and the Jesus of Matthew and Luke is not in whether to understand Jesus as "*a* son of God" or "*the* son of God." The significant area of difference in the Synoptic Gospels is in how and where he allegedly became "son of God."

Son of God in Jewish and Hellenistic thought

What is the difference in meaning of the expression "son of God" in Jewish and Greek cultures respectively? The ancient world, at the time in which the New Testament was written, was greatly influenced by Hellenistic culture. This led to a profound misunderstanding of the Hebrew phrase "son of God." Biblically, the term "son of God" does not designate a divine being, but rather a wholly human individual imbued with divine spirit. It refers to the person's function and character, as a man of God, not to his being God. As a result, Jewish thought about the nature of such an individual is anthropomorphic and metaphoric, not ontological. Speculative thought on a human as being (or becoming) God or a god ontologically, was strictly a Greek or Hellenistic notion. In Hellenistic thought sonship was understood to be primarily a matter of biology, a matter of being from the same substance. To this extent the virgin conception stories are best understood as accommodations to this Hellenistic idea that a son is like his father because he is of the same substance. Jesus, it was reasoned under Hellenistic cultural influences, was God manifest in the flesh because he was, to some extent, of divine substance.

While it is true that the concept of a man being a son of God is found in the Jewish Scriptures it is in a completely different sense than that found in the pagan world. Every Jew is authorized to call upon God as Father, for Israel has been designated God's child by God. Not so the other nations. One may surmise that it was because

Jesus was said to be obedient to God that he was originally called "son of God." Thus, while for the Greeks "son of God" meant from the same substance, for the Jews "son of God" could refer to one who obeys God. The two meanings suggest a possibility for misinterpretation when the Jewish phrase was used among Greek hearers.

Son of God in Christian theology

In the hands of Christianity, the biblical expression "son of God" was influenced by ontological speculations of Hellenistic and Egyptian origins. In the first century of the Common Era, the imperial cult of Caesar was the fastest-growing religion in the Mediterranean world where divinization and worship of rulers was standard. The emperors adopted the title "Son of God" with the god in question being their deceased, and newly deified, predecessor. Egyptian pharaohs were regarded as divine offspring of gods. In Egyptian mythology, the god Horus is called the son of Ra, the sun god. In almost every royal inscription from ancient Egypt, the pharaoh is also called "the son of Ra." Divine sonship was given to the pharaoh at his coronation. The dead pharaoh's heir was believed to become the incarnation of Horus, the son of Ra, upon the death of his predecessor.

The idea of the divine sonship of pharaoh did undergo change with time. But, the epithets "Son of Ra" and "Living Horus" continued to be used throughout the pharaonic period. They were even applied to foreign rulers, such as Alexander the Great and his successors, and the Roman Caesars. Divine pharaonic titles continued to be used well into the Christian era in Egypt. Did this affect Christian understanding of the title "son of God" as applied to Jesus in the New Testament? Did it contribute to the development of the incarnate "God the Son" in the trinitarian sense?

Christianity came to Egypt shortly after the death of Jesus. By the second and third centuries, it had spread throughout the country. It was because the Egyptians from pharaonic times through the Roman period believed their king was the "son of god" (that is, the incarnation of Horus, the son of Ra) that the concept of Jesus as the incarnate " son of God" found widespread support in Egypt. Under the further influence of Greek philosophical speculations the "son of

God" became, God the Son," one part of a trinitarian godhead.

By the time of the Council of Nicea in 325 C.E., Alexandrian Neoplatonist Christianity was a dominant force. It developed a highly mythologized Jesus, a divine ontological being. In the years between the Councils of Nicea and Chalcedon (451 C.E.), the advocates of Alexandrian Christianity grew in power and influence and, with the assistance of the secular authorities, the notion of Jesus having the being of god became the recognized orthodox Christian dogma. What the theologians of the Councils meant by the creedal title "Son of God" was far removed from what it meant to the Jewish proto-Christians who knew Jesus, to Paul, to the authors of the Synoptic Gospels and the author of the Gospel of John. The creeds spoke in Greek philosophical terms; the first followers of Jesus spoke in Jewish terms of the special and perhaps unique role their fully human teacher had in God's providence. In Paul's writings, influenced by Hellenism, Jesus achieves the status of an angelic being. This notion is also variously expressed in the Gospels, reaching its climax in the Fourth Gospel. Thus, under the influence of Greek and Hellenistic speculation, Christianity transformed Hebrew metaphor into Greek ontology.

When Jesus' earliest followers called him "son of God," the reference was to his obedience, not to his biological origin. This is also what is meant when Jesus is called God's son in Mark's baptism narrative (Mark 1:9-11). Through the introduction of the virginal conception this meaning loses its original significance in the baptism narratives of Matthew 3:16-17 and Luke 3:21-22. In Mark 1:9-11 the declaration of Psalms 2:7, "You are my son," is combined with Isaiah 42:1 ("Here is My servant ... I have put my spirit upon him."). According to the Gospel narratives, when John the Baptist baptizes Jesus, the heavens open up and the holy spirit or the spirit of God, depending on the Gospel, descended upon Jesus in the form of a dove (cf. the placing of God's spirit on the prophet—Isaiah 42:1), and a voice from heaven proclaims (as in Psalm 2), "You are My beloved son" (Mark 1:10-11, Matthew 3:16-17, Luke 3:21-22, John 1:32-34). What is found in the Gospels is the result of a transformation of the Jewish meaning of "son of God." The original sonship concept within Judaism as first applied to Jesus was soon supplanted by the notion that he was infused with a divine spirit at either his baptism or alleged resurrection. In a later development he was said to be an angelic son of God at conception. The trinitarian "God, the Son" concept is a post-New Testament idea.

[1] Exaggerated genealogical claims of Roman emperors were recorded by the Roman historian Suetonius (69-140 C.E.). He writes of Julius Caesar's praise of his deceased aunt, Julia:

And in the eulogy of his aunt he spoke in the following terms of her parental and maternal ancestry and that of his own father: "The family of my aunt Julia is descended by her mother from the kings, and her father's side is akin to the immortal gods; for the Marcii Reges [her mother's family name] go back to Ancus Marcius, and the Julii, the family of which ours is a branch, to Venus. Our stock therefore has at once the sanctity of kings, whose power is supreme among mortal men, and the claim to reverence which attaches to the gods, who hold sway over kings themselves." (Suetonius, *The Deified Julius* 6.1). (Loeb)

Concerning Galba, Suetonius writes:

Nero was succeeded by Galba, who was related in no degree to the house of the Caesars, although unquestionably of noble origin and of an old and powerful family; for he always added to the inscription on his statues that he was the great-grandson of Quintus Catulus Capitolinus, and when he became emperor he even displayed a family tree in his hall in which he carried back his ancestry on his father's side to Jupiter and on his mother's to Pasiphae, the wife of Minos. (Suetonius, *Galba* 2). (Loeb)

[2] Compare with the arthrous predicate nouns (that is, the definite article is before either noun) in the high priest's supposed question at the Sanhedrin trial: "Are you the Son of the Blessed [alternately "God"]?" (*ho huios tou enlogetou* in Mark 14:61; *ho huios tou theou* in Matthew 26:63). But, of course, the high priest is not calling Jesus "the Son of the Blessed [God]," but asking him if he thinks that he is. The specific question most likely derives from a Christian polemic, which saw fit to attribute this wording to the high priest.

[3] Classical Latin had no words corresponding exactly to our definite article *the* or our indefinite article *a*.

Chapter 54

SATAN'S TEMPTATION
(Matthew 4:1-11, Mark 1:13, Luke 4:1-13)

If Jesus is God as well as man how could Satan expect to tempt him? Mark simply states that Jesus was tempted by Satan (1:13) but Matthew (4:1-11) and Luke (4:1-13) elaborate the story. It is claimed that during Jesus' alleged forty days' sojourn in the desert, following his baptism by John, Satan tempted him with promises of an earthly kingdom if Jesus would only worship him. Was Satan so unaware of the complete nature of Jesus (as imagined by later Christians) that he entertained the thought that Jesus would join him in a dynamic dyad?

If Jesus is part of God, how could he possibly sin, and how could Satan possibly hope to tempt him? Satan's words would be meaningless. Surely, if the New Testament is correct, the earthly Jesus was incapable of committing as sinful an act as the worshiping of Satan. Indeed, unlike a mere mortal, it was decreed that the Gospels' Jesus follow exactly the life outlined for his earthly existence by the very deity of which supposedly he was an integral part. In assuming a human body, the Jesus of Christian theology knew what God's purpose for the future of mankind was and what was expected of him in order to bring this about. Did Jesus, the perfect god-man, have free will to sin while on earth? Obviously not! Had he failed to carry out God's plan, the entire timetable set forth by the Almighty would have been eternally disrupted. Lacking free will to do other than what he was programed to do, Jesus could not truly have been tempted.

It would be ridiculous for Satan, as one of God's creations, to promise the Gospel's Jesus, who supposedly was already divine and in control of the universe, a mere kingdom as a reward for worshiping him. As puffed up with pride as one might envision Satan to be, he is certainly not stupid. In the Gospel narrative Satan knew Jesus was not a mere human, given to flattery and subject to the temptations of the flesh. Jesus was not one who would accept worthless promises. Even if we suppose that Satan did make Jesus the most extravagant of offers, as reported by the Synoptic Gospels, it would not in the least have been a temptation to the divine Jesus of later Christianity. In view of the claim by Christians that Jesus was offered an earthly kingdom by God, as recorded in Psalm 2: "Ask of Me, and I will give the nations for your inheritance, and the ends of the earth for your possession" (Psalms 2:8), can anyone believe that a member of the Trinity would have difficulty in choosing between the two opposing offers? Certainly, Satan would not have wasted his time on such a futile endeavor. It is obvious that the account of Satan's attempt to tempt Jesus cannot be reconciled with the overall view of Jesus as held by Christians.

Of Jesus it is said: "For because he himself has suffered and has been tempted, he is able to come to the aid of those who are tempted" (Hebrews 2:18). It is also alleged that when Jesus was on earth, he was "tempted in all things as we are, yet without sin" (Hebrews 4:15). Men need to be strengthened at times of anguish (Luke 22:43) or temptation (Matthew. 4:11, Mark. 1:13); God does not. If Jesus were God in any manner of speaking it would be meaningless to tempt him. To say that that God feels temptation like a human would is absurd (Matthew 4:11, Mark.1:13). If Jesus was God as well as man at the time of his alleged temptation by Satan, how are these verses, and indeed the entire temptation episode, to be reconciled with the belief expressed by the author of James? He states, "Let no one say when he is tempted: 'I am being tempted by God'; for God cannot be tempted by evil, and He Himself does not tempt anyone" (James 1:13). If according to James, "God cannot be tempted by evil," then the Jesus who Christians claim is God cannot have been tempted by Satan. The entire Gospel episode of Satan's temptation of Jesus must therefore have not occurred.

In contrast to the Christian claims about Jesus, the God of Israel does not need to be tempted and suffer in order to be able to understand and forgive man's sins, because He is the all-knowing creator of man. This is poignantly expressed in the verse: "And the Lord said: 'I have surely seen the affliction of My people that are in

Egypt, and I have heard their cry because of their taskmasters; for I know their pains'" (Exodus 3:7). Isaiah reiterates this relationship between God and Israel: "In all their affliction He was afflicted" (Isaiah 63:9).

Chapter 55

JESUS MOVES FROM NAZAREH TO CAPERNAUM

(Matthew 4:13-16)

Matthew alleges that by moving from Nazareth to Capernaum to begin his ministry Jesus was fulfilling a prophecy from the Book of Isaiah. He writes:

> And having left Nazareth he came and took up residence in Capernaum beside the sea in the districts of Zebulun and Naphtali in order that there might be fulfilled what was spoken through Isaiah the prophet, saying: "The land of Zebulun and the land of Naphtali, by the way of the sea, on the other side of the Jordan, Galilee of the Gentiles. The people sitting in darkness saw great light, and those sitting in the region and shadow of death, light rose up to them." (Matthew 4:13-16)

The fallaciousness of the claim that Jesus' move fulfilled prophecy is best seen by comparing what Matthew writes with the actual words expressed by the prophet. Isaiah writes:

> For is there no gloom to her that was steadfast? Now the former has lightly afflicted the land of Zebulun and the land of Naphtali, but the latter has dealt a more grievous blow by the way of the sea, beyond the Jordan, in the district of the nations. (Isaiah 8:23)

> The people that walk in darkness have seen a great light; they that dwelt in the land of the shadow of death, upon them has the light shined. (Isaiah 9:1)

In quoting these two verses together, Matthew omits those parts which, if left in the text, would totally invalidate his claim. Based on Matthew's connection of these two verses, Christian translations of the Bible list them as Isaiah 9:1 and 9:2 respectively. But, these two verses do not belong together within the same chapter. In the

341

Jewish Scriptures, what is Isaiah 9:1 in the Christian versions of the Scriptures, with its reference to Naphtali and Zebulun, is found as the last verse of the eighth chapter, Isaiah 8:23, and completes the prophet's message up to that point. What is Isaiah 9:2 in the Christian versions of the Scriptures is the beginning of the ninth chapter, Isaiah 9:1, in the Jewish Bible, and starts a new part of the prophetic message. Reading in context what is Isaiah 9:1 in Christian Bibles one sees that it belongs to the eighth chapter of Isaiah. There the prophet speaks about the destruction, not long before, of the kingdom of Israel by the Assyrians. What is Isaiah 9:2 in Christian versions is a complete change, not only in subject matter, but also in form, as it is written in poetic style, whereas the verse Christians consider to be Isaiah 9:1 is written in prose. This accounts for the chapter divisions as found in Jewish Bibles, which follows the logical separation between the two chapters.

Matthew was so anxious to have as much of Jesus' career be part of prophecy that he combined the references to Zebulun and Naphtali and the reference to the light and darkness to support the claim that these were predictions of the beginning of Jesus' ministry. At the time he wrote his Gospel there were no formal chapter divisions placed within the biblical text, but it is self-evident from the context that his placing of these two verses in conjunction with each other is totally incorrect.

Chapter 56

JESUS AND DIVORCE
(Matthew 5:32, 19:8-9; Mark 10:2-12; Luke 16:18)

According to Matthew's Jesus, adultery is the only legitimate reason for divorce. He declares: "But I say to you that everyone who divorces his wife, except on account of fornication, makes her commit adultery; and whoever marries a divorced woman commits adultery" (Matthew 5:32). He contends that the reason this precept is not included in the Torah's commandments is: "Because of your hardheartedness, Moses permitted you to divorce your wives; but from the beginning it has not been this way" (Matthew 19:8). He then repeats that "whoever divorces his wife, except for fornication, and marries another commits adultery" (Matthew 19:9). Mark's Jesus is even more restrictive, declaring that under no circumstances is divorce to be granted: "Whoever divorces his wife and marries another commits adultery against her; and if she divorces her husband and marries another, she is committing adultery" (Mark 10:11-12). The same harsh criterion is set by Luke's Jesus: "Everyone who divorces his wife and marries another commits adultery; and he who marries one who is divorced from a husband commits adultery" (Luke 16:18).

Paul agrees with Jesus' command on divorce as expressed in the respective Gospels of Mark and Luke. He writes: "But to the married I give instruction, not I, but the Lord, that a wife should not leave her husband but if she does leave, let her remain unmarried, or else be reconciled to her husband, and that a husband should not send his wife away" (1 Corinthians 7:10-11). Moreover, in Romans 7:3, Paul states that if a woman marries another man while her first husband is still living, she is an adulteress.

Contrary to Matthew's Jesus, who allows divorce by reason of adultery, the Jesus of the respective Gospels of Mark and Luke, do not permit divorce under any circumstances. The addition or omission of adultery is an extremely important difference and leaves unanswered the question as to which statement, if any, is the actual teaching of

Jesus.   Paul supports the extremely rigid, legalistic declaration as found in the respective Gospels of Mark and Luke. He also directly attributes to Jesus this legislation, whose restriction goes beyond the law of divorce as stated in the Law of Moses (Deuteronomy 24:1-4). Jesus' command on the subject of divorce, in any of its variant forms, is an impractical legalism which, on examination, is found to be nonviable in society. It is no wonder that throughout history the followers of Jesus, in one way or another, have disregarded his command in any version.

Chapter 57

THE FORGIVING JESUS OF CHRISTIAN IMAGINATION
(Matthew 5:39; Luke 6:29, 23:34)

Turning the other cheek

Among the Christian folk-myths is to tell of the extraordinary pacifistic teachings of Jesus. To illustrate this, there are two verses that are often cited. The first is from the Gospel of Matthew: "Do not resist him that is wicked; but whoever slaps you on your right cheek, turn to him the other also" (Matthew 5:39). The second is from the Gospel of Luke: "To him that strikes you on the cheek, offer the other also" (Luke 6:29). Whatever one might think of the message, this sublime dictum was not practiced by Jesus himself. According to the Gospels, Jesus preached turning the other cheek (Matthew 5:39), loving one's enemies and praying for those who persecute you (Matthew 5:44), and forgiving those who wrong you (Luke 23:34). But, he himself never turned the other cheek.

Jesus responded to his opponents, not with passive resistance, but by answering criticism with criticism, reviling and threatening his adversaries (e.g., Matthew 15:1-20). Jesus never forgave anyone who wronged or criticized him. He only forgave those who wronged others.

On the cross, in a verse not found in the earliest New Testament manuscripts and clearly a later interpolation, he allegedly offered a general forgiveness of everyone: "Father, forgive them, for they do not know what they are doing" (Luke 23:34). That it is a later addition is also seen by investigating the internal evidence. A careful reading of the Gospels shows that this verse is not at all in agreement with Jesus' true feelings about forgiveness of ones enemies. Elsewhere, Luke records a statement by Jesus that is more in keeping with the true attitude the Gospels' Jesus showed toward his enemies: "But these enemies of mine who did not want me to reign over them, bring them here, and slay them in my presence" (Luke 19:27). Similarly, Matthew's Jesus expresses his feelings in a particularly merciless way when he says: "[S]o that there may come upon you all the righteous blood poured out upon the earth from the blood of righteous Abel to the blood of Zechariah son of Barachiah, whom you murdered between the Temple and the altar" (Matthew 23:35, cf. 2 Chronicles 24:21). Here Jesus condemns the Jews to suffering for "all the righteous blood poured out upon the earth" from a time even before the birth of Abraham, the father of the Jewish people. According to this passage, they are to suffer the penalty for the sins of murder of everyone else in the world since the dawn of history, as well as to suffer the penalty for their own sins of murder.

When an opportunity to personally forgive others presented itself he always declined. For example, instead of forgiving Judas for betraying him, he said: "But woe to that man through whom the Son of Man is betrayed! It would have been good for that man if he had not been born" (Matthew 26:24, Mark 14:21). In John 18:22-23, we find that Jesus, when beaten by an officer, instead of offering quietly his other cheek argues with him:

> But having said these things, one of the officers standing by gave Jesus a slap, saying: "Is that the way you answer the high priest?" Jesus answered him: "If I have spoken wrongly, bear witness concerning the wrong; but if rightly, why do you hit me?"

It is clear from the Gospels that Jesus never forgave anyone who wronged or criticized him. At best, he only forgave those who wronged others. Whenever an opportunity to personally forgive others who he felt wronged him presented itself, he always declined. For example, "he [Jesus] began to reproach the cities in which most of his miracles were done, because they did not repent. 'Woe to you, Chorazin! Woe to you Bethsaida! . . . Nevertheless I say to you, it shall be more tolerable for Tyre and Sidon in the judgment, than for you. And you, Capernaum, will not be exalted to heaven, will you? You shall descend to Hades; for if the miracles had occurred in Sodom which occurred in you, it would have remained to this day'" (Matthew 11:20-24, Luke 10:13-15). And we again mention the most egregious example of his unforgiving nature, which would have had great significance, that is, forgiving Judas who committed suicide in remorse. Instead of forgiving Judas for betraying him, he said: "But woe to that man through whom the Son of Man is betrayed! It would have been good for that man if he had not been born" (Matthew 26:24).

For his part, Paul did not submit meekly to the high priest Ananias' order that he be smitten on the mouth. He did not offer his cheek in compliance with Jesus' command. Instead, Paul swore at Ananias in direct contradiction of another of Jesus' alleged commandments: "Bless those who curse you, pray for those who mistreat you" (Luke 6:28), and his own statement: "Bless those who persecute you; bless, and do not curse" (Romans 12:14).

> And the High Priest Ananias commanded those standing beside him to strike him on the mouth. Then Paul said to him: "God is going to strike you, you whitewashed wall. And do you sit to judge me according to the Law, and in violation of the Law order me to be struck?" (Acts 23:2-3)

It is no wonder that the dictum to turn the other cheek, attributed to Jesus, is more spoken about by Christians than complied with?

Is such an unforgiving attitude as shown by Jesus and Paul in accord with the allegedly benign, kind, forgiving soul of Jesus as found in Christian theological myth? After observing Jesus' bitter hatred of those who disagreed with him is it any wonder why Christianity (in its many forms) has shown intolerance and persecuted anyone who doesn't agree with its religious beliefs.

Chapter 58

HOW GOOD IS CHRISTIANITY?
(Matthew 7:15-20, Luke 6:43-45)

The Gospels' Jesus declares:

> Beware of the false prophets who come to you in sheep's clothing, but inwardly are ravenous wolves. You will know them by their fruits. Grapes are not gathered from thorns, nor figs from thistles, are they? Thus, every good tree bears good fruit, but the rotten tree bears bad fruit. A good tree cannot produce bad fruit, nor can a rotten tree produce good fruit. Every tree that does not bear good fruit is cut down and thrown into the fire. So then, you will know them by their fruits. (Matthew 7:15-20; see also Luke 6:43-45)

In this passage, Jesus explains that what is good cannot possibly produce evil, and conversely, that which is evil cannot possibly produce good: "A good tree cannot produce bad fruit, nor can a rotten tree produce good fruit." Viewed from this perspective, Christianity cannot be considered good since so many wrongs have issued from its murderous intolerance of those not in theological agreement with it. Many Christians argue that the evils resulting to the world in the wake of Christianity are not really of Christian origin. This is tantamount to claiming that the bad fruit growing on a tree were not produced by the tree. It is Christianity in all its forms, denominations and sects that is spoken of. No amount of explaining can absolve Christianity from the innumerable wrongs stemming from the hegemony it has exercised over vast areas of the world in the course of its tortuous history.

But, wait someone might say. Look at all the good things Christians have done in the name of Jesus, such as building hospitals, sending medical missions to places in need and establishing orphanages. (If only baptism and belief in Jesus as one's savior from sin saves then "good works" counts for nothing. The only "good" Christianity recognizes is belief in Jesus.)

To this "good works" argument in defense of Christianity Matthew's Jesus answers:

> Not everyone who says to me: "Lord, Lord," will enter the kingdom of the heavens, but he who does the will of my Father who is in the heavens. Many will say to me on that day: "Lord, Lord, did we not prophesy in your name, and in your name cast out demons, and in your name perform powerful works?" And then I will declare to them: "I never knew you; depart from me, you who practice lawlessness." (Matthew 7:21-23)

How aptly this applies to Christianity in general, which has spoken in the name of Jesus and in his name "performed powerful works." Could Jesus possibly accept Christianity as his own? Jesus' core message is that if the tree is rotten, so will be the fruit it produces. He does not say some fruits will be good and some fruits will be bad; it is all or nothing. To be true to his own dictum that bad fruit can never be produced by a good tree, Jesus would have to disown and reject *all* of Christianity for the evil it has perpetrated in his name. Yet, even though he might reject Christianity, many of the horrors it has subjected the world to are the direct result of his teachings (e.g., Luke 19:27). Yes, indeed, "You will know them by their fruits."

Chapter 59

A CALL TO VIOLENCE

(Matthew 10:34-35; Luke 12:49-53, 19:27; Matthew 8:30-32, Mark 5:11-13, Luke 8:31-33; Matthew 21:12-13, Mark 11:15-17, Luke 19:45-46, John 2:13-16; Matthew 21:18-22; Mark 11:12-14, 20-25)

Jesus and violence

Christians maintain that Jesus fulfilled Isaiah's description of the suffering servant of the Lord as one who "had done no violence" (Isaiah 53:9). Isaiah's text is a description of the servant's (the nation of Israel's) life. But Christians take this phrase in an absolute literal sense and then refer it to Jesus. As such, one would expect Jesus to have never used violence, but that is not the case. He not only committed acts of violence himself, but advocated its use among his followers. If Jesus was truly non-violent he could not have uttered such violent words as: "Do not think that I came to bring peace on the earth; I did not come to bring peace, but a sword. For I came to set a man against his father, and a daughter against her mother, and a daughter-in-law against her mother-in-law" (Matthew 10:34-35).

Luke continues this theme of Jesus' call to violence:

I have come to cast fire upon the earth; and how I wish it were already kindled! But I have a baptism to undergo, and how distressed I am until it is accomplished! Do you suppose that I came to grant peace on earth? I tell you, no, but rather division; for from now on five members in one household will be divided, three against two, and two against three. They will be divided, father against son, and son against father; mother against daughter, and daughter against mother; mother-in-law against daughter-in-law, and daughter-in-law against mother-in-law. (Luke 12:49-53)

In this passage the allegedly non-violent Jesus proudly declares that his is a mission which will cause discord, disturb the universal peace, and bring war to the world. It was during this "first coming" that he calmly called for his opponents to be brought before him (he is the nobleman of the parable) for summary execution: "But these enemies of mine who did not want me to reign over them, bring them here, and slay them in my presence" (Luke 19:27). Is this love? Is this compassion? Is this nonviolence? Jesus' followers took to heart the message of this parable in their treatment of Jews and others deemed "enemies of Jesus."

Jesus is said to have permitted demons to enter a swine herd causing their death (Matthew 8:32, Mark 5:13, Luke 8:33), attacked merchants in the Temple area (Matthew 21:12, Mark 11:15-16, Luke 19:45, John 2:15), and cursed a fig tree for not bearing fruit out of season (Matthew 21:18-21, Mark 11:13-14),

The drowning of a herd of swine (Matthew 8:30-32, Mark 5:11-13, Luke 8:31-33)

One of the strangest miracles attributed to Jesus caused the drowning of a herd of swine. This tale is found in the Synoptic Gospels, which state:

> Now there was at a distance from them a herd of many swine feeding. And the demons began to entreat him, saying: "If you are going to expel us, send us into the herd of swine." And he said to them: "Go away!" And they came out, and went into the swine, and behold, the entire herd rushed down the steep bank into the sea, and died in the waters. (Matthew 8:30-32)

> Now there was a big herd of swine feeding there on the mountain side. And they entreated him, saying: "Send us into the swine so that we may enter them." And he gave them permission. And coming out, the unclean spirits entered the swine; and the herd rushed down the steep bank into the sea, about two thousand of them; and they were drowned in the sea. (Mark 5:11-13)

> And they were entreating him not to command them to depart into the abyss. Now there was a herd of many swine feeding there on the mountain; and the demons entreated him to permit them to enter the swine. And he gave them permission. And the demons came out from the man and entered the swine; and the herd rushed down the steep bank into the lake, and was drowned. (Luke 8:31-33)

By allowing the demons to enter and take possession of the herd of swine, Jesus was at fault for causing the death of the swine. To rationalize this act by asserting that certain unstated factors were involved has no basis in the Gospel presentations. There is no reason to accept the assumption of some Christians that either the owners of the swine were Jewish and thus were guilty of disobeying the Torah, or that the swine were the property of a Gentile in defiance of his Jewish neighbors. Other Christians maintain that the reason Jesus allowed the demons to enter the swine was because he knew the demons were right in implying that the time of their consignment to hell had not yet arrived. Yet, if Jesus were so insightful, we should expect that he also knew that the demon possessed swine would leap into the lake and drown. What happened to the demons at that point? Did they need to enter yet another life form? It would seem that Jesus could have assigned them to the next host without this short-lived intermediate stay in the swine. Still other Christians explain that the episode took place to teach a sense of proportion in life, that is, people are more important than swine. Thus, it should be remembered that those demons had first possessed certain individuals who were now cured of their demon possession. With no clear reason given for Jesus' action, the lesson is lost, if there ever was one to begin with. But, certain facts about this fictive tale are clear.

According to the New Testament, Jesus could expel demons from people without having to place them into another life-form (Matthew 9:33; Mark 1:39, 7:26-30; Luke 8:2, 13:32). Besides, the death of the animals was not necessary to confirm to the man (two men according to Matthew 8:28) that he was now rid of the demons, he would have sensed the difference. Moreover, Mark 1:34 asserts that Jesus had such power over demons that they could not speak without his permission. Indeed, the demons needed his permission to enter the swine (Matthew 8:31, Mark 5:12, Luke 8:32). By allowing the demons to enter and take possession of the herd of swine, Jesus was at fault for causing the cruel death of these animals. Since the demons, unlike humans, had no free will, but were subject to Jesus' will, he was culpable for the wanton death of the swine by reason of his giving permission for the demons to enter and take possession of them. We must, thus, accept the inescapable conclusion that Jesus was indeed responsible for the violent death of the swine. This was a needless, unjust, violent act perpetrated on dumb animals. It also unjustly deprived their owner of his property.

The geographic setting for the drowning of the swine episode presents a problem about whether this alleged incident ever happened. The Synoptic Gospels relate that Jesus and his disciples crossed the Sea of Galilee and went to Gerasa, "the country of Gerasenes, which is opposite Galilee" (Mark 5:1, Luke 8:26) or alternately to Gadara, "the other side into the country of the Gadarenes" (Matthew 8:28). Gerasa, where Mark and Luke locate the episode is about thirty miles southeast of the Sea of Galilee, which is the only large body of water in the region. Matthew changes the location to Gadara, six miles from the Sea of Galilee. Can pigs fly? A thirty-mile leap by the swine, into the Sea of Galilee, would be quite a miracle, in itself, but, certainly, a six-mile leap would be quite a feat as well.

Violence in the Temple (Matthew 21:12-13, Mark 11:15-17, Luke 19:45-46, John 2:13-16)

The Gospels inform us of the violence Jesus perpetrated in the Temple:

> And Jesus entered into the Temple and cast out all those who were selling and buying in the Temple, and overturned the tables of the moneychangers and the seats of those who were selling doves. And he said to them: "It is written, 'My house shall be called a house of prayer'; but you are making it a robbers' den." (Matthew 21:12-13)

> And they came to Jerusalem. And he [Jesus] entered into the Temple and began to cast out those who were selling and buying in the Temple, and overturned the tables of the moneychangers and the seats of those who were selling doves; and he would not allow anyone to carry a utensil through the Temple. And he was teaching and saying: "Is it not written, 'My house shall be called a house of prayer for all the nations'? But you have made it a robbers' den." (Mark 11:15-17)

> And he entered into the Temple and began to cast out those who were selling, saying to them: "It is written, 'And My house shall be

a house of prayer,' but you have made it a robbers' den." (Luke 19:45-46)

And the Passover of the Jews was near, and Jesus went up to Jerusalem. And he found in the Temple those who were selling oxen and sheep and doves, and the moneychangers seated. And he made a whip of ropes, and drove them all out of the Temple, with the sheep and the oxen; and he poured out the coins of the moneychangers and overturned their tables. And to those who were selling the doves he said: "Take these things away; stop making my Father's house a house of merchandise." (John 2:13-16)

Exactly when did Jesus carry out his attack on the Temple? Matthew and Luke have one time, Mark another, and John still a third. John's account alleges that the incident occurred on an earlier visit to Jerusalem than the one recorded in the Synoptic Gospels. However, all four canonical Gospels agree that Jesus used violent means to attack the commercial activity in the Temple courtyard. Whip in hand, he attacked the merchants in the Temple area causing an uproar. He overturned the tables of the moneychangers and the seats of those selling doves, and drove out of the Temple courtyard not only the merchants but also those purchasing sacrificial offerings along with the sheep and oxen used for this purpose.

Jesus' action was a preplanned violent assault. On his first day in Jerusalem, Jesus entered the Temple courtyard and "looked around at everything, then left" (Mark 11:11). The following day he returned to launch his surprise attack. Contrary to Mark, Matthew and Luke say that when Jesus first arrived in the city he proceeded directly to the Temple. They do not mention the earlier Temple visit. These two Gospels give the impression that Jesus' assault took place as a spontaneous reaction to condition he found upon entering the Temple. This difference is significant in that Mark's account shows that Jesus carefully studied the situation before making his plans. It was only then that he returned and disrupted the commercial activity in the Temple courtyard. Mark's account, in particular, shows that Jesus deliberately initiated the attack, and reveals the extent of his violent actions. Moreover, Jesus' disciples must have assisted him, as it would have been impossible for Jesus to have accomplished it all alone. Mark has Jesus take such complete control of the Temple courtyard that he prevented its use as a thoroughfare: "And he would not allow anyone to carry a utensil through the Temple" (Mark 11:16). Such control could only have been achieved with the help of his followers. Apparently the respective authors of Matthew and Luke suppress this information to hide the extent of Jesus' heavy-handed actions. They want to minimize the impression that Jesus was a man of violence. The glimpse of Jesus' deliberate use of violence that we get in the Gospel of Mark, in particular, speaks for itself.

The Synoptic Gospels have Jesus admonishing the merchants with a condemnation made by combining Isaiah 56:7 and Jeremiah 7:11. John's Jesus makes no such statement. Some Christians feel that the discrepancies show that there were two separate incidents of violence in the Temple involving Jesus.

Some might argue that Jesus was justified in attacking commercial activity in the Temple. But, before addressing that issue let it be clear that whatever the reason for his attack it was accompanied by the use of violence, which means he did not fulfill what is said of the servant of the Lord: "he had done no violence" (Isaiah 53:9). But what was this commercial activity in the Temple precinct? There was a need to exchange heathen coins depicting idolatry for those that could be donated to the Temple. Also, to bring animals for sacrifices from a distance was difficult, especially since they had to be blemish free. The proximity to the place of sacrifice meant less chance that the animal would be unsuitable.

During the several alleged Jewish interrogations and the trial before Pontius Pilate at which Jesus is said to have been questioned there is never any mention made of his violent attack. Surely, from the standpoint of the Gospel authors it was best not to mention the incident any more than necessary since it showed Jesus' violent nature.

They do, however, attempt to portray Jesus' righteous indignation at the alleged greed of the merchants, while minimizing the violent nature of his attack just a few days before his arrest. But, what Jesus is said to have done was not only a provocation, which disrupted certain commerce. It posed a threat that would automatically involve the Roman authorities. The Gospels want to show Jesus as a peaceful, nonviolent individual devoid of any wrongdoing. It is more than likely that his actions were motivated by something more than commercial activity in the Temple. As such, the pre-Gospel sources used this *indignation excuse* to cover-up an open rebellion against the Temple authorities and/or the Romans. The Gospel author's further sanitized their respective retelling of the incident. What other violent clashes he might have had with the authorities have been expunged.

In any case, the issue is not whether Jesus was right or wrong in violently attacking the merchants or if he was initiating a revolt. The issue is that Jesus used unequivocal violence. Mark gives some insight into what happened that is suppressed in later Gospels. In that Gospel we get an inkling of the riotous and ruthless actions undertaken by him and his followers in the Temple on that day. Jesus must have known that his Temple attack and his earlier provocative entrance into Jerusalem would not go unnoticed by both the Jewish and Roman authorities. Given the political and social condition of the time in Judea his actions were understood by these authorities and Jesus himself as the opening salvos of a revolt against Roman governance.

The cursing of the fig tree (Matthew 21:18-22; Mark 11:12-14, 20-25)

The authors of Matthew and Mark respectively tell a story about how a hungry Jesus curses a fig tree for not providing him with its fruit out of season:

> In the morning, as he was returning to the city, he became hungry. And seeing a lone fig tree by the road, he went to it, and found nothing on it except leaves only; and he said to it: "No longer shall there be any fruit from you." And the fig tree withered instantly. And seeing this, the disciples marveled, saying: "How did the fig tree wither instantly?" And Jesus answered and said to them: "Truly I say to you, if you have faith, and do not doubt, you shall not only do what was done to the fig tree, but even if you say to this mountain: 'Be lifted up and cast into the sea,' it shall happen. And everything you ask in prayer, believing, you shall receive." (Matthew 21:18-22)

> And on the next day, when they had departed from Bethany, he became hungry. And seeing at a distance a fig tree that had leaves,

he went to see if perhaps he would find anything on it; and when he came to it, he found nothing but leaves, for it was not the time of figs. And he answered and said to it: "May no one ever eat fruit from you again!" And his disciples were listening.... And when they were passing by early in the morning, they saw the fig tree withered up from the roots. And Peter, having remembered it, said to him: "Rabbi, behold, the fig tree which you cursed has withered." And Jesus answered saying to them: "Have faith in God. Truly I say to you that whoever says to this mountain: 'Be lifted up and cast into the sea,' and does not doubt in his heart, but believes that what he says is going to happen; it shall be granted him. Therefore I say to you, all things for which you pray and ask, believe that you have received them, and they shall be granted you. And whenever you stand praying, forgive, if you have anything against anyone; in order that your Father also who is in the heavens may forgive you your transgressions." (Mark 11:12-14, 20-25)

The Gospels relate a story in which Jesus became hungry while on the road to Jerusalem (Matthew 21:18, Mark 11:12). He sees a fig tree with leaves on it, but on approaching it he does not find any fruit on it, "for it was not the time of figs" (Mark 11:13). Jesus curses the fig tree and it withers either instantly (Matthew 21:20) or by the next morning (Mark 11:20-21).

It is the nature of the fig tree that even before the tree is covered with leaves, the *paggim* ("green figs") begin to develop and continue to grow during the summer months. The first ripe figs sometimes appear in the early summer (Song of Songs 2:13), many weeks after the leaves have appeared. So, even if there had been figs, as Jesus had expected, it was too early in the season for them to be ripe for eating. Jesus speaks to the tree as if it could understand him, but a tree has no mind or conscience of its own so it cannot be treated as deceptive and certainly cannot be held responsible for not producing fruit. Why then did Jesus take violent action against the tree? According to the Torah, not even during a time of war is one permitted to cut down a fruit-bearing tree (Deuteronomy 20:19). Jesus, in violation of the Torah, destroyed a tree he considered capable of bearing fruit as indicated by his statement: "May no one ever eat fruit from you again!" (Mark 11:14). This verse is alternately expressed as: "No longer shall there ever be any fruit from you" (Matthew 21:19).

When Jesus' disciples question him about his actions he says he did it to show what can be done by having faith (Matthew 21:21-22, Mark 11:2-24). But how does wanton destruction show faith? There is no moral lesson stated or even alluded to in this destructive act. If Jesus was all-powerful and all-loving, would it not have been proper for him to command the tree to give forth fruit rather than to command it to wither and die? Is it not hypocritical for him to tell his followers to forgive those with whom they have had differences ("And whenever you stand praying, forgive, if you have anything against anyone" — Mark 11:25) when he did not practice what he himself preached. He could not even forgive a tree for not bearing fruit out of season! In any case, Jesus' action was an act of violence not consistent with the Christian claim that Jesus is the suffering servant portrayed in Isaiah 53:9 and is completely non-violent in all his actions.

Chapter 60

HOW SOON THE SECOND COMING OF JESUS?
(Matthew 16:28, Mark 9:1, Luke 9:27)

How soon is shortly?

The Gospels' Jesus promises that "Truly I say to you, there are some of those who are standing here who will not taste death at all until they see the Son of Man coming in his kingdom" (Matthew 16:28; see also Mark 9:1, Luke 9:27). This statement records the early Christians expectation that Jesus was to return shortly to his contemporary generation. "This generation" appears fifteen times in the Gospels and always applies to Jesus' contemporaries (Matthew 11:16; 12:39, 41, 42, 45; 16:4; 23:36; Mark 8:12, 38; 9:19; 13:30; Luke 11:30, 50, 51; 17:25). That generation passed away without Jesus returning. Therefore, we are confronted by another unfulfilled promise by Jesus. The Gospel's Jesus did not return during the time period he himself specifically designated. Some are of the opinion that "this generation" means the generation alive when this prophecy comes to pass, which they believe has yet to occur. However, the text shows that Jesus was not speaking to an unspecified future generation; he was speaking to his contemporary disciples and directed this prophecy to them personally.

Even before the Gospels were written, Paul declared: "And the God of peace will crush Satan under your feet shortly" (Romans 16:20). Another pre-Gospel New Testament author writes: "For yet in a very little while, he who is coming will come, and will not delay" (Hebrews 10:37). A late New Testament author attributes the following statements to Jesus:

Do not seal up the words of the prophecy of this book, for the time is near. (Revelation 2:10)

Behold, I am coming quickly, and my reward is with me, to render to each one as his work is. (Revelation 22:12)

Yes, I am coming quickly. (Revelation 22:20)

What does Paul mean by the word "shortly" in Romans 16:20 or the author of Revelation 22:10, 12, 20 by "the time is near" and "I am coming quickly"? To understand what is meant we will investigate the information provided, from the perspective offered by Hebrews 10:37: "For yet a little while, he who is coming will come, and will not delay." This verse is derived in part from the Septuagint's rendering of Habakkuk 2:3. The Prophet Habakkuk wondered when divine righteousness would be vindicated in light of the suffering his people were enduring at the hands of the Babylonians. God answered Habakkuk and bade him to be patient, for, at a divinely designated time, the righteous in Israel would emerge triumphant from all the anguish to which they had been subjected. The Hebrew text reads:

> And the Lord answered me, and said: "Write the vision, and make it plain upon tablets, that a man may read it swiftly. For the vision is yet for the appointed time, and it declares of the end, and does not lie; though it tarry, wait for it, because it shall surely come, it will not delay. Behold, his soul is puffed up, it is not upright in him; but the righteous shall live by his faithfulness." (Habakkuk 2:2-4)

First century Christians were a diverse community living in daily expectation of the imminent return of Jesus. The author of Hebrews enthusiastically embraced this expectation. In Hebrews 10:37 he is solely concerned with the immediate future and his expectation that Jesus will return shortly: "For yet a little while he who is coming will come, and will not delay." He proclaims that Jesus would be returning in what was then the near future as time is reckoned in human terms. He utilizes some of Habakkuk's wording to convey his own message, but that has no significance for our discussion. We are concerned with the author of Hebrews' timing of the alleged second coming of Jesus. God informs Habakkuk that even when the wicked temporarily flourish one should be patient and wait, for faith in God will be vindicated. God promises that the vindication will come in its appointed time, not before, nor after. It is to come in God's own time.

This fits well into the scheme of history addressed by the psalmist's words that "a thousand years in Your sight are but as yesterday when it is past, and as a watch in the night" (Psalms 90:4). The author of Hebrews shows by his choice of the words, "for yet a little while," that he has a specific time period in mind for expecting the arrival of the second coming. In so doing, he highlights the failure of Jesus to return as predicted.

Mark's Jesus, after listing all the tribulations the world must go through before he returns a second time (Mark 13:5-29), declares: "Truly I say to you, this generation will not pass away until all these things take place" (Mark 13:30). Now that over two thousand years have passed, it is apparent that the quick return of Jesus expected by the early Christians never occurred. The promise that Jesus would return within a short time after the supposed resurrection to establish his kingdom can *never* be fulfilled.

The author of the Second Letter of Peter writing after the Gospels were written attempts to deal with the problem occasioned by the delay in Jesus' return by appealing to Psalms 90:4. Thus, 2 Peter 3:8 states: "But do not let this one fact escape your notice, beloved, that with the Lord one day is as a thousand years, and a thousand years as one day." However, the psalmist's words are not applicable to the situation under study. The author of 2 Peter 3:9, still basing himself on the psalmist, states that "the Lord is not slow about His promise, as some count slowness." This author does not consider the second coming as "slow" in coming when considered according to God's reckoning. This makes 2 Peter 3:9 irrelevant in seeking a solution to the problem. Jesus' promise to return was recorded in accordance with human determination of time ("this generation" — Matthew 24:34, Mark 13:30) not God's and must, therefore, come as specified by those human terms. There was to be fulfillment within the lifetimes of certain individuals alive at the time Jesus made the promise and following upon certain cataclysmic events which were to be witnessed by that generation. Jesus' promise of his quick return includes prolonging the lifetime of certain individuals until he returns (Matthew 16:28). Yet, none of his early followers are alive today and his promise to them never materialized. Also, these cataclysmic events never occurred and the time for their occurrence has long since passed.

The Gospels were written more than thirty years after the death of Jesus. Their authors were part of a generation that was dying out. How should they understand these words attributed to Jesus? Did Jesus mean that before the last apostle's death he would return? Wishing to express confidence in the fulfillment of the promised return Mark (followed by Matthew) hastens to add: "But of that day or hour no one knows, not even the angels in heaven, nor the Son, but the Father" (Mark 13:32, cf. Matthew 24:36). The inclusion of this verse seeks to halt speculation about when the end would occur. Nevertheless, the authors of Mark and Matthew respectively still expected the *parousia*, the second coming, before that generation died out, although the very writing of the Gospels implies a growing awareness that Jesus was not coming back as quickly as promised.

Jesus' vain promise to return quickly and his followers' vain hopes are both expressed in Revelation: "He who testifies of these things says: 'Yes, I am coming quickly.' Amen. Come, Lord Jesus" (Revelation 22:20). But the truth is that Jesus is never coming back.

Revelation declares that "the revelation of Jesus Christ ... must shortly take place" (1:1), that is, sometime around the end of the first century C.E. — not *now*, so many years later. One New Testament author expressed the expectation succinctly: "The end of all things is at hand [literally "has come near"]" (1 Peter 4:7). Indeed, in Revelation 22:7, 12 the subject of verse 13 (*the Alpha and the Omega*) says he is "coming quickly." The contexts in which the word *tacheos* (*"briefly* i.e. [in time] *speedily*, or [in manner] *rapidly*: - hastily, quickly, shortly, soon, suddenly)[1] is used in Revelation show that an imminent sudden return of Jesus was expected by its author. The earthly concept of time, that is, the speeds of everyday life are too slow in the divine sense of distance and duration. The psalmist expressed this in saying that to God, a thousand years is like an earthly day that has already passed (Psalms 90:4). The concept, *a fleeting moment for God*, considers time in eternal terms. Man cannot relate to a day of a thousand years; but he can relate to one of twenty-four hours. As a result, "shortly" used as a promised time interval to humans must be understood in its simplest earthly definition as occurring quickly in the near future or it is used deceptively. But, Jesus did not come back "shortly," within the timeframe designated by the Book of Revelation itself, this visionary experience (1:2, 22:8) is either false prophecy or the text cannot be speaking about Jesus in any form.

A prophecy unfulfilled

As we have seen, it is claimed that Jesus prophesied that certain unspecified individuals would not die until they would see either "the Son of Man coming in his kingdom" (Matthew 16:28), or "see the kingdom of God after it has come with power" (Mark 9:1), or "see the kingdom of God" (Luke 9:27). Jesus, addressing his disciples "privately" (Mark 13:3, Matthew 24:3) listed what was going to happen before his return. He then added, "Then shall they deliver you up to be afflicted and shall kill you and you shall be hated of all nations for my name's sake" (Matthew 24:9). Concerning this, Mark's version adds, "he that shall endure to the end, the same shall be saved" (Mark 13:13). Thus, it appears from this last remark that at least some of the disciples would survive and be present to witness the second coming and the end of time. The Synoptic Gospels, while in basic agreement on the wording of the first part of their respective verses differ, as indicated, on the wording of the second part. Mark is the most informative. It reads in the full literal verse: "Truly I say to you, there are some of those who are standing here who will not taste death at all until they see the kingdom of God having come [that is, after it has come] with power" (Mark 9:1). Apparently, the early Christian community was convinced of the imminent return of Jesus, as the Messiah, and the inauguration of the kingdom of God.

Christians, recognizing that fulfillment has not occurred, have sought to explain this failure by referring to the alleged transfiguration episode which follows, in the Synoptic Gospels, immediately after Jesus' prophecy. The assumption is made that the alleged transfiguration occurred directly after the prophecy. However, events recorded in the Gospels are not necessarily in the historic order in which they allegedly took place. Their present location in the Gospel narratives results from the work of a compiler seeking to make order out of the various unrelated sayings and events attributed to Jesus.

Attempting to explain away Jesus' failure

It is alleged that Jesus was not announcing the coming of his kingdom before all his contemporaries died, but a special revelation to certain of his disciples (Peter, James, and John). Jesus, then, was not announcing that certain people then living would see his return, but that some then living would see him in his "glory." For example, some Christians have said concerning Matthew 16:28 (see also Mark 9:1 and Luke 9:27): *"see the Son of Man coming in his kingdom"* that this was fulfilled when the disciples witnessed the transfiguration, that is, transformation (Matthew 17:1-8), which it is said is supposedly a miniature preview of the kingdom, with Jesus appearing in a state of glory.

The transfiguration supposedly gave the three disciples a miniature preview of Jesus' future exaltation and the coming kingdom. A miniature preview may serve as an illustration of an event, but is not the event itself. Mark 9:1 speaks of an actual event which, when it arrives, is to come with power, that is, something provided or endowed with unmistakable power. Those who are to live to see the fulfillment of the prophecy are not to die *until after* they see the actual kingdom of God arriving with power. These individuals who Jesus prophesied would not die until they would see the kingdom of God were told that they would be alive to see it *after* it had *already* come to power. A preview or glimpse of what the kingdom of God will be like would not fulfill the prophecy to keep certain individuals alive *"until* they see the kingdom of God having come with power." The phrase "having come with power" is pictured as a past event showing they are to still be alive "after it has come to power." The alleged transfiguration episode cannot be viewed as fulfilling the major promise of the prophecy that "there are some of those who are standing here who will not taste death at all until they see the kingdom of God having come with power." As we see, according to Mark, those referred to were to remain alive to see the kingdom of God not just in miniature preview, or early formation, but in its full intensity *"after* it has come with power," that is, having already come. This specific promise was not fulfilled.

Even if one considers the alleged transfiguration episode as a glimpse of the future kingdom of God, it still could never be the actual fulfillment of Mark 9:1. The phrase "until they see the kingdom of God having come with power" refers to the nature of the kingdom after it has come to fruition. At that time, the kingdom will manifest itself to appear actually endowed with supernatural power. Thus, Mark specifically describes an event, which is to occur after the kingdom of God has arrived in all its power and intensity not Jesus either before or after the alleged resurrection. What is alleged to have been shown at the transfiguration was a preview of things to come. It was not the actual event of the coming kingdom itself nor was it after the kingdom of God had already come with power. The specific moment following the arrival of the kingdom of God, when they are to see the coming kingdom arrive in all of its intensity, defines the time frame in which the prophecy of Mark's Jesus had to take place (not a so-called preview of things to come).

The very definition of the expression "kingdom of God" nullifies any connection between Mark 9:1 and the alleged transfiguration episode. No one definition can fully express the meaning of the phrase "kingdom of God." It refers to God's rule, God's sovereignty, God's will, the divine activity in the affairs of men and, in turn, their acceptance of His divine will. The alleged temporary transformation of Jesus, as a preview to his supposed future exaltation, does not provide a basis for contending the transfiguration came at that time endowed with power. If the purpose of the transfiguration episode is to represent Jesus' alleged future exaltation and power, that would still have nothing to do with Mark 9:1 despite the proximity of the verses to each other. Mark 9:1 not only signifies an expectation of the actual kingdom of God's arrival, not a facsimile, but indicates, as well, the time of the visual perception of that actual kingdom by those involved in the prophecy. The time limitation cited for the arrival of the kingdom of God endowed with actual power is before certain individuals, being addressed in the text, would die. It shows that the fulfillment of Jesus' prophecy is not to be found in some weak miniature representation of the kingdom of God. Matthew 16:28, Luke 9:27 and Mark 9:1 must be considered independently of the alleged transfiguration episode. Linkage of the two episodes is a desperate attempt to explain Jesus' statement, which was not fulfilled in the lifetime of those who heard him. Jesus' promise to his contemporaries must be taken as one more unfulfilled prophecy on his part. The respective proximity of these verses to the alleged transfiguration episode is of no consequence in understanding what was promised in this unfulfilled prophecy. Indeed, Paul and the respective authors of Hebrews and Revelation recount earlier traditions handed down before the Gospels were written and they confirm the promise and expectation of a quick return of Jesus *in their own day*.

Too little too late

Jesus never returned as promised! Why not blame the Jews? Indeed, some Christians say Jesus will not return until the Jewish people believe in him. They refer to Matthew's Jesus saying to a group of Jews: "For I tell you, you will not see my face until you say, 'Blessed is he who comes in the name of the Lord'" (Matthew 23:39). There you have it folks, Jesus can only come back if the Jews believe in him. The Jews have not cooperated! Despite all the violent and vile coercion and the missionary pretense and propaganda directed at them they have not succumbed to the pressure. The dubious result has been that the world has not been able to *enjoy* the malevolent return of Jesus to consign all those who do not believe in him to eternal damnation. Didn't Jesus know that the Jews would obstruct his plans when he promised a quick return to his then contemporaries?

As we have observed, the New Testament is filled with verses promising that Jesus is returning *soon* and *quickly* to that first century C.E. generation. Obviously, this expectation never occurred. It is not only that Jesus promised to make a quick return, his followers expected that return. With all the excuses Christians come up with to "explain" why the *second coming* never happened and their putting on of a *happy face* to show their enthusiastic faith in the imminent *expectation* of that return that never comes the question to ask Christian missionaries and wannabe missionaries is: How's that working out for you after 2000 years?

Did Jesus' first century C.E. followers expect his imminent return, as he promised, Jewish rejection or not?

- But this I say, brethren, the time has been shortened, so that from now on both those who have wives should be as though they had none, and those who weep, as though they did not weep; and those who rejoice, as though they did not rejoice; and those who buy, as though they did not possess; and those who use the world, as though they did not make full use of it; for the form of this world is passing away. (1 Corinthians 7:29-31)

- Let your moderation be known to all men. The Lord is at hand. (Philippians 4:5)

- You too be patient; strengthen your hearts, for the coming of the Lord is at hand. (James 5:8)

- The end of all things is at hand. (1 Peter 4:7)

- Children, it is the last hour; and just as you heard that antichrist is coming, even now many antichrists have arisen; from this we know that it is the last hour. (1 John 2:18)

- The revelation of Jesus Christ, which God gave him to show to his bond-servants, the things which must shortly take place … and heed the things that are written in it; for the time is near. (Revelation 1:1-3)

- I am coming quickly; hold fast what you have, in order that no one take your crown. (Revelation 3:11)

- And he said to me, "These words are faithful and true"; and the Lord, the God of the spirits of the prophets, sent His angel to show to His bond-servants the things which must shortly take place. And behold I am coming quickly." (Revelation 22:6-7)

- And he said to me, "Do not seal up the words of the prophecy of this book, for the time is near … Behold, I am coming quickly … to render to every man according to what he has done." (Revelation 22:10-12)

- He who testifies to these things says, "Yes, I am coming quickly." Amen, come Lord Jesus. (Revelation 22:20)

The passage of time has shown that the Jesus of the New Testament, the sole Jesus we have any information about, was wrong in predicting his quick return. No amount of Christian excuses will change that fact.

[1] See James Strong, *Strong's Exhaustive Concordance of the Bible*, Nashville: Abingdon, 1978, 5030.

Chapter 61

THE TRIUMPHAL ENTRY
(Matthew 21:8-11; Mark 11:8-11; Luke 19:36-38, John 12:12-13)

The Synoptic Gospels relate a tale of Jesus' triumphal entry into Jerusalem a few days prior to his crucifixion. They write:

> And most of the multitude spread their garments in the road, and others were cutting branches from the trees, and spreading them in the road. And the multitudes going before him and those who followed were crying out saying: "Hosanna to the son of David; blessed is he who comes in the name of the Lord; hosanna in the highest!" And when he had entered Jerusalem, all the city was stirred, saying: "Who is this?" And the multitudes were saying: "This is the prophet Jesus, from Nazareth in Galilee." (Matthew 21:8-11)

> And many spread their garments in the road, and others cut leafy branches from the fields. And those who went before and those who followed were crying out: "Hosanna! Blessed is he who comes in the name of the Lord; blessed is the coming kingdom of our father David; hosanna in the highest!" (Mark 11:8-11)

> And as he was going, they were spreading their garments in the road. As he was now getting near the descent of the Mount of Olives the whole multitude of the disciples started to rejoice and praise God with a loud voice for all the powerful works they had seen, saying: "Blessed is the King who comes in the name of the Lord; peace in heaven and glory in the highest!" (Luke 19:36-38)

The Gospel of John places the "triumphal entry" story at the beginning of Jesus' public career.

> On the next day the great multitude who had come to the feast, when they heard that Jesus was coming to Jerusalem, took the branches of the palm trees, and went out to meet him, and began to cry out: "Hosanna! Blessed is he who comes in the name of the Lord, and

the King of Israel." (John 12:12-13)

According to the account of the events surrounding the so-called triumphal entry found in the Synoptic Gospels, Jesus proceeded directly to Jerusalem (Matthew 21:1, Mark 11:1, Luke 19:28-29). Mark relates that he arrived late in the afternoon at which time he briefly entered the Temple compound and then went to Bethany, where he stayed overnight (Mark 11:11-12). It is on his return to Jerusalem the next day, Mark claims, that Jesus makes his assault on the Temple. However, according to Matthew and Luke, Jesus attacked the Temple immediately following his triumphal entry into Jerusalem, not the next day. John says the Temple attack occurred on a completely different date (cf. John 2:13-16 with John 12:12-13).

Matthew writes that when Jesus entered Jerusalem, the entire populace became excited (Matthew 21:8-11). The date of this alleged event was just a few days prior to Passover. This is the festival of freedom from bondage a highly volatile time of year in Roman occupied Jerusalem. As a result, the Romans were ever vigilant for any signs of insurrection. Therefore, they would have taken seriously a messianic procession shouting: "Hosanna to the son of David; blessed is he who comes in the name of the Lord; hosanna in the highest!" (Matthew 21:9; see also Mark 11:9-10, Luke 19:38, John 12:13). Nevertheless, the Gospels would have us believe that the Romans did not respond to Jesus' violent actions in the Temple. Jesus' actions and the cries of messianic fervor expressed by the crowds watching the procession, as described in the Gospels, would be seen by the Romans as nothing less than a call to revolt against Roman governance of Judea. According to Luke, it was Jesus' disciples who initiated this messianic demonstration: "As he was now getting near the descent of the Mount of Olives the whole multitude of the disciples started to rejoice and praise God with a loud voice for all the powerful works they had seen" (Luke 19:37). Therefore, this demonstration was not a spontaneous action by the common people, but a carefully orchestrated move by Jesus and his disciples calculated to promote religio-political agitation among the masses. In the passion accounts, the Gospels present Jesus as innocent as a lamb before Pilate.

Pilate, however, is portrayed as unable to withstand the pressure placed on him by the Jewish leadership to condemn the guiltless Jesus: "For he knew that because of envy they had handed him over" (Matthew 27:18, Mark 15:10). It is said that he wanted to release Jesus (Luke 23:20, John 19:12). Could this be true? Let us consider that it was Pilate's responsibility to be aware of any and all incidents which might lead to insurrection. He must have been informed of the open messianic display and tumult instigated by Jesus' triumphal entry into the city. Pilate would, thus, have considered Jesus a rebel deserving of death as a political criminal and would have dealt with him accordingly.

Not once, in the several inquiries at which Jesus is alleged to have been examined is there any mention by his enemies of his pretentious entry into Jerusalem. Surely, had the incident occurred it would have been used against him at one inquiry or another. Apparently, the Gospel authors felt it was best not to mention the incident at Jesus' trial before Pilate, as it constituted a provocation against Roman governance, and they wished to portray Jesus as a peaceful, nonviolent person who was not guilty of any wrongdoing.

Chapter 62

THE SPILLING OF RIGHTEOUS BLOOD
(Matthew 23:35)

The author of Matthew presents a statement said to have been uttered by Jesus, whose content is both incorrect and immoral. He writes:

> ...so that there may come upon you all the righteous blood poured out upon the earth from the blood of righteous Abel to the blood of Zechariah son of Barachiah, whom you murdered between the Temple and the altar. (Matthew 23:35; see also Luke 11:51)

The Jewish Scriptures relate that Zechariah, the son of Jehoiada the priest, was slain by the altar (2 Chronicles 24:20-21). There is no way that one can reconcile the person of Zechariah, the son of Jehoiada the priest, and Zechariah, the son of Berechiah (Zechariah 1:1). Zechariah, the son of Jehoiada, was slain during the reign of Joash, king of Judah (ca. 840 B.C.E.). The prophet, the son of Berechiah, did not prophesy until the second year of Darius (ca. 520), which followed the Babylonian captivity. There is no reason to think that Zechariah, the son of Berechiah, the son of Iddo, died in the manner described. The Jewish Scriptures do not indicate when, where, or how Zechariah, the son of Berechiah, died. However, it is obvious that the death described by the author of Matthew was suffered by another person, Zechariah, the son of Jehoiada.

Matthew, chapter 23, presents a stark illustration of its author's animosity toward the Jewish people. Matthew's Jesus begins with a scathing denunciation of the scribes and Pharisees and concludes with the horrendous burden of guilt he imposes upon the entire Jewish people. They are now to be considered responsible for all the shedding of righteous blood from the very dawn of humanity. In verses 1 through 33, Matthew's Jesus is attacking the scribes and Pharisees. They are called: hypocrites" and "blind guides" seven times. He then castigates them as "serpents," "brood of vipers," and "sons of hell." These imprecations are intended to counter any thought that the Pharisees are virtuous, sincere, God-fearing people and not Satan's earthly representatives. They are corrupt murders, uninterested in justice and mercy. The Pharisees are indiscriminately accused of being the "sons of those who murdered the prophets" (verse 31). That is, their Jewish ancestors, before there was even a Pharisaic party, killed the prophets, and they, despite all appearances to the contrary, are no better.

The context shows that Matthew's Jesus ends his direct attack on the scribes and Pharisees by declaring: "You serpents, you brood of vipers, how shall you escape the judgment of hell?" (Matthew 23:33). This is a transitional condemnation leading to the author of Matthew's primary focus of attack. Beginning at verses 34-35, the evangelist's attack is no longer directed specifically at the scribes and Pharisees. A sudden, subtle shift takes place: "Wherefore, behold, I send to you prophets and wise men, and scribes: and some of them you shall kill and crucify; and some of them you shall scourge in your synagogues, and persecute from city to city; that upon you may come all the righteous blood shed upon the earth, from the blood of righteous Abel to the blood of Zechariah son of Barachiah, whom you slew between the Temple and the altar."

A superficial reading of the text may lead one to believe verses 34-35 refer to the scribes and Pharisees, but this is not so. Who is actually being condemned and is to suffer for spilling "all the righteous blood," is clearly revealed in the verse (36) that follows immediately after the condemnation: "Truly I say to you, all these things shall come upon this generation." Matthew's Jesus is not speaking of the scribes and Pharisees alone but of the entire Jewish people (see also Luke 11:49-51). They became responsible for "all the righteous blood shed upon the earth," especially for the righteous blood of Jesus. Moreover, the phrase "this generation" does not confine punishment to Jesus' Jewish contemporaries alone. This is seen by the inclusion of all future Jewish generations in the statement: "His blood be upon us and our children" (Matthew 27:25).

Genea, commonly translated "generation," refers to "the whole multitude of men living at the same time … [and is] used especially of the Jewish race living at one and the same period."[1] The implication of translating *genea* incorrectly as "people," or "race" in conformity with some Christian commentators has contributed to Christian anti-Jewish feelings throughout the centuries. "Truly I say to you, all these things shall come upon this generation" (Matthew 23:36) limits the condemnation to the entire Jewish people of Jesus' day. Matthew's Jesus denounces his Jewish contemporaries as a "wicked and adulterous generation" (Matthew 16:4) and as a "faithless and perverse generation" (Matthew 17:17). By substituting "people" or "race" for "generation," these phrases become a condemnation of the Jewish people of *all* generations. Thus, "… all these things shall come upon this people" who are "a wicked and adulterous people" and are also a "faithless and perverse race." No time limitation is found in this rendering of Matthew 23:36. Undoubtedly, the author of Matthew believed in this eternal condemnation of the Jews, but he does not say it explicitly in the immediate context. In the Gospel of Matthew, the punishment for the murdered righteous, going back to the very dawn of history, is not confined to that one generation of Jews, but applies to both previous and future generations as well. However, the author's condemnation of *all* future generations of Jews who reject Jesus is implicit in verse 36. It is explicitly found in Matthew 27:25: "And all the people answered and said, 'His blood be upon us and our children!'" Verse 36 acts to bridge the accusation and connect previous, present and future generations together in being guilty of murder, especially that of Jesus.

The Gospel of Matthew has Jesus turn his wrath against "this generation," that is, the nation as a whole. But what is the nation of Israel being condemned for — individual sins, national sins, or sinful acts committed by part of the nation which reflect upon and must be borne by the whole nation? The astounding answer is none of these! Matthew's Jesus condemns the Jewish people for sins in which Israel had not participated. Matthew's Jesus goes so far as to condemn the entire nation for murders that were committed even before the birth of Abraham, the father of the Jewish people. According to Jesus, the Jewish people are to suffer for the murder of every righteous victim since the dawn of history. For Matthew's Jesus, it does not matter who murdered the righteous the Jews are still held accountable. All the Jewish people who did not follow Jesus are meant, not just factions within the nation. This is emphasized when Jesus couples his remarks with a characterization of their spiritual center as a place of murder: "O Jerusalem, Jerusalem, who kills the prophets and stones those who are sent to her![2] ... Behold, your house is being left to you desolate" (Matthew 23:37-38; see also Luke 13:34-35). Jerusalem is not the spiritual center of the Pharisees alone, but is representative of all Jews and their religious tradition. Thus, except for those Jews who accept Jesus, the Jews are considered inherently evil.

Some Christians say that the phrase "this generation," used by both Mathew's and Luke's Jesus, meant only the scribes and Pharisees and not all Jews. But, this does not rectify the basic injustice of the libel. Was the Gospels' Jesus justified in blaming the scribes and Pharisees, for wrongs neither they nor their ancestors committed? It is simply unreasonable to hold either the scribes or the Pharisees or their ancestors responsible for all the murders of the righteous committed from Abel onwards. The fact is that it is an unjust condemnation whether applied to the entire nation or to particular groups within the nation, such as the scribes and Pharisees. But, as we have seen, the author of Matthew had an even sinister intention. Compounding the injustice, the condemnation by Matthew's Jesus was not meant to refer merely to past generations or to "this generation," but to *all* future Jewish generations as well. There is no reason to think that the "guilt" of "this generation" for the spilling of the blood of all the righteous of the world from even before Abraham would be confined to "this generation" alone. Indeed, how much more so did the author believe was the guilt of future Jewish generations for the death of Jesus? In contrast, neither God nor His prophets ever explicitly or implicitly fault Israel in such an unreasonably sweeping way as Matthew's Jesus. Is it any wonder that Jews have been blamed for the world's ills when Jesus is said to have condemned them for "all the righteous blood shed upon the earth," since the slaying of Abel? Abel was slain by his brother, Cain (Genesis 4:8), before the Jewish people came into existence. Why are the Jews to bear responsibility for this act? Placing the responsibility for the death of Abel on the Jews puts them into the role of Cain despised by all creation.

374

[1] Joseph Henry Thayer, *A Greek-English Lexicon of the New Testament*, Grand Rapids, Mich.: Zondervan, 1979, p. 112.

[2] Very few instances of the killing of prophets are found in the Jewish Scriptures.

Chapter 63

THE JUDAS FICTION
(Matthew 26:14-15; 27:3-10, Acts 1:18-19)

The price of betrayal

The Gospel of Matthew is the only New Testament source that mentions the exact sum allegedly paid for the betrayal of Jesus. Its author writes:

> Then one of the twelve, the one called Judas Iscariot, went to the chief priests and said: "What are you willing to give me to deliver him to you?" And they paid him thirty silver pieces. (Matthew 26:14-15)

The giving of a supposed precise sum paid for the betrayal conforms to an expected feature of this Gospel. Its author makes a specific effort to show a detailed interconnection between the life of Jesus and biblical prophecy. In so doing he often takes a verse out of context and uses it as if it literally finds fulfillment in the events he describes. In the passage under study, the author of Matthew takes a verse out of context that is found in the Book of Zechariah. He uses it as if it was a prophecy that foretold the payment Judas was to receive for betraying Jesus to his enemies. The prophet says: "And I said to them: 'If it seems right to you, give me my wages, but if not, keep them.' So they weighed for my wages thirty pieces of silver" (Zechariah 11:12). Zechariah speaks here of himself. As the divinely appointed shepherd of Israel, he asks his wages of the people, who then pay him this paltry sum. There is no reason to connect this verse with Judas Iscariot. Moreover, this meager sum of thirty silver pieces would not have been enough for Judas to buy a field, as reported in Acts 1:18. The author of Matthew is once more claiming literal fulfillment where none exists. This time he enhances his story line by introducing a seemingly biblical text into his narrative. In this instance, he makes use of the thirty pieces of silver mentioned in Zechariah 11:13.

Judas Iscariot: A tale of two endings

Matthew continues his description of events following the death of Judas:

> Then when Judas, who had betrayed him [Jesus], saw that he had been condemned, felt remorse and returned the thirty silver pieces to the chief priests and the elders, saying: "I sinned when I betrayed righteous blood." But they said: "What is that to us? See to that yourself!" And he threw the silver pieces into the Temple and departed, and went off and hanged himself. And the chief priests took the pieces of silver and said, "It is not lawful to put them into the Temple treasury, since it is the price of blood." And they [the chief priests and the elders] counseled together and with the money bought the potter's field as a burial place for strangers. Therefore that field has been called the Field of Blood to this day. Then that which was spoken through Jeremiah the prophet was fulfilled, saying: "And they took the thirty silver pieces, the price of the one whose price had been set by the sons of Israel, and they gave them for the potter's field, as the Lord directed me." (Matthew 27:3-10)

Judas Iscariot is said to have repented his nefarious act. In his remorse, it is related, he attempted to return the thirty silver pieces paid for his betrayal. But the Jewish officials refused to accept the money. He then threw the silver pieces into the Temple, left the area, and hanged himself. The priests used the money to purchase a burial place for strangers: "Therefore," the author relates, "that field has been called the Field of Blood to this day."

However, a tradition totally at variance with that given by Matthew for the naming of the field is provided by the author of Acts:

> This man [Judas] acquired a field with the wages of his wickedness, and falling headlong he burst open in the middle, and all his intestines were poured out. And it became known to all the inhabitants of Jerusalem, so that in their own language that field was called Akeldama, that is, Field of Blood. (Acts 1:18-19).

In this passage, the field did not receive its name because the priests bought it for use as a burial ground for strangers, but rather because Judas met a bloody death there. According to the tradition found in Acts, Judas showed no remorse for his deed, did not attempt to return the silver pieces, and did not commit suicide. Instead, he used the betrayal money to purchase some land. His death is attributed to a violent fall.

But, Matthew's version of events is flawed still further. His alleged citation attributed to Jeremiah does not exist in the Book of Jeremiah or anywhere else in the Jewish Scriptures. It is Matthew's own creation, probably based on Zechariah 11:12-13, not Jeremiah. Jeremiah mentions a potter and his clay (18:1-6) and a field (32:6-9). But, the biblical references have no bearing on the erroneous citation. Furthermore, the author of Matthew, ever mindful to make the Jewish people responsible for the death of Jesus makes a subtle change in the text he takes from Zechariah. Matthew rephrases Zechariah's words. The prophet states: "So they weighed for my wages thirty pieces of silver. And the Lord said to me: 'Cast it into the treasury, the price that I was prized at of them.' And I took the thirty pieces of silver, and cast them into the treasury, in the house of the Lord" (Zechariah 11:12-13). Matthew's text (27:9) reads, "the price that I was prized of the sons of Israel." He changes Zechariah's unidentified "them" into *the sons of Israel*, that is, not unspecific individuals or "the chief priests and the elders" but "the Jews," as a specific group. This pseudo-biblical prophecy of a passion event continues Matthew's theme of placing culpability for Jesus' death upon *all* Jews.

There is no honest relationship between the passages found in Jeremiah and Zechariah and the passage found in the Gospel of Matthew. The biblical material from which Matthew crafts his counterfeit citation attributed to Jeremiah and the passage found in his Gospel are mutually exclusive, not parallel as he would have us believe.

Chapter 64

WAS THE LAST SUPPER A SEDER?
(Matthew 26:17-30, Mark 14:12-26, Luke 22:7-39, John 13:1-18:1)

The meal that never was

The Synoptic Gospels state that Jesus arranged to eat his last meal, commonly called The Last Supper, with the twelve apostles (Matthew 26:17-20, Mark 14:12-17, Luke 22:7-14). They present this last meal as a seder although no Gospel ever mentions that a lamb (Exodus 12:26-27) or bitter herbs (Exodus 12:8, Numbers 9:11) was part of the meal. The earliest New Testament reference to this meal is by Paul (1 Corinthians 11:23-25). He makes no connection between the last meal and the seder. The Synoptic Gospels describe only the Last Supper in a Passover context, never giving any indication in their respective accounts of the arrest, trials, crucifixion, death, and burial of Jesus that the day following this meal is Passover. In the context of an alleged Passover prisoner release custom the phrase "at a/ the feast" appears (Matthew 27:15, Mark 15:6, and the interpolation Luke 23:17) but gives no indication of whether this was to take place before or during the festival. The phrase may refer to any day during the festival and does not specify any one day in particular. Mark, the earliest of the Synoptic Gospels, turned the meal into a seder with the comment: "And on the first day of Unleavened Bread, when the Passover [lamb] was being sacrificed, his disciples said to him [Jesus], 'Where do you want us to go and prepare for you to eat the Passover?'" (Mark 14:12). From the sequence of events presented in the Gospels it would appear that the last meal occurred on a Thursday evening prior to Jesus' execution the next afternoon (that is, either on 14 Nisan or 15 Nisan).[1]

While the Synoptic Gospels portray the Last Supper as a Passover seder (15 Nisan), John's Gospel dates the Last Supper a day earlier (14 Nisan), making it a regular meal. The author of John has no intention of equating the Last Supper with the seder. At the beginning of his

Gospel, he has John the Baptist identify Jesus as the "lamb of God" (John 1:29). He now depicts Jesus as dying on the afternoon before the beginning of the Passover festival, at the same time as the lambs were being sacrificed in the Temple: "Now it was the day of preparation for the Passover; it was about the sixth hour (John 19:14).[2]

Apparently, either the Synoptic Gospels wanted to turn Jesus' last meal into a seder or John wanted to link Jesus' death with the slaughter of the paschal lambs. In any case, although all the Gospels agree that Jesus' death occurred on a Friday, neither date or only one date can be historically correct. From the Gospels' respective accounts we cannot know when Jesus died — the afternoon before Passover or the afternoon of the first day of the festival. It is also possible that Jesus' execution may have taken place on another day (Mark 14:1-2). Acceptance of one version over the other does not solve the issue of the historicity of either one. That is, there is no question of the historical existence of conflicting traditions but there is a question as to the historicity of the events they portray.

With a total disregard for consistency or scholarship, Christians accept the Synoptic Gospels' timing for the paschal meal but adopt the position held by the author of John that Jesus was crucified on the eve of Passover. The author of John does not connect the Last Supper with the seder. According to his sequence of events, the seder would have to follow the daylight hours during which Jesus was crucified. He writes:

> They [the priests] did not enter into the judgment hall in order that they might not be defiled, but might eat the Passover. (John 18:28)

> Now it [the day of the crucifixion] was the day of preparation for the Passover. (John 19:14)

These verses show that, according to John's chronology, Jesus was crucified on the afternoon preceding the seder. In that case, the Last Supper took place on the evening prior to that of the seder.

The author of John provides collateral evidence militating against the acceptance of the Synoptic Gospel's claim that the Last Supper was a seder. If this meal was indeed a seder we must then conclude that Jesus and his disciples did not observe the Torah injunctions against transacting business on a festival (Exodus 12:16; Leviticus 23:6-7; Numbers 28:17-18; Nehemiah 10:30, 32). Observant Jews would never handle money or conduct business transactions on a festival, yet John states: "For some [of the disciples] were supposing, because Judas had the money box, that Jesus was saying to him: 'Buy the things we have need of for the feast'; or else, that he should give something to the poor" (John 13:29). The disciples thought Judas had been instructed by Jesus to go and purchase things needed for the feast, but were not startled by what they presumed to be his order. Are we to assume that they were not observant of the Torah regulations, and that on the very seder night their leader, Jesus, was capable of ordering one of them to violate a fundamental commandment of God? How could the disciples even think that he who came to fulfill all the Law (Matthew 5:17) would ask anyone to violate that very Law? Furthermore, they must have known that Judas would find no shops open. Preparations for the paschal meal and the Passover festival, in general, would have been made prior to the holiday and not during the ceremony itself.

Did Judas, on Jesus' orders, go out to give charity? Some disciples thought this possible. But no observant Jew would give money, or ask someone to give it, on a festival. We must presume either that this was not the seder for which things may still need to be bought or that Jesus, lacking any regard for the Law of God, was capable of sending Judas out on an errand which violated that Law (cf. Nehemiah 10:32, 13:15-22). Under such circumstances Jesus could not be the Messiah.

Excuses, excuses and more excuses

There are those who contend that according to the lunar calendar the Last Supper was on a Tuesday night and that Jesus was crucified on Wednesday, the following day. If this were true why did the women wait until Sunday morning to come to the tomb rather than come on Thursday? A Wednesday crucifixion would also mean that the triumphal entry into Jerusalem, with Jesus riding a donkey, cutting of branches and business being transacted in the Temple, occurred on a Sabbath (John 2:1, 12). These are all Sabbath violations - and simply would not have occurred.

Another theory maintains that Jesus simply decided to celebrate the seder a day earlier, that is, on Thursday night (as in the Gospel of John), knowing that he would die prior to its proper celebration on the following night. There is nothing to support this reasoning except the realization of non-fulfillment.

There is also another attempt at harmonizing the different Gospel stories. John 18:28 says that the reason the priests did not enter the praetorium was "in order that they might not be defiled, but might eat the Passover." In light of John 19:14, "Now it was the day of preparation for the Passover," it is evident that, no matter why John reasons the priests did not enter Pilate's palace, the incident is supposed to have occurred prior to the paschal meal. John 19:14 leaves no doubt that John's Jesus was crucified on "the day of preparation for the Passover," that is, the afternoon prior to the paschal meal.

Some Christians argue that the Passover offering referred to in John 18:28 that the priests were concerned about is the chagigah offering of 15 Nisan. The chagigah of the fifteenth of Nisan could be eaten for two days and a night. This sacrifice in honor of the festival was to be offered on the first day of the Festival. However, if one did not do so, it could be offered during the intermediate days of Passover or the last day of the festival.[3] Consequently, these particular priests would still have occasion to fulfill their priestly duties. There is no excuse to cover up the simple fact that the claim that the Last Supper was a seder is to be seriously doubted.

---

[1] The days of the Jewish calendar run from the evening of one day to the evening of the next.

[2] According to the author of John, the crucifixion took place sometime after the "sixth hour" (John 19:14 ff.).

[3] Mishnah Chagigah 1:6.

Chapter 65

WAS JESUS A WILLING SACRIFICE FOR MANKIND'S SINS?
(Matthew 26:39, Mark 14:35-36, Luke 22:41-44)

According to the New Testament, Jesus came into the world expressly to offer himself as a willing sacrifice to atone for mankind's sins. Yet, he hesitates and prays for a reversal of the fate preordained for him. The Gospel narrative portrays Jesus' state of mind just a few hours before his crucifixion: "And going a little way forward, he fell upon his face praying and saying: 'My Father, if it is possible, let this cup pass from me. Yet, not as I will, but as you will'" (Matthew 26:39; see also Mark 14:35-36, Luke 22:41-44).

It is related that Jesus, supposedly one-third of the triune deity, needed an angel to strengthen him: "Then an angel from heaven appeared to him, strengthening him" (Luke 22:43). With his alleged divine pre-knowledge of why he had to die and of the rewards that would be his for obeying God, or himself, (Philippians 2:9-11), what reassurance did he need from a mere angel? Did he have to be reminded of his role and its rewards? Why the feelings of despair and failure? Jesus was in a state of agony (Luke 22:44) in which he tearfully cried out ("with loud crying and tears"), not for the sins of the world, but for himself to be saved from death (Hebrews 5:7). Jesus' alleged exclamation: "Yet, not as I will but as you will," shows that had it been his choice, he would not have undergone execution.

Although he seems to have submitted to God's will, in his final moments of life Jesus is said to have expressed feelings of frustration and abandonment (Matthew 27:46, Mark 15:34; cf. Luke 23:46, John 19:30) using the psalmist's words: "My God my God, why have you forsaken me?" (Psalm 22:2). In that last critical moment, Jesus who some say was an angelic being and others part of a triune deity expressed that he did not wish to be a sacrifice and die for the sins of mankind.

Chapter 66

THE TRIAL OF JESUS

(Matthew 26:57-27:24, Mark 14:53-15:15, Luke 22:54-23:24, John 18:12-19:16)

The Gospels' accounts of the trial proceedings against Jesus present the reader with four varied versions of those crucial events. While certain features of their respective narratives are similar, there are enough irreconcilable differences to question the veracity of their accounts.

Here are some questions that must be answered before one can even begin to consider the accounts of the trial proceedings as having any validity.

- Was Jesus, after his arrest in Gethsemane, first taken to the then high priest Caiaphas (so identified in Matthew 26:3, John 18:13), as indicated in Mark 14:53 and Luke 22:54, or was he first taken to Caiaphas' son-in-law, Annas, as John states (John 18:13)?

- Was there a Jewish trial before the entire Sanhedrin, as in Matthew 26:59 and Mark 14:55, or merely an inquiry by the Sanhedrin, as in Luke 22:66-71, or just private interrogations, first by Annas (John 18:13) and then by Caiaphas (John 18:24), as only John writes?

- Was there an additional morning meeting of the Sanhedrin convening expressly to confirm the decision of the night before, as in Matthew 27:1 and Mark 15:1, but which is not mentioned at all in either Luke or John? Is it not strange that in their respective narratives, Luke and John leave no time for this event to have occurred?

- Did the Jewish trial take place on the first night (Matthew 26:18-20, Mark 14:16-18, Luke 22:13-15) or morning (Luke 22:66) of Passover, as in the Synoptic Gospels or was it the day before Passover, as in John's Gospel (John 18:28, 19:14)?

- Are we to consider valid Luke's version, which has Pilate interrupt his own Roman trial proceedings to send Jesus to Herod Antipas, a Jew, for judgment (Luke 23:7)? Can one believe that Pilate would compromise his own power by sending Jesus to Herod Antipas, who, at that time, was not only himself subject to Rome but was still Pilate's enemy (Luke 23:12)?

- Did the witnesses testify that Jesus said "I am able to destroy this Temple" (Matthew 26:61) or "I will destroy this Temple made with hands" (Mark 14:58)? In other words, did Jesus claim, according to the accusations recorded by the Gospel authors, ability or clear intent?

- Did the high priest ask Jesus if he was the "Son of God" (Matthew 26:63, Luke 22:70) or the "Son of the Blessed" (Mark 14:61)?

- It is difficult to believe that Pilate, possessing enough military might to enforce any decision he desired, was compelled by a Jewish mob to order the execution of Jesus, whom he knew was innocent (Matthew 27:18, 20, 24; Mark 15:10, 14-15; Luke 23:14, 20, 24; John 19:12). We are told that he accepted the mob's demands for the release of a known rebel, Barabbas (Son of the Father), who had led an insurrection against Roman rule (Matthew 27:16, 20-21, 26; Mark 15:7, 15; Luke 23:18-19). If this was the case, Pilate had more to fear from the imperial wrath than from the Jewish accusation that if he released Jesus, he was not a friend of the emperor (John 19:12). Are we to believe the ludicrous situation the Gospels describe?

The factual discrepancies found in the various trial accounts produce a series of questions affecting the reliability of the Gospel narratives. We are confronted with a crucial New Testament event that is full of questionable information. But this is an ever-present Gospel phenomenon that is not confined to the trial episodes alone.

Chapter 67

HOW FALSE WERE THE "FALSE WITNESSES"?
(Matthew 26:59-61, Mark 14:55-59)

According to Mark, the Jewish religious authorities sought testimony that could condemn Jesus to death: "Now the chief priests and the whole Sanhedrin were seeking testimony against Jesus to put him to death, and they were not finding any" (Mark 14:55). Matthew inflames this allegation, claiming that the authorities deliberately sought false testimony: "Now the chief priests and the whole Sanhedrin were seeking false testimony against Jesus in order that they might put him to death" (Matthew 26:59). They then present their respective versions of the witnesses' testimony. Mark writes: "And some stood up and began to give false testimony against him, saying: 'We heard him say: "I will destroy this Temple made with hands and in three days I will build another not made with hands"'" (Mark 14:57-58). In his version, Matthew writes: "But later on two came and said: 'This man stated: "I am able to destroy this Temple of God and to rebuild it in three days"'" (Matthew 26:60-61). Matthew alters the statement, which the witnesses in Mark ascribe to Jesus. In his Gospel, the intention to destroy the Temple is now modified to one of ability to perform the act, that is, from "I will" to "I am able." Matthew also gives the exact number of witnesses as two, whereas Mark merely says "some" gave testimony.

Luke's Gospel omits completely the accusation that Jesus had threatened to destroy the Temple. According to him, Jesus was tried only on the charge of claiming to be the "Christ" or the "Son of God" (Luke 22:67-71). However, in Acts, attributed to Luke, Stephen is accused of saying that Jesus would destroy the Temple (Acts 6:14). John, writing much later, states that Jesus actually made a declaration quite similar to that which Mark and Matthew report as false testimony" "Destroy this Temple, and in three days I will raise it up" (John 2:19).

It is not surprising that Mark and Matthew do not agree on the exact wording of the testimony given by the witnesses. The fact is that rarely do these two Gospels use the same wording in describing their respective versions of events and quotations. As a result, it is impossible to say with certainty that the two witnesses definitely gave false testimony. Even these two Gospels cannot agree as to what the alleged false statements were supposed to have been. There is no reason to believe that the respective Gospels are recording what exactly the "false testimony" of the two witnesses was. While disagreeing with the wording in Mark, Matthew says there was no disagreement between the witnesses' testimonies (Matthew 26:60-62). What the witnesses testified to is in question. There is also the question of whether any of this took place or is just another fabrication to round out the already questionable trial episodes.

Added to the mix is the Gospel of John's informing us that there was a factual basis for the so-called "false testimony." As already mentioned, John quotes Jesus as saying: "Destroy this Temple, and in three days I will raise it up." This shows that according to John, there was a factual basis for the testimony (cf. Mark 13:2). The declaration by John's Jesus negates another accusation of "false witnesses," this time testifying as to hearsay evidence concerning Jesus bragging about destroying the Temple: "And they put forward false witnesses who said, 'This man [Stephen] incessantly speaks against this holy place and the Law. For we have heard him say that this Nazarene, Jesus, will destroy this place and alter the customs, which Moses handed down to us" (Acts 6:13-14).

One could never get the impression that there was a factual basis to the testimony from either Mark or Matthew. They do not mention Jesus as ever making such a statement. According to their description of the events, the witnesses devised the entire story. Yet from John we see not only that Jesus said something quite similar to the testimony, but, given the inconsistent manner in which Mark and Matthew transmit what was supposedly said there is a strong possibility that the witnesses may very well have quoted Jesus intent correctly. In actuality, it may be that it is the Gospel authors who distorted the record. One thing is certain. It suited Mark and Matthew to accuse the witnesses and the Sanhedrin of perversity.

In the final analysis, whether the evidence represents fact or fancy is not important. What is most significant is that nothing attributed by the witnesses to Jesus would have been considered blasphemous by a Jewish court. Perhaps his outburst was foolish and pretentious, but it was not one justifying his condemnation to death. Therefore, if there was any falsehood involved, it was on the part of Mark and Matthew seeking to condemn the Jewish leadership. It is likely that the inconsistencies in testimony are due to the prejudicial Gospel authors rather than to the witnesses. In principle, even John agrees with the witnesses that Jesus said he could rebuild the Temple after three days. Whether Jesus said: "I will" (according to Mark), "I am able" (according to Matthew), or "If you" (according to John), his declaration, in any form given, is merely an idle boast for which no one is liable to the death penalty. This testimony could never have been used to condemn Jesus. Having insufficient information as to what actually transpired in the time period that elapsed between the capture and the execution of Jesus, the Gospel authors fabricated a tale based on legendary material. This segment of their record cannot be accepted as historically accurate.

Oh, but wait! The Gospels' Jesus meant that after three days he would rise from the dead and it was to the temple of his body that he was referring. If so, then he was misleading his audience into believing something completely opposite from what he really meant. John's Jesus, speaking in a deceitful manner (cf. Isaiah 53:9) had declared: "Destroy this temple, and in three days I will raise it up" (John 2:19). The people were led to believe that he meant the Jerusalem Temple, but John says, "he was speaking of the temple of his body" (John 2:21). Jesus' own secret meaning was clearly hidden from those to whom he spoke. His audience did not infer that Jesus meant anything other than the Jerusalem Temple. The Gospels' Jesus was simply a deceiver.

Chapter 68

A RESURRECTION TALE
(Matthew 28:6-7, Mark 16:6, Luke 24:6, John 20:9)

Nobody saw what never happened

There are four often contradictory accounts of the alleged resurrection of Jesus provided by the respective Gospels. To explain this, it is said, the Gospel authors each saw the resurrection event from a different perspective. But this is incorrect. They could not see the resurrection event from different perspectives since they did not personally witness the supposed resurrection. In fact, nobody witnessed this supposed happening. Peter is alleged to have stated: "This Jesus God resurrected, of which we are all witnesses" (Acts 2:32), yet, not one witness is produced who actually saw the resurrection of Jesus.

The Gospel authors can only attest to an account they heard surrounding the body's disappearance. They had no direct knowledge of why it disappeared or what was the nature of its final disposition. They knew nothing more than that on Sunday morning it was claimed that the tomb was empty. They were not alone in their ignorance of the facts. There was no one who saw Jesus rise from the dead; all claims to that effect are hearsay. The disappearance of the body does not mean that there was a resurrection. The empty tomb explains nothing.

Matthew presents a typology from the Book of Jonah (Jonah 2:1, 1:17 in some versions) to support the claim that Jesus would rise on the third day. He cites Jesus as saying to the scribes and Pharisees: "For just as Jonah was three days and three nights in the belly of the sea monster, so will the Son of Man be three days and three nights in the heart of the earth" (Matthew 12:40). This typology allegedly foreshadows the burial and resurrection of Jesus. Yet the citation from Jonah contains an essential difference in comparison with Matthew's resurrection account. This difference destroys Matthew's attempt at an analogy.

According to all four Gospels, the crucifixion took place on a Friday and the resurrection on the following Sunday.[1] From this it would seem that Jesus was buried for three days (Friday, Saturday, Sunday). Matthew writes that according to prophecy, Jesus was to rise on the third day: "Then he opened their minds to understand the scriptures, and he said to them: 'Thus it is written, that the Christ should suffer and rise from the dead the third day'" (Luke 24:45, 46; see also Matthew 16:21; Mark 8:31, 10:34; Luke 9:22, 18:33). According to Jewish law, part of the day is equivalent to a full day, however, Matthew's Jesus promised to be buried specifically for three days and three nights. By using the phrase "three days and three nights," Matthew's Jesus indicated that he expected to be buried for three consecutive periods between dawn and dark (day) and dark and dawn (night), or approximately seventy-two hours. The Scriptures employ the phrase "three days" in a more general sense than that expressed by "three days and three nights." For example, "three days" does not necessarily include the period of day or night at either the beginning or end of the total time to be indicated. Therefore, when the phrase "three days" is meant to specifically include three days and three nights, and this is not evident from the text, it must be stated, as for example, "neither eat nor drink three days, night or day" (Esther 4:16). However, when the phrase "three days and three nights" is stated, it includes either all three days and all three nights or can be deficient in only parts of a day or night at the beginning or end of the entire period, but never of a full segment of day or night out of twenty-four hours (1 Samuel 30:11-13).

Although Jesus did not have to be buried exactly seventy-two hours, he did have to be buried at least on parts of three days and three nights. According to the Gospel narrative, Jesus died on a Friday at the ninth hour, which corresponds to about 3 P.M. The claim is made that Jesus rose three days later, on a Sunday. This would mean that he was buried during the daylight hours of three different days. If this is true, he was buried for only two nights.

Some Christians attempt to manipulate the Gospel narrative to show Jesus was buried on a Wednesday or Thursday so as to complete a seventy-two hour period within the allotted time. But, none of these explanations are sufficiently satisfactory to explain away the discrepancies.

John shows that Jesus' promise to rise after being buried three days and three nights was never fulfilled. According to Matthew, the women came to the tomb "as it began to dawn toward the first day of the week" (Matthew 28:1), Mark says, "they came to the tomb when the sun had risen" (Mark 16:2), and Luke says it was "at early dawn that they came to the tomb" (Luke 24:1). But, in John it states that it was not yet dawn when the body of Jesus disappeared from the tomb: "On the first day of the week Mary Magdalene came early to the tomb, while it was still dark, and saw the stone already taken away from the tomb" (John 20:1). Thus, according to the author of John, Jesus, having risen before the dawn of Sunday morning, was buried for only two days and two nights, that is, one full day (Saturday), part of another (Friday), and two nights (Friday and Saturday nights). This is contrary to the claim that in fulfillment of prophecy, Jesus was buried three days and three nights. The Gospels' evidence simply does not add up to three days, (that is, daylight hours) and three nights, as specifically promised by Jesus. Therefore, Jesus did not fulfill his very own prediction as recorded in the Gospels.

Another promise unfulfilled

Luke records that one of the two thieves crucified with Jesus questioned his claim to be the Messiah (Luke 23:39). In the version found in Matthew and Mark not one but both of the thieves revile Jesus (Matthew 27:44, Mark 15:32).[2] But, the inconsistencies continue, for Luke has Jesus promise the thief who, in this version, did not revile him that "today you shall be with me in paradise" (Luke 23:43). This promise contradicts Mark who states that Jesus arose on the first day of the week (Mark 16:9).[3] That was three days later (Luke 24:46)! In addition, it is claimed that Jesus "was taken up into heaven" at a date sometime after the crucifixion (Mark 16:19, Luke 24:51). Moreover, John says that after the resurrection Jesus said to Mary Magdalene: "Touch me not for I have not yet ascended to the Father" (John 20:17). Jesus' promise to the thief is completely untenable.

The soldiers at the tomb

Only Matthew alleges that the Jewish officials sent a contingent of soldiers to guard the tomb (Matthew 27:65-66). He writes that the Jewish enemies of Jesus, knowing of the latter's promise to rise from the dead on the third day, ask Pilate to send soldiers to guard the tomb. Is it not strange that Matthew should insist that Jesus' enemies not only knew of his promise but that they believed it as well?

The request of the Jewish officials that the tomb be guarded allegedly took place on the day following the crucifixion, which was the Sabbath and the first day of Passover (Matthew 27:62-64). In response to the request Pilate said to the officials: "You have a guard. Go make it as secure as you know how" (Matthew 27:65). Because of the holiness of the day, these soldiers could not have been organized and sent to the tomb by the Jews before the end of the Sabbath. Enough time, therefore, would have elapsed between the end of the Sabbath and the arrival of the soldiers for Jesus' body to have been quickly removed by some of his followers. In any case, the soldiers would have been poor witnesses to the events, for how could they know "all the things that had happened" (Matthew 28:11) when according to Matthew 28:4, they fainted on seeing the angel? If there was a contingent of soldiers, they found the tomb, on their arrival, already open and the body gone. Subsequently, the early Christians developed the story to include "miraculous" events as an answer to the Jews, who correctly surmised that some of Jesus' confederates were directly implicated in the body's disappearance.

Matthew advances a rather unlikely explanation of the general disbelief of the Jews in the resurrection story (Matthew 28:12-15). He says that the Jewish official bribed the soldiers sent to guard the tomb to say that they had fallen asleep and that while they slept, Jesus' disciples stole the body. Sleeping while on guard duty is an extremely serious offence for soldiers to commit, and it is unlikely that the soldiers would have let themselves be bribed into admitting something which could lead to their execution. Even though the Jewish officials promised to protect them from the consequences if Pilate heard that they had slept on duty, it is doubtful that the soldiers, be they Jewish or Roman, would have risked the chance. Pilate, harsh, brutal, and insensitive, was simply not the man the soldiers could expect to overlook a flagrant breach of their assigned duty.

The facts of how the body disappeared were branded as a lie by Matthew. His fabrication was necessitated by the need to preserve the Christian belief in the risen Christ. He must have agreed with Paul's admonition that without the resurrection "your faith is worthless" (1 Corinthians 15:17). Christianity is based not on the life and death of Jesus, but on the alleged resurrection. Since the facts would nullify the Christian faith, Matthew disqualifies the testimony of those Jews who knew the truth, accusing them of scheming and lying.

Who came to the tomb and when?

Which of Jesus' followers allegedly came to the tomb? Matthew says that Mary Magdalene and another woman named Mary came to view the burial place (Matthew 28:1). Mark relates that Mary Magdalene, Mary the mother of James, and Salome came to the tomb (Mark 16:1). Luke has Mary Magdalene, Joanna, and Mary the mother of Jesus, as well as "other women," at the tomb (Luke 24:10) with "the spices which they had prepared" (Luke 24:1). It would be unseemly for a male's body to be anointed for burial by women, as it would be for men to anoint a woman's body for burial.

John writes that Mary Magdalene came to the tomb, and the context shows that she was alone and not with any "other woman" (John 20:1). In John no reason is given for her being there since the body was already "anointed" by Joseph of Arimathea and Nicodemus (John 19:40). Women became the focal point of these stories because by the time the Gospels were written it was a well-established pre-Gospel story that the disciples had taken flight (Mark 14:50) to avoid being themselves crucified.

Matthew says that when Mary Magdalene and Mary arrived at the tomb an angel "approached and rolled away the stone and sat upon it," to the accompaniment of a great earthquake (Matthew 28:2). Mark claims that when the women arrived at the tomb they found the stone already rolled away, and no mention is made of an angel moving it for them or of a great earthquake (Mark 16:4). Luke also reports that the women found the stone already rolled away from the tomb, making no mention of its being moved by an angel or of an earthquake (Luke 24:2). John states that Mary Magdalene found the stone already moved from the entrance when she arrived at the tomb.

Counting angels

How many angels did Jesus' followers allegedly encounter at, or in, the tomb, one or two? Who rolled away the stone from before the tomb? Where were the angels when first seen? Which of Jesus' followers entered the tomb, and when did they do so? Which Gospel version is correct?

Mark claims that when "they entered into the tomb they saw a young man sitting on the right side wearing a white robe" (Mark 16:5). Luke says that when they entered into the tomb "two men stood by them in flashing clothing" (Luke 24:4). Well, which is it, Mark or Luke, one angel or two, sitting or standing? But, if this is not confusing enough, John gives his readers a little of both versions plus some additional contradictions to ponder. He says that Mary Magdalene ran to Simon Peter and the Beloved Disciple when she saw that the stone was rolled away from the tomb's entrance (John 20:1-2). She does not make any mention to them of seeing angels or experiencing an earthquake but expresses her feeling that evildoers had removed the body. John mentions that Mary Magdalene first looked into the tomb when she came back a second time. It was only then, John reports, that she saw "two angels in white sitting, one at the head and one at the feet, where the body of Jesus had been lying" (John 20:12). However, this occurred after the disciples left and not on an earlier visit to the tomb as in the other versions.

Where was Jesus while all this was going on? The Synoptic Gospels all agree that Mary Magdalene was told, "He is not here, for he was raised up" (Matthew 28:6, see also Mark 16:6, Luke 24:6). However, according to John, "she [Mary Magdalene] turned back, and saw Jesus standing" (John 20:14).

Let us now return to the problem involving angels. In Matthew the angel says, "go quickly and tell his disciples" (Matthew 28:7). In Mark the angel says, "tell his disciples and Peter" (Mark 16:7). But, according to Luke, they went to tell the disciples without being commanded to do so by the angels (Luke 24:9). John has Mary Magdalene tell the disciples what has happened before she sees the angels (John 20:2, 11-12). She further informed them that "we do not know where they have laid him." John, therefore, contradicts the claim that the angels provided the knowledge of the resurrection (Matthew 28:6, Mark 16:6, Luke 24:6). According to John, Jesus himself, not an angel, informs Mary Magdalene of his forthcoming ascension (John 20:17-18).

Mary Magdalene and a Jesus apparition

Where did Jesus allegedly appear to Mary Magdalene after his death? Matthew states that Jesus first appeared to Mary Magdalene and Mary after they had left the tomb and were on the road returning to Jerusalem to tell his disciples about the empty tomb. He writes: "Behold Jesus met them, saying: 'Hello.' And they approached and took hold of his feet and worshiped him" (Matthew 28:9). However, according to John, Jesus first appeared to Mary Magdalene while she was alone at the tomb, and he said to her: "Touch me not, for I have not yet ascended to the Father" (John 20:17). In this episode, Mary Magdalene, one of Jesus' most intimate followers, did not recognize him when he appeared to her, and had to be informed by the man she encountered at the tomb that he was Jesus (John 20:14-16). Disagreeing with John, Matthew says that an angel, not Jesus, was present at the tomb and told the two women, of whom Mary Magdalene was one, that Jesus had risen (Matthew 28:5-7). There is no room in Matthew's narrative for them both, or Mary Magdalene alone, as in John's version, to have met Jesus at the tomb. Mark merely records that Jesus appeared to Mary Magdalene first, but no geographic location is given for this alleged meeting (Mark 16:9). Luke's version does not mention an appearance by Jesus to Mary Magdalene, or any other woman, and leaves no room for one to have occurred (Luke 24:9-10). John alleges that Mary Magdalene, while alone at the tomb, grabbed Jesus by the feet (John 20:17), but Matthew's version has both Marys, while on the road to Jerusalem, grab his feet (Matthew 28:9). Although John's Jesus admonishes Mary Magdalene for touching him, Matthew's Jesus says nothing to the two Marys about their holding on to him.

Exactly where and to whom did Jesus appear — near the tomb to Mary Magdalene alone (John), on the road to both Marys (Matthew), at an undisclosed location to Mary Magdalene alone (Mark), or to neither one (Luke)? Did they or did they not touch him? What is one to believe about the veracity of any of this? The Gospel evidence presented to verify post-resurrection appearances by Jesus to his followers (never to skeptics or unbelievers) are vague, confused, and simply unreliable.

What does an empty tomb prove?

To prove that Jesus was resurrected various evidential materials have been produced. Contrary to Christian claims, this data does not furnish proof that Jesus was resurrected. Particular emphasis has been laid on the "empty tomb," supposedly an objective and verifiable fact. The assumption is made that if the body of Jesus could not be produced a miracle must have occurred. However, empty tombs have occurred more frequently in history than resurrections. As such, even if the tomb of Jesus was really empty on the Sunday after his Friday burial it would, in itself, not be a demonstrable fact verifying a resurrection. The emptiness of the tomb, if indeed it was empty, has no significance. This is especially true when one considers the witnesses and evidence presented in the New Testament to verify what is supposed to have occurred. What we get in the Gospel narratives is a highly incomplete substitute for factual evidence. The Gospels seek to substantiate their original claim to a resurrection with dubious sightings of the risen Jesus. That these apparitions may simply be products of outright fraud further complicates the very verification they seek to uphold. Acceptance of the trustworthiness of the post-resurrection appearance narratives depends on one's view of the resurrection accounts. If one believes the Gospel's resurrection stories, then the post-resurrection appearances will more than likely present no problem. If the resurrection accounts are not believable, then there is certainly not enough evidence to support the authenticity of the post-resurrection appearance stories on their own. In the end, the claim of the resurrection and of the sightings of the raised Jesus must be accepted on faith. They can never be accepted if judged by objective standards.

It has been argued that the absence of the body but the presence of linen wrappings shows that Jesus rose from the dead. In fact, only Luke and John (Luke 24:12, John 20:5) mention the finding of linen wrappings in the tomb. John adds a "cloth which was upon his head" (John 20:7). In any case, Luke and John prove nothing since the finding of these articles could as easily be the result of a hasty departure from the tomb by Joseph of Arimathaea and Nicodemus. If linen wrappings were really found in the tomb, they could either be leftover extras. In the rush to prepare for the burial, Joseph of Arimathaea would not have had time to measure off the exact amount of linen needed for wrapping the body. It is also conceivable that Nicodemus, unaware of what preparations Joseph of Arimathaea had made, may have also brought linen wrappings along with spices for the burial. In the rush to leave as quickly as possible, these linen wrappings were left behind.

The two most crucial New Testament witnesses of the final disposition of the body, Joseph of Arimathaea and Nicodemus (the latter only mentioned by John), are never mentioned again once the initial burial was complete. Reconstructing events as they actually occurred is difficult since the sparse New Testament information is burdened by legend, distortion, and censorship. In all likelihood, immediately after the Sabbath these two men, accompanied by servants, hastily removed the body from its temporary burial place, which had been quickly chosen because of the approaching Sabbath (John 19:41-42). Indeed, if they were fearful that the body might be mutilated, there was precedent for removal of the body even on the Sabbath (B.T. Shabbat 30b, 43b). In any case, they were never heard from again!

Following the story line, Joseph, described as a secret disciple (John 19:38), and Nicodemus apparently had no contact with "the women" or the disciples generally before, during, or after the crucifixion. This is seen from the behavior of the women, who kept at a distance from the Friday-afternoon burial party, not daring to approach them (Matthew 27:61, Mark 15:47, Luke 23:55). They certainly would have approached them had they been on good terms with either Joseph or Nicodemus. When the women arrived at the tomb on Sunday morning, they did not even know that the body was already anointed (Mark 16:1; Luke 23:56, 24:1; cf. John 19:39-40). Afterwards, when the resurrection claim was made, Joseph and Nicodemus, if they heard of it, did not, it seems, advise the claimants of its absurdity. In any case, the early-morning visitors to the tomb allegedly saw the discarded linen wrappings and, in their guilt-ridden, highly emotional state, thought they must have belonged to the missing Jesus. Thus, a legend was born.

According to the Gospels, the first claim that Jesus appeared after the resurrection was made by Mary Magdalene. The early Christian myth-makers, seeking to substantiate the resurrection tale, needed more proof than the account of the hysterical Mary Magdalene, from whom Jesus is said to have cast out seven demons (Mark 16:9). Her story was not believed by the apostles (Mark 16:11, Luke 24:11), even though Jesus had supposedly predicted his resurrection to his disciples when he set out for Jerusalem for the last time (Matthew 26:2). But the utility of her report was soon realized. An empty tomb does not prove what happened to its occupant, but if he is seen elsewhere the presumption is that his body and not just his spirit has risen. This led to the development of other resurrection apparitions. Forty days were added to Jesus' earthly stay, and they were then filled with a number of encounters between Jesus and his disciples. It was not a universal experience among a wide range of Jews and Jesus is never said to have appeared to anyone during those forty days who was not of his group of followers. "God raised him up on the third day, and granted that he should become visible, not to all people, but to witnesses who were chosen beforehand by God, to us, who ate and drank with him after he arose from the dead" (Acts 10:40-41).

Jesus apparitions "appear" to the disciples

Luke refers to a post-resurrection appearance by Jesus to a man named Simon: "The Lord was really raised up, and has appeared to Simon" (Luke 24:34). This could not be a reference to one of the apostles by that name, for the two followers from Emmaus, who reported this apparition to the apostles, found the eleven surviving apostles gathered together (Luke 24:33). We are therefore left with a claim that an otherwise unidentified person named Simon saw Jesus. It would seem from the text that he may have been one of the two followers of Jesus who allegedly met him on the road from Emmaus (Luke 24:13, Mark 16:12) and later reported this sighting to the apostles. In any case, these two followers did not immediately recognize Jesus (Luke 24:16), and as soon as "their eyes were opened and they recognized him he vanished from their sight" (Luke 24:31). There was no verification from the person they allegedly met on the road that he was Jesus. Therefore, this report remains, at best, only their personal feelings as to the identification of the stranger. Matthew and John make no mention of these two men. This story is plainly unreliable evidence shrouded in legendary material.

It is stated in the Gospels of Mark and Luke respectively that Jesus appeared to the eleven surviving apostles on the evening following the resurrection (Mark 16:14; Luke 24:33, 36). Contrary to this, John says that Thomas was not present and did not believe the other apostles' report when he heard it (John 20:24-25). Eight days later John claims, Jesus appeared to the eleven apostles specifically to end Thomas' skepticism (John 20:26-27). Strangely enough, no other Gospel mentions this second episode. It would certainly have been to their advantage not to omit an additional post-resurrection appearance. But this is more than an omission on the part of the Synoptic Gospel authors, for they attest to Thomas' presence, contrary to John, at the earlier gathering. They speak of the eleven gathered together, which must include Thomas.

Where did the eleven apostles first see Jesus after the resurrection? According to Matthew, an angel instructs Mary Magdalene to tell the disciples that "he is going before you into Galilee, there you will see him" (Matthew 28:7). Matthew then states that when Jesus met the women, after they departed from the tomb, and were on the way back to Jerusalem, he instructed them to "go, take word to my brethren to leave for Galilee, and there they will see me" (Matthew 28:10). Accordingly, the apostles "went into Galilee, into the mountain where Jesus had arranged for them. And when they saw him they worshiped, but doubted" (Matthew 28:16-17). At this first encounter with the supposed resurrected Jesus all of the disciples "doubted" (most English renderings add "some"). The nature of this doubt is not stated. Perhaps they questioned the manner of conjuring up the apparition that some claimed to see. It may be that they did not believe those who claimed to see Jesus and were attempting to stir up a mass hysteria in which others would follow suit (as was done by the disciples on Jesus' arrival in Jerusalem - Luke 19:37-38). Then, of course, there is the possibility that the incident never happened and is simply a faith-induced story that developed among Jesus' followers.

Mark states that it was an angel in the tomb, not Jesus, who informed Mary Magdalene and Mary that they should "go, tell his disciples and Peter, he is going before you into Galilee; there you will see him, just as he said to you" (Mark 16:5-7). Mark reports, contrary to Matthew's Gospel, that Jesus later changed his plans and "he appeared to the eleven themselves as they were reclining at the table, and he reproached them for their lack of faith and hardheartedness, because they did not believe those who had seen him after he had been raised up" (Mark 16:14).

Luke says that the women who came to the tomb were not informed by anyone about where Jesus would meet the disciples. Luke has the post-resurrection Jesus first appear to the eleven disciples as they were gathered together in Jerusalem (Luke 24:33, 36). Later that same day, Luke writes, Jesus "led them out as far as Bethany" (Luke 24:50), which is near Jerusalem, where "he was parted from them [and was carried up into heaven]" (Luke 24:51).[4]

According to John, Mary Magdalene, while standing outside the tomb, was commanded by Jesus to tell his disciples: "I ascend to my Father and your Father, and to my God and your God" (John 20:17). No mention is made to her about a forthcoming meeting with the disciples. Later, John has Jesus appear to them as they are gathered together in Jerusalem soon after Mary Magdalene had come to tell them what she saw that same day at the tomb (John 20:18-19). There is little or no agreement among the Gospels as to who was informed, when, and by whom, that Jesus would meet his disciples after the resurrection. The crucial question of whether Jesus' first alleged meeting with his eleven disciples after the crucifixion was in Galilee, as stated in Matthew (Matthew 26:32; 28:7, 10, 16-17), or in Jerusalem, as in Mark, Luke, and John (Mark 16:14; Luke 24:33, 36; John 20:19), still remains.

John relates how a stranger appeared on shore to seven of the apostles as they were fishing on the Sea of Galilee (John 21:1-22).

But mysteriously, the seven apostles did not actually recognize the stranger as being Jesus, even when they arrived back on shore. Then, instead of receiving confirmation from the stranger as to his identity, John says that they did not ask him who he was, "knowing that it was the Lord" (John 21:12). The only confirmation of the stranger's identity comes from the author of the Gospel. Again we have an instance where a stranger is said to have been an apparition of Jesus. With time the story was expanded still further to include a mythical conversation between Jesus and Peter. This is no surprise, since the later a Gospel was written, and John was the latest, the more details it contains concerning post-resurrection appearances. This Gospel incorporated much of the increased legendary material concerning appearances that was created as the years passed.

The narratives of the post-resurrection appearances found in John, chapters 20 and 21, reflect pre-Johannine accounts, as well as the author's revisions in accordance with what he perceived as the needs of his community and his own theological understanding.[5] John, chapter 21, in particular, affords a glimpse at how and why certain appearance stories were developed, expanded, and finally added to the Gospels. The appearance stories were developed to explain problems unresolved as a result of Jesus' death, as well as to give hope that Jesus was still alive and would eventually return (Acts 1:2-9).

Many New Testament scholars have recognized that chapter 20 originally closed John's Gospel and that chapter 21 is an addition to that Gospel. This chapter is variously ascribed to either a latter addendum by the author of the Gospel, himself, or to a later editor who was part of the Johannine community. In any case, a study of John, chapter 20, shows that verse 29 closes the accounts of the alleged resurrection appearances of Jesus and that verses 30-31 conclude the Gospel. The twentieth chapter in its form, structure, and purpose completes John's presentation of Jesus following his alleged resurrection. The mention in John 20:30 of many other signs that Jesus allegedly performed is presumably inclusive of resurrection appearances also. The statement that Jesus did "many other signs" shows that it is claimed that, for one reason or another, not all the available materials were included. It is evident from a comparison of the Fourth Gospel with the Synoptic Gospels that other non-recorded source material was in all likelihood known in the circles of those who fashioned the Fourth Gospel, but was not used. The author of John, as the Synoptic authors who preceded him, restricted his choice of material to those items, which he felt were especially instructive to his community. The Gospel authors selected from a body of material preserved orally or in writing. However, none of the authors of the four Gospels knew all the sources available that were believed to recount the words and deeds of Jesus.

New Testament scholars believe that the Gospel of John originated in a Christian community that formed around the person of the Beloved Disciple of John 20:2. This Gospel had great significance for those who held the Beloved Disciple in high esteem. Presumably, the appearance account of chapter 21 would not be excluded from his community's Gospel if that material existed when the Gospel was written. It featured a very crucial saying by Jesus about the Beloved Disciple. This appearance would certainly be an incident preciously preserved by this community specifically because it contained a significant statement concerning him. Indeed, according to chapter 21, the "saying ... went out among the brethren that that disciple would not die" (verse 23). But, it should not be assumed that this notion originated from an utterance said to have been enunciated by Jesus at a post-resurrection meeting with Peter. Had the author of the Gospel of John desired to include the supposed Sea of Galilee appearance, found in chapter 21, he would have composed chapter 20 differently and included it there. That appearance and its message are just too important to leave out. It is difficult to imagine that this appearance story would be excluded, for any reason, in the original redaction of the Gospel. The appearance account of chapter 21 was a late fabrication designed after the close of the Gospel of John to meet a serious communal need. Therefore, it is unlikely that the original author added chapter 21. It is more likely that someone other than the original author of the Fourth Gospel wrote the final chapter as the Gospel is presently constituted.

The author of the addendum chapter, had reason for his editing certain earlier episodal traditions said to date from Jesus' ministry and supplementing them with a resurrection appearance of his own design. Chapter 21 is structured in order to give the impression that the entire narrative takes place as a continuous single event. However, there are indications that the author has interwoven more than one source. Analysis of verses 1-14 shows that this unit is composed of two sources: a fishing episode in verses 2, 3, 4a, 6, 11 and an appearance with a meal in verses 4b, 7-9, 12-13. Verse 14 indicates that verses 1-14 formed a complete section in itself. The redaction of chapter 21, rather than fabricate an entirely new event, introduced and combined incidents from the sayings and deeds attributed to Jesus that were not previously used by the original author of the Gospel of John (cf. Luke 5:1-11); suitable alterations were introduced to transform them into resurrection appearances. But why was chapter 21 written? The answer has to do with the next section of this chapter.

As it now exists, chapter 21, written during a period of crises of faith, addresses the uncertainties, which must have beset the Johannine churches at a time after the Fourth Gospel had been completed. The Beloved Disciple, because he was the last of the disciples and greatly advanced in age, was commonly expected by "the brethren" to remain alive until Jesus' return (verses 22-23); but, he died. The most troubling aspect of his death was that it focused all the more on the failure of the expected return of Jesus, himself, to materialize. Jesus had not come "quickly" as earlier anticipated and now one of the signs or his imminent coming had failed the test of time. Chapter 21 was added to answer those who questioned what went wrong.

Clarification of the timing of the Beloved Disciple's death comes in the form of an answer given to Peter during an alleged post-resurrection appearance by Jesus. This appearance was composed sometime after the first twenty chapters of the Fourth Gospel had been completed. An ambiguous prediction concerning Peter's martyrdom, which occurred some thirty-five years earlier, is created vaticinium ex evento as a backdrop for the essential portion of this supposed post-resurrection narrative. "Follow me!" that is, become a martyr (verse 19), Jesus instructs Peter. At that moment, "Peter … seeing him [the beloved Disciple] said to Jesus, 'Lord, and what about this man?' Jesus said to him, 'If I want him to remain until I come, what is that to you? You follow me!' This saying therefore went out among the brethren that that disciple would not die; yet Jesus did not say to him that he would not die, but, 'If I want him to remain until I come, what is that to you?'" (verses 21-24). Thus, the belief that the Beloved Disciple would not die before the second coming is dismissed as a misunderstanding of Jesus' words rather than understood as a deep desire developed as he, the last of the disciples, advanced in age. The core of verses 20-23 is the saying of verse 22, which circulated among the Johannine churches independent of the rest of chapter 21 material. Explaining that the yearning revolving around the Beloved Disciple was due to a misunderstanding of what Jesus' had actually said raised morale. Had an elder of the Johannine church explained it, as such, there would still be doubt and uncertainty. There was a remedy for this. As redacted in chapter 21, there can be no doubt as to what Jesus is supposed to have said. Instead of an oral tradition as to what Jesus is supposed to have said there was now an authoritative written record of what were supposedly the actual words of the resurrected Jesus. The editor then reemphasizes the correct understanding. This rectification of what is described as a misunderstanding concerning the destiny of the Beloved Disciple was the central factor in the decision to add this chapter to the Fourth Gospel. The only place this rectification could fit into the already completed Gospel of John was at the end. It therefore had to take the form of a post-resurrection appearance story. The chapter was developed through the incorporation of incidents that were passed down by tradition as taken from the life of Jesus. The conclusion in verses 24-25 was in order to bring the chapter to an end and to establish the validity of the Gospel as a whole, thereby integrating the epilogue into that Gospel.

Far from being authored by the Beloved Disciple, chapter 21 is a later addition to the Gospel of John. Clearly, John 20 is the original final conclusion to this Gospel. The Beloved Disciple is introduced in John 21:24 as the author of the entire Gospel. Nevertheless, in John 21 there are linguistic differences between this chapter and John 1-20. For example, the use of the word "children" (verse 5) in addressing the disciples and "brothers" (verse 23) as a designation for followers of Jesus. The ultimate source of chapter 21 is from the imagination of a later redactor.

"Make disciple of all nations"

Writing the first chapter of Acts many years after the ascension supposedly occurred, Luke incorporated a great deal of legendary material into his account. Comparing his description of events to parallel accounts in the Gospels yields evidence of disagreement and conflicting traditions concerning the ascension tale.

Matthew quotes Jesus as addressing the apostles, at what was, according to him, the only post-resurrection meeting Jesus had with them: "Go therefore and make disciples of all the nations" (Matthew 28:19). Similarly, Mark relates that prior to Jesus' alleged ascension to a position at the right hand of God (Mark 16:19), he ordered the apostles to scatter throughout the world: "Go into all the world and preach the gospel to all creation" (Mark 16:15). This, Mark records, they proceeded to do: "And they went out and preached everywhere" (Mark 16:20). The wording shows that they did this immediately. There is no time provided for a later meeting of Jesus and all the apostles. However, according to Luke's version, when the ascension took place forty days after the resurrection (Acts 1:3, 9), the apostles were still all gathered together in Jerusalem. How could the apostles travel the great distances needed to comply with the accounts of Matthew and Mark, and return to Jerusalem within that short space of time? It is impossible for them to have scattered as Matthew and Mark claim and yet regroup in Jerusalem at the end of forty days. Travel conditions were just too difficult for that to have occurred. At the time of his alleged ascension Luke has Jesus instruct the apostles not to leave Jerusalem but "to wait for what the Father had promised" (Acts 1:4). Once the holy spirit came upon them they were to go out into the world (Acts 1:8). This conforms to what Luke says Jesus declared to the apostles at their first post-resurrection meeting" "You are to stay in the city [Jerusalem] until you are clothed with power from on high" (Luke 24:49). In contrast to Luke's statement, Matthew (who has the post-resurrection meeting take place in Galilee) and Mark assert that the apostles were already scattered throughout the world by the time forty days after the resurrection had passed. These variant Gospel traditions make it impossible to accept as serious evidence Luke's claim that the apostles saw Jesus forty days after the alleged resurrection.

The great omission

A most remarkable omission takes place in Paul's listing of those early followers of Jesus to whom he supposedly made appearances. He never mentions the alleged first witnesses — the women.

Paul's version of who saw the Jesus apparition

Paul's references to Cephas (1 Corinthians 15:5) and James (1 Corinthians 15:7) seeing Jesus could not be verified to the Corinthians. Does Cephas refer to Simon Peter, who at times was referred to as Cephas? Paul's words show a chronological sequence of appearances after the alleged resurrection, with the first to Cephas and then the surviving apostles meeting Jesus. However, at no time is the apostle Simon Peter, under any name, mentioned in the New Testament as seeing Jesus prior to the alleged appearance to the eleven apostles together. It may be that Paul was confused by a legend circulating in Christian circles, which Luke later incorporated into his Gospel, that someone named Simon saw Jesus (Luke 24:34). Paul, for unspecified reasons, may have claimed that this Simon referred to Simon Peter. However, it is evident from our earlier study of Luke 24:34 that the Simon who allegedly met Jesus was not Simon Peter.

Paul did not know that his letters would be preserved and eventually widely circulated and held sacred. Considering the time and conditions under which he wrote and that he expected Jesus to return shortly, Paul did not fear if his exaggerated statements were challenged. Those who denied his claims he simply accused of being false teachers (2 Timothy 4:14-18; Galatians 1:6-8). As the years went by it became a case of his word against theirs as his letters became increasingly accepted in the church as historical and theological truth.

But, in Paul's mentioning of Cephas and James respectively seeing a Jesus apparition he is unclear as to the identity of the individual being referred to. There are also discrepancies in the overall tale that he weaves when compared with other New Testament documents. There were at least three different men named James involved in the life of Jesus. Which one is supposed to have seen the resurrected

Jesus? When and where did Cephas and James see Jesus? And, as mentioned above, he never mentions the initial Jesus apparition witnesses — the women. He gives first sighting credit to Cephas.

Paul writes in 1 Corinthians 15:6, without giving a geographic location that "upward of five hundred brethren" saw Jesus and that most of them were still alive. There is no information provided to indicate whether the experience was a visionary revelation or an actual appearance in the flesh. Moreover, Paul does not tell his readers whether he was among the five hundred. Surely, he would say he was a witness to the event if he was there. Paul does not mention anyone by name that supposedly was there. He also does not mention if he had heard the story from one of the participants or if it was merely a story that was circulating among some Christian groups. This alleged post-resurrection appearance is conspicuously omitted in both the Gospels and Acts. Had the Corinthians wanted to verify Paul's statement, it would have been virtually impossible for them to do so given the ambiguous information he provides. The alleged incident has all the overtones of being an unverifiable story resulting from overzealous missionary activity seeking to bolster the resurrection claim.

The entire episode recording the speech and supposed martyrdom of the Samaritan oriented Stephen consists of questionable material.[6] It is doubtful that it ever took place and certainly not as described. In particular, while "full of the Holy Spirit" he is said to have seen "the glory of God, and Jesus standing at the right hand of God" (Acts 7:55). Thus, his vision adds a fourth member to the multi-person Christian god, that is, "the glory of God." In this light, Stephens alleged vision (Acts 7:55-56) was, at best, hallucination of a confused individual.

Paul claims that while undergoing some sort of seizure he heard Jesus (Acts 9:4-5, 22:7-8, 26:14-15; 1 Corinthians 15:8). This is not the most reliable verification of a Jesus apparition. It is more the self-explanation of an individual trying to cope with and understand his mental ailment.

The author of Revelation records visions he claims to have had of Jesus (Revelation 1:10-20). These are not claimed to be actual apparitions of a returned Jesus. The figure he sees does not look or sound like the Jesus the apostles knew and followed. Indeed, that is always the case with Jesus apparition claims. The author's visionary experience does not confirm that Jesus was resurrected, merely that his mind was capable of conjuring up an image of the way he thought the heavenly Jesus should look. Again all that the New Testament sources provide is an identification which is based on unsubstantiated evidence.

The implications of the discrepancies and questionable information associated with these declarations of post-resurrection appearances should not be underestimated. The information provided by the New Testament attempts to substantiate the claim of the resurrection and subsequent appearance of Jesus to certain of his followers, but this evidence is weak. The simple fact remains that the resurrection story is not based on any authentic historical evidence. There were no eyewitnesses; no one saw Jesus leave the tomb. There are only unsubstantiated third-hand reports. Significantly, the Gospels of Matthew and Luke differ most from each other at exactly those points where they could not follow Mark, the first written Gospel, namely, in their accounts of the infancy and resurrection appearances of Jesus. Those aspects of the story were not mentioned in Mark's narrative. The accounts of the resurrection and the encounters with the risen Jesus were developed after the events were supposed to have occurred. The belief in the resurrection existed first, but the stories to support this alleged event, and which are used to verify it, were later developments.

The notion that post-resurrection appearances took place resulted from a combination of myth and highly emotional expressions stemming from the deep yearnings of disappointment and guilt that the followers of Jesus felt after his death. On the other hand, with the many discrepancies that appear in the story, it is no wonder that the overwhelming majority of contemporary Jewish people dismissed the resurrection story and subsequent apparitions as fabrications by Jesus' followers.

Why the apparition stories developed

We see in the Gospels that there was a widespread folkloric belief in the reappearance of those already dead but not necessarily with the same features. The Gospels tell us that this belief was not unique to the Jesus movement. According to Mark, people were saying of Jesus: "John the Baptist has risen from the dead, and therefore these miraculous powers are at work in him [Jesus]" (Mark 6:14); and Herod said to his servants: "This is John the Baptist; he has risen from the dead; and that is why miraculous powers are at work in him" (Matthew 14:2); and when Jesus asked his disciples who people thought him to be they reported that "Some say John the Baptist; others Elijah; and still others Jeremiah, or one of the prophets" (Matthew 16:13-14). Luke writes: "Now Herod the tetrarch heard of all that was happening; and he was greatly perplexed, because it was said by some that John had risen from the dead, and by some that Elijah had appeared, and by others that one of the prophets of old had risen again" (Luke 9:7-8). It is said that when certain disciples encountered the post-crucifixion Jesus they did not recognize him but later realized it was Jesus: "And it came about that while they were conversing and discussing, Jesus himself approached, and began traveling with them. But their eyes were being prevented from recognizing him" (Luke 24:15-16). But later: "Their eyes were opened and they recognized him, and he vanished from their sight. And they said to one another: 'Were not our hearts burning within us while he was speaking to us on the road, while he was explaining the Scriptures to us?'" (Luke 24:31-32). "[S]he [Mary Magdalene] turned around and beheld Jesus standing and did not know that it was Jesus" (John 20:14). She not only thought he was "the gardener," but also did not even recognize his voice (John 20:15). Jesus had to tell her who he was (John 20:15-16). Again John writes that the apostles did not recognize Jesus (John 21:4) but they knew it was him (John 21:12). Mark, the earliest of the four Gospels (but in a section of that Gospel considered by many Christians as a later addition), provides a reason why the disciples did not recognize Jesus: "He appeared to them in a different form" (Mark 16:12).

According to Matthew, it was believed by contemporaries of the disciples that John the Baptist (Matthew 14:1-2) or prophets (Matthew 16:13-14) came back from the dead to walk among men. He also claims that when Jesus died "many of the saints who had fallen asleep were raised and came out of the tombs and entered the holy city and appeared to many" (Matthew 27:51-54). So, why not Jesus as well? To the disciples who remained loyal, Jesus most of all deserved to be raised up. Therefore, such a return suited Jesus all the more so! It is not surprising that some should claim to have felt his presence and others to have imagined seeing him physically in another form, or still others having visionary experiences where they imagined he had returned and spoken to them. Paul writing many years before the Gospels appeared speaks of his own experiences and earlier experiences by the disciples with the Jesus apparition in terms of visionary encounters. The Gospels intent is, however, to solidify the alleged visionary sightings into encounters with an actual physical being albeit with supernatural abilities. Interestingly, if this notion of return from the dead was widely believed, then claims of Jesus reappearing in some form or other would not create much surprise. People might not have accepted that he returned but would not dismiss the overall possibility of a return. Jesus was just not considered special enough to warrant a return except by his followers. Others, of course, rejected the notion of people being raised as described. In any case, for the followers of Jesus who thought of him as the Messiah, who more than Jesus was deserving of being raised from the dead? And in their hearts and minds they imagined that in some way it must be so.

As to the final resting place of the body, there is a lack of reliable information for arriving at a definitive answer. The body of Jesus is gone, but the many inaccuracies in the stories told of the alleged resurrection and post-resurrection encounters remain. This ambiguous claim calls into question the veracity of the claim that Jesus can give everlasting life to those who believe in him.

[1] Friday is referred to in the Gospels as the Day of Preparation, i.e., for the Sabbath, (cf. Matthew 27:62, Luke 23:54, and Mark 15:42 with Exodus 16:5. See also Josephus, Jewish Antiquities, VIII. 16. 163 [p. 273 (Loeb ed.)], where an edict from Caesar Augustus says: "… and that they [the Jews] need not give bond [to appear in court] on the Sabbath or on the day of preparation for it [Sabbath Eve] after the ninth hour.") This particular weekly Sabbath was also the first day of Passover. It should be noted that although Passover is referred to as a Sabbath in Leviticus 23:15, it is never called a Sabbath in the New Testament. In the New Testament the festivals are always designated by their names.

[2] The significance of the word lestai ("thieves," "brigands"), used in Matthew 27:38 and Mark 15:27), lies in the fact that it was a derogatory term for the Zealots, who, by armed action, opposed Roman rule of the Holy Land.

[3] Some of the oldest New Testament manuscripts omit Mark 16:9-20.

[4] Some manuscripts add the words in the brackets.

[5] F.F. Bruce writes that the Johannine "documents themselves point to the existence of what may be called a 'Johannine circle.'" (F.F. Bruce, Peter, Stephen, James, and John, Grand Rapids, Mich.: William B. Eerdmans, 1979, p. 143). See also Raymond E. Brown, The Community of the Beloved Disciple, New York: Paulist Press, 1979.

[6] See Gerald Sigal, Anti-Judaism in the New Testament, Philadelphia: Xlibris, 1994, pp. 237-255.

Chapter 69

THE BAPTISM FORMULA
(Matthew 28:19)

The baptism formula

Some Christians allege that the command by Matthew's Jesus to, "Go therefore, and make disciples of all nations, baptizing them in the name of the Father and the Son and the Holy Spirit" (Matthew 28:19) shows the existence of a triune deity. However, it is doubtful that the Gospel of Matthew originally made this claim. Even more uncertain is the notion that this directive was made by Jesus at the onset of the apostolic period (following the death of Jesus) or at any other time. Belief in a triune deity entered into Christian belief independent of the composition of the Gospel of Matthew. The trinitarian baptismal formula, as it is now found in this Gospel, is a post-apostolic period doctrinal expansion of the text.

Eusebius of Caesarea (c. 260 - c. 340) cites Matthew 28:19 at least twenty-one times in his writings,[1] but not as it appears today in the New Testament. He finishes the verse with the words "make disciples of all nations in my name" (cf. Luke 24:47 - "And that repentance and forgiveness of sins should be proclaimed in his [Jesus'] name to all nations, beginning from Jerusalem"). Eusebius, in his Ecclesiastical History (c. 324 C.E.) wrote:

> But the rest of the apostles, who had been incessantly plotted against with a view to their destruction, and had been driven out of the land of Judea, went unto all nations to preach the Gospel, relying upon the power of Christ, who had said to them, "Go ye and make disciples of all the nations in my name."[2]

Again, in his Oration in Praise of Emperor Constantine (c. 335 C.E.), he wrote:

> What king or prince in any age of the world, what philosopher, legislator or prophet, in civilized or barbarous lands, has attained so

great a height of excellence, I say not after death, but while living still, and full of mighty power, as to fill the ears and tongues of all mankind with the praises of his name? Surely none save our only Saviour has done this, when, after his victory over death, he spoke the word to his followers, and fulfilled it by the event, saying to them, "Go ye, and make disciples of all nations in my name."[3]

In his Demonstratio Evangelica (c. 314 C.E.), he wrote:

For he did not enjoin them "to make disciples of all the nations" simply and without qualification, but with the essential addition "in his name." For so great was the virtue attaching to his appellation that the Apostle says, "God bestowed on him the name above every name, that in the name of Jesus every knee shall bow of things in heaven and on earth and under the earth." It was right therefore that he should emphasize the virtue of the power residing in his name but hidden from the many, and therefore say to his Apostles, "Go ye, and make disciples of all the nations in my name."[4]

Eusebius, who supported the orthodox trinitarian position, was present at the Council of Nicaea and was involved in the debates concerning whether Jesus was part of the essence of God or a creation of God. If the manuscript of the Gospel of Matthew that he used read "in the name of the Father, and of the Son and of the Holy Spirit," and thus could be used to support the trinitarian position, he would not have quoted it so frequently as "in my name." Thus, it can be assumed that the earliest manuscripts read "in my name,"[5] and that the phrase was enlarged and officially adopted to reflect the orthodox position as trinitarian influence spread following the Council of Nicaea (325).

Eusebius lived at the great Christian library of Caesarea collected by Origen[6] and Pamphilus. He had access to codices of the Gospels containing the disputed verse which were much older than those now available.[7] Evidently, the text of Matthew 28:19 with which he was familiar read "Go ye, and make disciples of all the nations in my name." It is only sometime after he attended the Council of Nicaea that his writings contain any reference to the expanded version of the text. This version is found in two works written in his old age,

413

and entitled respectively, Against Marcellus of Ancyra, and About the Theology of the Church. The expanded reading is also found in a letter addressed by Eusebius, after the Council of Nicea, to his church in Caesarea. These citations of the expanded formula either reflect conformity to avoid accusations of heresy in the post-Nicene period or may be the result of interpolation by later copyists.

Can Eusebius' phraseology, "Go ye, and make disciples of all the nations in my name," be considered as decisive proof that the clause "baptizing them in the name of the Father and the Son and the Holy Spirit" was lacking in the manuscripts available to Eusebius? Perhaps, in writing "in my name" Eusebius was simply abbreviating the longer clause. What militates against this proposal is that Eusebius cites the shorter version so often that it is difficult to suppose that he is simply paraphrasing the text. Moreover, the shorter form agrees with the baptismal formula used by the apostles as described in the Book of Acts.

If Matthew 28:19 as found in modern versions is accurate, then the apostles ignored Jesus, since there is not a single occurrence of them baptizing anyone according to that formula. All the relevant passages in the New Testament show that in the early years of Christianity people were baptized "into Christ" (Galatians 3:27) or "in the name of Jesus," just as Eusebius' text said to do and not as directed by the present-day reading of Matthew 28:19. Thus, we find: "Peter replied, 'Repent and be baptized, every one of you, in the name of Jesus Christ for the forgiveness of your sins'" (Acts 2:38). "They had simply been baptized into the name of the Lord Jesus" (Acts 8:16). "So he ordered that they be baptized in the name of Jesus Christ" (Acts 10:48; see also Romans 6:3, Galatians 3:27). "On hearing this, they were baptized into the name of the Lord Jesus" (Acts 19:5). From these citations we see that this was the procedure followed, whether or not Jesus actually so ordered. In Acts, the apostles always use the name of "the Lord Jesus" or "Jesus Christ" in baptizing, but never any trinitarian type formula. It is difficult to imagine that the apostles would have disregarded a clear command of Jesus if they knew of it.

All the evidence shows that the references to the receiving of "the holy spirit" with baptism which are found in the New Testament do not refer to a third member of the triune deity. They refer to the spiritual gifts believed by Christians to be bestowed by God upon those who receive baptism in the name of Jesus (see Acts 1:8). It should be remembered that the Gospel of Matthew was written in the post-apostolic period. The notion of a triune deity was present among some Christians in the ante-Nicene period, but that does not prove that the existence of a triune deity was taught by the New Testament.[8] If the longer formula was used by the author of Matthew it would still not conform to apostolic usage. Their practice puts in doubt any thoughts that Jesus ever uttered these exact words. There is simply no passage in the New Testament which asserts that God is three in any sense whatsoever.

[1] Eusebius cites Matthew 28:19 many times in works written between 300-336 (as in his Commentaries on the Psalms and Commentaries on Isaiah, his Demonstratio Evangelica, his Theophania, his Ecclesiastical History, and his The Oration in Praise of Emperor Constantine), and always as "Go ye, and make disciples of all nations in my name.".

[2] Eusebius, Ecclesiastical History, 3. 5. 2, Trans. Arthur Cushman McGiffert, in Eds. Schaff and Wace, Nicene and Post-Nicene Fathers of the Christian Church, Grand Rapids: Eerdmans, Vol. 1, 1986, p. 138.

[3] Eusebius, The Oration in Praise of Emperor Constantine 16. 8, in Eds. Schaff and Wace, p. 607.

[4] Eusebius, Demonstratio Evangelica [The Proof of the Gospel], 3. 7, Trans. W.J. Ferrar, New York: the Macmillan Co., Vol. 1, 1920, p. 136.

[5] One scholar, George Howard, has found what may be an early Hebrew version of the Gospel of Matthew embedded in a fourteenth century Hebrew manuscript. The treatise, Even Bochan ("The Touchstone"), was written in Spain, by Shem-Tov Shaprut. Forced by Christian theologians and born-Jewish apostates to Christianity to debate the merits of Judaism verses Christianity, Jews in Europe, during the Middle Ages, wrote polemical works. The Even Bochan is Shem-Tov's polemical treatise against Christianity. As with many of these works, Shem-Tov's Even Bochan contains a Hebrew text of a Gospel. Until Howard's study of this work, it was thought that this Hebrew rendering of Matthew was a fourteenth century Hebrew translation of the Greek, or its Latin version. Although there are notable differences between the Greek and Hebrew texts he believes the similarities in arrangement and wording of the Hebrew and Greek texts of Matthew show that one text served as a model for the other. There is no evidence as to which came first, the Greek or the Hebrew, and Howard maintains that both works are originals,

neither a translation. Shem-Tov's Hebrew Matthew reads at 28:19, "Go and (teach [some manuscripts read "guard"]) them to carry out all the things which I have commanded you forever." This wording has some affinity to the phraseology in my name. (George Howard, Hebrew Gospel of Matthew, Macon, Ga.: Mercer University Press, 1995, p. 151.)

[6] In all of his writings, Origen (c. 185-c. 254) makes no mention of the supposed command to baptize using the triune name formula (although there are a number of obvious interpolations into his works that cite the expanded form of Matthew 28:19).

[7] There are no Greek New Testament manuscripts today earlier than the fourth century containing Matthew 28:19. Of the fourth century there are two post-Council of Nicaea manuscripts: the Vaticanus and the Sinaiticus — both have the expanded text. All other known New Testament Greek manuscripts are from the fifth century or later. The oldest Syriac manuscript containing the Gospel of Matthew is missing the folio which contained the end of Matthew. This is also true of the oldest Latin manuscript.

[8] There is indication that a threefold formula was already in use by some Christians during the second century, even if it was not in the New Testament itself. Justin Martyr (c. 100-165) wrote: "For, in the name of God, the Father and Lord of the universe, and of our Saviour Jesus Christ, and of the Holy Spirit, they then receive the washing with water. For Christ also said, 'Except ye be born again ye shall not enter into the kingdom of heaven'" (Justin Martyr, The First Apology of Justin 61, in Eds. Roberts and Donaldson, The Ante-Nicene Father, Grand Rapids: Eerdmans, Vol. 1, 1996, p. 183. Although Justin used the triune formula, it does not mean that it was in his text of the Gospel of Matthew. Interestingly, while not formally citing the short form of Matthew 28:19 he echoed it when he wrote that "daily some [of you Jews] are becoming disciples in the name of Christ, and quitting the path of error" (Dialogue With Trypho, 39).

Chapter 70

DID JESUS MISREAD THE SCRIPTURES?
(Mark 2:25-26)

It appears from the Gospel of Mark that Jesus misread the Scriptures. Its author writes:

> And he [Jesus] said to them: "Have you never read what David did, when he was in need and was hungry, he and those who were with him: How he entered into the house of God, when Abiathar was high priest, and ate the bread of presentation, which it is not lawful for anyone but the priests to eat, and he gave it also to those who were with him?" (Mark 2:25-26)

Mark, Matthew, and Luke all contend that David's companions also ate the holy bread (Matthew 12:4, Luke 6:4). But, from the question asked of David by the high priest, Ahimelech: "Why are you alone, and no man with you?" (1 Samuel 21:2), it is clear that David came alone to the high priest. On this point the Jesus of all three Synoptic Gospels are incorrect.

Also, the biblical text records that it was not Abiathar who was high priest at the time this episode occurred, but Abiathar's father, Ahimelech. Abiathar was the sole survivor of the slaughter of the priests at Nob, who were killed for having fed David. Matthew and Luke do not mention the name of the high priest (Matthew 12:3-4, Luke 6:3-4). As the story reads in Mark, Jesus misread the biblical text.

Chapter 71

A FAMILY'S VERDICT: "HE IS OUT OF HIS MIND"

(Mark 3:19-21, 31)

According to the Gospel of Mark, Jesus' family was of the opinion that he was deranged. This Gospel relates:

> And he [Jesus] came into the house; and the multitude gathered again, so that they were not able to eat bread. And when his relatives heard of this, they went out to lay hold of him; for they were saying: "He is out of his mind." ...And his mother and his brothers came, and standing outside they sent in to him to call him. (Mark 3:19-21, 31)

It is apparent that Jesus' own family, including his mother, did not consider him to be the Messiah and the Son of God. Not only did they not know of these fundamental beliefs of later Christianity, but they believed him to be mentally unbalanced.

On the occasion described by Mark, Jesus was informed that his mother and brothers were looking for him. His response displayed hostility toward them, and denied the importance of familial relationships (Mark 3:31-35, Matthew 12:46-50, Luke 8:19-21). His statement was an expression of resentment for their refusal to accept his messianic pretensions: "For neither did his brothers believe in him" (John 7:5). Thus, Jesus declared: "A prophet is not without honor except in his home town and among his relatives and in his house" (Mark 6:4). But, this story elicits serious questions about fundamental components of the birth narrative. How could Mary, the mother of Jesus, forget so quickly the visit of angels, magi and shepherds, or the prophecies of Anna and Simeon in the Temple, and most of all, her own impregnation by the "Holy Spirit"? And, needless to say, how could she forget, as some Christians tell the tale, her perpetual virginity.

Chapter 72

WHO DECLARED THE WORD OF GOD INVALID?

(Mark 7:9-13)

In an indirect way Mark's Jesus is made to criticize the Torah he is said to fulfill elsewhere (Matthew 5:17). The author of Mark writes:

> And he said to them: "You nicely set aside the commandments of God, in order that you may keep your own tradition. For Moses said, 'Honor your father and your mother'; and 'He who speaks evil of father or mother, let him surely die.' But you say, 'If a man says to his father or his mother, anything of mine you might have been helped by is Corban (that is, given to God),' You no longer permit him to do anything for his father or his mother; thus invalidating the word of God by your tradition which you have handed down; and you do many things such as that." (Mark 7:9-13)

Mark's Jesus attempts to discredit the Pharisees by accusing them of negating the law of God and following instead an invalid tradition of their own making. According to Jesus' explanation of this alleged man-made Pharisaic tradition, a man who had devoted all his property to God is, in effect, prohibited by them from providing for his parents. But apparently, Mark's Jesus was not familiar with the laws of the Torah. There it is written: "But any devoted thing which a man may devote to the Lord of all that he has, whether of man or beast, or of the field of his possession, shall not be sold, nor redeemed; every devoted thing is most holy to the Lord" (Leviticus 27:28). Jesus' quarrel is not with the Pharisees, but with the word of God as stated in the Torah. He is criticizing the Pharisees for their obedience to God's commandments, not for following a man-made commandment. Jesus' attack is an exaggerated misunderstanding of the Torah's commandments. It is doubtful that Jesus ever uttered this complaint. It is more likely that it part of the early church's polemic not only against the Pharisaic leadership but also against obedience to

419

the Torah as well. In any case, it is a theoretical argument unsupported by an actual occurrence.

Chapter 73

JESUS AND THE LAWS OF KASHRUT
(Mark 7:14-15, 18-19)

And calling the multitude to him again, he began saying to them: "Listen to me, all of you, and understand. There is nothing from outside the man which going into him can defile him; but the things which proceed out of the man are what defile the man...." And he said to them [the disciples]: "Are you not aware that whatever goes into the man from outside cannot defile him, because it does not go into his heart, but into his stomach, and goes out into the latrine?" Thus he declared all foods clean. (Mark 7:14-15, 18-19)

According to Mark, Jesus invalidated the biblical principle that there is a distinction between clean and unclean foods (Leviticus 10, Deuteronomy 14:3-21). Jesus reportedly says: "There is nothing from outside the man which going into him can defile him; but the things which proceed out of the man are what defile the man." This negation of the biblical distinction between permitted and prohibited foods is of great significance. Mark's Jesus presumptuously dismissed a fundamental biblical precept. Moreover, this statement is in direct contradiction of declarations Jesus supposedly made about the validity and permanence of the Torah that are found in the other Synoptic Gospels (Matthew 5:17-19, Luke 16:17).

Some Christians claim that what Jesus is stressing in his assertion is that there are many immoral things which proceed from within a person that defile him (Mark 7:20-23). Yet the fact is that Jesus' statement, as reported in Mark refers to the dietary laws of the Torah. Mark is explicit in declaring that Jesus meant specifically the nullification of the dietary laws of clean and unclean food. This is stressed in his editorial comment. Following his citation of Jesus' statement that "whatever goes into the man from outside cannot defile him, because it does not go into his heart, but into his stomach, and goes out into the latrine," Mark adds: "Thus he declared all foods clean." Whether Mark actually reproduced an actual saying of Jesus can never be known with certainty, but Mark's Jesus certainly was expressing the view of at least a faction within the early church (Luke 11:41; Acts 10:15, 11:9; Romans 14:14; Colossians 2:16). Although Mark's Jesus did not grant outright permission to eat unclean species, it was so understood by Mark. By denying the distinction between clean and unclean food, Mark's Jesus paved the way for his followers to declare invalid an important feature of God's Torah to Israel.

To further advance the antinomian branch of the early church the author of Acts tells a story about Peter:

> And he became hungry, and was desiring to eat; but while they were making preparations, he fell into a trance; and he beheld the sky opened up, and a certain object like a great sheet coming down, lowered by four corners to the ground, and there were in it all kinds of four-footed animals and crawling creatures of the earth and birds of the air. And a voice came to him, "Arise, Peter, kill and eat!" But Peter said, "By no means, Lord, for I have never eaten anything unholy and unclean." And again a voice came to him a second time, "What God has cleansed, no longer consider unholy." (Acts 10:10-15)

While in a trance, Peter is reluctant to disobey the dietary laws of the Torah. He is then reassured by the "Lord" that it is God's will that he partake of prohibited foods. With this story, the faction of the church that wanted to do away with observance of the Mosaic Law gave credence to their position and countered those in the early church who opposed the nullification of the Torah (Acts 15:5, Galatians 2:11-12).

Christianity in the name of Jesus Christ abolished the bulk of the laws of the Torah. Whether or not that nullification actually represented the position of Jesus of Nazareth becomes monumentally irrelevant. Christianity in all its variations is not a continuation or fulfillment of Biblical Judaism, Rabbinic Judaism or anything else represented by Judaism or being Jewish. If one believes Jesus (Yeshua, Yeshu, Yahoshua, etc.) is Messiah, unique, God, Son of God, risen from the dead that is simply not in accordance with biblical teachings.

Chapter 74

NEW TESTAMENT REFUTATIONS OF THE TRINITY DOCTRINE
(Mark 13:32)

The notion of a triune deity

In trinitarian Christian belief there are three conscious personalities existing in one divine being or substance: the union in one God of Father, Son and Holy Spirit as three infinite, coequal and coeternal persons; one God in three persons. Many Christian scholars acknowledge that the concept of the Trinity cannot be substantiated from the Jewish Scriptures. Nevertheless, there are misunderstandings of the Jewish Scriptures by some trinitarian Christians attempting to prove otherwise. This is especially true when on occasion angels speak as if they were God Himself, and even use His personal name, Y-H-V-H. A few examples of such occurrences involve Manoah and his wife (Judges 2:1; 13:21, 22), Jacob wrestling (Genesis 32:24-30; Hosea 12:3-5), Moses (Exodus 3:2ff.) and Gideon (Judges 6:12-14). What trinitarians sometimes attribute to Jesus or to "the Holy Spirit"[1] in the Jewish Scriptures is better explained as God manifesting Himself by means of an angelic messenger who speaks for Him in the first person ("I the Lord," etc.) and manifests His glory.

Inability to substantiate the Trinity doctrine from the Jewish Scriptures has led some Christians to say the concept must be derived from the New Testament. However, the allegation of a triune deity cannot be established even from the New Testament (despite some trinitarian interpolations). Careful examination of the evidence presented to prove the existence of a triune deity based on Jewish or Christian Scriptures is found to be without substance.

Compounding the exegetical problem for Christian laypersons reading the New Testament is the fact that the definite article is often added by translators to the term holy spirit. This leads readers to think that "the Holy Spirit" is referring to a separate person, a third person

423

of "the Holy Trinity" as taught by trinitarian theologians. There is a failure to understand "holy spirit" in the New Testament as a claim to either a manifestation of God's presence and power or of an angelic manifestation speaking on behalf of God.

The Master and the servant

There are many New Testament passages that refute the Christian doctrine of the Trinity. An examination of statements attributed to Jesus by the Gospels, shows that he never said he was God or a part of God. Jesus spoke of his Father in heaven as his God (John 20:17), to whom he attributed superior authority, knowledge and greatness (Matthew 20:23, Mark 13:32, John 14:28). The Trinity doctrine says "the Father" and "the Son" are coequal in power and substance, but what does the New Testament have to say?

The Gospels' Jesus did not consider himself equal to God, for it is said there were things that neither he nor the angels knew, but only God knew. Mark's Jesus says: "But of that day or the hour no one knows, neither the angels in heaven, nor the Son, but the Father" (Mark 13:32). Furthermore, when troubled by the prospect of imminent execution, Luke's Jesus displayed submission to God and prayed for help saying: "Father, if you are willing, remove this cup from me; yet not my will, but Yours be done" (Luke 22:42, cf., John 5:30). Are these verses from the Gospels consistent with the trinitarian claim that Jesus is in fact one in substance and power with God? Do they show agreement or equality of consciousness?

It is alleged that God did miracles and wonders through Jesus (Matthew 9:8; Acts 2:22, 10:38). If Jesus were God, the New Testament would simply say that Jesus did the miracles himself without having to make reference to God's input. The claim that it was God not Jesus who was the actual miracle maker shows that God is greater than Jesus. The claim that Jesus in heaven supposedly prays on behalf of those who follow him (e.g., Hebrews 7:25), yet that God accepts or rejects his petition shows a separation of ideation.

These verses are representative of the Gospels' teachings concerning Jesus' relationship with God. But there are other verses as well, which illustrate that the Trinity doctrine is not found in the New Testament. In Matthew 12:31-32 (see also Luke 12:10) it is stated:

"Therefore I say to you, every sin and blasphemy shall be forgiven men, but blasphemy against the spirit will not be forgiven. And whoever speaks a word against the Son of Man, it shall be forgiven him; but whoever speaks against the holy spirit, it shall not be forgiven him, neither in this age nor in that to come." Matthew's Jesus is here arguing with "the Pharisees who say he performs miracles with the help of "Beelzebul the ruler of the demons" (Matthew 12:24) and not as he claims by "[the] spirit of God" (Matthew 12:28). He sees this as their blasphemous denial of God's power, that is, His spirit, as manifested through His agent (Jesus). Jesus is not talking about an actual personage called "the Holy Spirit." Hence, we may reasonably presume that Jesus, if he is to be equated with the "Son of Man" (John 8:28), is not of equal status with an imagined "Holy Spirit" (supposedly the third member of the triune deity of Christianity). If both the Holy Spirit and Jesus were coequal persons in one deity, then there would be no difference between speaking against Jesus and speaking against the Holy Spirit.

Matthew says the mother of the sons of Zebedee requests of Jesus that her sons be given prominent positions to the right and left of him in his kingdom. Jesus responds that such decisions are not made by him, but by the Father. He says: "this is not mine to give, but it is for those for whom it has been prepared by my Father" (Matthew 20:20-23). Does this statement illustrate equality within the Trinity?

Matthew's Jesus declares: "Heaven and earth will pass away, but my words will not pass away. But of that day and hour no one knows, neither the angels of the heavens nor the Son, but only the Father" (Matthew 24:35-36; see also Mark 13:32). Do the various parts of the Trinity keep secrets from each other? How can the Father and Son be of one essence if the Father knows things of which the Son is ignorant?

Similarly, when asked (after his supposed resurrection) if he would "at this time" restore the kingdom of Israel (Acts 1:6) Jesus replied: "It is not for you to know times or seasons which the Father has placed in His own jurisdiction" (Acts 1:7). Are we to conclude that the "equal" partners of the triune godhead have powers and knowledge, which they do not share with each other? Even after his supposed resurrection, Jesus is still not all-knowing but is said to receive increments of knowledge from God. Thus, we find: "The revelation of Jesus Christ, which God gave him to show to his bond-servants, the things which must shortly take place" (Revelation 1:1). Even the pre-incarnate Jesus did not have the same degree of knowledge as God, the Father. If this pre-incarnate supernatural being is equated with the angel of the Lord as so many trinitarians allege then the following needs to be considered. The prophet Zechariah records that the angel of the Lord inquired of God: "O Lord of hosts, how long will You not have compassion on Jerusalem and on the cities of Judah" (Zechariah 1:12). Where is the equality of knowledge between the "equal" partners of the triune godhead?

Luke 2:52 says: "And Jesus kept increasing in wisdom and in physical growth, and in favor with God and men." Do the members of the Trinity have likes and dislikes about each other? Did Jesus, the perfect god-man, need to increase in favor with God, or shall we say with two-thirds of God?

John's Jesus does not consider himself equal with the Father as is illustrated in several verses. He acknowledges that "The Son can do nothing by himself; he can only do what he sees his Father doing; for whatever the Father does, these things the Son also does in like manner" (John 5:19). He adds: "I can do nothing on my own initiative. As I hear, I judge; and my judgment is just, because I do not seek my own will, but the will of Him who sent me" (John 5:30; see also John 6:38, Luke 22:42). Are some members of the allegedly coequal Trinity subservient, and less than equal, to other members? Although they have different wills ("I do not seek my own will"), do they obey without question the others' commands ("the will of Him who sent me")? John's Jesus admits to subordinating his own distinct will, yet according to the trinitarian doctrine they should all have the same will. Should one of the triune partners have to forgo his own will in favor of the will of another member of the Trinity? Should not they all have the exact same will? And, which member of the triune deity initiates the divine will?

John's Jesus says: "When you lift up the Son of Man, then you will know that I am he, and that I do nothing on my own initiative, but I speak these things as the Father taught me. And he who sent me is with me; He has not left me alone, because I always do the things that are pleasing to Him" (John 8:28-29). John's Jesus once more admits that "I did not speak on my own initiative, but the Father Himself who sent me has given me commandment, what to say, and what to speak" (John 12:49). Does the Son have a mind of his own or is he simply reiterating what he is told? Continuing in this vein Jesus says that what he is teaching is not his own ideas. He exclaims: "My teaching is not mine, but His who sent me" (John 7:16). Jesus could not say this if he were God because the instruction would then have been his to begin with.

John's Jesus says: "As the Father gave me command, even so I do" (John 14:31). Are we to presume that the Son has no authority without the consent of the Father? In the New Testament, there are numerous verses alleging that Jesus was given power and authority by "the Father." Yet, if he was an integral part of God, then he would have always had the power and authority that the New Testament says he was "given." Jesus was allegedly given "all authority" by the Father (Matthew 28:18). He was allegedly given "a name above every name" by the Father (Philippians 2:9). He was allegedly given work to accomplish by the Father (John 5:36). He was allegedly given the power to "raise up" those who believed in him by the Father (John 6:39-40, 10:28-29). He was allegedly given glory by the Father (John 17:22, 24). He was allegedly given his "cup" of suffering and death by the Father (John 18:11). The Father allegedly "seated" Jesus at His own right hand (Ephesians 1:20) and "appointed" him over the Church (Ephesians 1:22). These verses make no sense if Jesus is eternally "coequal" with the Father.

John quotes Jesus as saying: "I am going to the Father, because the Father is greater than I am" (John 14:28). Is this coequality within the Trinity? According to the New Testament, Jesus referred to God as "my God" both before and after his supposed resurrection (Matthew 27:46; John 20:17; Revelation 3:12). Thus, according to the New Testament, Jesus did not consider himself to be God or God's coequal, but instead recognized his subservience to God to whom he must go. As John's post-resurrection Jesus says to Mary Magdalene, "I ascend to my Father and your Father, and my God and your God" (John 20:17).

John's Jesus says: "Do you say of him whom the Father sanctified and sent into the world, 'You are blaspheming' because I said 'I am the Son of God'"? (John 10:36). The meaning of sanctify is "to make holy," specifically by setting something apart as holy (consecrate) or to make something free from sin (spiritually purified). This Gospel teaches that Jesus was "sanctified" by God before being sent into the world. It is claimed that Jesus was sanctified by God before entering the world, but God does not need to be sanctified! Does this sound like the alleged pre-incarnate Jesus and God were coequal?

The author of Hebrews writes that it was fitting that God should "make" Jesus "perfect through suffering" (Hebrews 2:10). According to this author, Jesus "learned obedience from the things which he suffered" (Hebrews 5:8). God is forever perfect, but Jesus is said to have needed to attain perfection through his suffering. If he was a sinless god-man this makes absolutely no sense. Why did Jesus have to learn to be obedient if he is God? An all-knowing God does not need to learn anything for He knows it already. Whom does Jesus have to obey? Do the equal members of the Trinity exercise authority, one over the other?

Paul states: "Christ is the head of every man, and the man is the head of a woman, and God is the head of Christ" (1 Corinthians 11:3). "You belong to Christ," Paul claims, but he goes on to say "Christ belongs to God" (1 Corinthians 3:23). As man is subservient to Christ, and woman to man, so Christ is subservient to God. One who is subservient to another cannot be equal to that individual.

In a prayer to God made by the disciples that is found in the Book of Acts, they refer to King David as God's "servant" (Acts 4:25). Later in that same prayer they call the alleged post-resurrection Jesus "your holy servant" (Acts 4:30). It is obvious that the disciples did not believe Jesus was God, but thought of him, like David, as a servant of God (cf. Matthew 12:18 and Acts 3:26).

Acts reports that Peter said that "God has made this Jesus ... both Lord and Christ" (Acts 2:36). It was God who it is alleged made

Jesus "both Lord and Christ" and "gave him the name that is above every name" (i.e., Lord of lords and King of kings"—Revelations 17:14, 19:16). If Jesus were part of the one-and-only God, he would not need God to exalt him for he would already be exalted. "Lord" (the Greek word is kyrios) is a masculine title of respect and majesty, and it is frequently used in the New Testament of others beside God and Jesus. Property owners are called lord (Matthew 20:8); heads of households are called lord (Mark 13:35); slave owners are called lord (Matthew 10:24); husbands are called lord (1 Peter 3:6); a son called his father lord (Matthew 21:30); the Roman emperor is called lord (Acts 25:26); Roman authorities are called lord (Matthew 27:63). The word, "lord" is not used at Acts 2:36 in the sense of God; rather, it refers to someone who has only attained a high station through the grace of God. The New Testament says Jesus earned positions of authority and as a result earned the names and powers that go along with these positions. How did he earn them? "[He] humbled himself and became obedient to the point of death—even on a cross. Therefore God also highly exalted him and gave him the name that is above every name" (Philippians 2:8-9). Such a one could not be God. Indeed, if Jesus were God, then by definition he was already "Lord," and it would be incorrect to say Jesus was "made" Lord.

Paul states "that Jesus Christ is Lord, to the glory of God the Father" (Philippians 2:11). Some Christians allege this shows that Paul taught that Jesus and God are equal. However, their claim is not correct. The complete passage shows Jesus in a subservient position to that of God:

> The attitude you should have is the one Christ had: Although he existed in the form of God he did not think that by force he should try to become equal with God. Instead, he emptied himself and took the form of a slave and came to be in the likeness of men. And being found in appearance as a man, he humbled himself and became obedient until death, even on a cross. For this reason God highly exalted him and gave him the name that is above every name. And so, in the name of Jesus every knee should bend of those in heaven and those on earth and of those underground. And every tongue should confess that Jesus Christ is Lord, to the glory of God

the Father. (Philippians 2:5-11)

According to this passage, Jesus "did not think that by force he should try to become equal with God," but instead "emptied himself and took the form of a slave, and came to be in the likeness of men." Having thereby humbled himself he went still further and in obedience to God underwent death on a cross. As a reward for lowering his (supernatural) status rather than trying to elevate himself to the status of God, Jesus was "highly exalted" by God because he did not seek equality with God (verses 6-9). The author of Acts shows that claiming Jesus was exalted does not mean he was God. He declares that "God ... raised up Jesus, whom you had put to death ... to His right hand as a prince and a savior ... [and] exalted [him] to His right hand a prince and a savior, to grant repentance to Israel, and forgiveness of sins" (Acts 5:30-31). The recipient of God's exaltation is not one who was or becomes equal with God, but is given certain powers as a reward for faithful service to God's will. These statements make no sense if Jesus were God, because then Jesus would have been praised for not seeking equality with himself! And, then, God is said to reward and exalt Himself!

Paul's Jesus is not equal to God but is a supernatural being that is considered to have been raised to an exalted position by God. He who is not equal to God cannot be God. Furthermore, Jesus is proclaimed Lord, but, in verse 11, Paul does not use "Lord" and "God" as synonymous terms. The simple fact is that Paul considers Jesus to be a highly honored supernatural agent, but does not make him equal with God. He is said to be in the "form of God" but not that he was God or even one-third of God. Jesus is said to be a lesser being who "did not think that by force he should try to become equal with God."

Paul says that in Jesus the "fullness [pleroma] of Deity dwells bodily" (Colossians 2:9). He alleges that God (the Deity) placed a full measure of divine qualities in Jesus. This is not the same as saying that Jesus is deity or that in him dwells the full essence — powers and attributes — of God. Earlier in Colossians, Paul states that God was pleased "for all the fullness to dwell in him [Jesus]" (Colossians 1:19). But, Paul is not claiming that all the divine attributes and nature dwell in

Jesus. Paul is speaking about Jesus being filled with spiritual attributes that will enable him to carry out all that God desires. Having "all the fullness" of God would not make one God. Paul also says that Christians should be filled with "all the fullness of God" (Ephesians 3:19), but this does not make Christians into God. Furthermore, if Jesus were God, there would be no point in saying that the fullness of God dwelt in him through an action of God, because, being God, he would already have the fullness of God within him.

Jesus, the man, is said to be the mediator between God and men. Paul writes, "For there is one God, and one mediator also between God and men, the man Christ Jesus" (1 Timothy 2:5). Jesus is called a "man," even after his alleged resurrection. Now, if this supposedly resurrected Jesus were himself God and acted in total accord with the other two-thirds of God, he could not be a mediator, an intermediary or conciliator, "between God and men." He could not be man's advocate and judge at the same time

Paul says that there is "one Lord, one faith, one baptism, one God and Father of all" (Ephesians 4:5-6). The "one Lord" is Jesus. The "one God" is the Father. In this passage there are two separate beings represented, not "one God" composed of Jesus and his Father. The fact is, there is no verse that says that Jesus and the Father are "one God." There is also no mention of the so-called "Holy Spirit" of the triune deity.

Revelation 11:15 states that "The kingdom of the world has become the kingdom of our Lord and of His Christ." Some Christians allege that this verse shows the equality of Jesus and God. This claim is incorrect. Significantly, "our Lord" in this verse is not Jesus but God Himself, and Jesus is clearly distinguished from God as "His Christ." While the term "Lord" is often used in the New Testament to refer to either God or Jesus, there is a difference between the two.

John's Jesus says: "I and the Father are one [hen]" (John 10:30). Trinitarians allege that this shows that they are one in essence. This claim is incorrect. This statement does not suggest either a dual or triune deity. What John's Jesus meant by the word hen ("one") becomes clear from his prayer concerning the apostles. He says: "That they may be one [hen], just as we are one [hen]" (John 17:22).

He means that they should be united in agreement with one another as he (Jesus) is always united in agreement with God, as stated: "I [Jesus] always do the things that are pleasing to Him [God]" (John 8:29). There is thus no implication that Jesus and God, or the twelve apostles are to be considered as of one essence. The lesser authority aligns his thoughts with the greater authority.

John claims that on hearing Jesus say: "I and the Father are one," the Jews accused him of making himself out to be a god: "For good works we do not stone you but for blasphemy, and because you, being a man, made yourself a god" (John 10:33). According to John, the Jews understood Jesus' words as an assertion, on his part, that he was a supernatural power ('elohim, i.e., a god). In answering the Jews, John's Jesus does not explain directly how he and the Father are one but explains rather that the concept of his being "a god" is not a farfetched idea. John has Jesus reply: "Has it not been written in Your Law, 'I said you are gods'?" (John 10:34). This is taken from Psalms 82:6, which reads: "I said: You are godlike beings ['elohim], and all of you sons of the Most High." By this explanation, John's Jesus wishes to show that there is nothing wrong in his claiming to be "a son of God" (John 10:36), for God declares this to be true of all the children of Israel. However, John's Jesus thinks himself to be in a closer relationship with God than any of the other "sons of the Most High." An important distinction needs to be made here. While Jesus is called the "Son of God" more than fifty times in the New Testament he is never called "God the Son."

John's Jesus explains that he is a messenger of God sent to do His bidding. He endeavors to convince the Jews that they misunderstand him, "whom the Father sanctified and sent into the world" (John 10:36). It is only because he is God's consecrated messenger, doing the works of his Father, that he believes himself to be "one" with God, strictly obedient to His every command (John 10:37-38). John's Jesus is so exact in his obedience to God's every desire that he claims "the Father is in me and I am in the Father" (John 10:38). At no time does he claim to be one in essence with God. Although he presents himself to be as one with God in will and purpose, John's Jesus never claims a unity of person or equality in substance with the Almighty.

In the final analysis, if Jesus were truly God Himself, there would be no need for him to be "sent" by anyone or anything.

John's Jesus states: "Even in your Law it has been written, that the testimony of two men is true [i.e., valid or admissible; see Deuteronomy 17:6, 19:15]. I am he who bears witness of myself, and the Father who sent me bears witness of me" (John 8:17-18). Does this passage show Jesus and God to be ontologically one? If Jesus and "the Father" were not two distinct entities how could they be considered two witnesses? If Jesus and God are one than there would in reality only be one witness. This statement also goes against the Torah's precepts. According to the Torah, the two witnesses do not include the testimony of the person being judged.

Hebrews says that Jesus is "not ashamed" to call his followers "brothers," because they "are all from one [Father]" (Hebrews 2:11). The text says they are "brothers" of Jesus and implicitly sons of God. It does not say they are "brothers of God." Jesus is no more part of God's essence than any other individual.

Revelation says: "I [Jesus] am the first and the last, and the living one; and I was dead, and behold, I am alive forevermore, and I have the keys of death and of Hades" (Revelation 1:17-18). By connecting this verse with Isaiah 44:6, "I am the first, and I am the last," some trinitarians claim to find proof that Jesus is God. However, while Revelation's author uses the prophet's language in creating his own phraseology there is no comparison being made with Isaiah's statement. He is expressing his belief that Jesus is the first and the last, not in terms of everlasting existence, but with regard to the manner of supposed resurrection. For this reason, the author calls Jesus "the firstborn of the dead" (Revelation 1:5). According to him, Jesus was the first one God raised from the dead to be "alive forevermore." He is also the last one whom God will raise directly in this manner, for now it is alleged that God has given the power to resurrect the dead, the "keys of death and Hades," exclusively to Jesus (see also John 5:21-22). These verses do not at all provide any ground for proclaiming Jesus as part of a triune deity.

John states: "Jesus said to him: 'Have I been so long with you, and yet you have not come to know me, Philip? He who has seen me has seen the Father; how do you say, "Show us the Father"?'" (John 14:9). If Jesus is actually God, this statement would contradict the assertion that "no man has seen God at any time" (John 1:18, 1 John 4:12; cf. Exodus 33:20). When John's Jesus says: "He who has seen me has seen the Father," it is not to be understood literally as actually seeing God in a physical sense. John claims Jesus is "the only begotten god ["son" in some manuscripts]" whose function is to explain God (John 1:18). He does not consider Jesus to be part of the Godhead, only a supernatural power who bridges the gulf between God and man.

In sum, the author of John does not consider Jesus to be a mere mortal, but neither does he believe that he is God. He considers Jesus to be God's most intimate messenger, the Logos, who (as Philo states) is made the most exact image of God, but is not God Himself. The New Testament teaches that Jesus died. Yet, even Paul admits at Romans 1:23 that God is "immortal." One who is immortal is not subject to death; such a being could not die for even a moment.

God: undivided and without equal

How did John's Jesus view the possibility of a division in the divine essence? Chapter 17 of the Gospel of John records a prayer, which its author attributes to Jesus. In verse 2 of this prayer, Jesus views himself as being sent by God, his Father, who "gave him authority over all mankind." But of his "Father" he is quoted, in verse 3, as saying that he is "the only true God." Jesus does not say, "We are the only true God," or even, "You Father and the Holy Spirit are the only true God," but refers his remarks solely to the God whom he depicts as "Father." Even assuming Jesus to have been God manifested in a human form, he still would be God, and as such, he would not have said that he was sent by God. Thus, by calling his Father not just the "true God" but "the only true God," he avows that he himself cannot be part of God. Jesus may claim to be united in oneness with God in doing only what the Almighty wishes, but he never asserts that he is part of the essence of God. If Jesus is of one substance with the Father, he could not say that the "Father" (verse 1), as differentiated from "Jesus Christ" (verse 3), is "the only true God." By definition, "only" must imply the singularity of God to the exclusion of all, including Jesus and the Holy Spirit. Thus, it is clear that Jesus himself confirms that the Father, not the Son or the Holy Spirit, is "the only true God."

According to Acts, Stephen claims to see a vision of God and Jesus just before his own death. While "full of holy spirit" he is said to see "the son of man standing at the right hand of God" (Acts 7:56). Thus, God and Jesus are portrayed as two separate beings. That which is a separate entity from God cannot be God.

Luke's Jesus spoke to a "certain ruler" who had called him "good," asking him, "Why do you call me good? No one is good except God alone" (Luke 18:18-19). If Jesus thought he was God, he would have complimented the man on his insight, just as he complimented Peter when Peter said he was "the Christ, the Son of the living God" (Matthew 16:15-16). Instead, Jesus gives the man a mild admonishment containing no recognition that there is any connection between calling him "good" and God alone being good.

Paul claims that "Christ" is the "image of God" (Colossians 1:15; 2 Corinthians 4:4). If Jesus is the image of God, then he cannot be God, because one cannot be an image of someone and the real person at the same time. If we see a photograph or a painting of a person, we see the individual's image, but the image is not the real person. If "Christ" is the image of God, as Paul alleges, then as God's image he could not be God.

Paul's Jesus: A savior but not God

The New Testament authors make a definite distinction between the one-and-only God and Jesus, never considering them one and the same. For instance, we find this distinction expressed in the statement: "Kindness and peace be multiplied to you in the knowledge of God and of Jesus our Lord" (2 Peter 1:2). This clarifies the meaning of the preceding verse, which reads, in part, "by the righteousness of our God and of [the] Savior Jesus Christ" (2 Peter 1:1). The author of these two verses indicates that he considers God and Jesus to be two distinct beings.

On occasion, the New Testament authors alternate their use of the term "savior," applying it to both God and Jesus. Thus, Paul, in Titus 1:3, calls God, "our Savior," and then in verse 4, differentiates between "God [the] Father and Christ Jesus our Savior." This does not show that God and Jesus are of one essence, but illustrates the function, which the New Testament authors believe Jesus has in God's relationship with humanity. This function can be seen from the following discussion of what some of the New Testament authors have to say about Jesus as savior.

Paul writes: "Awaiting the blessed hope and manifestation of the glory of the great God and of our Savior Christ Jesus" (Titus 2:13). He designates Jesus as "our Savior," but not as God Himself. Yet, even Paul could not deny that ultimately God is the true savior (Isaiah 43:11, 45:21; Hosea 13:4), which leads him to argue that God works through Jesus, as He worked, in former times, through others who were raised up as saviors (Judges 2:16; 3:9, 15; Nehemiah 9:27). Thus, God is still considered the ultimate and only source of salvation. However, salvation is now executed through Jesus. Accordingly, in Paul's letters we find the Father and the Son spoken of together in connection with salvation (1 Timothy 1:1; 2 Timothy 1:8-10; Titus 1:3-4, 2:10-13, 3:4-6). The author of Acts attributes to Peter a statement which indicates Jesus' position as a savior: "He is the one whom God exalted to His right hand as a leader and a savior" (Acts 5:31). This is also expressed in the statement: "the Father has sent the Son to be savior of the world" (1 John 4:14). In point of fact, even though Jesus is described as man's savior, God is described as Jesus' savior. The author of Hebrews writes: "In the days of his flesh, he offered up both prayers and supplications with loud crying and tears to the one able to save him from death, and he was heard because of his piety" (Hebrews 5:7). While Jesus is, for Paul and the other New Testament authors, the sole agent through which God deals with mankind, that is, man's Lord and Savior, he is not at all God.

"I am"

John's Jesus states: "'Abraham your father rejoiced to see my day; and he saw it, and was glad.' The Jews therefore said to him: 'You are not yet fifty years old, and have you seen Abraham?' Jesus said to them: 'Truly, truly, I say to you, before Abraham came into being, I am'" (John 8:56-58). Is the author of this Gospel claiming that Jesus is part of a triune deity when he has Jesus say, "before Abraham came into being, I am" (John 8:58)?

Trinitarians argue that the Greek words *ego eimi* ("I am"), allegedly spoken by Jesus, show that Jesus is God (see also John 8:24, 28). They arrive at their contention by connecting the phrase "I am" with the words spoken by God in Exodus 3:14 and often translated: "I AM THAT I AM…. Thus you shall say to the children of Israel: I AM has sent me to you." However, the literal and proper translation of this verse is: I WILL BE WHAT I WILL BE…. Thus you shall say to the children of Israel: I WILL BE has sent me to you."

Since John utilized the Greek Septuagint translation of the Bible in his writings, it cannot be assumed that John's Jesus is referring to the words in Exodus 3:14. Although Jesus actually spoke in Hebrew or Aramaic, not Greek, John recorded Jesus' alleged words in Greek. *Ego eimi* ("I am"), used by John's Jesus, is not the same as *ho on* ("The Being, The One Who Is"), which is used in the Septuagint's rendering of Exodus 3:14: "And God spoke to Moses, saying, I am THE BEING; and He said, Thus you shall say to the children of Israel: THE BEING has sent me to you." Even though ho on appears in the Gospel of John, it is never used as a title or name or exclusively as a reference to Jesus. In the Book of Revelation, also credited to John by Christian tradition, ho on appears five times (Revelation 1:4, 8; 4:8; 11:17; 16:5). Significantly, in each instance, it is used as a title or designation applied to God, not Jesus. Thus: "John to the seven churches that are in Asia: Grace to you and peace, from Him who is [ho on] and who was and who is to come; and from the seven spirits who are before His throne" (Revelation 1:4). That this verse refers to God and not Jesus is seen from the following verse, which continues the greeting by now including Jesus as one of those sending greetings. Hence, Revelation says, in verses 4 and 5 that greetings are sent by God, the seven spirits, and Jesus.

The author of Revelation writes: "'I am the Alpha and the Omega,' says the Lord God, 'who is [ho on] and who was and who is to come, the Almighty'" (Revelation 1:8). This verse also speaks of God, not Jesus. In Revelation 4:8, ho on is applied to "the Lord God, the Almighty," not Jesus, who, as the "Lamb" referred to in Revelation 5:6-7, comes to God, who is sitting on His throne. That they are two separate entities is seen from Revelation 5:13: "To the one sitting on the throne, and to the Lamb, be blessing and honor and glory and dominion forever and ever." In addition, ho on is applied to the "Lord God, the Almighty," not Jesus, in Revelation 11:17 and Revelation 16:5. That *ho on* in Revelation 16:5 refers to God and not Jesus can be seen from verse 7, which, referring to the subject of verses 5 and 6, states: "And I heard the altar saying: 'Yes, Lord God, the Almighty, true and righteous are Your judgments.'" These are further indications that ho on and ego eimi are not used as synonymous terms by John.

In John 8:56-58, John is expounding his belief that Jesus had a pre-human existence as God's special supernatural agent in heaven. John's Jesus is proclaiming in this passage that this pre-human existence began before Abraham was born: "Before Abraham came into being, I am." The fact of the matter is that the text does not at all indicate how long John's Jesus supposedly lived before Abraham. In no way is John's statement to be taken as identifying Jesus as part of God.

Jesus as an instrument of the Creator

Even the authors of John, Colossians, and Hebrews, who elevate Jesus to a point where he is viewed as the medium through whom things are done, do not claim that he is the Creator or part of a triune deity. They consider him the supernatural instrument through which the Creator works:

All things came into being through him, and apart from him not even one thing came into being. (John 1:3)

For in him all things were created in the heavens and upon earth, visible and invisible, whether lordships or governments or authorities. All things have been created through him and for him. (Colossians 1:16)

In these last days He has spoken to us by a Son, whom He appointed heir of all things, through whom also He made the ages. (Hebrews 1:2)

Do the preceding quotations from the New Testament show

oneness of substance and coequality within the christological concept of a triune deity? On the contrary, they show that the various members of the so-called Trinity could not be considered one or coequal. These authors did not view Jesus as equal to God, but rather as the being through which God relates to His creation.

The Jewish Scriptures inform us that only God, who is "from everlasting to everlasting," is eternal, and has no beginning (Psalms 90:2). The New Testament refers to Jesus as, "the beginning [arche] of the creation of God" (Revelation 3:14). Revelation's author does not imply that Jesus always existed. The word "beginning" expresses the idea of a starting point in time. This clarifies John 1:1, "In the beginning was the Word," referring to the beginning of creation. John does not state that Jesus was eternally with God, only that he existed for an unspecified time before being used as the means through which God's creative works were accomplished. It is only after creation began that John's Jesus became God's spokesman, the Word. The suggestion that Jesus is the author of the creation, and in that sense the beginning, does not accord with the meaning of the word arche. The claim that arche means the originating source of creation has no New Testament support. New Testament usage demonstrates that arche is not used in Revelation 3:14 in the sense of causing anything to come into being, but rather as a reference to the first thing created by God.

The Greek word *arche*, "beginning" or "origin" refers to the commencement of a thing, not its authorship. It indicates primacy in time, and primacy in rank, but not primacy in the sense of causing anything to exist. The authors of the New Testament considered Jesus a created being, the first so made by God. Paul writes that "he is the image of the invisible God, the firstborn of all creation…. And he is before all things" (Colossians 1:15-17).

The New Testament regards Jesus as the one through whom God rules the universe. It also attributes to Jesus the attaining of his exalted position only at the behest of God (Philippians 2:9). But what we are mainly concerned with here is that the wording of Revelation 3:14 does not at all establish Jesus as being the eternal Creator of the universe. It does not show Jesus to be the author or origin of creation.

It should be understood that there is a difference in meaning between saying one is the "head," "chief," "prince," or "ruler" of creation, and saying he is the "beginning" or architect of creation. Primacy in creation, as the first being created by God, and primacy over creation, as the one through whom God rules the creation, are two distinct attributes that the authors of the New Testament applied to Jesus. One does not naturally follow from the other.

In Revelation 3:14 *arche* is properly translated as "beginning" to indicate the author's belief that Jesus was the first being created. A further example of this usage may be found in Colossians 1:18. There, Jesus is called "the beginning [*arche*], the first born from the dead," indicating Paul's belief that Jesus is the first one of those who will be resurrected from the dead, "in order that he might come to have first place in everything." As we have seen, Paul's Jesus, the so-called "the beginning of the creation of God," is thought to be the first thing created by God, "the firstborn of all creation" (Colossians 1:15) through whom everything else was created. The very fact that Jesus' existence is connected with the beginning of creation nullifies the claim that Jesus is God. What is begotten cannot be eternal, and what is not eternal cannot be equal to God; moreover, that which is created by God cannot be God.

John expounds the belief that Jesus had a pre-human existence as the Word who was "in the beginning with God" and through whom "all things came into being." John emphasizes this belief throughout his entire Gospel (John 1:1-3; 17:5, 24). He describes Jesus as "an only begotten from a father" (John 1:14) and "the only begotten Son of God" (John 3:18; see also John 3:16, 1 John 4:9). John's belief in Jesus as "the only begotten Son of God" rests, as does Paul's belief, on the contention that Jesus is the only being created directly by God. All other creatures were created through Jesus. He is the image of the invisible God, the firstborn, and chief among all creation (Colossians 1:15-17). He is even higher than the ordinary angels (Hebrews 1:3-13). Yet, despite the exalted position to which John raised Jesus, he, like Paul, did not consider him part of the one-and-only God. According to Paul, Jesus became the "Son of God" by his supposed resurrection from the dead: "And who through the spirit of holiness was declared with power to be the Son of God by his resurrection from the dead: Jesus Christ our Lord" (Romans 1:4).

The New Testament's Jesus is never recognized as God or part of God, only as the "Son of God," that is, one who is the first thing created by God and who is in close relationship with God. In fact, even after his alleged resurrection Jesus is still referred to by the term "Son of God" (Revelation 2:18), nothing more. This is not surprising, since in the New Testament Jesus always speaks of himself, and is spoken of by others, as separate and distinct from God. Nowhere in the New Testament, including the Gospel of John, where it specifically mentions the Word becoming flesh, is the claim made that Jesus is God incarnate, a combination of God and man.

Some Christians, believing Jesus to be God incarnate, see an important significance in John's use of the Greek verb *eskenosen*, translated "dwelt," in John 1:14: "And the Word became flesh, and dwelt among us." This verb is akin to the noun meaning "dwelling," "tent," "booth," "tabernacle." These Christians interpret this word to indicate that Jesus was God in spirit while tabernacling, that is, dwelling in, a human body, this incarnation making him a god-man. However, usage of this verb, by the author of John, does not imply that Jesus is the incarnation of God. The author of the Second Letter of Peter uses the same manner of expression: "And I consider it right, as long as I am in this dwelling [*skenomati*], to stir you up by way of reminder, knowing that the laying aside of my dwelling [*skenomatos*] is imminent, as also our Lord Jesus Christ has made clear to me" (2 Peter 1:13-14). Does the author of this letter mean, by the use of the Greek noun *skenoma*, "dwelling," "tabernacle," that Peter also is an incarnation, a god-man? The author most certainly does not intend to express such an opinion. What the author wishes to express is that Peter would remain alive for a short time longer in his human body, and that is all. Therefore, word usage indicates that John 1:14 does not support the incarnation of God doctrine.

Syncretic roots of Paul's Jesus

Much of Christianity is the development of Paul and his theological descendants, who presented the pagans with a diluted form of Judaism in Hellenized garb. It is true that the Hellenistic Jewish philosophy of Philo paved the way to such a syncretism, but Philo certainly would have been shocked at the resulting distortion which followed in Paul's wake. Philo expected the Messiah, but he never identified the Messiah with the Logos, as was done by later Christian theology. For Paul, who is influenced by Philonic philosophy, the Christ is:

> [T]he image of the invisible God, the firstborn of all creation. For in him all things were created, in the heavens and upon earth, visible and invisible, whether lordships or governments or authorities. All things have been created through him and for him. And he is before all things, and in him all things hold together.... For it was [God's] good pleasure for all the fullness to dwell in him, and through him to reconcile all things to Himself.... He [Jesus] has now reconciled you in his fleshly body through death, in order to present you before Him [God] holy and blameless and beyond reproach. (Colossians 1:15-22)

Paul's view is that Jesus is not God. He is God's first creation and the means by which God acts in the universe. He sees Jesus as the temporary incarnation of a preexistent heavenly being. Jesus, for Paul, is in the image of God. He is the link between God and man and the agent for man's redemption. He intercedes with God on man's behalf and, as heavenly advocate, pleads man's cause before God (Romans 8:34; see also Hebrews 7:25, 9:24; 1 John 2:1). He is the mediator between man and God: "For there is one God, and also one mediator between God and men, a man Christ Jesus" (1 Timothy 2:5). Paul further states: "But for us there is but one God, the Father, from whom are all things, and we exist for Him; and one Lord, Jesus Christ, through whom are all things, and we exist through him" (1 Corinthians 8:6). Trinitarian theology misunderstood Paul's Father-Son relationship. Paul says that the Father is "the God of our Lord Jesus Christ." He is the God and Father of Jesus, not his equal (Ephesians 1:3, 17). If there is one God and one Lord, then there are two separate beings, and they are not of the same nature or substance nor are they equal.

In all of his writings, Paul does not identify Jesus with God or portray him as equal to God. In fact, he says that in the future, the

Son will be subject to the Father. He says: "And when all things are subjected to him, then the Son himself will also be subjected to the One who subjected all things to him, that God may be all in all" (1 Corinthians 15:28). In Philippians 2:9, Paul writes of Jesus that it is God who "highly exalted him," which means that God did not make him His equal. Even after his exaltation, Jesus continues to remain subject to God. It is obvious that if Jesus is "highly exalted" by God, he must have first occupied an inferior position in relation to God. Since his prior position was lower than God's, and at best, he will attain a level where he will still be "subject to the One who subjected all things to him," he could not be part of or equal to that "One."

Subordination and subjection

Wherever the relationship of Jesus to God is treated in the New Testament, Jesus is always represented in a subordinate position. This subordinate role can be seen in the fact that Jesus views himself as a messenger: "He who receives you receives me, and he who receives me receives Him who sent me" (Matthew 10:40; see also John 5:36). Jesus acknowledges his subordination and subjection to God when he declares that God is greater than he is (John14:28), that he does nothing on his own initiative, speaking and doing only what God has taught him (John 8:28-29) and seeking not his own will, but the will of the God who sent him (John 5:30, 6:38).

Obviously, John's Jesus is not God, whose will is to be done, but is lower than God, doing God's will in accordance with Philo's conception of the Logos as a heavenly being distinct from God. In accordance with Philo's concept of the Logos as the mediator between God and mankind, John's Jesus said: "You are seeking to kill me, a man who has told you the truth, which I heard from God" (John 8:40). To the apostles he reveals the source of his alleged knowledge: "I have called you friends, because all the things which I have heard from my Father I have made known to you" (John 15:15). John's Jesus repeatedly speaks of himself as being sent by God and being taught by God.

But Jesus cried out and said: "He who believes in me does not believe in me, but in Him who sent me. And he who beholds me beholds

443

the One who sent me.... For I did not speak on my own initiative, but the Father Himself who sent me has given me commandment as to what I should say and what I should speak. And I know that His commandment is life everlasting. Therefore the things I speak are just as the Father has spoken to me, thus I speak." (John 12:44-50)

John's Jesus acknowledges that "A slave is not greater than his master, neither one who is sent greater than the one who sent him" (John 13:16). As God is greater than Jesus in sending him, so Jesus is greater than his disciples in sending them. Jesus tells them: "As the Father has sent me, I also send you" (John 20:21). The one who has greater authority sends the one who has less authority. John's Jesus himself disavows any triune coequality with God. He says: "This is everlasting life, that they may know You, the only true God, and Jesus [the] Christ whom You have sent" (John 17:3). The true God is superior to, separate and distinct from Jesus. That is why Paul writes: "there is but one God, the Father ... and one Lord, Jesus Christ" (1 Corinthians 8:6).

John's Jesus commands his followers to do "greater works" than his own. He declares: "He who believes in me [Jesus], the works that I do shall he do also; and greater works than these shall he do; because I go to the Father" (John 14:12). This statement is absurd if he were God, because then he would be instructing his followers to do greater works than God does.

The New Testament Jesus: A distinct supernatural agent

Despite the distinctiveness with which God and Jesus are regarded in the New Testament, most Christians are under the misconception that God and Jesus form two-thirds of a triune deity. Partial responsibility for this error goes to the New Testament authors because a number of designations for Jesus in the New Testament are the same as those given to God in the Jewish Scriptures. The resulting confusion as to whether certain New Testament passages refer to God or to Jesus helped to produce the belief in a triune deity. That Jesus, considered by the New Testament authors to be the link between God and His creation, is called by some of the same designations that are applied to God is understandable. After all, the New Testament authors believed that God had conferred a tremendous amount

444

of power upon this supernatural agent. So why not, as well, some of His names, which express certain facets of His being? But it is nevertheless clear that although God in the New Testament interacts with the world He created solely through His "firstborn," the latter is still subservient to God. Because of the exalted yet subservient position in which they envision Jesus, the New Testament authors do not believe it compromises God's status to apply some of His names to Jesus (cf. Ephesians 1:21, Philippians 2:9, Hebrews 1:4). The use of common names is not intended to show that Jesus is of one substance with God, but that God is giving Jesus the authority to act in some capacity on His behalf.

The Alpha and the Omega

In Revelation we find the verse: "I am the Alpha and the Omega,2 says the Lord God, who is and who was and who is to come, the Almighty" (Revelation 1:8). Alpha is the first letter of the Greek alphabet and Omega the last letter. This description is ascribed to God who verse 6 says is "his [Jesus'] God and Father." Verse 8 in the King James Version[3] reads: "'I am Alpha and Omega, the beginning and the ending,' saith the Lord, 'which is, and which was, and which is to come, the Almighty.'" In this verse, the King James Version and its derivative translations leave out the words ho theos ("the God") and use only *kyrios* ("Lord") giving the impression that the text is referring to Jesus when Alpha and Omega are distinctly applied here to the "Lord God" and not to Jesus. The word "God" is found in the best ancient manuscripts and, as a result, many modern versions do include the word "God."[4] As is clear from the context, the author of Revelation applies these words to God and not to Jesus. Thus we find: "Grace and peace to you from Him who is, and who was, and who is to come, and from the seven spirits before his throne, and from Jesus Christ, who is the faithful witness, the firstborn from the dead, and the ruler of the kings of the earth" (Revelation 1:4-5). Confusion became more pronounced as exegetical study of the New Testament intensified the connection between the so-called "Lord Jesus" and "the Lord God." But, there is a definite separation between God, "who is, and who was, and who is to come," and Jesus.

Those who rely on the King James Version or its derivative

445

translations are further misled by its rendering of Revelation 1:11. The King James Version mentions the Alpha and Omega in verse 11, which in context implies that it refers to Jesus. This text reads: "Saying, I am Alpha and Omega, the first and the last: and, What thou seest, write in a book, and send it unto the seven churches which are in Asia; unto Ephesus, and unto Smyrna, and unto Pergamos, and unto Thyatira, and unto Sardis, and unto Philadelphia, and unto Laodicea." The title, Alpha and Omega, is absent in the best ancient manuscripts and, as a result, is not included in most modern translations.[5] This verse should read: "Write what you see in a book and send it to the seven churches, to Ephesus and to Smyrna and to Pergamum and to Thyatira and to Sardis and to Philadelphia and to Laodicea."

Revelation 1:17 and 2:8 do not contain the words the Alpha and the Omega. In these verses the author of Revelation uses *protos* ("first") and *eschatos* ("last") which imply the same thought as the phrase the Alpha and the Omega. Revelation 1:17 reads: "When I saw him, I fell at his feet as though dead. But he laid his right hand upon me, saying, 'Fear not, I am the first and the last.'" Revelation 2:8 reads: "And to the angel of the church in Smyrna write: 'The words of the first and the last, who died and came to life.'" Jesus is called the arche or "beginning" of the creation of God (Revelation 3:14) and considered as the *prototokos* or "first begotten" spiritual son (Hebrews 1:6). Only in Revelation 21:6 is Jesus called the Alpha and the Omega. Verse 6 reads, "And he said to me, 'They have occurred! I am the Alpha and the Omega, the beginning and the end. To the thirsty I will give from the fountain of the water of life without payment.'" Jesus becomes the Alpha and the Omega and the *arche* ("beginning"; see Revelation 3:14, "the beginning of the creation of God") as well as the *telos* ("end"). This supposedly points to when Jesus is to become the Alpha and the Omega. In this phrase, the Greek collective neuter plural *gegonan*, "they have occurred," promotes the concept that there is a progressive process by which Jesus advances in stature when given increased powers and authority that in the past were exclusive to Almighty God. Nevertheless, in the Book of Revelation, Jesus is not God's equal at any point in time. What is recorded in Revelation is a vision of an imagined second return of Jesus. In this vision Jesus refers to himself as "the Alpha and the Omega, the beginning and the end" (Revelation 21:6). This title was not applied initially to Jesus. It becomes his reward signifying the power and authority invested in him for faithful service to God.

In Revelation we see Jesus portrayed again as the Alpha and Omega, the first and the last, the beginning and the end. Jesus supposedly says:

> I am the Alpha and the Omega, the first and the last, the beginning and the end. Blessed are those who wash their robes, that they may have the right to the tree of life and that they may enter the city by the gates. Outside are the dogs and sorcerers and fornicators and murderers and idolaters, and every one who loves and practices falsehood. I Jesus have sent my angel to you with this testimony for the churches. I am the root and the offspring of David, the bright morning star. (Revelation 22:13-16)

As conceived by the author of Revelation, Jesus is given these titles as part of his delegated power from God. As the *protos* of the creation he is now called the Alpha; as the *eschatos* of the creation he is now called the Omega.

In Revelation, the title the Alpha and the Omega is applied in different verses to refer to either God or Jesus in their own respective ways. Therefore, the title can be applied to either one of them or to both of them. It is unnecessary to make the two of them into "one God" in order to explain this phrase. In the New Testament, the titles "Lord," "Savior," and "King of kings and Lord of lords" apply to both God and Jesus respectively (cf. 1 Timothy 6:14-16 where the title is attributed to God with Revelation 17:14, 19:16 where it is said to apply to Jesus). As with "Lord," "Savior" and "King of kings and Lord of lords," the title the Alpha and the Omega is thought by the author of the Book of Revelation to fit both. God is the beginning and the end of all things because he is uncreated and eternal: the first and the last, the beginning and the end. The title the Alpha and the Omega is applied to Jesus based on the New Testament belief that the pre-incarnate being that was later called Jesus was the first and last thing created directly by God and that the incarnate Jesus was the first and last being resurrected directly by God. Once created,

Jesus became the intermediary between God and His creation. In this depiction, Jesus is the firstborn from the dead and all others will be raised by him at the end of the ages when God will judge the world through him.

But, the title the Alpha and the Omega does not yet belong to Jesus. The author of Revelation has only seen things transpire in a vision. At his expected second coming Jesus supposedly will attain this title from God who has held it heretofore. Then there will be "a new heaven and a new earth" (21:1), "the holy city, new Jerusalem, coming down out of heaven from God" (21:2), Jesus dwelling among "his peoples" (21:3), and no more tears, death, mourning, crying, or pain (21:4). However, what is significant concerning the trinitarian claim is that the relationship between God and Jesus is clearly stated throughout the Book of Revelation as being of two completely separate beings (21:22). The "Holy Spirit" is not even mentioned in this book.

The events of this last book of the New Testament which supposedly contain "the revelation of Jesus Christ ... must shortly take place" (Revelation 1:1), that is, sometime around the end of the first century C.E. — not now in our own time. One New Testament author expressed the expectation succinctly: "The end of all things is at hand [literally "has come near"]" (1 Peter 4:7). Jesus supposedly exclaims: "I also will keep you from the hour of testing, that [hour] which is about to come upon the whole world.... I am coming quickly, hold fast what you have, in order that no one take your crown" (Revelation 3:10-11). Indeed, in Revelation 22:7, 12 the subject of verse 13 (the Alpha and the Omega) says he is "coming quickly." The contexts in which the word tacheos, "briefly i.e. (in time) speedily, or (in manner) rapidly: hastily, quickly, shortly, soon, suddenly," is used in the Book of Revelation shows that an imminent sudden return of Jesus was expected while his contemporaries were still alive. Needless to say, this never happened.

John 1:1

It is in John that the nature of the Logos (the Word) is explicitly stated. The first verse of John, as translated in the King James Version, reads: "In the beginning was the Word [ho logos], and the

Word was with God [ton theon, accusative case of *ho theos*], and the Word was God [*theos*]" (John 1:1). In the Greek this is: *En arche en ho logos, kai ho logos en pros ton theon, kai theos en ho logos.* The Greek sentence ends with the crucial phrase: *kai theos en ho logos* ("and god was the Word"). We are concerned here with the Greek noun *theos* ("god") written without the definite article. This contrasts with the first mentioning of this noun expressed by *ton theon*, the accusative case of *ho theos* ("the God"), that is, the noun theos preceded by the definite article ho.

In this verse, reference is made to God and the Logos, not to three beings. When John 1:1 refers to the Word as "god," there is really no basis for concluding that he is the second person of a triune deity. This is evident from the Greek text, where, as we have just seen, the definite article *ho* appears before the first mention of God in the sentence, but is omitted before the second. The presence of the definite article before the noun suggests an identity, a personality, whereas its absence merely suggests a quality about someone. In the New Testament, the definite article usually precedes the noun theos when it denotes the one-and-only God. Since the Greek definite article is omitted before the second mention of theos, no proof for the existence of a triune deity can be accurately adduced from this verse. The omission of the definite article before the second mention of *theos* causes the word *theos* to act merely as an adjective that describes the nature of the Word. It thus serves as a predicate adjective rather than as a predicate noun. For this reason, some translators render John 1:1 as "the word was deity" or "was divine." This is quite different from the trinitarian view that the Word was God and was identical with God. If the Word was toward God, or with God, or for God, it is impossible to say that it was God. If it was God, it could stand in no relationship to God.

John is expressing his belief that Jesus, the Word, was not "the God" but "a god." It should not be considered unusual that a New Testament author refers to Jesus as a "god" since he is considered to be the supernatural agent that is the decisive link between God and His creation. The term "god" is applied even to the evil angel Satan, "the god of this world" (2 Corinthians 4:4). Indeed, Paul says: "there are many gods and many lords but for us there is but one God, the Father ... and one Lord, Jesus Christ" (1 Corinthians 8:5-6). Since referring to Jesus as a god would not make him, in any way, part of the one-and-only God, the proper translation of John 1:1 should be: "In the beginning was the Word, and the Word was with [literally "toward"] God, and the Word was a god." There is no reason to assume that the need for a definite article is understood from the context in order to be able to translate the end of the verse as, "and the Word was [the] God." John means that the god mentioned here was not the only god, i.e., a supernatural being.

It follows that it should be quite acceptable to render theos en ho logos as "the Word was a god" for here John is expressing his belief about the quality or nature of the Word. He is not identifying the essence of the Word as being one with God. For John *ho theos* and *ho logos* are not interchangeable terms. If they were, he could not say, "the Word was with God." John's Word is a supernatural being but he is not the Deity.

The trinitarian argument that the second *theos* in John 1:1 does not require the article to be considered definite can only be motivated by theological considerations, whereas to translate the word *theos* as "a god" (a celestial being) is consistent with the New Testament's general explanation of Jesus' relationship to God. There is no reason to assume that the absence of a definite article is implied or understood. The absence of the article is intentional and essential to express John's belief. Similarly, in Revelation 19:13, attributed to the author of the Gospel of John, Jesus is called "the Word of God" (literally "the Word of the God," *ho Logos tou Theou*), not "God the Word." Under the influence of Philo's teachings, John did not promulgate the idea that the Word was "the God," but that he was, as the firstborn Son of God, a second "god" (celestial being). God and Logos are not interchangeable terms. For this reason, in John 1:1, God is referred to as the God and the Logos as a god to show the difference between the two. John deliberately omitted the definite article in the predicate in order to describe who or what the Word was in relation to God, i.e., a god, a supernatural power, but not the God.

It was not difficult for the Hellenistic Gentile mind to picture human salvation as being brought about by the incarnation of the Word in the form of Jesus. The pagans of Asia Minor believed that the Son of God, Hermes, had come down in disguise to dwell among men. Acts records how in Lystra, Paul and Barnabas were identified with Hermes and Zeus (Acts 14:12). In John's time (after 81 C.E.), the emperor Domitian insisted that he be regarded as God, son of the supreme God, and be addressed as "our Lord and our God." It was, therefore, quite understandable for John to have Thomas adore the allegedly risen Jesus as "my Lord and my God" (John 20:28). This could have been employed as a Christian polemic against Domitian's claim to divinity.

As to the claim that Thomas' alleged exclamation: "My Lord and my God" is proof of Jesus' divinity, a grammatical analysis of the original Greek will disprove it. It reads in Greek: Ho kyrios mou kai ho theos mou ("The Lord of me and the God of me"). Moule states:

> In John 20:28 Ho kyrios mou kai ho theos mou, it is to be noted that a substantive [e.g., God] in the Nominative case used in a vocative sense [indicating the person addressed, e.g. Jesus] and followed by a possessive [e.g., of me] could not be anarthrous [i.e., without the definite article] ...; the article before theos may, therefore, not be significant.[6]

Because of this grammatical rule, the definite article before theos is, in this instance, of no conclusive value for proving that Thomas referred to Jesus as the God. A better understanding of John's rendition of Thomas' words may be seen by comparing them with Paul's usage of the words God and Lord: "But for us there is one God, the Father, from whom are all things, and we exist for Him; and one Lord, Jesus Christ, through whom are all things, and we [exist] through him" (1 Corinthians 8:6). Paul speaks of two separate and distinct entities. Indeed, Thomas' words may be taken literally as an exclamation referring to both: "The Lord of me [is Jesus] and the God of me [is Y-H-V-H]." Alternately, Thomas' words may very well mean that Jesus is referred to as a specific supernatural power, who exerts dominion over him ("my lord") as his guardian angel ("my god"), and not to God Himself. In the light of the evidence presented by the New Testament, it is clear that this alleged statement of Thomas' in no way refers to Jesus as the Eternal God of Israel.

The impersonal nature of holy spirit

The spirit of God is not a being with its own identity and separate consciences. It is divisible and able to be distributed as God sees fit. For example, God took of the spirit that was upon Moses and put it upon the seventy elders of Israel (Numbers 11:17-25). David prayed that God's "holy spirit" not be removed from him (Psalms 51:13). It was also measured out differently to different people; hence Elisha could pray to receive a "double portion" of spirit (2 Kings 2:9). It was not given to all and therefore its presence was noteworthy (Genesis 41:38).

Isaiah declares that when the Messiah comes "the spirit of the Lord shall rest upon him, the spirit of wisdom and understanding, the spirit of counsel and might, the spirit of knowledge and of the fear of the Lord (Isaiah 11:2). These "spirits" are symbols of the intense God given power of insight and judgment with which the Messiah will judge and reign. They are not separate beings nor the third member of a triune deity, the "Holy Spirit." The Hebrew usage of "the spirit of God" never refers to an infinite, coequal and coeternal being separate from, but at the same time a part of, God Almighty.

The impersonal nature of holy spirit is also reflected in New Testament belief. Peter, on the day of Pentecost, reportedly quoted from Joel 2:28 where God says: "[I] will pour out of My spirit." The Greek rendering reads literally "from the spirit of Me," that is, "some of My spirit," or "part of My spirit," or "a portion from My spirit" (Acts 2:17). Elsewhere it says: "We know that we live in Him and He in us, because He has given us of His spirit" (1 John 4:13). Does this sound like coequality or what is being expressed is that the spirit of God is a separate personage within the framework of a triune deity?

Establishing paternity

In Matthew's version of the alleged conception of Jesus story (Matthew 1:18) it states that Mary "was found to be with child by holy spirit [with no definite article before "holy spirit"]." In Luke's version of this story it says that the angel "said to her [Mary], 'Holy spirit [with no definite article] will come upon you,' and the power

GERALD SIGAL

of the Most High will overshadow you" (Luke 1:35). If holy spirit and power of the Most High are synonymous terms used here in a parallel structure then Luke can allege that "for this reason the holy offspring shall be called the Son of God (verse 35). But, if they are two separate entities then who is the father of Jesus—the holy spirit or God?

It may be that the "father-son" phraseology is a convenient way of trying to explain the relationship between God and Jesus. However, if "a holy spirit" (or alternately "the Holy Spirit") is a separate person within the triune deity, yet part of that triune entity, one might say that God, the Father, is the father of the Son, and that the Holy Spirit is also the father of the Son. But, if the Son is no less part of the triune deity than the Father and the Holy Spirit then, in essence, the Son fathered himself.

The problem with 1 John 5:7-8

It would seem that one of the best New Testament proofs for the Christian doctrine of a triune deity is found in 1 John 5:7-8. However, this conclusion depends on which translation of the New Testament you are using. Many modern translations do not include this supposed proof of a trinitarian deity.

As rendered in the King James Version of the Bible, it reads: "For there are three that bear record in heaven, the Father, the Word, and the Holy Ghost: and these three are one. And there are three that bear witness in earth, the spirit, and the water, and the blood: and these three agree in one." However, these verses do not occur in any reliable Greek New Testament manuscript. There is simply no manuscript authority to support this interpolation. The words added to the text begin in verse 7 with "in heaven" and include every word through "in earth." Whatever its source, the crucial passage does not appear in any of the early manuscripts and is of much later origin than the original authorship of 1 John.

Pneuma, "spirit" and parakletos, "helper"

The Greek word for spirit (pneuma) has many different meanings, the correct one being determined only from the context of each occurrence. In Greek pneuma, is neuter, as are all pronouns referring

453

to the spirit, making them necessarily impersonal. Those New Testament translations which render the "spirit" as "He" instead of "it" do so because of trinitarian beliefs (e.g., John 14:17). If the translators had properly rendered the neuter pronouns of "the spirit of the truth" found in John 14 through 16 as "it," "its," "itself" and "which" instead of "He," "His," "Him," "who," and "whom," (John 14:17, 26; 15:26; 16:7-8, 13-15) there would not be this false sense that there is personality attributed to the holy spirit.

In his last discourse to his disciples, John's Jesus speaks of the "helper" who will come to encourage the faithful after he has gone to the Father. Since "helper" (*parakletos*) is a masculine word in Greek, trinitarian translators render the following pronouns as "he" and "him." The same "helper" is, however, synonymous with "the spirit of the truth" and the texts should be rendered as follows:

> If you love me, you will keep my commandments, and I will ask the Father and He will give you another helper to remain with you until the [coming] age, the spirit of the truth, which the world cannot receive, because it does not see it or know it [*auto*, neuter agreeing with spirit]. But you know it [*auto*] because it remains with you and will be in you. I will not leave you as orphans, I will come to you.... But the helper, the holy spirit, which the Father will send in my name, it [*ekeinos*, masculine in Greek to agree with *parakletos*, but translated as "he" only if it is assumed a person is meant] will teach you all things and remind you of all things that I said to you. (John 14:15-26)

Since the "helper" may be distributed at the request of the "Son" and is subservient to the wishes of the "Father" it is not a person distinct from and equal to the Father or the Son.

So-called pathetic fallacies, attributing personal qualities, gender, feelings, and actions to things that have no real personal consciousness are common in the Jewish Scriptures. For example, Wisdom is personified in Proverbs 8 and 9, yet no literal person named "Wisdom" was actually beside God as He created the world (Proverbs 8:30). Similarly, in the Gospel of John the spirit of God is personified as a *parakletos*, "helper," "advocate" (14:16, 26; 15:26; 16:7). The personal pronouns used agree grammatically with the nature of the figurative title. But, the personification does not mean the subject has substance or is a person. The *parakletos*, as with the "spirit of the truth," and "spirit" requires the neuter "it" to reflect the impersonal nature of what its referent is. A writer or a poet can, however, employ a figurative expression in the use of pronouns. When in the Gospel of John poetic personification is being employed with reference to the "helper" the reader needs to understand such usage to be a mere figure of speech. It is implicit in the text of John 16:13 that this "helper" is "sent." It is explicit that it "does not speak on its [his] own initiative" and is instructed ("whatever it [or he] hears it [or he] will speak"). Used in this context, it is supposedly the heaven sent insight taking the place of Jesus who is to go to the Father (John 14:12). It is "another helper" in lieu of the departed Jesus who is to lead the disciples to a deeper knowledge of the gospel and enable them to undergo trials and persecution. It is by no means meant by the author of John to be considered a personage coequal to the sender. Parakletos is also applied to Jesus in the sense of him being a heavenly advocate or intercessor for his followers: "If anyone sins, we have an advocate (*parakletos*) with the Father, Jesus Christ the righteous" (1 John 2:1). But, in this context it is not used as if it were a personification.

Paul writes that "The spirit intercedes for us" (Romans 8:26), but also identifies who this spirit is in the context of this passage: "Christ Jesus ... intercedes for us" (Romans 8:34). He also writes: "But whenever a man turns to the Lord, the veil is taken away. Now the Lord is spirit, and where the spirit of the Lord is, there is freedom" (2 Corinthians 3:16-17). The veil is a reference to Exodus 34:34, "But when Moses went in before the Lord to speak with Him, he took the veil off." Christians are divided as to whether "the Lord" in verse 17 refers to God or Jesus although Exodus 34:34 refers to *Y-H-V-H*. In any case, Paul's words can be best understood as leaving no room for a separate entity called the "Holy Spirit."

The term "spirit" is used in several different ways in the New Testament, but none of them supports the contention that it refers to a coeternal, coequal being within a triune structured deity. It simply expresses a belief held by the author of the Gospel of John that by this "spirit," this thought implant, Jesus would allegedly still be present: "I will come to you" (14:18); "I am in you" (14:20); and "I will show myself" (14:21). By this spirit his work with them would supposedly continue: "It will teach you" (14:26); "It will remind you of everything I have said" (14:26); "It will testify about me" (15:26); "It will convict the world of guilt" (in preparation for his judgment — 16:8); "It will guide you into all truth" (16:13); "It will give glory to me by taking what is mine and making it known to you" (16:14). But, despite the use of the pronoun he when referring to spirit in Christian translations it is not a person!

The author of 1 John writes that "We are from God; he who knows God listens to us; he who is not from God does not listen to us. By this we know the spirit of truth and the spirit of error" (1 John 4:6). If the *parakletos*, the "spirit of the truth" (John 14:17) were a person, then "the spirit of the error" in 1 John 4:6 would also have to be a person, given that the two are directly contrasted. The fact is that what is meant is that each "spirit" represents the mental influence under which a person acts, but neither is a person in itself.

In the New Testament, the Spirit of God is simply God's *dunamis* (power) in action. The "Holy Spirit" does not have an independent personality. It is merely a way of speaking about God's personally acting in history. In the New Testament it is also used of the allegedly risen Jesus' personally acting in the life of the Church. The New Testament nowhere represents the spirit as having an independent personality.

Leaving out reference to the holy spirit

In the opening salutation of Paul's letters to various churches (Romans through Thessalonians) he sends personal greetings from "God the Father and the Lord Jesus Christ." If "the Holy Spirit" were an integral and personal part of a triune deity, then why does He not send His personal greetings as well? Obviously, Paul never contemplated that there was such a person. If there were a third person involved, would not the supposedly divinely inspired Paul have known about it and included Him in his greetings to the churches? When Paul does include additional persons in his greetings, salutations and adjurations, he names "the elect angels," not "the Holy Spirit" (1

Timothy 5:21; cf. Luke 9:26 and Revelation 3:5). It is ludicrous to think that Paul would consistently omit mention of the third person of the Trinity, if he believed it to exist.

In the other New Testament letters, every one of the authors identifies himself with "God the Father" and "the Lord Jesus Christ," but not one does so with "the Holy Spirit." But, if they were ignorant of the existence of the doctrine of a triune deity then their apostleship was faulty at best, and at worst they were teaching heresy. No; their failure to clearly teach the existence of a triune deity shows that the doctrine of the Trinity was not a belief of the early church. 1 John 1:3 says that for followers of Jesus fellowship is with "the Father and with His Son, Jesus Christ." Why is the Holy Spirit left out?

In the eternal city of Revelation 21 and 22, both God and Jesus are presented as a featured fantasy. Each is pictured as sitting on his throne (Revelation 22:1). If "the Holy Spirit" is a "coeternal" member of a triune deity, why does it have no seat of authority on the final throne? This is consistent with the New Testament belief that there is one God, "the Father," and one "Lord, Jesus Christ." There is no such separate person known as "the Holy Spirit." In point of fact, the notion of the Holy Spirit never appears in the Book of Revelation.

Is the Trinity Doctrine a New Testament teaching?

Paul, speaking of Jesus says, "[F]or in him all the fullness of deity dwells in bodily form" (Colossians 2:9). Whether Paul is teaching a form of dualism or that this supposed supernatural power that has indwelled Jesus has become God's unique representative to mankind is a dispute for Christians to ponder. Suffice it for us to ask, if God was in the incarnate Jesus and was one with Jesus ontologically why is it that God knew things of which Jesus had no knowledge (Matthew 24:36, Mark 13:32, Acts 1:7)? Why is it that John's Jesus says: "I go to the Father; for the Father is greater than I" (John 14:28)? The author/authors of the Gospel of John recognized that Jesus was not part of the essence of God. John's Jesus says: "Now this is eternal life: that they may know you, the only true God, and Jesus, whom you have sent" (John 17:3). Yes, this Gospel's author taught that God the Father was the one and only God, and unlike the later trinitarians he taught that Jesus was a separate entity sent by God. John's Jesus believes himself to be so exact in his obedience to God's every desire that he claims "the Father is in me and I am in the Father" (John 10:38). But, at no time does he claim to be one in essence with God. Although he presents himself to be at one with God in will and purpose, John's Jesus never claims a unity of person or equality in substance with the Almighty. In the final analysis, were Jesus truly God Himself, there would be no need for him to be "sent" by anyone or anything.

And last but not least, consider this. According to New Testament theology, Jesus came into the world expressly to offer himself as a willing sacrifice to atone for mankind's sins. Yet, he hesitates and prays for a reversal of the fate preordained for him. The Gospel narrative portrays Jesus' state of mind just a few hours prior to his crucifixion: "And going a little way forward, he fell upon his face praying and saying: 'My Father, if it is possible, let this cup pass from me. Yet, not as I will, but as you will'" (Matthew 26:39; see also Mark 14:35-36, Luke 22:41-44). It is related that Jesus, supposedly one-third of the triune deity, needed an angel to strengthen him: "Then an angel from heaven appeared to him, strengthening him" (Luke 22:43). With his alleged divine pre-knowledge of why he had to die and of the rewards that would be his for obeying God (Philippians 2:9-11), or himself, what reassurance did he need from a mere angel? Did he have to be reminded of his role and its rewards? Why the feelings of despair and failure? Jesus was in a state of agony (Luke 22:44) in which he tearfully cried out, not for the sins of the world, but to be saved from death (Hebrews 5:7). Jesus' alleged exclamation: "Yet, not as I will but as you will," shows that had it been his choice, he would not have undergone execution. Although he seems to have submitted to God's will, in his final moments of life Jesus is said to have expressed feelings of frustration and abandonment (Matthew 27:46, Mark 15:34; cf. Luke 23:46, John 19:30) using the psalmist's words: "My God my God, why have you forsaken me?" (Psalms 22:2). In that last critical moment, Jesus who some say was a supernatural power and others part of a triune deity expressed that he did not wish to die. He did not want to become a sacrifice for the sins of mankind.

The New Testament does not teach the doctrine of the Trinity. However, even if it did, this doctrine would still be false since it does not conform to the teachings of the Jewish Scriptures. God is an absolute one who is neither a duality, a trinity, a quaternary, nor any other composite being. The transformation of Jesus into part of a triune deity is a chimera, an unfortunate distortion of Jewish biblical text, the New Testament, and the Philonic Logos used in conjunction with pagan motifs. Christians have been misled into worshiping Jesus as the divine God the Son. Combined with this is the notion of the "Holy Spirit" as part of a coeternal, coequal deity. These concepts, in truth, have no place in a discussion of the ontological being of God.

Attempts to explain the doctrine of a triune deity can only be made by the use of extra-biblical terminology. But, this can only mask, not resolve, the many contradictions of Scripture and logic inherent in the Trinity doctrine. Every verse quoted by those attempting to "prove" the existence of a triune deity or that Jesus is God Almighty can be understood, within the context of the original language sources of the New Testament, to refute that false doctrine.. The absolute indivisible oneness of God stands on a solid foundation.

Tritheism or trinitarianism?

Trinitarians may insist that there is only one God and indeed the vast majority of those who hold to this doctrine truly believe there is one God, but do they worship one God? The point of contention is their further claim that there is one Godhead existing in three persons. The problem is that this is not the God described in the Jewish Scriptures nor the New Testament where they assume this trinitarian teaching is to be found. The relationship they propose between God the Father, God the Son and God the Holy Spirit is not one of a Godhead existing in three persons, but one of tritheism, three independent gods of unequal status. It should be noted that neither trinitarianism nor tritheism is in concert with the New Testament's teaching on the relationship of God, Jesus and the holy spirit.

Theoretically, trinitarians profess to believe there is one indivisible God, not three gods. But, they say:

The Father is God.

The Son is God.
The Holy Spirit is God.
The Father is not the Son.
The Father is not the Holy Spirit.
The Son is not the Holy Spirit.

In applying this statement of faith to the actual teachings of the New Testament the result is tritheism.

How is that possible? The New Testament teaches that there is only one Being who is God and that the pre-incarnate Jesus was his first creation. The Gospels' Jesus in his alleged incarnate form is not part of the Godhead and Jesus always physically separates himself from God in describing their relationship. Moreover, the so-called post-resurrection Jesus is always portrayed in the New Testament as a physically separate entity from God. That is, not as one of three persons existing as an indivisible God. The Father and Son are always distinguished with the Father superior to the Son in position and knowledge. In the New Testament, Jesus is never referred to as God the Son, but only as the son of God. As for the role of the so-called Holy Spirit it simply has none as a separate coequal and eternal entity.

[1] Since there is no mixture of upper and lower case letters in Greek Septuagint and New Testament manuscripts no accurate distinction can be made by a reference to the Greek biblical manuscripts or to New Testament manuscripts to decide if the upper case "Holy Spirit," a proper noun referring to God or a lower case "holy spirit," referring to an impersonal force, is meant.

[2] Christians differ as to what the phrase means. More than likely the phrase designates the whole of anything from the beginning to the end.

[3] The Greek text used for the King James Version was edited by Erasmus (1466-1536). It was a poorly edited volume containing hundreds of typographical errors and many of its readings supporting Christian doctrines, although sometimes ancient, are not found in the better and more ancient manuscripts. An example of Christian scribal interpolation to support trinitarianism is the King James Version of the New Testament reading at 1 Timothy 3:16. It reads, "God [Theos] was revealed in the flesh" in conformity with some later manuscripts, but the reading of this verse in the ancient manuscripts is "[he, Jesus,] who [hos] was revealed in the flesh." (See B.F. Westcott and F.G.A. Hort, Introduction to the New Testament in the Original Greek, Peabody, Mass.: Hendrickson Publishers, 1988, pp. 133-135.)

[4] The word "God" is found in the oldest Greek manuscripts, including the Alexandrine, Sinaitic, and Codex Ephraemi Rescriptus.

[5] The title, the Alpha and the Omega is not found in the oldest Greek manuscripts of Revelation 1:11, including the Alexandrine, Sinaitic, and Codex Ephraemi Rescriptus.

[6] C.F. Moule, An Idiom Book of New Testament Greek, Cambridge: University Press, 1977, p. 116.

Chapter 75

WHO IS A CHRISTIAN?
(Mark 16:16-18)

A question that has provoked much bloodshed and strife in the world, especially among those calling themselves Christians, is: "Who is a Christian?" In answering this question, Jesus is alleged to have said:

> He that believes and is baptized will be saved, but he that believes not will be condemned. And these signs will follow those that believe: in my name they will cast out demons, they will speak with tongues, and with their hands they will pick up serpents, and if they drink anything deadly it will not harm them at all. They will lay hands upon the sick and they will recover. (Mark 16:16-18)

Who is the true believer in the teachings of Jesus? Is it the Roman Catholics, Greek Orthodox, Baptists, Pentecostals, Jehovah's Witnesses, Methodists, Latter Day Saints, Episcopalians, Seventh-Day Adventists, Lutherans, Quakers, or any of the other thousands of sects and denominations calling themselves not only Christian but the true church in possession of the true teachings of Jesus to the exclusion of all others. Who is correct? Who is actually a true Christian? The answer to this perplexing question appears to be given by Mark's Jesus (Mark 16:16-18).

According to this passage, the true Christian can cast out demons, speak with tongues, pick up serpents, drink anything deadly, and heal the sick. These are the promises made by Jesus to all the faithful, not only of his generation, but of all generations. The Christian is told by Jesus that he/she possesses the ability to bring all of these miraculous deeds to pass. The formula for success is simple? "Believe!" Paul switches the parameters of the promise to make it seem that fulfillment was possible. He maintains that people are given different levels of ability to perform miraculous deeds, depending on the amount of grace bestowed upon them. All believers, Paul states, share in the miraculous works of the few since they are all part of "one body in Christ" (Romans 12:3-8, 1 Corinthians 12:4-31). This is a feeble attempt, on the part of Paul, to reinterpret Jesus' promise in a way that explains why his guarantee to all the faithful never came about. According to Jesus' promise, however, all believers are given unqualified grace and ability to perform the miraculous. The believer himself performs the miracles; he does not share in them vicariously through a mystic union of the entire church body. The promise, coming directly from Jesus, vitiates any attempt to disavow or modify these abilities by any Christian spokesman.

But can the Christian actually perform these miraculous abilities? No, of course not! Yet everyone who believes Jesus is the true Messiah has been guaranteed by him the power to cast out demons, speak with tongues, pick up serpents, drink anything deadly, and heal the sick. Even non-true-believing Christians are, according to Jesus, able to perform miracles in his name. Matthew's Jesus says: "Many will say to me on that day: 'Lord, Lord, did we not prophesy in your name, and in your name cast out demons, and in your name perform powerful works?' And then I will declare to them: 'I never knew you, depart from me, you who practice lawlessness'" (Matthew 7:22-23). Thus, according to Matthew, even those who claim to perform miracles in the name of Jesus are not necessarily following him. How then can one tell who is a real Christian? Those who profess to believe in Jesus cannot do all the categories of miracles Jesus promised they would be able to do. Their strong belief will not enable them to cast mountains into the sea, as Jesus promised, no matter how strongly they believe (Matthew 21:21, Mark 11:23). Yet, Jesus did promise that his followers would be able to do all of them. And there is no time limit on his promise - whether in his day or in the present.

What is the reason for the Christian inability to fulfill the promises made to them by Jesus? Christians cannot perform these miraculous abilities because Jesus' claims have no validity. His own mouth testified against him. According to his own words, there is no such person as a Christian (follower of Jesus) since a Christian should be able to do all the things enumerated in Mark 16:16-18. To believe Jesus is the Messiah and the son of God and that he can give everlasting life to those who believe in him is to stretch one's credulity to inadmissible limits.

Chapter 76

LUKE'S CENSUS
(Luke 2:1-5)

Now it came about in those days that a decree went out from Caesar Augustus, that a census be taken of all the inhabited earth. This was the first census taken while Quirinius was governor of Syria. And all were proceeding to register for the census, everyone to his own city. And Joseph also went up from Galilee, out of the city of Nazareth, to Judea, to the city of David, which is called Bethlehem, because he was of the house and family of David, in order to register, along with Mary, who was engaged to him, and was pregnant. (Luke 2:1-5)

Background

Both Matthew (2:16) and Luke (1:5) place Jesus' birth during the last years of Herod the Great's reign (c. 6-4 B.C.E.). But Luke includes a conflicting date as well, the year of a census conducted under Quirinius (Luke 2:1-2). Luke places the birth of Jesus, "while Quirinius was governor of Syria." Quirinius was not the governor of Syria, an area that included Judea, while Herod reigned (contrary to Luke 1:5, 26; 2:2). At the time mentioned Quintilius Varus held that office.[1] Quirinius was not appointed governor until 6 or 7 C.E.[2] There are Christians who argue the Quirinius was governor before 4 B.C.E. as well as later on. But there is no proof for this contention. The list of Roman governors for the period before the birth of Jesus does not contain the name Quirinius.

The census

The claim that the Romans conducted an empire-wide census in the manner described in the Gospel of Luke is historically impossible. According to this Gospel, the Romans ordered that the people being enumerated should return to the towns of their ancestors rather than register in the towns in which they actually resided. If information about the ancestral towns was essential to the Romans, they would merely have required the people to supply the names of their ancestral towns. It should be understood that some of these places of origin were outside the area of Roman geographic control. Was it really necessary to compel people to travel to their ancestral town sometimes hundreds of miles away? The alleged Roman demand presumes that the people all knew their ancestral origins. It would also have caused the disruption of normal family life in the many cases where husbands and wives had to set off in opposite directions in order for each to return to their "own city."

What Luke describes would create a chaotic situation of unprecedented size. The people involved would have had to travel throughout the length and breadth of the Roman Empire, clogging the roads and disrupting the smooth running of the imperial system in every province of the Empire. In the course of their journey, they would be traveling, for the most part, over extremely poor roads once they left the major Roman highways. Available services to travelers would be strained to the breaking point. Certainly in the eastern provinces, of which Judea was a part, such a census would present a serious military danger, for the Parthians, then Rome's strongest antagonist in the region, would have had an excellent opportunity to attack. Roman soldiers on the march would find it extremely difficult to make their way through the clogged roads with their tremendous mass of civilians on their way to or from registration. It is difficult to imagine the Romans as so incompetent or unrealistic as to throw the entire Empire into such a chaotic state by carrying out the census described by the author of this Gospel. And for what other purpose would this census be administered than to create a tax roll? But, how self-defeating this interruption in commerce and agriculture would be and the loss in revenue would be staggering. Indeed, taxes are paid where one lives not where one's ancestors lived leaving no reason for this absurd claim of a census being taken.

It is also unusual that an event of this size would go unnoticed. Yet, no contemporary record mentions this thoroughly useless and disruptive census or the turmoil it would have created. If this census occurred in Judea or Galilee it is strange that Josephus never mentioned it in any of his literary works. It is obvious that the author of Luke introduced this incredulous tale to explain still another legendary tale, namely, how it came about that Joseph and Mary, she in an advanced state of pregnancy, went to Bethlehem at that time.

A journey of a thousand years

According to Luke's narrative, Joseph's journey had to do with the fact that David lived in Bethlehem approximately one thousand years before, and it is alleged that Joseph was of "the house and lineage of David." For Joseph, the ancestral home did not even mean Jerusalem, which served as residence of the Davidic dynasty for some five hundred years. There is no reason to assume that in the post-exilic period the descendants of David returned to Bethlehem rather than Jerusalem or that they owned land in that town or its environs. Interestingly, Luke makes no mention of one having to go to a place where he owned property. As we have seen, Joseph makes the journey to Bethlehem, not because he was required to return to his home city, but, rather, because it was the home city of his remote ancestor. This reason is somewhat farfetched to say the least.

Contriving history

The utilizing of the census narrative supplied the necessary reason for Joseph and Mary, who were not yet married to leave their respective homes in Nazareth. This move Luke claims resulted in the birth of Jesus in Bethlehem. The historicity of this story is questionable. As we have noted, there is no evidence of one empire-wide census under Augustus or of a census requirement that people be registered in their ancestral cities. Luke's narrative says: "This was the first census taken while Quirinius was governor of Syria" (Luke 2:2). The one and only census conducted while Quirinius was governor of Syria was a regional census that affected Judea and Galilee, and took place in 6-7 C.E. According to Josephus, Rome did take a census, at this time, of people who lived in Judea, Samaria and Idumea, but not Galilee. Josephus records: "Now the territory subject to Archelaus [Judea, Samaria and Idumea] was added to the province of Syria, and Quirinius ... was sent by Caesar to take a census of property in Syria."[3] He makes no mention of the need to travel to register in one's ancestral home. This census was taken some ten years after the death of Herod the Great, during whose reign Jesus was most likely born. This census was taken because Archelaus, Herod's son, had been deposed and the province of Judea was now governed directly by Rome. Galilee was not a Roman province, but remained a semi-independent Roman tetrarchy, under Archelaus' brother Herod Antipas. As such, it would not be subject to a Roman census. Thus, Luke's Mary and Joseph, who lived in Nazareth, located in Galilee would not have been affected by Quirinius' census, which concerned the inhabitants of Judea but not Galilee. Bethlehem was located in Judea.

[1] Josephus, Jewish Antiquities XVII. 5.2 [89].

[2] Jewish Antiquities XVII. 13.4 [355], XVIII. 1.1 [1].

[3] Jewish Antiquities XVII. 13.5 [355].

Chapter 77

THE SHORT MEMORIES OF MARY AND JOSEPH
(Luke 2:46-50)

There is a remarkable incident that occurs in the Gospel of Luke that highlights the fictive nature of the Gospel narrative. On a return trip from Jerusalem, Joseph and Mary realize that Jesus is not in the caravan. They return to Jerusalem to search for him:

> And it came about that after three days they [Joseph and Mary] found him in the temple, sitting in the midst of the teachers, both listening to them, and asking them questions. And all who heard him were amazed at his understanding and his answers. And when they saw him, they were astonished; and his mother said to him, "Son, why have you treated us this way? Behold, your father and I have been anxiously looking for you." And he said to them, "Why is it that you were looking for me? Did you not know that I must be about my father's business?" And they did not understand the statement he made to them. (Luke 2:46-50)

Why is this incident remarkable? It is because after being visited by angels, Mary remaining a virgin until after Jesus' birth, witnessing the magi giving fabulous riches to the baby Jesus, fleeing into Egypt to protect Jesus, hearing the prophecies of Anna and Simeon about the baby Jesus, Luke's Joseph and Mary are dumbfounded by Jesus' statement in this verbal exchange with the teenage Jesus. Joseph did not understand and Mary did not understand for the simple reason that none of the above ever happened.

Chapter 78

JESUS AND FORGIVENESS
(Luke 23:34; John 7:53-8:11)

The preaching and the practice

Luke's Jesus says: "Father, forgive them, for they do not know what they are doing" (Luke 23:34). This sentence is not found in the earliest manuscripts of the Gospel of Luke and all indications are that it is an interpolation. That it is a later addition is evident from internal evidence. A careful reading of the Gospels shows that this verse is not at all in consonance with Jesus' true feelings about forgiveness of enemies. Elsewhere, Luke records a parable attributed to Jesus that is more in keeping with Jesus' true attitude toward his enemies. He declares: "But these enemies of mine who did not want me to reign over them, bring them here, and slay them in my presence" (Luke 19:27). This expresses Jesus' actual attitude on the subject of forgiveness. Similarly, Matthew's Jesus expresses his feelings in a particularly merciless way when he says: "So that there may come upon you all the righteous blood poured out upon the earth from the blood of righteous Abel to the blood of Zechariah son of Barachiah, whom you murdered between the Temple and the altar" (Matthew 23:35). Here Jesus condemns the Jews to suffering for "all the righteous blood poured out upon the earth" from a time even before the birth of Abraham, the father of the Jewish people. According to this passage, they are to suffer the penalty for the sins of murder of everyone else in the world since the dawn of human history. And of course, Jesus never forgave Judas for leading the authorities to him. Is such an unforgiving attitude in accord with the allegedly benign and kind soul of Jesus of Nazareth, the Prince of Peace?

Yes, Luke's Jesus instructs others, even God, to forgive, but there is not one instance in all the Gospels where he personally forgives anyone or anything (e.g., a fig tree - Mark 11:12-14, 11:20-25; Matthew 21:18-22) that he feels wronged him.

The forgiveness that never was

Some Christians point to John 7:53-8:11, as an example of Jesus' forgiveness of sinners. It is a story where the wrong doing was not against Jesus. The tale is about a woman caught in adultery and there is much controversy over its authenticity. Was this story originally included in the Gospel of John or is the story of the adulterous woman forgiven by Jesus a later insertion into the text? The earliest Greek manuscripts do not include this story. No churchman commented on this passage until the twelfth century, and even then it was to comment that accurate Greek manuscripts did not contain it. Among the manuscripts that do contain the section, either wholly or in part, there are variations of placement. Some manuscripts put it after John 7:36, others after John 21:25, and some even place it in the Gospel of Luke (after Luke 21:38 or 24:53).

There is internal evidence, too, that John 7:53-8:11 is not original to the text. For one thing, the inclusion of this passage breaks the flow of the Gospel narrative. Reading from John 7:52 to John 8:12 (skipping the controversial section) makes perfect sense. Also, the vocabulary used in the story is different from what is found in the rest of the Gospel of John. For example, John never refers to "the scribes" - except in John 8:3. There are thirteen other words in this short passage that are found nowhere else in the Gospel of John. The fact is that the inclusion of this passage is not supported by the best manuscript evidence. In any case, it is another example where Jesus personally forgave those who wronged others but never those who wronged him.

Chapter 79

A BONE OF CONTENTION
(John 19:33, 36)

The author of the Gospel of John writes:

But coming to Jesus, when they saw that he was already dead, they did not break his legs.... For these things occurred, in order that the Scripture might be fulfilled: "Not a bone of him shall be broken." (John 19:33)

Some Christians maintain that this verse is a fulfillment of Psalms 34:21 (verse 20 in some versions), which states: "He guards all his bones; not one of them is broken." However, the psalmist's words are simply too general in nature to have specific application to Jesus, and there is thus no proof that they constitute a typology of an event in his life. In fact, John did not consider Psalms 34:21 the scriptural prooftext for the events he describes. He refers instead to the scriptural sources which he feels are more specific and meaningful for his purposes. John does not give the exact scriptural reference to which he is alluding, but it is evident that he is not using Psalm 34 as the typology for the claim that the soldiers did not break Jesus' bones. This author, in claiming that the soldiers did not break Jesus' legs, is alluding to one of the restrictions regarding the paschal lamb (Exodus 12:46, Numbers 9:12), for he believes that Jesus was "the Lamb of God who takes away the sins of the world" ("John 1:29). John attempts to portray Jesus within the context of the Passover celebration by representing him as the paschal sacrifice and, as such, fulfilling a biblical commandment which deals specifically with the bones of the paschal lamb. He sees the death of Jesus, the so-called "Lamb of God," which occurred just prior to the Passover festival, as the climax of his view of the paschal lamb. According to John, the paschal lamb was sacrificed on the day before Passover as a prefiguring of Jesus, who, in his opinion, also died the day before Passover. It should be noted that according to those who believe that the Last Supper was the seder Jesus would have died on the first day of Passover, not the previous day.

The New Testament claim is that Jesus was a sacrifice by which mankind can obtain atonement from sin. In doing so, he has been compared to the paschal lamb that was offered as a remembrance of God's passing over the Israelites when He slew the Egyptian firstborn (Exodus 12:26-27). But this analogy is fallacious because the paschal sacrifice is not at all offered for the atonement of any sin. More properly, Jesus should have been put to death not the day before Passover (according to John) or on the first day of Passover (according to the Synoptic Gospels), but rather on YomKippur, the Day of Atonement. On that day, the sacrifice was offered for the express purpose of obtaining forgiveness of sin for the entire nation (Leviticus 16:7-10, 21-22, 24, 29-30).

In his effort to show the literal fulfillment of the Jewish Scriptures in the life of Jesus, John informs his readers that not one bone of Jesus' body was broken. This was supposed to have occurred in conformity with the divine command not to break any of the bones of the paschal lamb (Exodus 12:46, Numbers 9:12). If we are to be literal, let us also be consistent. The most striking inconsistency in the hypothesis of Jesus' supposed sacrificial death is the fact that the Jewish Scriptures decry the horrific practice of human sacrifice (e.g., Leviticus 18:21, 20:2-5). Even disregarding the unequivocal opposition to human sacrifice, there is the question of the commandment: "Whatever has a blemish that you shall not offer" (Leviticus 22:20). Any potential sacrifice that is maimed in any way is not qualified (Leviticus 22:19, 22). Just prior to his crucifixion, Jesus was whipped and beaten (Matthew 27:26, 30; Mark 15:19; John 19:3). Moreover, Jesus was circumcised in the flesh, a practice that according to Paul, constitutes "mutilation," katatome (Philippians 3:2). Indeed, he even likens circumcision to castration (Galatians 5:12). Therefore, although Jesus is depicted as an "unblemished and spotless lamb" (1 Peter 1:19), the most perfect of all sacrifices (Hebrews 9:14), his "mutilation" would disqualify him, as it would any sacrifice. Not only did the injuries just prior to his execution disqualify Jesus, but by disparaging circumcision in the flesh, Paul inadvertently rendered Jesus, almost from his very birth, as unfit for playing a sacrificial role!

Christians are selective in choosing scriptural confirmation. They ignore those facts that conflict with their claims. They disregard those biblical commandments that would explicitly disprove their allegations. If John 19:33 shows a physical fulfillment of prophecy, we must insist that it be shown how Jesus fulfilled all of the scriptural precepts regarding the physical fitness of a sacrificial animal. If John insists on the unbroken state of Jesus' bones at the time of his death, as a fulfillment of biblical prophecy, then we must equally insist on the biblical requirements of the need for a perfect body with no mutilations or abrasions. This requirement could not be fulfilled because Jesus was neither "unblemished" nor "spotless." The body of Jesus was marred in such a manner that it could not symbolize, or actually be a substitutionary sacrifice in accordance with the Scriptures.

Some Christians attempt to spiritualize the mention of Jesus "shedding his blood," making it a metaphorical statement of Jesus' ability to do what the atonement feature of the sacrificial system did. However, when the First Epistle of Peter claims that redemption was brought about "with precious blood, like that of an unblemished and spotless lamb" (1 Peter 1:18-19) the mention of blood can only refer to the actual blood of the physical body of Jesus. John must also be referring to the physical nature of Jesus as well. If actual shedding of blood were not meant why the need for his execution!

In summation: Being human, and moreover, wounded and mutilated, Jesus was not in a proper physical state to be suited for a sacrifice. To consider Jesus in a sacrificial role would violate the laws concerning sacrifices. In any case, treating Jesus as representing the paschal lamb does not give him any power to atone for sins since the purpose of the paschal lamb had nothing to do with the atonement of sins. All in all, there is no legitimate reason for identifying the death of Jesus with the atonement of sins.

Chapter 80

GAMALIEL'S SPEECH
(Acts 5:34-39)

Acts 5:34-39: But a certain Pharisee named Gamaliel, a teacher of the Law, respected by all the people, stood up in the Council and gave orders to put the men outside for a short time. And he said to them, "Men of Israel take care what you propose to do with these men. For some time ago Theudas rose up, claiming to be somebody, and a group of about four hundred men joined up with him. And he was slain; and all who followed him were dispersed and came to nothing. After this man Judas of Galilee rose up in the days of the census, and drew away some people after him, he too perished, and all those who followed him were scattered. And so in the present case, I say to you, stay away from these men and let them alone, for if this plan or action should be of men, it will be overthrown, but if it is of God, you will not be able to overthrow them; or else you may even be found fighting against God."

The historicity of this episode as presented in Acts is questionable. If this self-serving story is true, Gamaliel most likely made his speech before 35 C.E. Gamaliel is said to refer to two revolts. Theudas led the first "After this man [i.e., Theudas] Judas of Galilee rose up in the days of the census." Judas met his death (6 C.E.) when he opposed the census conducted in Judea by Quirinius.[1] Luke's chronology would place Theudas' revolt sometimes before 6 C.E. However, according to Josephus,[2] a Theudas revolted sometime after Gamaliel is supposed to have made his impassioned appeal. The revolt led by this Theudas occurred in 45 or 46 C.E. Was the Theudas mentioned by Josephus different from the Theudas cited by Gamaliel in Acts? Gamaliel's Theudas must have made some impact or else citing him, over thirty years later, would have had no effect on his audience. As such, it is unlikely that Josephus would not have mentioned this supposedly earlier Theudas as well. We may conclude that there was only one Theudas who rebelled and that he lived after Gamaliel allegedly spoke.

Gamaliel's pronouncement before the Council, whether actually made or not, encapsulates the general Jewish attitude toward the first century proto-Christian community of Jerusalem, which followed the teachings of the apostles: "And so in the present case, I say to you, stay away from these men and let them alone, for if this plan or action should be of men, it will be overthrown, but if it is of God, you will not be able to overthrow them; or else you may even be found fighting against God." The presumption may have been that when they would see that Jesus did not return as expected these transgressors would abandon their misguided beliefs.

The author of Acts, writing in the post-war period (c. 85), attributes to Gamaliel his own comment that is directed more against those who followed the apostles than at the "unbelieving" Jews. He artfully introduces his disdain for that part of the church that kept closer to common Judaism. The author of Acts writes: "And so in the present case" (verse 38a), as a reference to the apostles and their followers. He intends to differentiate between what the apostles taught and what the Hellenistic branch of the church was teaching. It is the author's judgment on the post-war disposition of the Jerusalem church: "for if this plan or action should be of men, it will be overthrown." It is precisely the Jerusalem church that disappears after 70 C.E. Indeed, by the second century the Jewish-born Christians were reduced to a marginalized minority within the church. It is the Hellenistic Gentile church, from which all present-day Christian groups are descended that the author has in mind when he cites, "but if it is of God, you will not be able to overthrow them; or else you may even be found fighting against God." The testimony of Acts is that the Jerusalem church, whose leadership had been closest to Jesus and his teachings, was "overthrown" because it was not of God.

[1] Jewish War II. 17. 8 [433].

[2] Jewish Antiquities XX. 5. 1 [97-98].

Chapter 81

STEPHEN'S HISTORICAL REVISIONISM

(Acts 7:14-16, 42-43, 46)

In the speech attributed to Stephen in the Book of Acts the protagonist said to be Christianity's first martyr delivers an oration much of which is historical revisionism of apparently Samaritan origin. Stephen declares:

> And Joseph sent and called to him Jacob his father and all his relatives, seventy-five souls; and Jacob went down into Egypt. And he died, he and our fathers, and they were removed to Shechem and were laid in the tomb that Abraham had bought for a sum of silver from the sons of Hamor in Shechem. (Acts 7:14-16)

Jacob's family that came down to Egypt, inclusive of Joseph and his sons, numbered seventy persons, not seventy-five (Genesis 46:27, Exodus 1:5, Deuteronomy 10:22). The number seventy-five agrees with the present-day (Christian corrupted) Septuagint but not with the Masoretic or Samaritan biblical texts.

There are a number of instances where Samaritan traditions are used or alluded to in Stephen's speech. In one such instance, Shechem, the Samarian religious center — their alternative to Jerusalem — is given added significance. Stephen makes Abraham the purchaser of a piece of ground at Shechem, in effect transferring the burial place of the patriarchs from Hebron in Judea to Shechem in Samaria. The Masoretic text (and the Septuagint Version) identifies Hebron as the location of the burial cave (Machpelah) that Abraham purchased from Ephron the Hittite (Genesis 23:1-20) and where Abraham, Isaac and Jacob were buried (Genesis 23:1-20). However, Stephen locates the burial cave of "Jacob ... and our fathers" in Shechem, bought from "the sons of Hamor [Gr. Emmor]" by Abraham (Acts 7:15-16). By claiming that Jacob and his sons were buried in a tomb that Abraham bought in Shechem, he infers that Abraham and Isaac were likewise buried there (cf. MT Genesis 49:29-32). The Jewish Scriptures state that Jacob was buried in Hebron, in the cave of Machpelah, which Abraham purchased from Ephron the Hittite for four hundred silver shekels (Genesis 23:16, 49:29-33, 50:13). Joseph was buried at Shechem, in the piece of ground which Jacob had purchased for a hundred silver shekels from the sons of Hamor (Genesis 33:19, Joshua 24:32). According to Josephus, the other sons of Jacob are buried at Hebron. He writes: "His [Joseph] brethren also died after sojourning happily in Egypt. Their bodies were carried some time afterwards by their descendants [and their sons] to Hebron and buried there.[1] The claims Stephen makes appear, for the most part, to be based on traditions of Samaritan origin. The Samaritans claimed "they are descended from Joseph"[2] and traced "their line back to Ephraim and Manasseh, the descendants of Joseph."[3] In any case, his revisionism is not supported by any other source.

Stephen's speech also reflects a Samaritan bias in interpretation of biblical history from Abraham to Solomon. In tracing a history of Jewish apostasy, Stephen makes reference in Acts 7:42 to worshiping "the host of heaven, as it is written in the book of the prophets." This alludes to Jeremiah 7:18 and 19:13 — the prophecy that Jerusalem and its Temple will be destroyed. In Acts 7:42-43 Stephen connects this statement with a version of Amos 5:25-27 which is apparently based on the Septuagint rendering, but which contains notable variations. The changes that he makes in the text are justified neither by the Masoretic text nor the Septuagint, nor by historical reality. Both the Masoretic text and the Septuagint version of the verse from the Book of Amos foretell the Assyrian exile of the northern kingdom of Israel (from whose tribes the Samaritans claimed descent). The place of their captivity is described as "beyond Damascus" (Amos 5:27). Stephen deliberately substitutes "beyond Babylon" for "beyond Damascus" (Acts 7:43). This makes the prophecy refer rather to the southern kingdom of Judah, and connects the Jews with the idolatrous generation Amos speaks of. As Stephen tells it, the apostasy from true worship that occurred in the wilderness, at the time of the exodus from Egypt, caused the downfall of the kingdom of Judah (Acts 7:41-42).

Stephen now makes another revision of history. In Acts 7:46, Stephen states: "And David found favor in God's sight, and asked that he might find a dwelling place for the house of Jacob." This apparently alludes to Psalms 132:5: "Until I find out a place for the Lord, a dwelling-place for the Mighty One of Jacob." However, as Stephen expresses it, David shows his interest in building a "dwelling place [skenoma] for the house of Jacob," that is, it is David's desire to build a national capital. This contrasts with the Masoretic text of the psalm, in which David's desire is to build a national sanctuary, "a dwelling place for the Mighty One of Jacob." One should not be confused by the many modern New Testament versions of Acts 7:46 that read "God of Jacob," which is found in the Septuagint. The earliest New Testament manuscripts read "house of Jacob." Thus, Stephen declares that it was not David's intention or desire to build a Temple. Stephen's purpose is to denounce Solomon's Temple as being "made with hands" (Acts 7:48) and being built against the wishes of God. This expressed the Samaritan position — the illegitimacy of the Jerusalem Temple and those who worshiped there.

¹ Jewish Antiquities II. 8. 2 [199].

² Jewish Antiquities IX. 14. 3 [291].

³ Jewish Antiquities XI. 8. 6 [341].

Chapter 82

CAN YOU TRUST PAUL?
(Acts 18:1-3)

Paul had one goal in his missionary endeavors and that was to convert Jew and Gentile alike to his theological teachings about Jesus. He had no qualms about being a hypocrite if it achieved his goal. On a number of occasions recorded in the New Testament, Paul lays himself open to the charges of hypocrisy and mendacity. A case in point is his circumcising of Timothy. Acts describes the circumstances:

> And he [Paul] came also to Derbe and to Lystra. A disciple was there, named Timothy, the son of a Jewish woman who was a believer; but his father was a Greek. He was well spoken of by the brethren at Lystra and Iconium. Paul wanted Timothy to accompany him; and he took him and circumcised him because of the Jews that were in those places, for they all knew that his father was a Greek. (Acts 18:1-3)

How could Paul have circumcised Timothy? In Galatians Paul makes it clear that in his estimation circumcision has no value, especially for one such as Timothy who already was a follower of Jesus. At best, circumcision is worthless; at worst, the act of circumcision might lead to the erroneous belief that salvation is possible through works of the law. Paul tells the Galatians that he opposed the circumcision of Titus, his Gentile traveling companion (Galatians 2:3-4), but he then has Timothy circumcised in order to make him his traveling companion. At the Jerusalem council of Acts 15 led by James, the church leadership adopted Paul's view that Gentile converts to Christianity need not be circumcised. However, they made no such concession concerning Jews. Titus was a Gentile, therefore, he need not be circumcised. Timothy, however, was a Jew. Apparently the Jews of Derbe, Lystra and Iconium and Asia Minor followed the rabbinic teaching that the status of the offspring of intermarriage is determined matrilineally.

479

Acts 16 begins with Paul's circumcision of Timothy. Timothy was circumcised, Acts says, "because of the Jews, all of whom knew that his father was a Greek." In order to win Jews, Paul felt he had to behave like a Jew; this is summed up in Paul's statement: "To the Jews I became as a Jew, in order to win Jews ... I have become all things to all men, that I may by all means save some" (1 Corinthians 9:20-22). In addition, he said: "What then? Only that in every way, whether in pretense or in truth, Christ is proclaimed; and in this I rejoice. Yes, and I will rejoice" (Philippians 1:18). He also stated: "I did not make myself a burden to you, nevertheless, trickster [crafty fellow] that I am, I took you in by deceit (2 Corinthians 12:16). Paul's statements make him out to be a sycophant and a hypocrite?

On the surface, Paul's circumcision of Timothy seems irreconcilable with his theology. However, Paul was ready to make temporary concessions in order to make converts for Jesus. If Paul could make himself a Jew to the Jews, that is, observe Jewish law when in their presence, why could he not circumcise Timothy "because of the Jews"? In Paul's mind the circumcision did not render Timothy subject to the law. In fact, it was for Paul a theologically meaningless act and was solely for the benefit of the mission. It was a circumcision justified by practical reasons to advance Paul's missionary agenda. Paul's public displays of loyalty to the law, including his circumcision of Timothy, are consistent with his deviousness.

The plain meaning of Acts 16:3 is clear. "Because of the Jews that were in those places, for they all knew that his father was a Greek" implies that Timothy was uncircumcised because his father was a Gentile and he was being brought up as a Gentile. However, the Jews all knew that Timothy's mother, Eunice, was Jewish (2 Timothy 1:5) and therefore they considered Timothy to be Jewish as well; they also knew that his father was a Greek and therefore that Timothy was uncircumcised. Although Timothy is mentioned a dozen times in the New Testament (aside from Acts 16:1-3), not a single passage implies that he was a Jew by birth. Even the two passages that speak of his home life (2 Timothy 1:5 and 3:15) do not imply that he was a Jew. They do not even imply that his mother was a Jew.

The phrase "because of the Jews in that vicinity" implies that, were it not for them, Paul would have left Timothy uncircumcised. Paul obviously felt compelled by the circumstances to become as a Jew in order to gain converts among the Jews, but his true feeling was that circumcision was an unnecessary act both for Jews and for Gentiles. This implication confirms the charge that Luke's Paul tries to deny by circumcising Timothy: "[A]nd they have been told about you that you teach all the Jews who are among the Gentiles to forsake Moses, telling them not to circumcise their children or observe the customs" (Acts 21:21).

Paul was proud of the deceptions he espoused in order to bring people to believe in the chimerical celestial being that he called Christ Jesus. This fictitious being whose story was originally based on events surrounding the execution by crucifixion of one Jesus of Nazareth became the center of his theological speculations. His belief more than likely stemmed from trauma due to illness that left him convinced that he was visited by this other-worldly being. However, his methods of spreading his newly conceived beliefs often were knowingly dishonest, but for him the end justified the means to bring about what he considered the greater good. Is such a man to be trusted to teach the will of God?

Chapter 83

ABRAHAM AND FAITH
(Romans 4:9-16)

Paul's agenda called for obtaining mass Gentile acceptance of Jesus as their Lord and Savior. To do this necessitated his nullification of the Torah's commandments. He therefore preached the following message:

> Is this happiness then upon the circumcised, or also upon the uncircumcised? For we say: "Faith was reckoned to Abraham as righteousness." How therefore was it reckoned? While he was circumcised or uncircumcised? Not while circumcised, but while uncircumcised. And he received the sign of circumcision, a seal of the righteousness of the faith which he had while uncircumcised, that he might be the father of all who believe without being circumcised, that righteousness might be reckoned to them; and a father of circumcision to those who not only are of the circumcision, but who also follow in the steps of the faith of our father Abraham which he had while uncircumcised. For it was not through law that Abraham or his seed had the promise that he should be heir of the world, but through the righteousness of faith. For if those who adhere to law are heirs, faith has been made void and the promise has been nullified. For the Law brings about wrath, but where there is no law, neither is there transgression. For this reason it is by faith, in order that it might be according to undeserved kindness, so that the promise may be certain to all the seed, not only to those who are of the Law, but also to those who are of the faith of Abraham, who is the father of us all. (Romans 4:9-16)

According to Paul, both Jews and Gentiles can achieve righteousness by faith alone without any need for the Torah. His conclusion is based on the premise that Abraham was considered righteous by God without his observance of the Mosaic Law. The Scripture states: "And he believed in the Lord; and He counted it to him for righteousness" (Genesis 15:6). Since this statement preceded

482

God's command to Abraham to circumcise his household, Paul argues, even that practice is not needed. He rationalizes that Abraham was circumcised (Genesis 17:10-11) not in obedience to the Law, but rather as a sign of the faith which he had prior to circumcision. Paul argues that since God's promise to Abraham "that he should be heir of the world" was made prior to the command to circumcise, the true heirs of the promise are not the circumcised, but the uncircumcised, that is, the Gentile church (Galatians 3:6-9, 29). Paul then concludes that it is faith not works which renders one just before God (Galatians 2:16, 3:23).

Paul's aim was to convert Jews and Gentiles to his beliefs. His overall guiding principle to achieve this was that the end justified the means. Thus he declared:

> And to the Jew I became as a Jew, that I might win Jews; to those under the law, as under the law, though not being myself under law, that I might win those under law. To those who are without law, as without law, though not being without the law of God but under the law of Christ, that I might win those without law. To the weak I became as weak, that I might win the weak: I have become all things to all men, that I may by all means save some. (1 Corinthians 9:20-22)

It was immaterial to Paul if deceptive means were used to bring about belief in Jesus. Thus, he says: "Whether in pretense or in truth, Christ is proclaimed; and in this I rejoice, yes, and I will rejoice" (Philippians 1:18). It simply did not matter to him if he distorted the meaning of the Scriptures. Paul's allegation, that Abraham was promised that he would be the "heir to the world" (a phrase not found anywhere in the Jewish Scriptures), "through the righteousness of faith" rather than "through law" builds a fallacious argument for the nullification of the Torah. His implication is that he is going back to a pristine belief system — "the faith of Abraham" that is open "to all the seed" and not just to "those who are of the Law." Paul desires to do away with the Torah reasoning that "where there is no law, neither is there transgression." That is, you can't sin if there is nothing to say that what you did was wrong. Of course, he will then substitute his own list of admonitions for his followers.

God's promises made to Abraham prior to his circumcision are posited on God's foreknowledge of Abraham's future actions. Thus, God declares: "For I have known him, to the end that he may command his children and his household after him, that they may keep the way of the Lord, to do righteousness and justice; to the end that the Lord may bring upon Abraham that which He has spoken of him" (Genesis 18:19). Significantly, the promises given to Abraham were to be fulfilled, not through all the "multitude of nations" that would descend from him, nor through spiritual followers, made up of the uncircumcised, i.e., the Gentiles, but specifically through, and for, only one nation: Israel (Genesis 28:13-15).

Paul's allegations are at odds with Genesis 26:3-5. In this passage, God first reveals some of the blessings that Abraham's descendants are to receive. He then gives the reasons for these blessings to be "because Abraham obeyed My voice, and kept My charge, My commandments, My statutes, and My laws." Although the particular commandments, statutes, and laws that Abraham kept are not listed, it is clear that Abraham did not live by faith alone. He earned His exalted position by practicing a good part of the Torah that was later revealed to his descendants on Mount Sinai: God's commandments, statutes and laws.

It was only with Abraham's circumcision and the establishment of the covenantal relationship that the promise to be "the father of a multitude of nations" (Genesis 17:5), made prior to circumcision, was able to be fulfilled. Indeed, it was through the circumcised Abraham that "all the nations of the earth will be blessed" (Genesis 18:18).

Did God demand of Abraham and his descendants faith alone without actual deeds? As previously stated, God Himself declares: "For I have known him, to the end that he may command his children and his household after him, that they may keep the way of the Lord, to do righteousness and justice; to the end that the Lord may bring upon Abraham that which He has spoken of him" (Genesis 18:19). Whatever God will command, in the way of works, the children of Abraham will do. As such, once the Torah was formally given to Abraham's descendants, on Mount Sinai, it became incumbent upon every generation of Israelites. What was actually demanded of Abraham, and serves as an example for his descendants, was a balance of faith and works. Abraham's faith was reflected in his positive deeds.

What Paul advocates is retrogression to a time before God revealed His will. He presumes that this lawless period is preferable to one in which God revealed His law. However, God's promise to make Abraham "the father of a multitude of nations," made prior to his circumcision, was actually contingent upon him and his descendants adhering to the act of circumcision. The fulfillment of all the promises God made to Abraham, both those made before circumcision and those made after, is contingent upon obedience to God's will, not simply to faith alone.

Paul's misguided teaching is objected to by the author of the Letter of James. Paul declares: "By works of law no flesh will be justified in His sight" (Romans 3:20), and "For if Abraham was justified by works, he has something to boast about; but not before God" (Romans 4:2). On the contrary, the Letter of James disagrees, stating that Abraham was measured by his works: "Was not Abraham our father justified by works, when he offered up Isaac his son upon the altar?" (James 2:21). It declares: "Faith without works is useless" (James 2:20); therefore, "a man is justified by works, and not by faith alone" (James 2:24). James goes so far as to say "faith without works is dead" (James 2:26).

If all God ever demanded of Abraham was faith alone, there would be no need for Him to command circumcision as a sign of the covenant between Himself and all generations of Abraham's Israelite descendants. Moreover, there would have been no reason for God to praise Abraham's obedience to His will (Genesis 26:5). Paul's analysis is unsound and without any merit whatsoever.

Chapter 84

THE NEED TO BE SAVED FROM ORIGINAL SIN
(Romans 5:12, 18-19)

Paul writes concerning the origin and consequences of sin:

> Therefore just as through one man sin entered into the world, and death through sin, and so death spread to all men, because all sinned. (Romans 5:12)

> So then as through one transgression there resulted condemnation to all men; even so through one act of righteousness there resulted justification of life to all men. For as through the one man's disobedience the many were made sinners, even so through the obedience of the one the many will be made righteous. (Romans 5:18-19)

Christian doctrine alleges that because of Adam's sin humanity has a sinful nature. By his disobeying God and eating of the Tree of Knowledge, it is said, Adam brought hereditary sin into the world, tainting all his descendants with what is called Original Sin. Thus, man is alleged to be a sinner from birth, separated spiritually from a holy God. Consequently, man has to be saved from sin and reconciled to God. Left to himself, this doctrine alleges, man can do nothing to overcome sin, for he is hopelessly involved in it. Atonement must be provided for him through means of a sinless sacrifice. The doctrine then maintains that Jesus was the only permanent sacrifice ever provided by God. It then concludes that the only way to achieve freedom from sin is by believing in Jesus as the mediating savior whose sacrificial death brings salvation to those who put their faith in him. In sum, this doctrine regards the death of Jesus as the only act of atonement which can redeem man from his sinfulness.

A discussion of whether man is a sinner by nature or not is

of no consequence. At some point in one's life an individual does sin, the problem is how one attains divine forgiveness and rejoins the fellowship of God. In the Torah, two means of redemption are offered to the sinner: animal sacrifice with prayerful contrition or prayer with a contrite spirit alone. In any case, reconciliation through sincere repentance in which the sinner pledges to rectify his waywardness and lead a righteous life is one means that is open at all times to all humanity. In opposition to this biblical process of atonement the doctrine of original sin claims that man is incapable of doing anything to earn his own salvation. It claims that since no man is completely righteous he cannot justify himself before God. Humanity can receive salvation only through grace, by an unmerited act of kindness bestowed by God upon him. This undeserved kindness, it is asserted, can only be received by those who accept Jesus as their savior (Ephesians 2:8-9).

Christians cite numerous verses to adduce proof for their contention that no man is righteous and that man cannot justify himself before God. The Christian explanation of these verses, though specious in their reasoning, needs to be examined. Among these verses cited is Psalms 51:7 (verse 5 in some versions): "Behold, I was brought forth in iniquity, and in sin did my mother conceive me." Christians claim that this verse shows that man is born in a state of sin. This allegation is without foundation. There is no reason to assume that David considers himself to be a sinner at birth. Rather, David's remark is a hyperbolic expression of the deep sense of guilt which he felt as a result of his carnal sin with Bathsheba. Even if one is to insist that David is saying that he has been a sinner since his birth, not just prone to sin, the all-important concept in this psalm is that David and all Israel could approach God directly and ask for forgiveness. The repentant sinner may demonstrate his contrition through certain specific sacrifices and confession and prayer, or through confession and prayer alone. While sacrifices accompanied by repentant prayer were a valid means of repentance when the Temple stood, subsequent to its destruction atonement was still attainable for the sinner as he could still approach God in contrite repentant prayer and ask for forgiveness of sins and receive atonement.

Christians referring to Psalms 53:3-5, argue that no one is righteous. There the psalmist states:

> God has looked down from heaven upon the children of men, to see if there is anyone who understands, who seeks after God. Every one of them is unclean, together they have become impure, there is no one who does good, not even one. Have the workers of wickedness no knowledge, who eat up My people as they eat bread, and call not upon God?

To understand the message of this psalm reference must be made to Psalm 14, which is another version of this psalm. In both psalms, the psalmist speaks of two groups. The first are "the workers of wickedness" who attack the second group, God's people. This second group, designated by God as "My people," is identified in Psalms 53:7 as Israel. The psalmist does not indicate, in either psalm, a universal unrighteousness on the part of mankind. This fact is illustrated in Psalms 14:5: "For God is with the righteous generation." What is described in these psalms is how widespread wickedness is in the world, and the difficulties Israel faces in a Godless world. Still, God looks down from heaven upon mankind and waits for those who truly seek Him. He never refuses to listen to those who approach Him with sincerity: "The sacrifice of the wicked is an abomination to the Lord; but the prayer of the upright is His delight" (Proverbs 15:8).

As a further illustration of their contention that no man is righteousness, Christians make use of Ecclesiastes 7:20: "For there is not a righteous man upon earth, that does good, and sins not." However, a perusal of this verse shows that it does not at all state that man is essentially unrighteous. On the contrary, it implies that there are many righteous persons, but that even the righteous may at one time or another fall prey to sin. In any case, he does not forfeit his status as a righteous person since the means for repentance are always available to the truly penitent, without recourse to anyone but God.

Endeavoring to prove their point, Christians have made reference to other biblical verses as well. Citing Isaiah, they incorrectly contend that our sins have separated us from God. The prophet says: "But your iniquities have separated between you and your God, and your sins have hid His face from you, that He will not hear" (Isaiah 59:2). Isaiah addresses himself here to a specific group at a particular time. If this was a general statement applicable to any and all sinners, who would be exempt? Even the patriarchs and Moses sinned. If God will not hear the sinner, David's confession would have been for naught, and Hezekiah would have died fifteen years earlier than he actually did. There is no justification for assuming, on the basis of this verse, that anyone who sins is completely separated from God. God most certainly hears and accepts the prayers of the repentant sinner.

Christians argue that no man can justify himself before God. In support of this allegation, they quote Psalms 143:2: "And do not enter into judgment with Your servant, for in Your sight no man living is righteous." But this understanding of the verse is faulty. The psalmist knows that if God judged mankind by the absolute standards of justice, no man could exist. That is why God always tempers justice with mercy. In his appeal to God for vindication, David is cognizant of this truth. Therefore, he does not despair, but is encouraged by the knowledge that God forgives the truly repentant.

This psalm is a prayer for deliverance and guidance. In verse 2, David is asking God not to judge him by the rules of strict justice, for on that accounting, neither he nor anyone else could stand unacquitted. Instead, he asks God to judge him with mercy by answering him in His faithfulness and righteousness: "O Lord, hear my prayer, give ear to my supplications. In Your faithfulness answer me, and in Your righteousness" (Psalms 143:1). When compared with God "no man living is righteous," but it is not expected of man to be on the superlative level of God: "If You, Lord, should mark iniquities, O Lord, who could stand? But with You there is forgiveness, that You may be feared" (Psalms 130:3-4). The record of the Jewish Scriptures is a testimony to God's boundless mercy by which the repentant sinner obtains forgiveness.

Job's friend, Eliphaz the Temanite, expresses a thought similar to that expressed by the psalmist in Psalms 143:2. Eliphaz says:

> What is man, that he should be clean or he who is born of a woman, that he should be righteous? Behold, He puts no trust in His holy ones; yea, the heavens are not clean in His sight. How much less one

that is abominable and impure, man who drinks iniquity like water! (Job 15:14-16)

Christians argue that this shows that man is totally unclean in God's sight. As a result, they insist that man cannot approach God directly for forgiveness. This construction contains a subtle change in the implication of the text. Again, what Eliphaz is saying is that, compared to God, nothing in the universe can be considered "clean," i.e., guiltless. Nothing can approach the perfection of God. But that does not mean that man cannot come directly before God. Eliphaz does not say that God has cast off humanity without any means of attaining forgiveness for sins committed. The biblical record consistently stresses that despite the damaging effects of sin, the sinner may personally approach God through sincere repentance: "Return, O backsliding children, says the Lord" (Jeremiah 3:14).

Christians contend that Ezekiel 18:4: "The soul that sins, it shall die," is proof that man is left in a hopeless state of sin unless he accepts Jesus as his savior. The context of the verse and, in fact, the entire thrust of the biblical message, teaches us something entirely different. The biblical message is clear for all to read. Ezekiel teaches us that each man is responsible for his own sins. He does not merely say that "the soul that sins, it shall die" but adds: "The son shall not bear the iniquity of the father with him, neither shall the father bear the iniquity of the son with him; the righteousness of the righteous shall be upon him, and the wickedness of the wicked shall be upon him" (Ezekiel 18:20). The remedy for sin is then clearly shown in the following verse: "But if the wicked turn from all his sins that he has committed, and keep all My statutes, and do that which is lawful and right, he shall surely live, he shall not die" (Ezekiel 18:21). Moreover, God says in verse 22: "None of his transgressions that he has committed shall be remembered against him; for his righteousness that he has done he shall live." But this is contingent on the person's sincere repentance as God says: "he should return from his ways, and live" (verse 23). Since people will, at times, unwittingly sin, animal sacrifice and the contrite heart are offered by the Torah as a means of atonement, with the stipulation that the person resolve to live up to all of God's statutes. To keep "all My statutes" does not mean that remission of sin is contingent upon the future keeping of all the commandments on the part of the repentant sinner. What is meant by this requirement is that the repentant person must pledge to keep all the commandments in the future. By this pledge the repentant sinner sincerely resolves to make every effort to conduct himself thereafter in accordance with all God's laws. "All" does not mean one will never sin again, but that when one does he will avail himself of all of the biblical atonement options available at that time for redemption from sin.

"There is no man that does not sin" (1 Kings 8:46). Indeed, "Who can say: 'I have made my heart clean, I am pure from my sin'?" (Proverbs 20:9). That is why God provided us with the means of cleansing ourselves from sin through repentance. This calls upon the repentant sinner to undergo genuine remorse for his past misdeeds and to pledge himself to improve his ways in the future by making every effort to keep away from all his past transgressions. However, if righteous acts are done insincerely as an attempt to hide unrepentant iniquities, "all our righteousnesses are as a polluted garment" (Isaiah 64:5).

This last statement is taken by Christians to mean that righteous acts are ineffective in bringing about atonement for sin. However, as indicated by the context, these words were only meant to apply to those who are insincere in the performance of good deeds. Since the verse is preceded by the verse wherein the prophet bemoans the disappearance of those "who joyfully performed righteous deeds, those who remembered You in Your ways" (Isaiah 64:4), it becomes clear that in the contrasting verse that follows, the prophet describes graphically the insincere acts of those who act hypocritically. As an integral part of organic Israel, Isaiah includes himself among the sinners, as Moses did in the incident of the Golden Calf (Exodus 34:9). All Israelites, whether individually innocent or guilty, share in the collective responsibility of the nation as a whole (Daniel 9:4 ff., Ezra 9:6 ff., Nehemiah 1:5 ff.).

To claim that man has no power to initiate the process of atonement or that man's righteous deeds have no meaning to God is tantamount to saying God contradicts Himself. The Christian belief

491

that atonement can only be effected through Jesus runs counter to the provisions for atonement prescribed in the Jewish Scriptures. First and foremost, God and no one else, provides the means of reconciliation and fellowship (2 Chronicles 7:14), which precludes any claim for atonement through the death of Jesus. In contrast to the Christian concept that man is hopelessly entrapped in sin, the Jewish Scriptures provide ample testimony that, although man may have an inclination towards evil (Genesis 8:21), the means of personal salvation are always at hand. God says to humanity: "sin is couching at the door; and it desires you, but you may rule over it" (Genesis 4:7). The Christian's question, "Are you saved?" is thus a question having no basis in the Jewish Scriptures. It is an alien concept whose origin lies in the New Testament and has no bearing on the spiritual life of the Jew.

It is interesting that neither Adam nor Eve is ever alluded to in the prophetic books or psalms as the source for suffering. Suffering is never attributed to anything that occurred in the Garden of Eden. No claim is made that human failures to live up to God's wishes result from the actions of the first couple. The biblical message is that people suffer collectively only because of wrongs they undertook willfully and that engulf the innocent as well as the guilty. Mankind's suffering is never attributed to an inherent condition as the descendants of Adam and Eve.

Of Jesus it is said: "For because he himself has suffered and has been tempted, he is able to come to the aid of those who are tempted" (Hebrews 2:18). In contrast, the God of Israel does not need to be tempted and suffer in order to be able to understand and forgive man's sins, because He is the all-knowing creator of man. This is poignantly expressed in the verse: "And the Lord said: 'I have surely seen the affliction of My people that are in Egypt, and I have heard their cry because of their taskmasters; for I know their pains'" (Exodus 3:7). God forgave sin before Jesus appearance, and continues to forgive without any assistance from the latter. It is no wonder that many centuries before the time of Jesus, Isaiah declared: "Israel is saved by the Lord with an everlasting salvation" (Isaiah 45:17).

Chapter 85

BORN UNDER THE LAW
(Galatians 4:4)

Conceived in sin

Paul alleges that "God sent forth His Son, born of a woman, born under the law" (Galatians 4:4). If one presumes that in the case of Jesus a conception without a man's help took place, as claimed by Matthew and Luke, then there is the problem that he was not born in accordance with the Law. As recorded in the New Testament, Jesus' birth violates the Torah's precepts on what constitutes adultery. Mary did not conceive by her betrothed, Joseph. Thus, she committed adultery "under the law" (Deuteronomy 22:23-24). As a result, the Christian claim that Jesus was born of a woman engaged to a man, yet had holy spirit as his father, must be considered to refer to him as an offspring of an illicit union (mamzer).

The Torah does not allow for God to seduce a maiden, even through the medium of holy spirit. This is not a discussion of what God's powers are capable of doing, but what restraints He puts on Himself. What would be the worth of a moral code that is violated by God Himself? Note that Paul never claims Jesus was born of a virgin. Stories of seduction of a female by a god are found in pagan mythology, not the Jewish Scriptures. Such a statement made in reference to the God of Israel shows the significant influence pagan thought had and has on Christian theology.

Chapter 86

HATING THE JEWS NO MORE THAN IS NECESSARY
(1 Thessalonians 2:15)

Hatred, not by accident

It is not by some historical fluke that the centuries since the establishment of Christianity have seen so much hatred of Jews and Judaism by so many followers of Christianity and by others influenced by Christian teachings.

Many Christians deny that the Gospels contain anti-Jewish and anti-Judaism statements. They insist the New Testament only teaches love. Other Christians suggest that to comprehend the original intent of the Gospels and other additions to the New Testament canon we need to approach them within their own historical context of the first century C.E. It is maintained that that would give a better understanding of the text within the framework of the culture. It is said that much if not all of the New Testament is Jewish literature. Jews are told that the Gospels are written in the best of Jewish tradition. Yes, even the way they condemn the Jews is said to be so very Jewish.

The truth behind the veil of Christian hypocrisy

Is it so Jewish when Paul describes the Jews as those "who killed both the Lord Jesus and the prophets … they displease God and oppose everyone" (1 Thessalonians 2:15)? This judgment is defended by a comparison of the Gospels' description of Jewish vindictiveness to the description of the benign attempt by Pontius Pilate to free Jesus. Matthew has "all the [Jewish] people" demanding Jesus' execution, when Pilate (otherwise known for his cruelty) literally washes his hands of any involvement in spilling innocent blood. In response, the Jews are said to shout: "[H]is blood be on our heads and on our children" (Matthew 27:25). Then there is the so typically Jewish response of John's Jesus who tells the Jews: "You are from your father the devil, and you choose to do your father's desires" (John 8:44). Whatever happened to the supposedly forgiving Jesus who it is claimed said, "For if you forgive men for their transgressions, your heavenly Father will also forgive you" (Matthew 6:14). Was John's Jesus having a schizophrenic happening? Was Jesus a sinner for not being personally forgiving as Matthew's Jesus continues, "But if you do not forgive men, then your Father will not forgive your transgressions" (Matthew 6:15). Was John's Jesus a sinner for separating himself from the Jewish people when he referred to the Torah as "your law" (John 8:17, 10:34) not "our law" or "the law"? Perhaps, this is why he died - for his own sinful transgressing nature. This is no ordinary vindictive "Old Testament" prophet, but the supposed loving forgiving Jesus (that is, others should forgive, he never forgave anyone who he felt slighted him).

What we are told is going on is that Jesus and the New Testament authors are indulging in the traditional language of polemics that were then prevalent among Jewish groups. The New Testament's anti-Jewish polemics is said to be comparable to passages in the Dead Sea Scrolls, where those excoriated are fellow Jews. Similarly, the works of Josephus and Philo have nothing but denunciation in describing those with whom they disagreed.

If this is true, then what is wrong with saying that when the vindictive language found in the New Testament was written it was normal if harsh rhetoric? The difference is essentially this: the bitter theological conflicts between different Jewish groups stayed within the confines of the Jewish community. Even the biblical prophets who denounced the sins of those within the wider community of Israel did not disassociate themselves from the community and they also confined their remarks to within the community. Paul's harsh words about Jews were addressed to Gentiles. The vindictive words of Matthew and John are constructed so as to condemn all non-Christian Jews and were put to writing when the church was predominantly Gentile. If these words were actually spoken by Jesus then the question is how was he better than other group leaders? Especially if with his wisdom he knew that his followers would use

495

these words to bring down vicious persecution of the Jews. The so-called historical context argument has no validity as we see that the purpose of these statements was to incite outsiders to hate and vilify Jews and Judaism. But most of all we ask: "Where was the supposed love and forgiveness of the imaginary Gospels' Jesus." Where is the love for one's enemies when it came to the scribes and Pharisees and when he condemned the Jewish people for all the sins of the world going back to Cain and Abel (Matthew 23:35-36)? And, last but not least, where was the forgiveness of Judas? Instead Jesus said of Judas: "Woe to that man through whom the Son of Man is betrayed. It would have been good for that man if he had not been born" (Matthew 26:24). The followers of Jesus certainly learned the lesson Luke's Jesus taught concerning his Jewish enemies: "But these enemies of mine who did not want me to reign over them, bring them here, and slay them in my presence" (Luke 19:27).

When all is said, the fact is that we do not know what Jesus really said rather than what was attributed to him by his followers. Whether Jesus used harsh and vindictive language as just one more preacher wandering the land is an intellectual/historical curiosity, but holds little practical significance for the ensuing Christian blood-lust directed at the Jewish people. For those who generated the texts and their followers there was never a desire simply to record what once was said and understand them in relation to the polemic rhetoric of the time they were spoken. The texts were not composed to satisfy historical curiosity. What is significant for Jewish-Christian relations in subsequent centuries down to the present is how the New Testament author's used words attributed to Jesus and further enhanced by they themselves to attack the Jewish people and Judaism.

Chapter 87

ABUSING ISAIAH 53
(1 Peter 2:21-24)

With an obvious reference to Isaiah 53, the author of 1 Peter 2:21-24 writes:

> [S]ince Christ also suffered for you, leaving you an example for you to follow in his steps, who committed no sin, nor was any deceit found in his mouth; and while being reviled, he did not revile in return. While suffering he uttered no threats, but kept entrusting himself to Him who judges righteously; and he himself bore our sins in his body on the cross that we might die to sin and live to righteousness; for by his wounds you were healed.

Let us review Jesus' lifetime record concerning these issues as the Gospels record them:

- Christ also suffered for you (unverifiable claim)
- leaving you an example for you to follow in his steps (A vindictive Jesus never forgave anything negative done to himself cf. Matthew 26:24, Luke 19:7)
- who committed no sin (unverifiable claim)
- nor was any deceit found in his mouth (cf. Matthew 13:13-15, Luke 8:10, John 18:20-21 with Matthew 16:20; John 2:19-21)
- while being reviled, he did not revile in return (cf. Matthew 23:3-35, John 8:44)
- while suffering he uttered no threats (But what about his threats of violent retribution on cities that rejected his message? - Matthew 11:20-24, Luke 10:13-15; and, of course, there is the missed opportunity to bestow upon the person of Judas what could have been the classic personal forgiveness example (Matthew 26:24). To hs enemies, Jesus promised nothing but retribution.
- but kept entrusting himself to Him who judges righteously (cf. Matthew 27:46)

- he himself bore our sins in his body on the cross that we might die to sin and live to righteousness (unverifiable claim)
- for by his wounds you were healed (unverifiable claim)

There is an important lesson to be learned in this New Testament tale of deception. It is an awareness about not only how the Gospels are replete with Jesus' lies and deceptions but that the appeal of the entire Christian missionary enterprise is based on lies and deception to its core. The Christian application to Jesus of verses and phrases based on Isaiah 53 are shown to be disingenuous from their own New Testament Scriptures.

Can you trust a Christian missionary? Consider Paul's example that has been followed in one way or another by Christian missionaries and would-be missionaries throughout the centuries:

> To the Jews I became as a Jew, that I might win Jews; to those who are under the Law as one under the Law (though not being myself under the Law) that I might win those who are under the Law; to those who are without law, as one without law, though not being without the law of God but under the law of Christ that I might win those who are without law. To the weak, I became weak that I might win the weak. I have become all things to all men that I may by all means save some. And I do all things for the sake of the gospel, that I may become a fellow partaker of it. (1 Corinthians, 9:20-23)

> I did not make myself a burden to you, nevertheless, trickster [crafty fellow] that I am, I took you in by deceit. (2 Corinthians 12:16)

There is total dishonesty on the part of Paul advocating that the end justifies the means; a program of lies and deceit that is the Christian missionary gold standard.

Chapter 88

NOAH AND BAPTISM
(1 Peter 3:20-21)

The author of 1 Peter writes:

> [W]hen the patience of God was waiting in the days of Noah, during the constructing of the ark, in which a few, that is, eight persons, were saved through water. And corresponding to that, baptism now saves you. (1 Peter 3:20-21)

The author of the First Letter of Peter alleges that the great flood recorded in Genesis 6-8 is a foreshadowing of the rite of baptism. He establishes a supposed analogy in which baptism saves the believer as water saved Noah and his family. But, a simple reading of the flood story reveals that Noah and his family were not saved through water, but from water. Such careless use of the Jewish Scriptures obviously proves nothing in support of the contention of the author of 1 Peter.

In any case, we who believe in the one God of Israel, without the errors associated with a belief in Jesus, are saved from the waters of baptism.

Chapter 89

THE MISSING TRIBE
(Revelation 7:4-8)

The author of the Book of Revelation writes:

> And I heard the number of those who were sealed, a hundred and forty-four thousand, sealed out of every tribe of the sons of Israel: Out of the tribe of Judah twelve thousand sealed; out of the tribe of Reuben twelve thousand; out of the tribe of Gad twelve thousand; out of the tribe of Asher twelve thousand; out of the tribe of Naphtali twelve thousand. Out of the tribe of Manasseh twelve thousand; out of the tribe of Simeon twelve thousand; out of the tribe of Levi twelve thousand; out of the tribe of Issachar twelve thousand; out of the tribe of Zebulun twelve thousand; out of the tribe of Joseph twelve thousand; out of the tribe of Benjamin twelve thousand sealed. (Revelation 7:4-8)

This author alleges that twelve thousand people were to be selected from each of the twelve tribes of Israel to constitute a select group numbering one hundred and forty-four thousand. This group is to be the "first fruits" of Jesus' millennial reign (Revelation 14:1, 4). The author enumerates the twelve tribes as being: Judah, Reuben, Gad, Asher, Naphtali, Manasseh, Simeon, Levi, Issachar, Zebulun, Joseph, and Benjamin. The twelve sons of Jacob, from whom the tribes of Israel are descended, should have been listed, but one of the names listed is Manasseh, the son of Joseph and a grandson of Jacob.

In listing Manasseh, the text leaves out Dan, the son of Jacob, without offering any explanation for this omission. As a rule, when Joseph is listed as one of the tribes, it automatically includes Manasseh. (We presume that Revelation takes the tribe of Joseph to be a reference to the tribe of Ephraim.) Many unsatisfactory solutions have been suggested, by Christians to explain why Dan is left out of the list. It is alleged, for example, that the Antichrist[1] will come from the tribe of Dan, but no relevant scriptural proof for this assertion is shown.

500

GERALD SIGAL

It is also suggested that the use of the phrase ek pases, "out of every," signifies that the whole group is to be considered as an entity whether there is an omission or not.

According to this explanation, the author's intention is to show that he does not mean "out of every one of the tribes. This interpretation is not based on the plain meaning of the text, which shows that the author's intention is to list every one of the twelve tribes of Israel; this inadvertently is not done. The fact remains, whether intentionally or not, that the tribe of Dan is omitted from the list, and there is no satisfactory reason for this omission.

[1] Antichrist is the term used by the Johannine Letters for those who deny "Christ" (1 John 2:18-22; 2 John 7). These letters speak of many "antichrists." The term is often personified to identify one particular individual who is supposed to appear shortly before the alleged second coming of Jesus.

BIBLIOGRAPHY

Abegg Jr., Martin, et al, eds. and trans. *The Dead Sea Scrolls Bible: The Oldest Known Bible.* San Francisco: HarperSan Francisco, 1999.

Anderson, Robert. *The Coming Prince.* London: Pickering and Inglis, 12th edition, 1929.

The Apocrypha and Pseudepigrapha of the Old Testament in English, ed. R.H. Charles, vol. 2. Oxford: Clarendon Press, 1913.

The Book of Isaiah, ed. Moshe H. Goshen-Gottstein. Jerusalem: Magnes Press, 1975.

Brown, Raymond E. *The Community of the Beloved Disciple.* New York: Paulist Press, 1979.

Bruce, F.F. *Peter, Stephen, James, and John.* Grand Rapids, Mich.: William B. Eerdmans, 1979.

Burrows, Millar. *The Dead Sea Scrolls of St. Mark's Monastery, "The Isaiah Manuscript and the Habakkuk Commentary,"* vol. 1. New Haven: The American Schools of Oriental Research, 1950, Plate VI.

Clement of Alexandria. *Stromata*, eds. Roberts and Donaldson. The Ante-Nicene Fathers, vol. 2. Grand Rapids: Eerdmans, 1996.

Dio Cassius. *Roman History*, trans. E. Cary, vol.8. Loeb Classical Library, London: Heinemann, 1925.

Eusebius. *Ecclesiastical History*, trans. Arthur Cushman McGiffert, in eds. Schaff and Wace, *Nicene and Post-Nicene Fathers of the Christian Church*, vol. 1. Grand Rapids: Eerdmans, 1986.

——. *The Oration in Praise of Emperor Constantine*, eds. Schaff and Wace, *Nicene and Post-Nicene Fathers of the Christian Church*, vol. 1. Grand Rapids: Eerdmans, 1986.

——. *Demonstratio Evangelica* [The Proof of the Gospel], trans. W.J. Ferrar, vol. 5. New York: the Macmillan Co., 1920.

Ginsberg, Christian D. *Introduction to the Massoretico-Critical Edition of the Hebrew Bible.* (reprint) New York: Ktav Publishing House, 1966.

Hoehner, Harold. *Chronological Aspects of the Life of Christ.* Grand Rapids: Zondervan, 1976.

502

The Holy Bible: New International Version, Grand Rapids, Mich.: Zondervan, 1978.

Howard, George. *Hebrew Gospel of Matthew*. Macon, Ga.: Mercer University Press, 1995.

Jerome. *Epistulae (Letters of Saint Jerome)*. Eds. Quasten and Burqhadt. New York: Paulist Press, 1963.

Josephus. *Works*, trans. H. St. J. Thackery, R. Marcus, A. Wikgren, and L.H. Feldman. Loeb Classical Library, 9 vols. Cambridge, MA: Harvard University Press, 1926-1965.

Justin Martyr, *Dialogue With Trypho*, eds. Roberts and Donaldson. *The Ante-Nicene Fathers*, vol. 1. Grand Rapids: Eerdmans, 1996.

————. *The First Apology of Justin*, eds. Roberts and Donaldson, *The Ante-Nicene Fathers*, vol. 1. Grand Rapids: Eerdmans, 1996.

King James Version of the Bible. Grand Rapids: Zondervan, 1992.

Kittel, R. Biblia Hebraica. Stuttgart: Deutsche Bibelgesellschaft, 1997.

Maimonides. *Commentary on the Mishnah (Mishnah Torah)*. New York: Large Rambam Publishing, 1962.

Marshall, Howard I. *The Gospel of Luke*. Grand Rapids: Eerdmans. 1978.

Midrash Rabbah, eds. J. Theodor and Ch. Albeck, 3 vols. Jerusalem: Wahrmann, 1965.

Mishnayoth, trans. Philip Blackman. New York: The Judaica Press, 1965.

Moule, C.F. *An Idiom Book of New Testament Greek*. Cambridge: University Press, 1977.

Origen. *Contra Celsum*, trans. Henry Chadwick. Cambridge: Cambridge University Press, 1965.

Pesikta Rabbati, trans. William G. Braude, 2 vols. New Haven: Yale University Press, 1968.

Philo. *The Works of Philo*, trans. C.D. Younge. Peabody, Mass.: Hendrickson Publishers, 2000.

Pilgrim of Bordeaux. *Itinerarium Burdigalense (Corpus Christianorum*, Series Latina [CCL] 175, ed. P. Geyer and O. Cuntz [Turnout: Brepols, 1965]), trans. Wilkinson, *Egeria's Travels*.

Preus, A. *Science and Philosophy in Aristotle's Biological Works*. Hildersheim: Georg Olms Verlag, 1975.

Proto-Gospel of James 19:1-20; in J.K. Elliott, trans., *The Apocryphal New Testament*, Oxford: Clarendon Press, 1993.

Robertson, A.T. *A Harmony of the Gospels.* New York: Harper, 1950.

Schaberg, Jane. *The Illegitimacy of Jesus.* San Francisco: Harper and Row, 1987.

Seder Olam Rabbah. Ma'ayan HaChochma. Jerusalem, 1955/1956.

Sifre. Jerusalem, 1978.

Sigal, Gerald. *The Jew and the Christian Missionary: A Jewish Response to Missionary Christianity.* New York: Ktav Pubishing House, 1981.

——. *Anti-Judaism in the New Testament.* Philadelphia: Xlibris, 2004.

——. *Trinity Doctrine Error: A Jewish Analysis.* Bloomington, IN.: Xlibris, 2006.

——. *Isaiah 53: Who is the Servant?* Bloomington, IN.: Xlibris, 2007.

—— –. *The Blood Atonement Deception: How Christianity Distorted Biblical Atonement.* Bloomington, IN.: Xlibris, 2010.

—— –. *The Resurrection Fantasy: Reinventing Jesus.* Bloomington, IN.: Xlibris, 2012.

—— –. *The Virgin Birth Myth: The Misconception of Jesus.* Bloomington, IN.: Xlibris, 2013.

——. *The 70 Weeks of Daniel (9:24-27).* Bloomington, IN.: Xlibris, 2013.

Soloveitchik, Joseph. *Days of Deliverance: Essays on Purim and Hanukkah*, eds. Eli D. Clark, Joel B. Wolowelsky, Reuven Ziegler. Jersey City: Ktav Publishing House, 2007.

Strong, James. Strong's *Exhaustive Concordance of the Bible*, Nashville: Abingdon, 1978.

Syon, Danny. "Gamla–Portrait of a Rebellion," *Biblical Archaeology Review* (18), January/February 1992: 31.

Tacitus. *Histories*, trans. John Jackson. Loeb Classical Library. Cambridge, MA.: Harvard University Press. 9th edition,1988.

Talmud, Babylonian, ed. I. Epstein. London & New York: Soncino Press, 1935.

Talmud, Jerusalem. Zhitomer edition. (reprint) Jerusalem: Bene Ma'arav, 1979/80.

Tanchuma. Jerusalem: 'or Hachaim, 1998.

Tertullian. *On the Flesh of Christ*, eds. Roberts and Donaldson, *The Ante-Nicene Fathers,* vol. 18. Grand Rapids: Eerdmans, 1996.

Thayer, Joseph Henry. *A Greek-English Lexicon of the New Testament*, Grand Rapids, Mich.: Zondervan, 1979.

Ulrich, E. (ed.), *Discoveries in the Judaean Desert: Psalms to Chronicles*, Vol. 16, Oxford: Clarendon, 2000.

Van Iersel, Baas. "The Finding of Jesus in the Temple: Some Observations on the Original Form of Luke ii 41-51a," *Novum Testamentum* 4 (1960): 161-173.

Westcott, B.F., and Hort, F.G.A. *Introduction to the New Testament in the Original Greek*. Peabody, Mass.: Hendrickson Publishers, 1988.

Scriptual Index
The Jewish Bible

511

Scriptual Index
The New Testament

Index of Names and Subjects

42969010R10300

Made in the USA
Middletown, DE
19 April 2019